Championship BBQ Secrets
for
Real Smoked Food

Karen Putman

Robert
ROSE

For complete cataloging information, see page 358.

Disclaimer
The recipes in this book have been carefully tested by our kitchen and our tasters. To the best of our
knowledge, they are safe and nutritious for ordinary use and users. For those people with food or
other allergies, or who have special food requirements or health issues, please read the suggested
contents of each recipe carefully and determine whether or not they may create a problem for you.
All recipes are used at the risk of the consumer.

We cannot be responsible for any hazards, loss or damage that may occur as a result of any recipe use.

For those with special needs, allergies, requirements or health problems, in the event of any
doubt, please contact your medical adviser prior to the use of any recipe.

Design & Production: PageWave Graphics Inc.
Editor: Sue Sumeraj
Recipe Tester: Jennifer MacKenzie
Proofreader: Sheila Wawanash
Indexer: Gillian Watts
Photography: Colin Erricson and Mark T. Shapiro
Food Styling: Kate Bush
Prop Styling: Charlene Erricson

Cover image: World Championship Ribs (page 251)

We acknowledge the financial support of the Government of Canada through the Book Publishing
Industry Development Program (BPIDP) for our publishing activities.

Published by Robert Rose Inc.
120 Eglinton Avenue East, Suite 800, Toronto, Ontario, Canada M4P 1E2
Tel: (416) 322-6552 Fax: (416) 322-6936

Printed in Canada
3 4 5 6 7 8 9 CPL 14 13 12 11 10

Contents

Preface 4
North American Regional Barbecue. 6
The Art of Smoking 7

Brines, Rubs, Marinades, Bastes and Sauces. 18
Getting Started. 72
Vegetables, Fruits, Cheese and Nuts 96
Fish and Shellfish 146
Poultry 192
Pork 224
Beef 270
Lamb 310
Specialty Smoking 332

Glossary. 355
Source Guide 356
Index 359

Preface

WHEN I HEAR THE WORD "barbecue," I don't think of hot and fast grilling over direct heat, as you would cook a hamburger or a steak on your backyard grill. I think of foods cooked next to a fire, low and slow, flavored with wood smoke. Succulent, finger-lickin' ribs. Dark, deep and meaty brisket. Salmon bronzed with alder smoke. That's barbecue!

I got interested in slow-smoked foods — real North American barbecue — by a happy chance. In 1984, a man I worked with talked me into entering the American Royal Barbecue Contest in Kansas City, Missouri. With my husband, Putter, and a few friends, I entered the contest with a borrowed cooker, or "rig." We took second place in the lamb category with a smoked lamb kabob served on saffron rice, and I was hooked.

Along the way, I've smoked everything there is to smoke, except maybe watermelon. I still compete in barbecue contests in my free time, having won the "Oscars" of the barbecue world: the American Royal, the Jack Daniels and two international contests in Lisdoonvarna, Ireland. My competition team is named "Flower of the Flames," the same name as the line of barbecue sauces I started to bottle and sell in 1988, when Ardie Davis (known in barbecue circles as Remus Powers, Ph.B. — that's a doctorate in barbecue philosophy!) called me a "pioneer of fruit-based sauces." I still like concocting new sauce recipes. In my regular working life, I'm a chef who has entered and won lots of recipe contests.

I've smoked on just about every kind of equipment, both good and very, very bad. In the mid-1990s, Putter and I entered a contest in Florida, drove down there with coolers full of 300 pounds of meat, and rented a cooker ahead of time. That smoker was a big rust bucket. It had holes in it everywhere you looked. Putter took 12 boxes of aluminum foil and started rolling up foil into balls to stuff those holes. He patched it all up. We did a test run to see if the temperature would hold, and it did. So we put our food on and hoped for the best. And we won the grand championship that year!

At a chef's contest in Belgium, I wanted to smoke chicken and salmon. But the equipment they gave me was a flat restaurant outdoor grill. So I made my own smoker, again with aluminum foil. I tented the grill and made a chimney.

This is all to demonstrate that you can get delicious results from any equipment you have. It's all in the technique: Keep the temperature at a steady, low and slow heat. Add enough wood for good flavor, but not so much that you have a bitter, acrid result. And flavor your food before, during and/or after smoking with brines, rubs, marinades, bastes, mops and sauces.

Every barbecuer develops his or her own style after a while. Here's mine:

1. I marinate or use a dry rub to flavor the food before smoking.

2. I use fruit woods such as apple, cherry and peach, sometimes in combination with oak, sugar maple or pecan, for a sweeter smoke flavor.

3. I spray my food with a fruit juice or citrus spray during smoking, or use a basting mixture of some kind, or both.

4. I follow up with a sauce with a touch of sweetness that provides a counterpoint to the slightly bitter flavor of the smoke.

5. I use a Tucker Cooker for hot-smoking, a SmokinTex® for cold-smoking.

However, any of the recipes in this book can be modified for the equipment and wood of your choice. The wood you use depends on your area and what is plentiful and not too expensive. You want a hard wood, not a soft one such as pine, which will add a bitter, resinous flavor to food. What makes smoking fun for me is experimenting with rubs, woods, temperatures and so forth. Once you get the basics down, you can let your imagination run wild. Smoking is constant creativity.

The Flower of the Flames team now consists of me; my husband, Putter; my sister, Ronna Keck; her husband, Bill; and my friends Cathy Jones, Tim Lanagin and Kevin Fatino. I also belong to the 'Que Queens, an all-female barbecue team that competes in Battle of the Sexes barbecue contests against a men's team... whenever they can get a team together. Several other barbecue teams have spun off from my team's experience in cooking with me at contests, and I'm happy about that. I love to share the experience. I get excited when people I've mentored end up winning a contest.

When you've had a chance to try some of the recipes in this book, I'd like to hear from you, too. Send me an email at **chefkp2003@aol.com**.

Happy smoking!

Karen Putman

North American Regional Barbecue

PEOPLE ACROSS NORTH AMERICA love barbecue, but everywhere you go they do it a little differently. The result is an amazing bounty of hot- and cold-smoked recipes. Here are some of the regional specialties that inspired the recipes in this book:

United States

- **New England:** Maple- or corn cob–smoked fish and shellfish; Cheddar; pork; barbecued "baked" beans paired with maple-sweetened barbecue sauces.

- **The Carolinas:** Pork shoulder blade roast; whole hog; pork butt with vinegar- or mustard-based barbecue sauces and slaw. The pork is either "pulled" apart with forks, chopped or minced.

- **Memphis:** "Wet" (with sauce) or "dry" (without sauce) barbecued ribs; spicy rubs; cold-smoked catfish; a touch of bourbon in sweeter barbecue sauces.

- **Kentucky:** Famous for barbecued lamb and mutton barbecue from Owensboro. The sauce is either tomato-based or a unique "black" sauce that is peppery hot.

- **Kansas City:** A melting pot of styles. Ribs; brisket with "burnt ends" (the twice-smoked thin ends of a brisket flat); turkey; lamb ribs; spicy, smoky tomato- and fruit-based barbecue sauces.

- **Texas:** Tender brisket; beef clod (shoulder); ribs; tangy vinegar or coffee mops; Southwest-style rubs and sauces; pinto beans for barbecued bean dishes; chili peppers. Tex-Mex style includes barbecued cabrito (young kid goat), served as tacos in flour tortillas.

- **California:** Santa Maria–style smoked tri-tip (big beef roast) over red oak; lots of herb flavors; lamb; smoked chicken with herb- or citrus-based sauces.

- **Pacific Northwest:** Fish and shellfish; lamb; Chinese-style ribs; Asian-style sauces.

Canada

- **Maritime Provinces:** Cold- and hot-smoked shellfish; salmon; cod paired with maple-sweetened brines or marinades and French-inspired sauces; slow-smoked bean dishes with salt pork and a touch of maple syrup.

- **Ontario:** Pork ribs with a sweet touch of maple syrup and sugar; maple-smoked freshwater fish; tomato-based, maple-sweetened sauces.

- **Prairie Provinces:** Lake fish such as walleye and whitefish; beef brisket; Calgary Stampede barbecued beef; upland game birds; tomato-rhubarb barbecue sauce. Russian Mennonite and other ethnic influences.

- **British Columbia:** Cold- and hot-smoked salmon; salmon "candy"; halibut; oysters; Asian-style sauces; barbecue "poutine," or pulled pork over french fries, topped with cheese curds and tomato-based barbecue sauce.

The Art of Smoking

FOR THOUSANDS OF YEARS, wood-smoke flavor has been used to enhance and modify the taste of foods, as well as to preserve meats. Think of smoked sausage, bacon smoked with apple wood, or alder-smoked salmon.

When the lignin, or the fiber in wood, starts to smolder, it releases many phenolic flavor chemicals. Some provide a "burnt sugar"–like note. Others act as preservatives, which help to prevent spoilage. Each type of hard wood has a slightly different flavor, from the very deep and bitter mesquite to the very light and almost sweet peach.

This book covers two types of smoking: hot-smoking and cold-smoking. In hot-smoking, you cook foods at a temperature above 200°F (100°C). Most of the recipes in this book are for hot-smoking. Cold-smoking is the less common of the two methods and is usually reserved for fish, shellfish, fruits and vegetables. It is done at a temperature well below 200°F (100°C). The colors stay true, and the food does not soften and wilt, as in hot-smoking.

I recommend learning how to hot-smoke before you move on to cold-smoking, because hot-smoking is more accessible and you have a wider range of recipes and flavors to work with.

Hot-Smoking

Hot-smoked food cooks, turns opaque and takes on a burnished or blackened appearance, changes color and takes on a wood-smoke flavor. Think barbecue ribs, brisket, pork butt, smoked whole turkey.

To get started with hot-smoking, you need a heat source, a way to control the heat and a way to enclose the food with the heat and smoke. You can use a charcoal grill, a charcoal, gas or electric bullet smoker, a gas grill, a wood pellet grill, a ceramic or Kamado-style grill or a big smoking rig as a hot smoker. A kettle grill with a lid will get you started. I've used all types of equipment over the years, and have had to create my own sometimes. Of course, you'll be setting this equipment up outside, away from anything flammable and in a protected spot so wind won't be a factor.

The Best Smoker for You

The best smoker for you is determined by the amount of space you have, where you live (city, suburb, country), the kind of fuel you want to use, the amount of cooking surface you need and how much money you want to spend. Are you a "backyarder" — a person who mainly wants to make great barbecue for family and friends in the backyard? Or do you have visions of entering barbecue contests, perhaps becoming a "ribber" (a person who is hooked on smoking the perfect slab of ribs and "smoking" the competition)?

Some of the most popular units for backyard use are charcoal kettle grills and bullet smokers (so named because their shape, accommodating three tiers, resembles a bullet). They are moderately priced, ranging from under $50 to $250. Backyarders also use electric-fired wood pellet grills, ceramic smokers, smoker ovens and gas grills with two or more burners. There are even gas grills that can adapt to cooking with charcoal or charcoal and gas at the same time. Passionate backyard barbecuers may use medium to large smoking rigs or pit smokers with a firebox on the side, as their competition buddies do. These larger rigs can start at $1,000 and go way, way up.

Many of these smokers can be purchased at hardware stores, home improvement stores and barbecue shops in your area. Some hardware stores and barbecue shops even carry the bigger rigs. You can also track down professional-style smokers through a barbecue society publication or online. Check out the Source Guide on page 356 for details on some smoker manufacturers.

Preparing the Fire

If you can prepare a fire in a grill, you can prepare a fire in a smoker. The difference is that you will be preparing an indirect fire, a heat source that will be not directly under the food you want to smoke, but farther away from it. You'll also be keeping the temperature to around 225°F to 250°F (110°C to 120°C), rather than at the higher temperatures used for grilling.

Before you get started, the smoker should be clean and the rack(s) lightly oiled (use vegetable oil and a long-handled brush). Assemble everything you need to prepare your fire and have it close at hand.

How you prepare the fire depends on the type of equipment you have. Some general guidelines follow; for more information, consult the manufacturer's instruction manual for your grill or smoker.

Charcoal grill

Use charcoal briquettes or hardwood lump charcoal to start a fire in a metal charcoal chimney (available at discount and home improvement stores, as well as barbecue and grill shops). Start the fire by stuffing newspaper in the bottom of the chimney and filling the cylinder with charcoal. Place the chimney on the grill rack and light the newspaper. Watch for a few moments to make sure the briquettes have started to catch fire, then let them smolder for 20 to 30 minutes.

When the coals begin to ash over, lift off the grill rack and dump them into the bottom of the grill. Depending on the type of charcoal grill and grill rack you have, you can create an indirect fire in one of two ways. If you have a smaller grill with a one-piece grill rack, use a long grill spatula to push the briquettes over to one side of the grill. Half of the grill will have briquettes, the other half will not. The briquette side is the direct side; the side without the briquettes is the indirect side. If you have a larger grill with a hinged grill rack, you can instead brush the charcoal into the center of the grill so that the briquettes form a band down the center.

If you use a water pan (see page 14), place it on the bottom of the grill, next to the coals. If your grill has a one-piece grill rack, add wood to the coals now (see "Adding Wood to the Fire," page 12). (If your grill has a hinged rack, you can add the wood after you've placed your food on the rack.) Place the grill rack back over top.

Use grill thermometers to monitor the temperature on both sides of the grill as your food is smoking. Ideally, smoking is done at a temperature of 225°F to 250°F

(110°C to 120°C), measured on the indirect side. Getting your temperature to stay in that range is where the main technique of smoking comes into play (see "Monitoring and Adjusting the Temperature," page 14).

Charcoal will last 30 to 45 minutes before it starts to die out, and it takes 30 minutes for charcoal to start and ash over in the charcoal chimney, so you should light another batch of charcoal whenever you dump a new batch of coals into the grill, or soon after. (Once the food is on the smoker, you'll be placing the charcoal chimney on a non-flammable surface such as your cement patio or driveway.) Estimate how long your food has to cook by looking at the recipe, then figure out how much charcoal refilling you'll need to do.

Ceramic or Kamado-style grill

The Kamado-style smoker has a ceramic firebox for the very little amount of charcoal placed in its inner compartment. Start the charcoal by placing two or three crumpled pieces of newspaper on the bottom, lighting the newspaper and placing enough charcoal on top. The paper burns, and the charcoal should settle just below the air holes in the fire box. Practice with a small amount of charcoal as you learn to regulate the heat. When the coals begin to ash over, add wood to the coals (see "Adding Wood to the Fire," page 12).

Use a grill thermometer to monitor the temperature in the grill as your food is smoking. Again, you want to aim for a temperature of 225°F to 250°F (110°C to 120°C), so practice regulating your fire (see pages 14–15 for details) before you start cooking.

There is no room for a water pan in this type of grill, so you'll want to spray your food with fruit juice as it smokes (see page 14).

Charcoal bullet smoker

Use charcoal briquettes or hardwood lump charcoal to start a fire in a metal charcoal chimney (available at discount and home improvement stores, as well as barbecue and grill shops). Start the fire by stuffing newspaper in the bottom of the chimney and filling the cylinder with charcoal. Place the chimney on the top tier and light the newspaper. Watch for a few moments to make sure the briquettes have started to catch fire, then let them smolder for 20 to 30 minutes.

When the coals begin to ash over, dump them into the bottom third of the smoker. Use a long grill spatula to spread the briquettes evenly. Because you will be placing the food on the top tier of this smoker, far away from direct heat, this is still considered an indirect fire.

If you use a water pan (see page 14), place it on the middle tier of the smoker. Add wood to the coals after you place your food on to smoke (see "Adding Wood to the Fire," page 12).

Use a grill thermometer to monitor the temperature in the smoker as your food is smoking. Ideally, smoking is done at a temperature of 225°F to 250°F (110°C to 120°C). Getting your temperature to stay in that range is where the main technique of smoking comes into play (see "Monitoring and Adjusting the Temperature," page 14).

Charcoal will last 30 to 45 minutes before it starts to die out, and it takes 30 minutes for charcoal to start and ash over in the charcoal chimney, so you should light another batch of charcoal whenever you dump a new batch of coals into the grill, or soon after. (Once the food is on the smoker, you'll be placing the charcoal chimney on a non-flammable surface such as your cement patio or driveway.) Estimate how long your food has to cook by looking at the recipe, then figure out how much charcoal refilling you'll need to do.

Electric or gas-powered bullet smoker

This type of equipment is great for the beginner who wants smoke flavor without having to tend a charcoal fire. You don't get the true smoke flavor you do from charcoal, but the flavor you get is pretty good. To prepare this fire, simply place your wood around or near the electric coils or gas flame in the bottom third of the smoker (see "Adding Wood to the Fire," page 12) and turn on the electricity or gas so that the wood begins to smolder. If you use a water pan (see page 14), place it on the middle tier of the smoker.

Gas grill

Yikes! I can't believe I wrote that. Because I'm a competition barbecuer, slow-smoking on a gas grill would not be my first, second or even third choice. If you want to slow-smoke a brisket or pork shoulder blade roast, for example,

you might need to have your gas grill on for up to 10 hours. That just isn't practical. Also, food smoked on a gas grill is not as flavorful as food smoked over charcoal.

You can, however, get a decent smoke flavor on vegetables, cheese, fish or shellfish using a gas grill. And these only take about an hour to slow-smoke. So these instructions are for those foods only.

To prepare a fire in a gas grill, you need a grill with at least two burners. Simply turn one burner (or half of the burners) to medium-high, and leave the other burner (or half of the burners) off. If you use a water pan (see page 14), place it closer to the side that's not turned on. Use a metal or foil container filled with dry wood chips or pellets for the wood-smoke flavoring (see "Adding Wood to the Fire," page 12), and place it on the direct side (over the flame) so that the wood will smolder.

Wood pellet grill

This type of grill uses electricity to spark and flame the wood pellets that are used as fuel and flavoring. The wood pellets, which come in all different wood flavors, are augured from the bin down to the firing mechanism. Because the flame is far away from the grill/smoker rack, this is considered an indirect fire. So all you have to do is plug in the grill, make sure the bin is filled with pellets (and keep checking on that) and set the temperature gauge. There is enough moisture in the pellets that you don't need a water pan, but a spray of fruit juice from time to time never goes amiss.

Professional-style smoker or smoker oven

When you get really serious about slow-smoking or start to compete in barbecue contests, you usually graduate from a charcoal kettle grill to a charcoal bullet smoker, then on to one of these larger smokers. A big-rig smoker has a firebox off to one side and an enclosed chamber with smoker racks on which you place the food. There are many different styles of professional smokers available, some of which you can tow behind your car or truck, like my Tucker Cooker.

Use charcoal briquettes or hardwood lump charcoal to start a fire in a metal charcoal chimney (available at discount and home improvement stores, as well as barbecue and grill shops). Start the fire by stuffing newspaper in the bottom of the chimney and filling the cylinder with charcoal. Place the chimney on the top smoker rack and light the newspaper. Watch for a few moments to make sure the briquettes have started to catch fire, then let them smolder for 20 to 30 minutes.

When the coals begin to ash over, dump them into the firebox. Use a long grill spatula to spread the briquettes evenly. Because the firebox is far away from the food in the smoking chamber, this is considered an indirect fire.

If you use a water pan (see page 14), place it on one of the smoker racks. Add wood to the coals after you place your food on to smoke (see "Adding Wood to the Fire," page 12). The bigger the firebox, the bigger the pieces of wood you'll use for wood-smoke flavoring. Barbecuers cut dry sticks or logs of wood to fit the dimensions of their firebox. With a big rig, you would not use the smaller wood chips, pellets or chunks.

Use grill thermometers to monitor the temperature on both sides of the grill. Ideally, smoking is done at a temperature of 225°F to 250°F (110°C to 120°C), measured on the indirect side. Getting your temperature to stay in that range is where the main technique of smoking comes into play (see "Monitoring and Adjusting the Temperature," pages 14–15).

Charcoal will last 30 to 45 minutes before it starts to die out, and it takes 30 minutes for charcoal to start and ash over in the charcoal chimney, so you should light another batch of charcoal whenever you dump a new batch of coals in the grill, or soon after. (Once the food is on the smoker, you'll be placing the charcoal chimney on a non-flammable surface such as your cement patio or driveway.) Estimate how long your food has to cook by looking at the recipe, then figure out how much charcoal refilling you'll need to do.

A big smoker might use about 100 pounds (45 kg) of charcoal at a barbecue contest, where you're smoking pork butt, brisket, ribs, chicken and more. I've kept three charcoal chimneys going the whole time, just to keep the fire going and the temperature steady in the rig. What I like about the Tucker Cooker I have now is that it's so efficient. I can get through a contest with just two bags of charcoal!

Varieties of Hardwood Flavors

Always look for seasoned hard wood that has been dried for at least six months. You can find woods common to your area at barbecue shops, home improvement stores, orchards and firewood cutters. When you need specialty woods such as whispering oak or pear, turn to mail-order sources (see the Source Guide, page 356).

Alder: A light, aromatic flavor; great with seafood. *Pacific Northwest.*

Apple: A sweet, aromatic flavor that is good with chicken or pork. I like to use apple in combination with hickory, oak, pecan or other fruit woods. *North America.*

Cherry: A deep, sweet flavor, delicious with beef tenderloin, pork, chicken or lamb. *North America.*

Grape: A fruit wood harvested when grape vines are pruned. Medium smoke flavor. *Vineyard areas of North America.*

Hickory: The traditional flavor of smoked foods. *North America.*

Maple: A medium smoke flavor. I especially like sugar maple. *Eastern North America.*

Mesquite: The strongest, smokiest flavor, best suited to beef, especially brisket. I like to use mesquite in combination with fruit woods or pecan to lighten up the smoke flavor. *Texas and the American Southwest.*

Oak: A medium smoke flavor that's not bitter. I especially like whispering oak. *North America.*

Peach: A lighter, more delicate flavor than apple. *North America.*

Pecan: A medium smoke flavor, less pronounced than hickory but more than oak. Pecan is great for grilling with a kiss of smoke. *Midwest.*

Adding Wood to the Fire

When you're slow-smoking at a low temperature, the flavor comes from smoldering hard woods — such as hickory, cherry, oak, mesquite and pecan — which are placed on or near the fire. Wood comes in several different forms, and the type of smoking equipment you have determines how you use it.

Shredded chips

In a charcoal grill or smoker, scatter dry chips directly on the coals. In a gas-powered bullet smoker, make an aluminum foil packet to enclose dry chips, then poke holes in the packet and place it near the gas flame. In a gas grill or an electric bullet smoker, put dry chips in a metal smoker box or make an aluminum foil packet to enclose them, then poke holes in the packet. Place the smoker box or the packet on the grill rack over the heat in a gas grill or near the electric coil in an electric smoker. (Some gas grills have a special built-in place where the smoker box goes; consult the manufacturer's instruction manual for your grill.)

Pellets

Wood pellets (bits of compressed sawdust) must be used dry; if you moisten them, they disintegrate instead of smoldering. In a charcoal grill or smoker or a gas-powered bullet smoker, make an aluminum foil packet to enclose the pellets, then poke holes in the packet and place it directly on the coals or near the gas flame. In a gas grill or an electric bullet smoker, put pellets in a metal smoker box or make an aluminum foil packet to enclose them, then poke holes in the packet. Place the smoker box or the packet on the grill rack over the heat in a gas grill or near the electric coil in an electric smoker. (Some gas grills have a special built-in place where the smoker box goes; consult the manufacturer's instruction manual for your grill.) Wood pellets must be replenished about once an hour (the wood pellet grill does this automatically).

Chunks

These are bigger pieces of aromatic wood, 4 inches (10 cm) wide. Barbecuers argue about whether soaking wood chunks gives you more smoke. I sometimes soak them before using, but not always. Wood chunks are most often placed directly on hot coals or around, but not touching, the electric coil in an electric bullet smoker or the gas flame in a gas-powered bullet smoker. They are too big to use with a gas grill.

Sticks or logs

These larger pieces of wood are cut to fit the dimensions of the firebox in a competition-style rig and are placed right on the hot coals. Sticks and logs are used dry.

Adding the right amount of wood to get the right amount of smoke flavor is another technique that requires practice. In general, the smaller the smoking chamber (the enclosed area in which your food is smoking), the less wood you use, and the lighter the smoke flavor you want, the less wood you use.

- In a charcoal grill or a bullet smoker, start with about 1 cup (250 mL) of wood chips, ⅓ cup (75 mL) of wood pellets or anywhere from three to eight chunks of wood; replenish as necessary.

- In a gas grill, start with about 1 cup (250 mL) of wood chips or ⅓ cup (75 mL) of wood pellets; add more wood when the chips or pellets have smoldered and are spent. You won't be smoking anything for very long on a gas grill anyway, so you won't have to worry about replenishing the wood over more than a two-hour period.

- In a wood pellet grill, simply fill the bin with wood pellets and keep checking to make sure the bin doesn't empty completely. The pellets are automatically fed to the flames while your food is cooking.

- In a professional-style smoker, start with 15 to 20 chunks of wood, or three sticks of wood cut to fit the firebox; replenish as necessary.

It's always best to err on the side of less, rather than more, as food with too much smoke flavor is acrid and inedible. Once you see how much smoke flavor you get, you can always increase the wood the next time.

You have more control over the wood-smoke flavor when you use charcoal, because wood smolders and burns better and more completely. If you use a gas or electric bullet smoker or a gas grill, you will end up with wood that has charred but has not completely burned. That's why barbecuers on the contest circuit use charcoal.

Adding Moisture During Smoking

For the tenderest, most flavorful barbecue, you need to add moisture to the smoking chamber during cooking. You can do that in one of two ways.

The most common method is to use a water pan, which is simply a metal or disposable aluminum pan filled with water. Use the largest pan that will fit in your equipment. Place the water pan on or near the heat source (see "Preparing the Fire," pages 8–11, for where to place it in your equipment). The water will heat and steam. Some

barbecuers fill the water pan with apple juice, cider or even beer. I'm not sure how much flavor that really adds, but it sure smells great!

The second method is to fill a plastic spray bottle with fruit juice or nectar and spray the food as it smokes, every 30 minutes or so. (Just open the lid, quickly spray the food, then close the lid, so you lose as little heat and smoke as possible.) If I use this method in a recipe, I recommend a fruit juice or nectar in the ingredients list.

Monitoring and Adjusting the Temperature

The best way to judge a smoker's temperature is with a thermometer. If a thermometer is not built in to your smoker, use a candy thermometer (or two, or three). Place the stem of the thermometer through the holes where the hot exhaust escapes. (Many beginners use duct tape to fasten thermometers to the smoker, with the stems sticking through the holes.)

When you're starting out, it's much more common to have to find ways to lower the temperature than to raise it. If you're stuck at 300°F (150°C), and you want to get down to 250°F (120°C), here's what you do:

- On a charcoal grill, bullet smoker or ceramic smoker, close the baffles on the side vents (or open the lid as a last resort — you'll lose wood-smoke flavor).

- On a gas-powered bullet smoker, turn the flame to low.

- On a gas or wood pellet grill, turn the temperature dial to lower the temperature.

- On a professional-style smoker, close the baffles on the side vents.

If you need to raise the temperature, here's what you do:

- On a charcoal grill, bullet or ceramic smoker, open the baffles on the side vents or add more charcoal.

- On a gas-powered bullet smoker, turn the flame up a little.

- On a gas or wood pellet grill, turn the temperature dial to raise the temperature.

- On a professional-style smoker, open the baffles on the side vents or add more charcoal.

Keeping your grill lid closed while smoking will help you keep a steady temperature. Competition barbecuers check the temperature every 15 minutes or so to make sure they're smoking at a fairly constant 225°F to 250°F (110°C to 120°C). You don't have to be quite so vigilant in the backyard.

How to Smoke

Once you have prepared your fire, you will either put your food on the smoker rack first, then add the wood to the coals, or the reverse, depending on your equipment. Close the lid and start smoking. After about 10 minutes, check to make sure you can smell wood smoke. If you can't, open the lid to see if the wood is starting to smolder. If not, place the wood closer to the heat source.

Smoke with the lid or hood closed as much as possible. This will trap the heat, allowing it to circulate. With the hood down, your food will cook faster and you'll conserve fuel.

If you're using a charcoal smoker, check periodically — about once every 30 minutes — to make sure you have enough charcoal. You'll know when to replenish because your temperature will start going down. Some barbecuers just add charcoal to the smoldering coals already in the smoker, others always have backup charcoal in the charcoal chimney, hot and ready to go. The timing of starting the charcoal and having it ready when the coals are spent is something you'll have to practice with your equipment.

If you're using a water pan, check periodically — about once every hour — to make sure it has enough liquid and you have enough charcoal or wood.

Check periodically — about once every 3 hours — to see if you need more wood. If you sniff your food and it has a good wood-smoke aroma, don't add more wood. Foods such as pork butt or brisket may only need to smoke for 3 to 5 hours, but they need to slow-cook for longer.

Smoking Timetable

Smoking times are subject to the weather. On a hot, still day, your food will cook more quickly. On a cold, windy day, your food will cook more slowly. The better you can control the heat and the temperature of your smoker in any kind of weather, the better the food you'll produce.

Smoking times also depend on the type of equipment you're using. If you're using a small smoker, such as a kettle grill or a bullet smoker, your food will cook more quickly than it will in a professional-style smoker.

The general rule for hot-smoking is 30 minutes per pound. You'll need to calculate the total weight of the food you have on the smoker. For example, you might be smoking 5 lbs (2.5 kg) of chicken and 5 lbs (2.5 kg) of ribs, or 10 lbs (5 kg) total. In this case, the chicken and ribs should be done in 5 hours.

Use the suggested cooking times given in each recipe as a guideline, but also keep an eye on your food while it's smoking and use a meat thermometer to gauge doneness where appropriate. I always recommend allowing extra time — an hour, perhaps — when smoking any kind of food. You never know!

Storing Smoked Food

Most smoked food can be stored in the refrigerator for up to 1 week or in the freezer for up to 3 months. More delicate smoked fish, fruits and vegetables should be frozen for only up to 1 month. I don't advise freezing smoked cheese.

Cold-Smoking

Cold-smoking is usually reserved for fish, shellfish, fruits and vegetables because cold-smoked food is more preserved than cooked. It stays translucent, doesn't change color and takes on a light wood-smoke flavor. Think thinly sliced smoked salmon, or lox, and smoked scallops.

Cold-smoking is difficult to do at home because you need a smoker capable of keeping a constant low temperature. You'll need special equipment, whether you buy a cold smoker or fashion your own (see below). I use a SmokinTex® (see the Source Guide, page 356), a box-like stainless steel smoker that has a temperature range of up to 250°F (120°C), so you could also use it to hot-smoke foods.

The cold-smoking recipes in this book result in foods with a cold-smoked flavor and appearance, but they are not meant to preserve foods (a lengthy process that must be done with specialized equipment). Cold-smoking at temperatures under 80°F (27°C) is usually a commercial rather than a home-based activity.

Acquiring a Cold Smoker

Because cold-smoking is very specialized, you'll have to do some research online or through your barbecue society to learn what might be the right equipment for you and how to purchase it. If you feel adventurous, however, you could try to convert the equipment you have to cold-smoking. For information on how to do this, visit **www.virtualweberbullet.com/coldsmoker.html**. Or, if you're handy, you could convert a filing cabinet into a cold smoker. To find out how, visit **www.downsizer.net/Projects/Curing_and_Smoking/Filing_Cabinet_Hot%10 Cold_smoker/**.

The Cold-Smoking Process

The cold-smoking process is similar to hot-smoking in that you prepare the food with marinades or rubs before smoking, you use wood for flavor and you keep the temperature constant during smoking. But there are a few differences:

- You don't use a water pan or spray the food while smoking; the whole point of cold-smoking is to remove moisture, not add it. Likewise, you do not need to baste or mop.

- Moist foods such as fish and shellfish are usually brined before smoking to remove moisture, but are not marinated.

- Vegetables, cheeses and fruits are not usually brined or seasoned.

- You don't glaze foods with sauce, as there is not enough heat to set the glaze.

For information on preparing a fire, consult the manufacturer's instruction manual for your cold smoker.

How Much Wood?

On the equipment I use, the rule of thumb is 2 oz (60 g) of wood chips per 1 lb (500 g) of food. Read the instruction manual for your cold smoker and follow the manufacturer's guidelines until you come up with your own.

Controlling the Temperature

With cold-smoking, you have to control the temperature of both the smoker and the smoke. I start my cold smoker at 200°F (100°C) to get the wood to smolder, then adjust the temperature as needed for the recipe. The smoke needs to cool before it reaches the food. In the SmokinTex®, a cold plate sits over the firebox and keeps the heat from going up into the unit. You set a pan of ice on the cold plate to keep the smoke cool. Consult the manufacturer's instruction manual to learn more about regulating the temperature of your cold smoker.

Brines, Rubs, Marinades, Bastes and Sauces

BUILDING FLAVOR LAYERS and ensuring moist and tender results in your smoked foods begins before the smoking process with brines, rubs and marinades. It continues during smoking with bastes and mops, and ends with the final brush of barbecue sauce or glaze or a spoonful of a complementary finishing sauce. Each recipe will tell you which methods work best, but feel free to try any or all of these techniques as you develop your own style of barbecuing.

- *Before Smoking:* Immerse foods in a brine, soak in a marinade, brush with a slather or sprinkle with a dry rub.

- *During Smoking:* Use a buttery baste or mop for foods that could dry out during smoking, such as salmon or chicken breasts. Use a vinegary or coffee-laced mixture to cut the fatty taste in brisket or pork shoulder blade, and a citrus spray for oily fish. During the last hour of smoking, brush on barbecue sauce or a glaze to create a lacquered, shiny appearance on the food.

- *After Smoking:* Serve more barbecue sauce or a finishing sauce or salsa to complement the smoky flavor in the food. Or offer Barbecuer's Aioli (page 71), a garlicky homemade mayonnaise, with smoked lobster, scallops or shrimp.

BRINES

Maple Mustard Brine 21
Orange, Garlic &
    Brown Sugar Brine 22
Tennessee Bourbon Brine 23
Brine for Beef 24
Beer & Brown Sugar Brine 25

RUBS AND PASTES

All-Purpose Barbecue Rub 27
New Mexico–Style Rub 27
Savory Brown Sugar Rub 28
Aromatic Poultry Rub 29
Every-Flavor Spice Rub 30
Ancho-Herb Dry Rub 30
Honey & Spice Rub 31
Flower of the Flames Rib Rub . . . 32
Brown Sugar Rib Rub 33
Sassy, Spicy Pork Rub 34
Onion & Garlic Dry Rub 34
Fresh Herb & Spice Paste 35
Fresh Garlic & Herb Paste 35

MARINADES

Chipotle Marinade 36
Soy-Sherry Marinade 37
Lime Cola Marinade 37
Lime & Lager Marinade 38
Bay Leaf Marinade 38
Orange & Soy Marinade 39
Fresh Orange &
    White Balsamic Marinade . . . 39
Onion Soy Marinade 40
Easy Asian Marinade 40
Coffee Lime Marinade 41
Blackberry Merlot Marinade 41
Maple Honey Marinade 42
Mediterranean Marinade 42
Sesame Marinade 43

BASTES

All-Purpose Mop 44
Rich & Delicious Brisket Mop 45
Beefy Barbecue Mop 46
Sweet Orange Baste 46
Sweet & Spicy Rib Baste 47
Buttery Brown Sugar
    & Lime Basting Sauce 48

BARBECUE SAUCES AND FINISHING SAUCES

Flower of the Flames
    Raspberry Barbecue Sauce . . . 50
Vinegar-Style Barbecue Sauce . . . 51
Bourbon Barbecue Sauce 52
Texas-Style Barbecue Sauce 53
Texas Spit 54
Kansas City–Style
    Barbecue Sauce 55
Sugar-Free Barbecue Sauce 56
North Carolina–Style
    Barbecue Sauce 57
Memphis-Style Barbecue Sauce . . 58
Tangy Mustard Barbecue Sauce . . 59
Mustard & Marmalade
    Barbecue Sauce 60
Honey Mustard
    Barbecue Sauce 61
Apple Ancho Barbecue Sauce . . . 62
Cherry Chipotle
    Barbecue Sauce 63
Peachy Barbecue Sauce 64
Apricot, Apricot, Apricot
    Barbecue Sauce 65
Easy Apricot Barbecue Glaze 66
Apricot Maple Glaze 66
Barbecue Glaze 67
Red Currant Sauce 67
Blackberry Merlot Sauce 68
Citrus Demi-glace 68
Fresh Blueberry &
    Ginger Sauce 69
Herbal Balsamic Jelly 70
Barbecuer's Aioli 71

Brines

For moist, flavorful results, many chefs and barbecuers recommend immersing food in brine, a salty solution that can contain flavoring agents such as mustard, wine, spices, herbs and other seasonings. A brine can transform chicken, pork or even a whole turkey into a mouthwatering masterpiece. Many types of seafood, such as salmon and swordfish, also benefit from brining.

What's brining?

Brining is the process of soaking meat, poultry or seafood in a salty tenderizing solution. Thanks to salt's natural ability to draw out food's true flavors and juices, brining adds an extra amount of seasoned moisture and helps the food retain flavor and tenderness throughout the slow-smoking process. When brining is done properly, your food will not taste salty. It will simply be juicier than usual.

You can use any kind of salt for a brine, but many chefs and barbecuers prefer kosher salt or sea salt because it does not contain the iodine often found in table salt. Non-iodized salt has a cleaner and purer taste.

With brining, you have to plan ahead. Foods can take up to 48 hours to brine before smoking. Some barbecuers take a shortcut by using veterinary syringes (available at veterinary supply houses) to inject the brine solution into briskets, pork loins and pork shoulder blades right before smoking. There are also specialized kitchen flavor injectors now available at specialty kitchenware stores.

A simple solution

To make the most basic of brines, mix 3 tbsp (45 mL) non-iodized salt with 4 cups (1 L) water.

How to brine

- Use approximately 4 cups (1 L) brine for every pound (500 g) of meat.

- Place the meat, poultry or fish in a non-metallic container big enough to allow it to be fully immersed in the solution. (For smaller meats, such as fish fillets, pork chops or chicken legs and thighs, you can use a large sealable plastic bag.) Cover (or seal) and let soak in the refrigerator at a rate of 1 hour per pound (500 g).

- Drain, discarding brine, pat dry and smoke as you normally would, without any change in temperature or technique.

Maple Mustard Brine

This flavorful brine makes smoked pork loin or shoulder blade extra juicy, as with Pork Loin Roast in Maple Mustard Brine (page 244). It's also delicious on salmon and whitefish.

MAKES ABOUT 8 CUPS (2 L)

TIPS

To use on a pork loin roast, see page 244.

• • •

To use on salmon, swordfish or whitefish, use the full recipe on several large fillets, or use half a recipe on one large fillet; brine (see instructions, page 20) for 1 to 2 hours before smoking.

• • •

To halve the ingredients for this brine, use 6 tbsp (90 mL) maple syrup and half of each of the other ingredients.

¾ cup	pure maple syrup	175 mL
½ cup	kosher salt	125 mL
2 tbsp	Dijon mustard	25 mL
1 tbsp	coarsely ground black pepper	15 mL
1½ tsp	hot pepper flakes	7 mL
1 tsp	dried rosemary	5 mL

1. In a large saucepan, bring 8 cups (2 L) water, maple syrup, salt, mustard, pepper, hot pepper flakes and rosemary to a boil over high heat. Remove from heat and let cool.

Orange, Garlic & Brown Sugar Brine

There is a touch of sweetness in this brine, which works well with chicken (see Whole Chicken in Orange, Garlic & Brown Sugar Brine, page 195) or fish, especially salmon.

MAKES ABOUT 6 CUPS (1.5 L)

TIPS

To use on a whole chicken, see page 195.

• • •

To use on salmon or swordfish, use the full recipe on several large fillets or use half a recipe on one large fillet; brine (see instructions, page 20) for 1 hour before smoking.

• • •

To use on a whole turkey, double the recipe; brine (see instructions, page 20) for 48 hours before smoking.

1 cup	orange juice	250 mL
1 cup	packed brown sugar (dark or light)	250 mL
½ cup	kosher salt	125 mL
2 tbsp	garlic powder, or to taste	25 mL
1 tbsp	coarsely ground black pepper	15 mL

1. In a large saucepan, bring 4 cups (1 L) water, orange juice, brown sugar, salt, garlic powder and pepper to a boil over high heat, stirring to dissolve sugar. Remove from heat and let cool.

Tennessee Bourbon Brine

It may make you weep to discard the bourbon after your food has finished brining, but that's the way it goes. This is a great brine for smaller foods, such as a salmon fillet, pork chops (see Tennessee Bourbon–Brined Pork Chops, page 248) or bone-in chicken thighs and legs. It's a bit strong for chicken or turkey breast. This brine would be expensive to double or triple to use on a pork loin or shoulder blade, but if money's no object, go right ahead!

MAKES ABOUT 1 1/2 CUPS (375 ML)

TIPS

To use on pork chops, see page 248.

• • •

To use on salmon or swordfish, use a full recipe on each large fillet; brine (see instructions, page 20) for 1 hour before smoking.

• • •

To use on bone-in chicken thighs and legs, use a full recipe for every 4 thighs and/or legs; brine (see instructions, page 20) for 2 to 3 hours before smoking.

1 cup	bourbon	250 mL
1/2 cup	packed brown sugar (dark or light)	125 mL
1 tbsp	kosher salt	15 mL
1 tsp	garlic powder	5 mL
1 tsp	coarsely ground black pepper	5 mL
1/2 tsp	dried thyme	2 mL

1. In a small bowl, mix bourbon, brown sugar, salt, garlic powder, pepper and thyme until sugar has dissolved.

Brine for Beef

When you use this brine on a large brisket, tri-tip or beef roast, you'll get a beefier, juicier result.

TIPS

To use on a whole brisket or a large tri-tip or beef roast, use a full recipe; brine (see instructions, page 20) for 12 to 48 hours before smoking.

• • •

If you can't wait days for your beef to brine, let the brine mixture set for 1 hour after heating, then strain out the bay leaves and peppercorns and use a veterinary syringe or flavor injector to inject the meat with the brine.

3	bay leaves	3
3 cups	cider vinegar	750 mL
½ cup	kosher salt	125 mL
⅓ cup	packed dark brown sugar	75 mL
1 tbsp	whole black peppercorns	15 mL

1. In a large saucepan, bring bay leaves, 4 cups (1 L) water, vinegar, salt, brown sugar and peppercorns to a boil over high heat. Remove from heat and let cool.

Beer & Brown Sugar Brine

This brine produces a deep, dark, rich flavor that is perfect for beef, game or even meaty fish such as swordfish or tuna.

**MAKES ABOUT
4 CUPS (1 L)**

TIPS

To use on beef flank steak or venison chops, use a full recipe; brine (see instructions, page 20) for 6 to 10 hours before smoking.

● ● ●

To use on swordfish or tuna, use a full recipe on 2 to 3 pounds (1 to 1.5 kg) fish fillets; brine (see instructions, page 20) for 2 to 4 hours before smoking.

4 cups	brown ale	1 L
½ cup	kosher salt	125 mL
½ cup	packed dark brown sugar	125 mL
¼ cup	pickling spice	50 mL

1. In a large saucepan, bring ale, salt, brown sugar and pickling spice to a boil over high heat, stirring to dissolve sugar. Remove from heat and let cool.

Rubs and Pastes

A dry rub is a seasoning mixture containing salt, sugar, dried herbs, spices and dried chilies. It's used to create a flavorful crust or "bark" on foods destined to be smoked. Many barbecuers add paprika or chili powder to their dry rubs to add color to the smoked food.

No fresh or moist ingredient is used in a dry rub; that's why you'll see unusual ingredients like honey powder or carrot powder in some of these rubs. You can find these ingredients at better spice stores (or see the Source Guide on page 356).

You want fresh dried ingredients for your dry rubs, not old, tired and tasteless spices and herbs that have sat on the grocery store shelves for ages. That's why I buy my herbs and spices in bulk, so I can smell how fresh they are. I also buy herbs and spices from well-known herb and spice businesses, even if I have to mail-order them.

Once you add a fresh or moist ingredient, the mixture becomes a paste rather than a rub. A paste is generally a dry rub mixture with olive oil and/or fresh garlic and herbs added. A paste is brushed over foods destined for the smoker and helps keep them moist during cooking.

How to make and use a dry rub or paste

To make a dry rub, just mix all the ingredients together in a bowl. I usually marinate foods first, then remove them from the marinade and sprinkle on the dry rub. Other barbecuers might brush the food with olive oil, then sprinkle on a dry rub. Still others might brush foods like brisket or pork shoulder blade with a mustard slather — as simple as prepared yellow mustard straight from the jar or a mixture of Dijon mustard and mayonnaise — then sprinkle with the dry rub; they let the food sit until the surface feels tacky to the touch (about 30 minutes), then put it on the smoker.

You make a paste the same way — mix all the ingredients together in a bowl. Again, I like to marinate my foods first, then spread a paste over them before putting the foods on the smoker. You can also just spread on the flavoring paste and smoke the food without marinating or brining. A flavoring paste is also delicious on foods you might grill or put on the rotisserie, because the olive oil helps keep them moist.

How to store a dry rub or paste

Place dry rubs in a sealable plastic bag or a jar and store in a dark, cool, dry place for up to 6 months. Place pastes in an airtight container and store in the refrigerator for up to 3 days.

All-Purpose Barbecue Rub

This seasoning mixture tastes great on anything you want to slow-smoke: pork ribs, whole chickens, beef brisket — you name it!

MAKES ABOUT ½ CUP (125 ML)

TIP

You can buy jalapeño pepper powder and ancho chili powder at better herb and spice emporiums, by mail order or online (see the Source Guide, page 356).

2 tbsp	fine kosher or sea salt	25 mL
2 tbsp	granulated sugar	25 mL
1 tbsp	packed dark brown sugar	15 mL
2 tsp	ancho chili powder (see tip, at left)	10 mL
2 tsp	sweet Hungarian paprika	10 mL
1 tsp	ground cumin	5 mL
1 tsp	MSG (optional)	5 mL
½ tsp	onion powder	2 mL
½ tsp	garlic powder	2 mL
¼ tsp	jalapeño pepper powder (see tip, at left)	1 mL

1. In a small bowl, combine salt, sugar, brown sugar, chili powder, paprika, cumin, MSG (if using), onion powder, garlic powder and jalapeño pepper powder.

New Mexico–Style Rub

For an authentic Southwest flavor, add this mixture to barbecued beans, pork, lamb or beef.

MAKES ABOUT ½ CUP (125 ML)

TIP

To get the best blend of flavors, pair a hot rub like this one with a sweeter sauce such as Apricot, Apricot, Apricot Barbecue Sauce (page 65) or Peachy Barbecue Sauce (page 64).

¼ cup	chili powder	50 mL
1 tbsp	onion powder	15 mL
1 tbsp	ground cumin	15 mL
2 tsp	kosher salt	10 mL
1½ tsp	dried oregano	7 mL
1 tsp	garlic powder	5 mL
1 tsp	cayenne pepper	5 mL

1. In a small bowl, combine chili powder, onion powder, cumin, salt, oregano, garlic powder and cayenne.

Savory Brown Sugar Rub

This lip-smackin' good rub is wonderful on ribs. But try it on pork loin or shoulder blade too.

**MAKES ABOUT
¾ CUP (175 ML)**

TIPS

You can buy ancho pepper powder at better herb and spice emporiums, by mail order or online (see the Source Guide, page 356).

● ● ●

To get the best blend of flavors, pair a sweet rub like this one with a hotter sauce such as Cherry Chipotle Barbecue Sauce (page 63).

¼ cup	kosher salt	50 mL
¼ cup	granulated sugar	50 mL
3 tbsp	packed dark brown sugar	45 mL
1 tbsp	ancho chili powder (see tip, at left)	15 mL
1 tbsp	paprika	15 mL
1½ tsp	ground cumin	7 mL
1½ tsp	MSG (optional)	7 mL
¾ tsp	onion powder	3 mL
¾ tsp	garlic powder	3 mL
¾ tsp	coarsely ground black pepper	3 mL
¼ tsp	cayenne pepper	1 mL

1. In a small bowl, combine salt, sugar, brown sugar, chili powder, paprika, cumin, MSG (if using), onion powder, garlic powder, black pepper and cayenne.

Aromatic Poultry Rub

Sprinkle this rub on chicken, turkey, game birds (pheasant, quail, partridge, grouse, etc.) or Cornish game hens, then smoke for a sweet and spicy result.

MAKES ABOUT 1 CUP (250 ML)

TIPS

You can buy dried orange zest at better spice emporiums, or grate it yourself and spread out in a single layer on a baking sheet lined with waxed paper, aluminum foil or parchment paper. Let dry at room temperature for about 24 hours, or until completely dry.

* * *

To build a customized rub, start with salt and brown sugar, then add chili powder or paprika for color, then your herbs and spices. For heat, add cayenne pepper, jalapeño pepper powder or hot pepper flakes.

¼ cup	fine kosher or sea salt	50 mL
3 tbsp	packed brown sugar (light or dark)	45 mL
2 tbsp	dried orange zest (see tip, at left)	25 mL
1 tbsp	onion salt	15 mL
1 tbsp	freshly ground black pepper	15 mL
1 tbsp	freshly ground white pepper	15 mL
1 tbsp	chili powder	15 mL
1 tbsp	dried marjoram	15 mL
1 tbsp	poultry seasoning	15 mL
1 tbsp	ground lemon pepper	15 mL
1 tbsp	MSG (optional)	15 mL

1. In a small bowl, combine salt, brown sugar, orange zest, onion salt, black pepper, white pepper, chili powder, marjoram, poultry seasoning, lemon pepper and MSG (if using).

Every-Flavor Spice Rub

Hot, cool, mellow, spicy, sweet, savory — this dry rub has it all. Try it on chicken thighs, game birds, turkey and pork.

MAKES ABOUT ¼ CUP (50 ML)

TIP

This recipe can be doubled, tripled or quadrupled to use with larger cuts of meat.

2 tbsp	packed brown sugar	25 mL
1 tbsp	kosher salt	15 mL
2 tsp	ground coriander	10 mL
1 tsp	freshly ground black pepper	5 mL
1 tsp	dried thyme	5 mL
1 tsp	ground allspice	5 mL
1 tsp	ground cinnamon	5 mL
½ tsp	cayenne pepper	2 mL

1. In a small bowl, combine brown sugar, salt, coriander, black pepper, thyme, allspice, cinnamon and cayenne.

Ancho-Herb Dry Rub

Try this rub on a pork loin or shoulder blade for a savory flavor. It's also good on chicken, turkey and game birds.

MAKES ABOUT 3½ CUPS (875 ML)

TIP

Add a little moisture to a dry seasoning rub, and it becomes a paste. Add lots of moisture, as in vinegar, olive oil or wine, and the rub becomes a marinade.

2 cups	packed brown sugar (light or dark)	500 mL
⅓ cup	fine kosher or sea salt	75 mL
¼ cup	sweet Hungarian paprika	50 mL
¼ cup	ancho chili powder (see tip, page 28)	50 mL
¼ cup	onion powder	50 mL
¼ cup	garlic powder	50 mL
1 tsp	dried mint	5 mL
1 tsp	dried basil	5 mL
1 tsp	dried thyme	5 mL

1. In a medium bowl, combine brown sugar, salt, paprika, chili powder, onion powder, garlic powder, mint, basil and thyme.

Honey & Spice Rub

This sweet and spicy rub tastes great on pork, chicken and turkey.

TIPS

You can find honey powder at better spice emporiums or online (see the Source Guide, page 356). If you can't find it, substitute an equal amount of granulated maple sugar.

• • •

You can find granulated garlic at well-stocked supermarkets or online (see the Source Guide, page 356).

3 tbsp	fine kosher or sea salt	45 mL
3 tbsp	packed brown sugar (light or dark)	45 mL
2 tbsp	MSG (optional)	25 mL
2 tbsp	honey powder (see tip, at left)	25 mL
1 tbsp	sweet Hungarian paprika	15 mL
1 tbsp	freshly ground black pepper	15 mL
1½ tsp	granulated garlic (see tip, at left)	7 mL
1¼ tsp	ground lemon pepper	6 mL
1 tsp	cayenne pepper	5 mL
1 tsp	chili powder	5 mL
½ tsp	dry mustard	2 mL
¼ tsp	ground cinnamon	1 mL

1. In a small bowl, combine salt, brown sugar, MSG (if using), honey powder, paprika, black pepper, garlic, lemon pepper, cayenne, chili powder, mustard and cinnamon.

Flower of the Flames Rib Rub

Here is my own rib rub, which helped me win a world championship in the ribs category at an international barbecue contest held in Limerick, Ireland. This rub has a magical blend of salt, sugar, spices and herbs.

MAKES ABOUT 5 CUPS (1.25 L)

TIP

If you wish, use a clean electric coffee grinder to grind celery seeds and dried oregano to a fine powder for this rub.

1 cup	sweet Hungarian paprika	250 mL
¾ cup	fine kosher or sea salt	175 mL
½ cup	freshly ground black pepper	125 mL
½ cup	chili powder	125 mL
½ cup	ground cumin	125 mL
½ cup	packed brown sugar (light or dark)	125 mL
½ cup	garlic powder	125 mL
¼ cup	granulated sugar	50 mL
¼ cup	ground celery seeds	50 mL
2 tbsp	ground oregano	25 mL

1. In a medium bowl, combine paprika, salt, pepper, chili powder, cumin, brown sugar, garlic powder, sugar, celery seed and oregano.

Brown Sugar Rib Rub

Slow-smoked pork ribs really benefit from a spicy rub with medium heat. A good rub accentuates the sweetness of the pork, while helping to create a crusty exterior. I also like this rub on slow-smoked salmon.

MAKES ABOUT 3½ CUPS (875 ML)

TIP
You can find granulated garlic at well-stocked supermarkets or online (see the Source Guide, page 356).

2 cups	packed dark brown sugar or granulated maple sugar	500 mL
½ cup	fine kosher or sea salt	125 mL
¼ cup	sweet Hungarian paprika	50 mL
¼ cup	chili powder	50 mL
¼ cup	ground lemon pepper	50 mL
¼ cup	granulated garlic (see tip, at left)	50 mL
1 tbsp	freshly ground black pepper	15 mL
1 tsp	dried basil	5 mL
1 tsp	dried thyme	5 mL

1. In a medium bowl, combine brown sugar, salt, paprika, chili powder, lemon pepper, garlic, black pepper, basil and thyme.

Sassy, Spicy Pork Rub

Here's a savory rub that accentuates and contrasts with the sweet flavor of smoked pork ribs, pork shoulder blade and pork loin. It's also great on chicken wings!

MAKES ABOUT
²/₃ CUP (150 ML)

TIP

To get the best blend of flavors, pair a hot rub like this one with a sweeter sauce such as Apricot, Apricot, Apricot Barbecue Sauce (page 65) or Peachy Barbecue Sauce (page 64).

3 tbsp	fine kosher or sea salt	45 mL
3 tbsp	packed dark brown sugar	45 mL
1 tbsp	freshly ground black pepper	15 mL
1 tbsp	sweet Hungarian paprika	15 mL
1 tbsp	MSG (optional)	15 mL
1½ tsp	garlic salt	7 mL
1 tsp	ancho chili powder (see tip, page 28)	5 mL
½ tsp	onion salt	2 mL
½ tsp	dry mustard	2 mL

1. In a small bowl, combine salt, brown sugar, pepper, paprika, MSG (if using), garlic salt, chili powder, onion salt and mustard.

Onion & Garlic Dry Rub

Hearty and satisfying, with onion and garlic, this dry rub is great on smoked beef brisket or any cut of beef you put on the smoker.

MAKES ABOUT
3½ CUPS (875 ML)

TIP

Carrot powder is available at better spice emporiums or online (see the Source Guide, page 356). If you can't find it, increase the paprika by 2 tsp (10 mL).

2 cups	packed brown sugar (light or dark)	500 mL
½ cup	fine kosher or sea salt	125 mL
¼ cup	sweet Hungarian paprika	50 mL
¼ cup	onion powder	50 mL
¼ cup	garlic powder	50 mL
¼ cup	chili powder	50 mL
2 tsp	carrot powder (see tip, at left)	10 mL
2 tsp	freshly ground black pepper	10 mL

1. In a medium bowl, combine brown sugar, salt, paprika, onion powder, garlic powder, chili powder, carrot powder and pepper.

Fresh Herb & Spice Paste

A dry rub contains all dry ingredients. Because this recipe contains fresh herbs, it's more like a paste that you spread over foods. Its hearty flavor makes it delicious on beef, pork or game destined for the smoker or the grill.

MAKES ABOUT 1 CUP (250 ML)

Make ahead

Place in an airtight container and store in the refrigerator for up to 3 days.

¼ cup	finely minced onion	50 mL
¼ cup	minced fresh parsley	50 mL
3 tbsp	kosher salt	45 mL
3 tbsp	cracked black pepper	45 mL
2 tbsp	minced garlic	25 mL
1 tsp	minced fresh basil	5 mL
1 tsp	minced fresh thyme	5 mL
1½ tsp	dry mustard	7 mL

1. In a small bowl, combine onion, parsley, salt, pepper, garlic, basil, thyme and mustard.

Fresh Garlic & Herb Paste

Spread this luscious paste on chicken breasts, whole chicken, turkey breast, fish fillets or shrimp before smoking. Heavenly!

MAKES ABOUT ⅓ CUP (75 ML)

Make ahead

Place in an airtight container and store in the refrigerator for up to 3 days.

4	cloves garlic, minced	4
2 tbsp	minced fresh rosemary	25 mL
2 tbsp	olive oil	25 mL
1 tbsp	minced fresh mint	15 mL
1 tsp	kosher salt	5 mL
½ tsp	cracked black pepper	2 mL

1. In a small bowl, combine garlic, rosemary, oil, mint, salt and pepper.

Marinades

Marinades add a lot of flavor to food. A marinade can be a complex mixture of 25 ingredients or a simple bottle of your favorite vinaigrette. Typically, marinades have a higher proportion of an acid ingredient, such as vinegar or citrus juice. Vinaigrettes have a higher proportion of fat, usually from olive oil or another vegetable oil. But either is good for marinating foods before smoking. Make sure to marinate fish and shellfish only as long as the recipe dictates. The high acid content in marinades could "cook" the delicate seafood into ceviche, which is delicious but not what you want here!

Chipotle Marinade

This zesty marinade is wonderful on chicken wings, pork and beef.

MAKES ABOUT 1½ CUPS (375 ML)

Make ahead

Pour into a glass jar with a tight-fitting lid and store in the refrigerator for up to 3 days.

2	cloves garlic	2
2	canned chipotle peppers in adobo sauce (2 tbsp/25 mL sauce reserved)	2
¼ cup	sherry vinegar or white wine vinegar	50 mL
¼ cup	balsamic vinegar	50 mL
½ tsp	kosher salt	2 mL
⅔ cup	olive oil	150 mL
	Freshly ground black pepper	

1. In a food processor or blender, process garlic, chipotle peppers, reserved adobo sauce, sherry vinegar, balsamic vinegar and salt until smooth. With the motor running, add oil in a slow, steady stream through the feed tube until all the oil is incorporated. Season to taste with pepper and pulse to blend.

Soy-Sherry Marinade

The sweet/savory combination in this marinade goes well with small quantities of chicken, fish or pork.

TIP

Jalapeño pepper powder is available from better spice emporiums or online (see the Source Guide, page 356). If you can't find it, substitute about 1/2 tsp (2 mL) hot pepper sauce.

2	cloves garlic, minced	2
3 tbsp	soy sauce	45 mL
1 tbsp	dry sherry	15 mL
1 tsp	Worcestershire sauce	5 mL
1 tsp	dry white wine	5 mL
1 tsp	freshly squeezed lime juice	5 mL
1 tsp	granulated sugar	5 mL
1/4 tsp	jalapeño pepper powder (see tip, at left)	1 mL

1. In a small bowl, combine garlic, soy sauce, sherry, Worcestershire sauce, wine, lime juice, sugar and jalapeño pepper powder.

Lime Cola Marinade

This marinade is wonderful with brisket, ribs, pork loin and chicken.

TIPS

Serrano chili peppers can be found in Mexican markets and well-stocked supermarkets.

• • •

If you can't find lime-flavored cola, use regular cola (not diet) and increase lime zest to 1 tbsp (15 mL) and lime juice to 1/2 cup (125 mL).

8	cloves garlic, coarsely chopped	8
3	green onions, minced	3
1	serrano chili pepper, chopped	1
3 cups	lime-flavored cola	750 mL
1/2 cup	bottled Italian dressing	125 mL
1/4 cup	minced fresh cilantro	50 mL
2 tsp	grated lime zest	10 mL
1/4 cup	freshly squeezed lime juice	50 mL
2 tbsp	kosher salt	25 mL
1 tsp	freshly grated black pepper	5 mL

1. In a large bowl, combine garlic, green onions, serrano pepper, cola, dressing, cilantro, lime zest and juice, salt and pepper.

Lime & Lager Marinade

If you like the combination of lime and lager at the pub, you'll love it with smoked shrimp, scallops and chicken.

**MAKES ABOUT
2½ CUPS (625 ML)**

TIPS
You'll need 6 to 8 medium limes to make ¾ cup (175 mL) juice.

• • •

You can multiply most marinade recipes to match the quantity of food you want to marinate.

8	garlic cloves, minced	8
1 cup	lager beer	250 mL
¾ cup	freshly squeezed lime juice	175 mL
¼ cup	olive oil	50 mL
1 tbsp	minced canned chipotle pepper	15 mL
1½ tsp	Worcestershire sauce	7 mL
1 tsp	soy sauce	5 mL
1 tsp	powdered chicken stock base	5 mL
½ tsp	minced fresh mint	2 mL
½ tsp	minced fresh basil	2 mL
½ tsp	freshly ground black pepper	2 mL

1. In a medium bowl, combine garlic, beer, lime juice, oil, chipotle pepper, Worcestershire sauce, soy sauce, powdered chicken stock, mint, basil and pepper.

Bay Leaf Marinade

Deep and aromatic, this marinade is good with ostrich or meaty game birds.

**MAKES ABOUT
1½ CUPS (375 ML)**

TIP
To get the best and freshest nutmeg flavor, use a whole nutmeg and grate a pinch into the marinade.

4	whole cloves	4
3	cloves garlic, minced	3
3	bay leaves	3
1 cup	chicken stock	250 mL
½ cup	red wine vinegar	125 mL
½ tsp	poultry seasoning	2 mL
Pinch	ground nutmeg	Pinch
Pinch	dried oregano	Pinch

1. In a small bowl, combine cloves, garlic, bay leaves, chicken stock, vinegar, poultry seasoning, nutmeg and oregano.

Orange & Soy Marinade

When you add soy sauce to a marinade, you get a salty, savory flavor and a lovely color. I like this marinade with fish and shellfish.

MAKES ABOUT 1 2/3 CUPS (400 ML)

Make ahead

Cover and store in the refrigerator for up to 1 week (but best when used right away).

2	cloves garlic, minced	2
1/2 cup	soy sauce	125 mL
1/2 cup	orange juice	125 mL
1/4 cup	chopped fresh parsley	50 mL
1/4 cup	ketchup	50 mL
2 tbsp	freshly squeezed lime juice	25 mL
1 tsp	ground ginger	5 mL
1 tsp	dried Italian seasoning	5 mL

1. In a small bowl, combine garlic, soy sauce, orange juice, parsley, ketchup, lime juice, ginger and Italian seasoning.

Fresh Orange & White Balsamic Marinade

Try this easy marinade on a meaty fish fillet or steak, such as tuna or swordfish, before smoking or grilling. The fresh orange flavor cuts the oiliness of the fish, while adding a wonderful flavor. It's also good on pork, chicken and shellfish.

MAKES ABOUT 1 CUP (250 ML)

TIP

One medium orange should yield more than enough juice, but you'll need 2 oranges to get enough zest. Use the leftover orange for garnish.

1	clove garlic, minced	1
2 tbsp	grated orange zest	25 mL
1/4 cup	freshly squeezed orange juice	50 mL
1/4 cup	olive oil	50 mL
3 tbsp	soy sauce	45 mL
2 tbsp	minced shallots	25 mL
1 tbsp	white balsamic vinegar	15 mL
Pinch	freshly ground black pepper	Pinch

1. In a small bowl, combine garlic, orange zest and juice, oil, soy sauce, shallots, vinegar and pepper.

Onion Soy Marinade

When you get good at slow-smoking, people will start asking you to lend your barbecuing talents to school and church events, weddings… you name it. When you slow-smoke in quantity, you need large-volume recipes like this one. This savory/sweet marinade is great on pork of all kinds, from ribs to tenderloin. The combination of soy and sesame oil gives it a slightly Asian flavor.

MAKES ABOUT 20 CUPS (5 L)

TIPS

To get the quantity of ingredients you need without a high cost, shop at wholesale clubs or restaurant supply stores.

• • •

To make 5 cups (1.25 L) puréed onion, purée 8 cups (2 L) chopped onions (about 10 onions) in a food processor, in batches as necessary.

10 cups	soy sauce	2.5 L
5 cups	granulated sugar	1.25 L
5 cups	puréed onion (see tip, at left)	1.25 L
2 cups	olive oil	500 mL
1½ cups	sesame oil	375 mL
1 cup	garlic powder (8 oz/250 g)	250 mL
⅓ cup	cracked black pepper	75 mL

1. In a very large bowl or a stockpot, combine soy sauce, sugar, onion, olive oil, sesame oil, garlic powder and pepper, stirring to dissolve sugar.

Easy Asian Marinade

This all-purpose marinade imparts an Asian flavor to vegetables, chicken, fish, pork, lamb, beef and game intended for the smoker. It's especially good on pork tenderloin and salmon.

MAKES ABOUT 1¾ CUPS (425 ML)

Make ahead

Cover and store in the refrigerator for up to 1 week (but best when used right away).

⅓ cup	Worcestershire sauce	75 mL
¼ cup	soy sauce	50 mL
¼ cup	rice vinegar	50 mL

1. In a small bowl, whisk together 1 cup (250 mL) water, Worcestershire sauce, soy sauce and vinegar.

Coffee Lime Marinade

I developed this marinade for a contest, and I love it on just about anything, but especially on chicken.

MAKES ABOUT 1⅓ CUPS (325 ML)

TIP
You'll need 3 to 4 medium limes to make ¼ cup (50 mL) juice.

1	clove garlic, minced	1
½ cup	brewed coffee, cooled	125 mL
¼ cup	freshly squeezed lime juice	50 mL
¼ cup	vegetable oil	50 mL
¼ cup	hot pepper sauce	50 mL
¼ cup	chopped fresh cilantro	50 mL
½ tsp	kosher salt	2 mL

1. In a small bowl, combine garlic, coffee, lime juice, oil, hot pepper sauce, cilantro and salt.

Blackberry Merlot Marinade

Delicious with quail, venison, pheasant or any other game, this marinade has a darkly intriguing flavor.

MAKES ABOUT 3 CUPS (750 ML)

TIP
Blackberry merlot is a blackberry-flavored wine beverage available from a few different wine producers. Look for it where wines or coolers are sold. If you can't find it, substitute any other dark, semisweet, fruity wine.

6	green onions, minced	6
4	cloves garlic, minced	4
3	sprigs fresh thyme	3
2 cups	blackberry merlot wine (see tip, at left)	500 mL
½ cup	olive oil	125 mL
3 tbsp	rice vinegar	45 mL
2 tbsp	kosher salt	25 mL
1 tsp	freshly ground black pepper	5 mL

1. In a medium bowl, whisk together green onions, garlic, thyme, wine, oil, vinegar, salt and pepper.

Maple Honey Marinade

A little sweet, a little savory, this marinade is delicious with game, exotic meats such as ostrich, and lamb or pork. Use pure maple syrup for the best flavor.

**MAKES ABOUT
1 1/2 CUPS (375 ML)**

Make ahead

Cover and store in the refrigerator for up to 1 day (but best when used right away).

4	cloves garlic, minced	4
1/2 cup	diced onion	125 mL
1/2 cup	pure maple syrup	125 mL
1/4 cup	olive oil	50 mL
1/4 cup	liquid clover honey or other amber honey	50 mL
2 tbsp	kosher salt	25 mL
1/4 tsp	cracked black pepper	1 mL

1. In a small bowl, whisk together garlic, onion, maple syrup, oil, honey, salt and pepper.

Mediterranean Marinade

With garlic, fresh herbs, lemon juice and olive oil, this marvelous marinade does wonders for anything you want to smoke, from vegetables to game. (It's also good on foods you want to grill.)

**MAKES ABOUT
2 1/2 CUPS (625 ML)**

Make ahead

Cover and store in the refrigerator for up to 1 day (but best when used right away).

6	cloves garlic, minced	6
1/3 cup	packed fresh thyme sprigs	75 mL
1/4 cup	packed fresh rosemary leaves	50 mL
1 1/2 cups	olive oil	375 mL
1/2 cup	freshly squeezed lemon juice	125 mL
1 1/2 tbsp	kosher salt	22 mL
Pinch	freshly ground black pepper	Pinch

1. In a medium bowl, combine garlic, thyme and rosemary. Whisk in oil, lemon juice, salt and pepper until blended.

Sesame Marinade

I love using this marinade on chicken or fish before it goes on the smoker or the grill. This recipe makes a lot of marinade — enough for several whole chickens or salmon fillets. If you don't need this much, cut the recipe in half.

MAKES ABOUT 6 CUPS (1.5 L)

TIPS

Use a fine, sharp-toothed grater, such as those made by Microplane® to grate the gingerroot.

⚬ ⚬ ⚬

To make 1¼ cups (300 mL) puréed onion, purée 2 cups (500 mL) chopped onions (about 2 onions) in a food processor.

⚬ ⚬ ⚬

Make sure to look for dark sesame oil. The lighter version will not be toasted and will not have the same flavor.

⚬ ⚬ ⚬

Make ahead

Pour into airtight containers and store in the refrigerator for up to 1 week (but best when used right away).

2½ cups	soy sauce	625 mL
1¼ cups	granulated sugar	300 mL
1¼ cups	puréed onion (see tip, at left)	300 mL
1 cup	vegetable oil	250 mL
½ cup	toasted sesame oil (see tip, at left)	125 mL
2 tbsp	garlic powder	25 mL
1 tbsp	cracked black pepper	15 mL
1 tsp	grated gingerroot	5 mL

1. In a large bowl, whisk together soy sauce, sugar, onion, vegetable oil, sesame oil, garlic powder, pepper and ginger until well blended.

Bastes

When you're smoking food for hours, even at a low temperature, it can dry out. That's where bastes and mops come in handy. You simply use a basting brush, a never-used-before paint brush or dish mop, or a clean cloth and baste the food. Generally, fatty foods such as brisket or pork shoulder blade get a tangy baste or mop, with a higher proportion of vinegar or coffee, to perk up the flavor. Lean foods such as poultry or fish get a more buttery baste to give them a golden look and a luscious flavor.

All-Purpose Mop

As you can see, this recipe makes a lot, so use it when you have a large quantity of food to smoke, such as for a contest or a large family gathering.

MAKES ABOUT 24 CUPS (6 L)

Make ahead

Pour into airtight containers and store in the refrigerator for up to 1 week.

16 cups	chicken stock	4 L
4 cups	Worcestershire sauce	1 L
2 cups	cider vinegar	500 mL
2 cups	butter	500 mL
3 tbsp	MSG (optional)	45 mL
3 tbsp	kosher salt	45 mL
3 tbsp	dry mustard	45 mL
2 tbsp	garlic powder	25 mL
2 tbsp	chili powder	25 mL
2 tbsp	hot pepper sauce	25 mL

1. In a stockpot, combine chicken stock, Worcestershire sauce, vinegar, butter, MSG (if using), salt, mustard, garlic powder, chili powder and hot pepper sauce; bring to a simmer over medium-low heat. Simmer for 10 minutes to let flavors blend. Keep warm by the smoker and baste food during the smoking process.

Rich & Delicious Brisket Mop

The butter adds moisture, while the vinegar and apple juice perk up the flavor in this luscious mop.

MAKES ABOUT 2½ CUPS (625 ML)

TIPS

Keep the mop in a disposable aluminum pan by your smoker so the butter stays melted.

• • •

Use a dish mop (a wooden-handled, yarn-ended tool used to clean food off dirty plates) to apply this mixture to a slow-smoking brisket, beef roast, beef ribs or whatever else you're smoking.

½ cup	unsalted butter	125 mL
1¼ cups	apple juice	300 mL
½ cup	finely chopped onions	125 mL
½ cup	cider vinegar	125 mL
¼ cup	packed brown sugar	50 mL
¼ tsp	cayenne pepper	1 mL

1. In a medium saucepan, melt butter over medium-high heat. Add fruit juice, onions, vinegar, brown sugar and cayenne; bring to a boil. Remove from heat and transfer to a disposable aluminum pan. Keep warm by the smoker and brush on brisket as it is smoking.

Beefy Barbecue Mop

Use this mop on a flank steak, brisket or beef roast during smoking.

**MAKES ABOUT
1⅔ CUPS (400 ML)**

TIP
Serrano chili peppers can be found in Mexican markets and well-stocked supermarkets.

2	cloves garlic, minced	2
1 cup	beef stock	250 mL
¼ cup	cider vinegar	50 mL
3 tbsp	barbecue sauce (store-bought or see recipes, pages 50–65)	45 mL
2 tbsp	Worcestershire sauce	25 mL
2 tbsp	olive oil	25 mL
1 tsp	minced serrano chili peppers	5 mL

1. In a small bowl, combine garlic, beef stock, vinegar, barbecue sauce, Worcestershire sauce, oil and serrano peppers. Keep warm by the smoker and baste food during the smoking process.

Sweet Orange Baste

Slather this wonderful baste over chicken, pork or fish while it's smoking to keep it moist and delicious.

**MAKES ABOUT
1¼ CUPS (300 ML)**

TIP
Why amber honey? Most honey you buy at the grocery store, such as clover honey, will be an amber color, which indicates a medium flavor and sweetness. Light honeys made from blossoms have a more flowery, sugary flavor; darker honeys such as sunflower have a deep, almost sulphurous flavor.

6 tbsp	amber liquid honey	90 mL
3 tbsp	soy sauce	45 mL
3 tbsp	ketchup	45 mL
3 tbsp	Worcestershire sauce	45 mL
3 tbsp	freshly squeezed orange juice	45 mL
2 tsp	dry mustard	10 mL
½ tsp	kosher salt	2 mL
Pinch	freshly ground black pepper	Pinch

1. In a small bowl, combine honey, soy sauce, ketchup, Worcestershire sauce, orange juice, mustard, salt and pepper. Keep warm by the smoker and baste food during the smoking process.

Sweet & Spicy Rib Baste

Just as the title says, this baste is a sweet and spicy way to keep ribs moist, especially at the end of their smoking time. This recipe makes enough for several slabs of ribs.

MAKES ABOUT 6 CUPS (1.5 L)

TIP

Keep a disposable aluminum pan as close to the heat of your smoker as possible, and place your baste (or a plastic jar of honey) inside. That way, your baste stays warm and it's within easy reach. The aluminum pan ensures that, if you spill any baste, you won't have a mess.

3	cloves garlic, minced	3
2 cups	chopped onions	500 mL
2 cups	ketchup	500 mL
1 cup	cider vinegar	250 mL
¾ cup	packed brown sugar	175 mL
¼ cup	prepared yellow mustard	50 mL
2 tbsp	hot pepper sauce	25 mL
2	oranges, seeded and sliced	2

1. In a blender or food processor, purée garlic, onions, ketchup, vinegar, brown sugar, mustard and hot pepper sauce until smooth. Transfer to a large saucepan, add orange slices and bring to a simmer over medium heat. Simmer, stirring occasionally, for 15 minutes to let flavors blend. Keep warm by the smoker and baste ribs frequently during the last hour of smoking.

Buttery Brown Sugar & Lime Basting Sauce

This buttery, flavorful baste is delicious with salmon and other fish.

TIP

Jalapeño pepper powder is available from better spice emporiums or online (see the Source Guide, page 356). If you can't find it, increase the amount of jalapeño pepper sauce to ½ tsp (2 mL).

1	clove garlic, minced	1
¼ cup	butter, melted	50 mL
¼ cup	packed brown sugar	50 mL
1 tbsp	onion salt	15 mL
2 tsp	freshly squeezed lime juice	10 mL
2 tsp	dry white wine	10 mL
¼ tsp	jalapeño pepper sauce	1 mL
¼ tsp	jalapeño pepper powder (see tip, at left)	1 mL

1. In a small bowl, combine garlic, butter, brown sugar, onion salt, lime juice, wine, jalapeño pepper sauce and jalapeño pepper powder. Baste fish or shellfish after 15 minutes of smoking.

Barbecue Sauces and Finishing Sauces

Barbecue Sauces

Barbecue sauces are meant to complement smoked meats, poultry, fish, shellfish, game and vegetables. You can taste sauces alone, and they might taste mighty fine, but the whole point is to match them to the flavor of the foods you've smoked.

Barbecue sauces can have tomato, mustard or vinegar as a base, with herbs, spices and other ingredients added to round out the flavor. They go well with traditional barbecued meats: whole chicken and turkey, pork ribs, pork shoulder blade, beef brisket, and beef and lamb ribs. Barbecue sauce is great in a barbecued bean dish too, which you can also put on the smoker (see recipes, pages 75, 126 and 127).

When I had my own barbecue sauce company under my competition name, Flower of the Flames, I specialized in fruit-based barbecue sauces. Why? Well, I like them, for one thing. And for another, everybody likes a little sweetness, and this flavor helps balance the somewhat bitter taste you get from wood smoke.

When I create my own sauces, I like to start with a fruit such as apple, cherry or blackberry and go from there. I add something sour (usually vinegar), ketchup for texture, and spices and herbs that complement the fruit and the rub on the meat, poultry or fish.

I like a milder sauce with a spicy rub, and a spicy sauce with a milder marinade or rub. Contrast is what you're after. But some of the same flavors need to carry through from the marinade or rub to the sauce.

Finishing Sauces

A finishing sauce is a little more elegant than a barbecue sauce. I like these to have a touch of sweetness as well. But their colors and flavors are more sophisticated.

Flower of the Flames Raspberry Barbecue Sauce

This is the sauce I used to bottle and sell, and to my mind, it goes with everything! Fruity, spicy, sassy, sweet and just plain ole good.

MAKES ABOUT 4½ CUPS (1.125 L)

Make ahead

Pour into airtight containers and store in the refrigerator for up to 1 week.

2	cloves garlic, minced	2
2 cups	fresh or frozen raspberries	500 mL
1 cup	granulated sugar	250 mL
1 cup	ketchup	250 mL
1 cup	tomato sauce	250 mL
¼ cup	packed brown sugar	50 mL
¼ cup	raspberry vinegar	50 mL
¼ cup	Worcestershire sauce	50 mL
2 tbsp	fancy molasses	25 mL
2 tbsp	barbecue seasoning mix (such as All-Purpose Barbecue Rub, page 27)	25 mL
1 tbsp	cracked black pepper	15 mL
1 tbsp	garlic powder	15 mL
1 tbsp	onion powder	15 mL
¼ tsp	celery seeds	1 mL
Pinch	cayenne pepper	Pinch

1. In a large saucepan, bring garlic, raspberries, sugar, ketchup, tomato sauce, ½ cup (125 mL) water, brown sugar, vinegar, Worcestershire sauce, molasses, seasoning mix, black pepper, garlic powder, onion powder, celery seeds and cayenne to a boil over high heat, stirring to dissolve sugar. Reduce heat and simmer, stirring occasionally, for 45 minutes to let flavors blend. Strain through a fine-mesh sieve, if desired.

Vinegar-Style Barbecue Sauce

This is the vinegar-based Carolina sauce traditionally served on pulled pork sandwiches. It's also good on steamed spinach and collard greens.

MAKES ABOUT 4 CUPS (1 L)

Make ahead

Cover and store in the refrigerator for up to 1 week.

4 cups	white vinegar	1 L
1/3 cup	hot pepper flakes	75 mL
1/3 cup	granulated sugar	75 mL
1 1/2 tbsp	kosher salt	22 mL

1. In a large glass bowl, combine vinegar, hot pepper flakes, sugar and salt. Let stand at room temperature for 3 to 4 hours to let flavors blend. Strain through a fine-mesh sieve, if desired.

Bourbon Barbecue Sauce

A shot or two of bourbon can make all the difference! Serve this sweet and tangy tomato-based sauce with pork, chicken or game birds.

MAKES ABOUT 1½ CUPS (375 ML)

Make ahead

Pour into an airtight container and store in the refrigerator for up to 1 week.

1 tbsp	olive oil	15 mL
2	cloves garlic, minced	2
½ cup	minced onion	125 mL
1 cup	tomato purée (about half of a 15-oz/425 g can)	250 mL
⅔ cup	amber liquid honey	150 mL
3 tbsp	cider vinegar	45 mL
2 tbsp	bourbon	25 mL
1 tsp	dry mustard	5 mL
1 tsp	kosher salt	5 mL
¼ tsp	jalapeño pepper powder	1 mL

1. In a saucepan, heat oil over medium heat. Add garlic and onion; sauté until transparent, about 5 minutes. Add tomato purée, ½ cup (125 mL) water, honey, vinegar, bourbon, mustard, salt and jalapeño pepper powder. Reduce heat to medium-low and simmer, stirring occasionally, for 30 minutes to let flavors blend. Strain through a fine-mesh sieve, if desired.

Texas-Style Barbecue Sauce

Yee-haw! There's lots of Texas-style flavor in this tangy, hearty, tomato-based sauce. It's best served with smoked beef brisket, ribs, flank steak, tenderloin or prime rib. Whether you dunk your smoked German sausage, your tender brisket or your smoked beef shoulder (clod or chuck) in this sauce, it's bound to be tasty.

MAKES ABOUT 3½ CUPS (875 ML)

Make ahead

Pour into airtight containers and store in the refrigerator for up to 1 week.

4	bay leaves	4
2	stalks celery, minced	2
2	cloves garlic, minced	2
1 cup	ketchup	250 mL
½ cup	rice vinegar	125 mL
¼ cup	vegetable oil	50 mL
¼ cup	Worcestershire sauce	50 mL
2 tbsp	minced red onion	25 mL
1 tbsp	granulated sugar	15 mL
1 tsp	chili powder	5 mL
1 tsp	dry mustard	5 mL
¼ tsp	kosher salt	1 mL
Pinch	freshly ground black pepper	Pinch

1. In a medium saucepan, combine bay leaves, celery, garlic, 1½ cups (375 mL) water, ketchup, vinegar, oil, Worcestershire sauce, red onion, sugar, chili powder, mustard, salt and pepper and bring to a simmer over medium-low heat. Simmer, stirring occasionally, for 20 minutes to let flavors blend. Strain through a fine-mesh sieve, if desired.

Texas Spit

Texans definitely have a way with words and fun with their barbecue. Use this sauce as a baste or glaze, or as a finishing sauce, whichever takes your fancy. It's delicious with a Texan's favorite barbecue dish: smoked brisket.

MAKES ABOUT 3½ CUPS (875 ML)		

Make ahead

Pour into airtight containers and store in the refrigerator for up to 1 month.

2 tbsp	unsalted butter	25 mL
2	onions, finely chopped	2
2	cloves garlic, minced	2
½ cup	ketchup	125 mL
⅓ cup	packed brown sugar	75 mL
⅓ cup	Worcestershire sauce	75 mL
¼ cup	prepared steak sauce	50 mL
2 tbsp	cider vinegar	25 mL

1. In a medium saucepan, melt butter over medium-low heat. Add onions and garlic; sauté for 5 minutes, but do not allow them to brown. Stir in ½ cup (125 mL) water, ketchup, brown sugar, Worcestershire sauce, steak sauce and vinegar; bring to a boil over medium-high heat. Reduce heat and simmer, stirring occasionally, for 20 minutes to let flavors blend.

Kansas City–Style Barbecue Sauce

Kansas City's favorite sauce is tomato-based, with spices and a touch of smoky flavor that goes well with ribs, brisket or sausage from the smoker.

MAKES ABOUT 5 CUPS (1.25 L)

Make ahead

Pour into airtight containers and store in the refrigerator for up to 1 month.

4 cups	ketchup	1 L
1 cup	cider vinegar	250 mL
1 cup	packed dark brown sugar	250 mL
¼ cup	soy sauce	50 mL
¼ cup	fancy molasses	50 mL
2 tbsp	dry chili seasoning or chili powder	25 mL
1 tbsp	liquid smoke (optional)	15 mL
2 tsp	dry mustard	10 mL
½ tsp	ground allspice	2 mL
¼ tsp	cayenne pepper	1 mL
¼ tsp	freshly ground black pepper	1 mL

1. In a large saucepan, combine ketchup, vinegar, brown sugar, ½ cup (125 mL) water, soy sauce, molasses, chili seasoning, liquid smoke (if using), mustard, allspice, cayenne and black pepper. Bring to a boil over medium-high heat, stirring to dissolve sugar. Reduce heat and simmer, stirring occasionally, for 45 minutes, until sauce is thickened.

Sugar-Free Barbecue Sauce

I don't usually recommend particular brands in my recipes, but in this case, when you want to be very careful about any sugar added, it's time to read the labels. Canned tomato products sometimes contain sugar, so when I want to serve this sauce to friends with diabetes, I use Contadina tomato purées, which contain no sugar or salt.

MAKES ABOUT 5 CUPS (1.25 L)

Make ahead

Pour into airtight containers and store in the refrigerator for up to 1 month.

2	cans (each 15 oz/425 g) tomato purée	2
1 cup	pineapple juice	250 mL
1 tbsp	minced garlic	15 mL
2 tsp	onion powder	10 mL
2 tsp	garlic powder	10 mL
1 tsp	freshly ground black pepper	5 mL
1 tsp	freshly ground white pepper	5 mL
1 tsp	liquid smoke	5 mL
¼ tsp	cayenne pepper	1 mL
¼ cup	unsalted butter	50 mL
	Artificial sweetener (optional)	

1. In a large saucepan, combine tomato purée, pineapple juice, garlic, onion powder, garlic powder, black pepper, white pepper, liquid smoke and cayenne. Bring to a boil over medium–high heat. Reduce heat and simmer, stirring occasionally, for 10 minutes. Add butter and artificial sweetener (if using) and simmer, stirring occasionally, until butter has melted and mixture is well blended.

North Carolina–Style Barbecue Sauce

People in different regions of North Carolina might prefer different types of sauces — whether mustard-, vinegar- or ketchup-based — but barbecue lovers all agree that smoked pork (ribs, shoulder blade, whole hog) is what it tastes best on.

MAKES ABOUT 4 CUPS (1 L)

Make ahead

Pour into airtight containers and store in the refrigerator for up to 1 month.

1½ cups	packed dark brown sugar	375 mL
½ cup	butter	125 mL
3	cloves garlic, minced	3
1	small onion, chopped	1
1½ cups	prepared steak sauce	375 mL
1 cup	ketchup	250 mL
½ cup	rice vinegar	125 mL
1 tbsp	celery seeds	15 mL
1 tbsp	dry mustard	15 mL
1 tsp	minced jalapeño pepper	5 mL

1. In a large, deep skillet, melt brown sugar and butter over medium-high heat until bubbly. Whisk until lumps are gone. Reduce heat to medium and add garlic, onion, steak sauce, ketchup, vinegar, celery seeds, mustard and jalapeño pepper. Reduce heat and simmer, stirring often, until thick enough to coat the back of a spoon, about 15 minutes.

Memphis-Style Barbecue Sauce

If you go to a barbecue joint in Memphis, Tennessee, and order ribs, you'll be asked an important question: "Wet or dry?" Wet means with sauce; dry means without, or with the sauce on the side. This tangy, spicy sauce tastes great with ribs, either way.

MAKES ABOUT 3½ CUPS (875 ML)

Make ahead

Pour into airtight containers and store in the refrigerator for up to 1 month.

3	cloves garlic, minced	3
2 cups	ketchup	500 mL
1 cup	chopped onions	250 mL
1 cup	red wine vinegar	250 mL
½ cup	prepared yellow mustard	125 mL
½ cup	packed dark brown sugar	125 mL
½ tsp	hot pepper sauce	2 mL

1. In a medium saucepan, combine garlic, ketchup, onions, vinegar, mustard, brown sugar and hot pepper sauce over medium-low heat. Simmer, stirring occasionally, for 30 minutes, or until slightly thickened.

> The Memphis in May barbecue contest is one huge pork fest, with competition barbecuers showing off their best ribs, pork shoulder blade, whole pork shoulder and whole hog to the judges.

Tangy Mustard Barbecue Sauce

This mustard-based barbecue sauce is traditionally served with slow-smoked pork ribs, pork shoulder blade or whole hog.

Make ahead

Pour into an airtight container and store in the refrigerator for up to 1 week.

1 cup	prepared yellow mustard	250 mL
1 cup	rice vinegar	250 mL
¼ cup	granulated sugar	50 mL
2 tbsp	butter	25 mL
1 tbsp	Worcestershire sauce	15 mL
1 tsp	kosher salt	5 mL
1 tsp	freshly ground white pepper	5 mL
½ tsp	jalapeño pepper sauce	2 mL

1. In a small saucepan, combine mustard, vinegar, sugar, butter, Worcestershire sauce, salt, pepper and jalapeño pepper sauce; bring to a boil over medium-high heat. Reduce heat and simmer, stirring occasionally, for 15 minutes to let flavors blend.

Mustard & Marmalade Barbecue Sauce

Honey and orange marmalade make this sauce sweet. Dijon and dry mustards make it hot. Together, the sweet and hot flavors taste great on smoked pork or salmon.

MAKES ABOUT 1½ CUPS (375 ML)

TIP

Use a prepared barbecue seasoning mix, or try the All-Purpose Barbecue Rub (page 27).

● ● ●

Make ahead

Pour into an airtight container and store in the refrigerator for up to 6 months.

1 cup	Dijon mustard	250 mL
½ cup	apple juice	125 mL
¼ cup	liquid clover honey or other amber honey	50 mL
¼ cup	orange marmalade	50 mL
2 tbsp	tomato paste	25 mL
1 tbsp	dry mustard	15 mL
1 tsp	barbecue seasoning mix (see tip, at left)	5 mL
¼ tsp	freshly ground black pepper	1 mL
Pinch	cayenne pepper	Pinch

1. In a medium saucepan, bring Dijon mustard, apple juice, honey, marmalade, tomato paste, dry mustard, seasoning mix, black pepper and cayenne to a boil over medium–high heat, stirring occasionally. Reduce heat and simmer, stirring occasionally, for 20 minutes to let flavors blend.

Honey Mustard Barbecue Sauce

Smoking adds a note of bitterness to foods, so using a sweet, hot finishing sauce like this one makes all the flavors come together at the end.

TIP
You can find granulated garlic at well-stocked supermarkets or online (see the Source Guide, page 356).

• • •

Make ahead

Pour into an airtight container and store in the refrigerator for up to 6 months.

1 cup	liquid clover honey or other amber honey	250 mL
²/₃ cup	cider vinegar	150 mL
½ cup	Dijon mustard	125 mL
¼ cup	balsamic vinegar	50 mL
¼ cup	light corn syrup	50 mL
2 tbsp	tomato paste	25 mL
2 tbsp	freshly squeezed lemon juice	25 mL
1 tsp	fine kosher or sea salt	5 mL
½ tsp	granulated garlic (see tip, at left)	2 mL

1. In a medium saucepan, bring honey, vinegar, mustard, corn syrup, tomato paste, lemon juice, salt and garlic to a boil over medium-high heat, stirring occasionally. Reduce heat and simmer, stirring occasionally, for 30 minutes, or until slightly thickened and flavors have blended.

Apple Ancho Barbecue Sauce

The fruity, spicy flavors in this barbecue sauce really complement pork and poultry dishes. It's also delicious with smoked squash.

MAKES ABOUT 2½ CUPS (625 ML)

TIPS

You can use either sweetened or unsweetened applesauce and apple juice — it's up to you!

• • •

You can buy ancho chili powder and jalapeño pepper powder at better herb and spice emporiums, by mail order or online (see the Source Guide, page 356).

• • •

Make ahead

Pour into airtight containers and store in the refrigerator for up to 1 month.

6 tbsp	butter	90 mL
1	clove garlic, minced	1
¼ cup	minced onion	50 mL
1 cup	ketchup	250 mL
¾ cup	applesauce	175 mL
½ cup	packed brown sugar (light or dark)	125 mL
¼ cup	cider vinegar	50 mL
¼ cup	apple juice	50 mL
2 tbsp	Worcestershire sauce	25 mL
2 tsp	ancho chili powder (see tip, at left)	10 mL
1½ tsp	liquid smoke	7 mL
1 tsp	fine kosher or sea salt	5 mL
1 tsp	freshly ground black pepper	5 mL
¼ tsp	jalapeño pepper powder (see tip, at left)	1 mL
¼ tsp	celery seeds	1 mL

1. In a medium saucepan, melt butter over medium-high heat. Add garlic and onion; sauté until softened, about 5 minutes. Stir in ketchup, applesauce, brown sugar, vinegar, apple juice, Worcestershire sauce, chili powder, liquid smoke, salt, pepper and jalapeño pepper powder; bring to a boil. Reduce heat and simmer, stirring occasionally, for 30 minutes to let flavors blend.

Cherry Chipotle Barbecue Sauce

Try this sauce on a smoked chicken or pulled pork sandwich. Delicious!

MAKES ABOUT 5 CUPS (1.25 L)

TIP

Look for cherry juice in bottles or cartons in the fruit juice section of well-stocked supermarkets and health food stores.

• • •

Make ahead

Pour into airtight containers and store in the refrigerator for up to 6 months.

2 cups	ketchup	500 mL
1 cup	cherry preserves	250 mL
1/2 cup	cherry juice (see tip, at left)	125 mL
1/2 cup	packed brown sugar (light or dark)	125 mL
3 tbsp	cider vinegar	45 mL
1 1/2 tbsp	chipotle pepper sauce	22 mL
1 tbsp	Worcestershire sauce	15 mL
1 tsp	minced garlic	5 mL
1 tsp	onion powder	5 mL

1. In a medium saucepan, bring ketchup, cherry preserves, cherry juice, brown sugar, vinegar, chipotle pepper sauce, Worcestershire sauce, garlic and onion powder to a boil over medium-high heat. Reduce heat and simmer, stirring occasionally, for 10 minutes to let flavors blend.

Peachy Barbecue Sauce

This lovely, fruity barbecue sauce is especially good on chicken, pork, game and lamb. This recipe makes a lot of sauce, so you might want to bottle some and give it as a gift.

MAKES ABOUT 6 CUPS (1.5 L)

TIP

If you can't find peach purée, make it yourself by puréeing canned peaches in a blender or food processor. You'll need about one 15-oz (425 mL) can of sliced peaches, drained, to make 1 cup (250 mL) peach purée.

* * *

Make ahead

Pour into airtight containers and store in the refrigerator for up to 2 months.

4 cups	barbecue sauce (store-bought or see recipes, pages 50–63)	1 L
1 cup	peach purée	250 mL
¼ cup	butter, melted	50 mL
¼ cup	orange juice	50 mL
¼ cup	pineapple juice	50 mL
¼ cup	dry sherry	50 mL

1. In a large bowl, combine barbecue sauce, peach purée, butter, orange juice, pineapple juice and sherry.

Apricot, Apricot, Apricot Barbecue Sauce

Apricot preserves, syrup and nectar provide a triple dose of fruity flavor in this luscious barbecue sauce. Slather it over ribs, pork shoulder blade, game birds, rabbit or chicken for a sweet finish.

MAKES ABOUT 2¼ CUPS (550 ML)

TIPS

Look for apricot nectar in bottles or cartons in the fruit juice section of well-stocked supermarkets and health food stores.

• • •

Look for apricot syrup where syrups for pancakes or ice creams are shelved at the grocery store.

• • •

Make ahead

Pour into an airtight container and store in the refrigerator for up to 1 week.

¼ cup	olive oil	50 mL
2	cloves garlic, minced	2
2 tbsp	grated onion	25 mL
½ cup	apricot preserves	125 mL
½ cup	apricot nectar (see tip, at left)	125 mL
½ cup	tomato sauce	125 mL
¼ cup	cider vinegar	50 mL
¼ cup	apricot syrup (see tip, at left)	50 mL
2 tbsp	Dijon mustard	25 mL
1 tbsp	packed brown sugar	15 mL
1 tsp	Worcestershire sauce	5 mL
1 tsp	kosher salt	5 mL
Pinch	cayenne pepper	Pinch

1. In a medium saucepan, heat olive oil over medium-high heat. Add garlic and onion; sauté until translucent, about 5 minutes. Stir in apricot preserves, apricot nectar, tomato sauce, vinegar, apricot syrup, mustard, brown sugar, Worcestershire sauce, salt and cayenne. Reduce heat and simmer, stirring occasionally, for 15 minutes to let flavors blend.

Easy Apricot Barbecue Glaze

Here's an easy glaze that tastes great on poultry, pork and game birds.

MAKES ABOUT 1¾ CUPS (425 ML)

Make ahead

Pour into an airtight container and store in the refrigerator for up to 1 month.

1 cup	apricot preserves	250 mL
¼ cup	pure maple syrup	50 mL
¼ cup	packed brown sugar	50 mL
3 tbsp	cider vinegar	45 mL
2 tbsp	dry mustard	25 mL

1. In a small bowl, combine apricot preserves, maple syrup, brown sugar, vinegar and mustard, stirring until sugar is dissolved.

Apricot Maple Glaze

The flavors of apricot and maple have a natural affinity for each other. Try this combination with smoked game birds, rabbit, sausage, poultry, pork and lamb.

MAKES ABOUT 1½ CUPS (375 ML)

TIP

Look for apricot nectar in bottles or cartons in the fruit juice section of well-stocked supermarkets and health food stores.

• • •

Make ahead

Pour into an airtight container and store in the refrigerator for up to 1 month.

1 cup	apricot nectar (see tip, at left)	250 mL
¼ cup	pure maple syrup	50 mL
¼ cup	packed brown sugar	50 mL
2 tbsp	teriyaki sauce	25 mL
1 tsp	grated gingerroot	5 mL

1. In a small bowl, combine apricot nectar, maple syrup, brown sugar, teriyaki sauce and ginger, stirring until sugar is dissolved.

Barbecue Glaze

This hearty all-purpose glaze will put a savory sheen on smoked meats.

TIP
If you can't find shallots,
use the white parts of
green, or spring, onions.

1½ tbsp	cornstarch	22 mL
1 cup	chicken stock	250 mL
2 cups	barbecue sauce (see recipes, pages 50–65, or store-bought)	500 mL
¼ cup	minced shallots	50 mL
1 tbsp	minced garlic	15 mL
½ tsp	dried thyme	2 mL
Pinch	freshly ground white pepper	Pinch

1. In a small bowl or cup, dissolve cornstarch in 2 tbsp (25 mL) water; set aside.

2. In a medium saucepan, bring chicken stock to a boil over medium-high heat. Whisk in cornstarch mixture until sauce thickens. Add barbecue sauce, shallots, garlic, thyme and pepper. Reduce heat and simmer, stirring gently, for 5 minutes to let flavors blend. Keep warm by the smoker to brush on meats during the last hour of smoking.

Red Currant Sauce

Tart, tangy, yet buttery, this rosy sauce goes well with smoked lamb, chicken and pork.

TIP
Red currant jelly adds
a touch of sweetness to
sauces and bastes and
adds a glazed effect to
your meat. It's also good
with game meats.

¼ cup	unsalted butter	50 mL
1	jar (10 oz/300 g) red currant jelly	1
¼ cup	packed brown sugar	50 mL
¼ cup	ketchup	50 mL

1. In a medium saucepan, melt butter over medium heat. Stir in red currant jelly until it melts, then stir in brown sugar and ketchup until sugar melts. Simmer, stirring, for 5 minutes to let flavors blend. Serve warm.

Blackberry Merlot Sauce

Serve this deeply delicious sauce with smoked game birds, venison or beef.

**MAKES ABOUT
2 CUPS (500 ML)**

See page 112 for instructions on hot-smoking red onion. See page 98 for instructions on cold-smoking red onion.

1	clove garlic, minced	1
3 cups	frozen blackberries	750 mL
1/2 cup	granulated sugar	125 mL
1/4 cup	hot- or cold-smoked red onion (see tip, at left)	50 mL
1/4 cup	blackberry merlot wine (see tip, page 41)	50 mL
1 tbsp	amber liquid honey	15 mL

1. In a medium saucepan, combine garlic, blackberries, sugar, red onion, wine and honey; bring to a boil over medium-high heat. Boil gently until reduced by half. Serve warm.

Citrus Demi-glace

For a true taste of haute cuisine from the smoker, finish your smoked beef or pork tenderloin with this luscious yet easy sauce.

**MAKES ABOUT
1 CUP (250 ML)**

TIP

You'll need 2 to 3 medium limes to yield 3 tbsp (45 mL) juice.

1/2 cup	beef stock	125 mL
3 tbsp	freshly squeezed lime juice	45 mL
3/4 cup	unsalted butter, cut into 12 cubes	175 mL

1. In a small saucepan, bring beef stock to a boil over medium-high heat. Stir in lime juice and boil until reduced by one-third, about 7 minutes. Reduce heat to medium-low and whisk in butter, 1 cube at a time, until smooth and silky. Remove from heat and serve immediately.

Fresh Blueberry & Ginger Sauce

Oh my! You could just eat this with a spoon, but save some to serve with smoked Cornish game hen, duck or pheasant.

MAKES ABOUT 5 CUPS (1.25 L)

TIP

Keep batches of this in the freezer to have on hand for the holidays or to give as a gifts from your kitchen.

• • •

Make ahead

Spoon into airtight containers and store in the refrigerator for up to 3 days or in the freezer for up to 3 months. Reheat gently in a saucepan over the stove or smoker.

3 cups	fresh blueberries	750 mL
½ cup	packed dark brown sugar	125 mL
½ cup	ketchup	125 mL
½ cup	rice vinegar	125 mL
1 tbsp	soy sauce	15 mL
1 tsp	minced garlic	5 mL
½ tsp	minced gingerroot	2 mL
	Kosher salt and freshly ground black pepper	

1. In a blender or food processor, purée blueberries, brown sugar, ketchup, rice vinegar, soy sauce, garlic, and ginger until fairly smooth. Season to taste with salt and pepper.

Herbal Balsamic Jelly

This jelly is great as a glaze on all meats, but especially on lamb and beef.

MAKES ABOUT 4½ CUPS (1.125 L)

Make ahead

Store in the refrigerator for up to 6 months.

4	cloves garlic, chopped	4
1½ cups	balsamic (or white balsamic) vinegar	375 mL
1½ cups	packed fresh herbs (such as thyme, basil and mint)	375 mL
1	package (1.75 oz/49 to 57 g) regular powdered fruit pectin	1
4 cups	granulated sugar	1 L

1. In a large, deep saucepan, bring garlic, vinegar, herbs and 2¼ cups (550 mL) water to a boil over high heat. Remove from heat and let steep for 10 minutes.

2. Strain herb mixture through a cheesecloth-lined sieve into a bowl, then measure out 3 cups (750 mL) of the infused liquid and let cool to room temperature. Return to the saucepan. Add pectin and bring to a boil over high heat, stirring. Add sugar and return to a boil, stirring until sugar dissolves. Boil hard for 1 minute. Remove from heat. Skim off the foam and pour into small jelly jars. Cool, then twist on lids.

Barbecuer's Aioli

Aioli, a garlicky mayonnaise from the south of France, tastes wonderful served with smoked lobster, scallops, shrimp or any smoked fish.

Make ahead

Cover and store in the refrigerator for up to 3 days.

This recipe contains raw egg yolks. If the food safety of raw eggs is a concern for you, use pasteurized eggs. Many grocery stores now carry pasteurized eggs in their shells.

2	egg yolks	2
4	cloves garlic, minced	4
1 cup	extra-virgin olive oil	250 mL
	Kosher salt and freshly ground black pepper	
2 tsp	freshly squeezed lemon juice	10 mL

1. In a medium bowl, using a wire whisk, beat egg yolks well. Stir in garlic. Gradually pour in oil in a thin stream, whisking constantly, until the mixture turns light and creamy. Season to taste with salt and pepper. Stir in lemon juice.

Getting Started

SLOW-SMOKING, OR CREATING traditional barbecue, is a technique, not a recipe. It's a technique that you gradually begin to master after lots of practice, practice, practice.

Here is a short chapter of easy slow-smoking recipes for the beginner. Although these recipes are simple, they're also sophisticated enough to please the most advanced barbecue competitor.

Remember, regulating your temperature and keeping it as steady as possible is the key to great barbecue. When you're starting out, add wood only for the first 3 hours, then see how smoky your food tastes. You can always add more wood, but you can't always subtract the acrid, bitter flavor food can get when it has smoked for too long.

If you want hands-on guidance or help locating woods or other supplies, check out your local barbecue society and attend one of their classes. To gain some experience, you can also volunteer to help a barbecue team at a contest or rib fest. To find a barbecue society or association, check out **www.bbqsearch.com**, then click on "Associations" to locate one in your area. Many of these groups have newsletters with recipes, tips and information on upcoming contests and the newest equipment.

Here are some other good resources:

- Kansas City Barbeque Society: **www.kcbs.us**
- Canadian Barbecue Association: **www.canadianbarbecueassociation.com**
- International Barbeque Cookers Association: **www.ibcabbq.org**
- Pacific Northwest BBQ Association: **www.pnwba.com**
- Memphis Barbecue Association: **www.memphisinmay.org**. Click on "Barbecue Association."

STARTER RECIPES

Soft Cheese 74
Barbecued Beans. 75
Stuffed Mushrooms 76
Potatoes. 77
Tomatoes 78
Chicken Breasts 79
Chicken Wings. 80
Italian Sausage. 81
Baby Back Ribs. 82
Pork Tenderloin 84

Pork Chops. 85
Pork Shoulder Blade 86
Beef Brisket Flat. 88
Standing Rib Roast. 89
Leg of Lamb. 90
Salmon Fillet 91
Tuna Steak 92
Whole Trout 93
Scallops 94
Shrimp 95

> **Tip:** If you get too much smoke flavoring and your food is somewhat bitter, you can rescue it. To get rid of the bitter, pungent flavor, rub honey and barbecue sauce all over the meat, wrap it well in foil and let it slow-cook for another hour in the smoker.

Soft Cheese

A fresh mozzarella or goat cheese tastes even better when kissed with smoke. At 225°F to 250°F (110°C to 120°C), even a soft cheese stays firm and gets deliciously smoky. From trial and error, I have found that it's essential to spray or brush the cheese with olive oil before smoking; if you don't, an unappetizingly dry brown skin forms on the cheese. You quarter the cheese to get more surface area: more surface area, more smoke flavor.

SERVES 4

Recommended wood: pecan or hickory

TIPS

Use a good, but not top-quality cheese for smoking. A wonderful artisanal cheese can stand on its own, but a kiss of smoke will elevate that log of chèvre you bought at the grocery store to heavenly flavor.

· · ·

Use smoked cheese crumbled on pizzas or salads, sliced in sandwiches or spread on bruschetta.

· · ·

Make ahead

Place in an airtight container and store in the refrigerator for up to 1 week.

¼ cup	olive oil	50 mL
8 oz	goat cheese, cream cheese or mozzarella cheese, quartered	250 g

1. Prepare a fire in your smoker. *(For instructions, see pages 8–11.)*

2. Place oil in a shallow bowl. Dip each cheese portion in oil, coating evenly, then place in a disposable aluminum pan.

3. Add wood to the coals and wait until smoke is fragrant, 5 to 10 minutes. Place pan on the smoker rack and close the lid. Smoke at 225°F to 250°F (110°C to 120°C) for 1 hour, until fragrant with smoke.

Barbecued Beans

If you like baked beans, you'll love them on the smoker. Bite-sized pieces of smoked meats — such as slow-smoked pork, brisket or sausage — add to the smoky flavor.

SERVES 6 TO 8	Recommended wood: hickory, oak or apple	

TIP

This casserole can be baked in a 350°F (180°C) oven for 1 hour, or until bubbly, but you won't get the smoky flavor or taste.

4 cups	canned pork and beans	1 L
1½ cups	tomato-based barbecue sauce (store-bought or see recipes, pages 50, 52–58 and 62–63)	375 mL
1 cup	chopped smoked meat (such as sausage, pork butt, brisket) or more to taste	250 mL
½ cup	packed brown sugar	125 mL
½ cup	diced onion	125 mL
¼ cup	ketchup	50 mL
2 tbsp	prepared mustard	25 mL
	Kosher salt and coarsely ground black pepper	

1. Prepare a fire in your smoker. *(For instructions, see pages 8–11.)*

2. In a disposable aluminum pan, combine pork and beans, barbecue sauce, meat, brown sugar, onion, ketchup and mustard. Season to taste with salt and pepper.

3. Place pan on the smoker rack, add wood to the coals and close the lid. Smoke at 225°F to 250°F (110°C to 120°C) for 2 hours, or until bubbling and fragrant with smoke.

Stuffed Mushrooms

These little appetizers can become addictive, so smoke more than you think you need for your party. Just double or triple the recipe as needed.

SERVES 8 TO 10	**Recommended wood:** hickory or apple

TIP

This appetizer can be baked in a 350°F (180°C) oven for 30 minutes, or until bubbly, but you won't get that smoky flavor.

24	large mushrooms, cleaned	24
1 tbsp	vegetable oil	15 mL
8 oz	herbed or seasoned cream cheese	250 g
½ cup	freshly grated Parmesan, Romano or Asiago cheese	125 mL
½ cup	chopped fresh parsley	125 mL
	Kosher salt and coarsely ground black pepper	

1. Prepare a fire in your smoker. *(For instructions, see pages 8–11.)*

2. Stem mushrooms and place caps stem side up on a baking sheet that will fit in your smoker. Chop stems.

3. In a skillet, heat oil over medium-high heat. Sauté mushroom stems until softened, about 8 minutes. Transfer to a bowl and stir in cream cheese, Parmesan and parsley. Season to taste with salt and pepper. Stir to combine well. Fill each cap with the mixture.

4. Place baking sheet on the smoker rack, add wood to the coals and close the lid. Smoke at 225°F to 250°F (110°C to 120°C) for 1 to 1½ hours, or until bubbling and fragrant with smoke.

Potatoes

Potatoes in the smoker? You bet. It's just like baking them, only at a lower temperature. Although I wouldn't set up my smoker just for potatoes or tomatoes, I throw a few in when I'm smoking something else because these vegetables are so good with a wood-smoke flavor. Smoked potatoes make a wonderful casserole or potato salad. They're also good simply served with a dab of butter or sour cream and sprinkled with salt and pepper.

SERVES 4	Recommended wood: your choice

TIPS

While any wood will work with this recipe, hickory, oak or pecan wood lend a hearty flavor to potatoes.

• • •

If you want to hurry these potatoes along a bit, either par-bake or microwave them until they're halfway done, then put them on the smoker for an hour or so to finish cooking.

4	baking or sweet potatoes, halved lengthwise	4
	Olive oil for drizzling	
	Kosher salt and freshly ground black pepper	

1. Prepare a fire in your smoker. *(For instructions, see pages 8–11.)*

2. Place potatoes cut side up in a disposable aluminum pan. Drizzle with oil and season to taste with salt and pepper.

3. Place pan on the smoker rack, add wood to the coals and close the lid. Smoke at 225°F to 250°F (110°C to 120°C) for 2 hours, or until potatoes are tender and smoky.

Tomatoes

Tomatoes really benefit from a little time on the smoker. They soften, take on a burnished look and develop a wonderful smoky aroma. Roma tomatoes and beefsteak tomatoes also work well.

SERVES 4	Recommended wood: your choice

TIPS

Roma tomatoes are also called plum tomatoes or Italian plum tomatoes.

• • •

After larger tomatoes have smoked, remove the peel and seeds and chop into a smoked tomato concassé that you can add to soups, savory flavoring butters or casseroles.

• • •

You can smoke cherry tomatoes still attached to the branch for a wonderful visual and taste effect. They'll be done in about 45 minutes.

• • •

Smoking with a hard wood such as hickory, maple, oak or pecan gives vegetables a fuller smoke flavor.

• • •

Make ahead

Place in an airtight container and store in the refrigerator for up to 1 week or in the freezer for up to 3 months.

4	beefsteak tomatoes, halved (or 8 Roma tomatoes, halved lengthwise)	4
	Olive oil for drizzling	
	Kosher salt and coarsely ground black pepper	

1. Prepare a fire in your smoker. *(For instructions, see pages 8–11.)*

2. Place tomatoes cut side up in a disposable aluminum pan. Drizzle with oil and season to taste with salt and pepper.

3. Add wood to the coals and wait until smoke is fragrant, 5 to 10 minutes. Place pan on the smoker rack and close the lid. Smoke at 225°F to 250°F (110°C to 120°C) for 1 hour, or until tomatoes are softened and fragrant with smoke.

Chicken Breasts

Serve these deliciously easy bone-in chicken breasts hot as an entrée or let them cool, remove the skin and bones and chop up the chicken for wonderful sandwiches or salads.

SERVES 4	Recommended wood: apple, cherry, pear or peach	

TIPS

Smoking with a fruit wood such as apple, cherry, pear or peach brings out the sweetness in poultry and pork.

• • •

The smaller the smoking chamber on your equipment, the sooner your food will be done. If you're using a kettle grill or a bullet smoker, your chicken breasts might be done in 1½ hours. If you're using a bigger rig or a genuine smoker, they might take 2 hours.

4	bone-in chicken breasts, skin on	4
	Olive oil for brushing	
¼ cup	dried Italian seasoning	50 mL
2	lemons, thinly sliced	2

1. Prepare a fire in your smoker. *(For instructions, see pages 8–11.)*

2. Place chicken in a disposable aluminum pan. Brush with oil, sprinkle with Italian seasoning and top with lemon slices.

3. Place pan on the smoker rack, add wood to the coals and close the lid. Smoke at 225°F to 250°F (110°C to 120°C) for 1½ to 2 hours, or until a meat thermometer inserted in the thickest part of a breast registers 170°F (75°C).

Chicken Wings

Chicken wings are a great way for beginners to learn the art of smoking, as they are inexpensive and take only about 1½ hours to smoke.

SERVES 6 TO 12

Recommended wood: combination of sugar maple and cherry

TIPS

Serve as an appetizer or a casual entrée.

● ● ●

The smaller the smoking chamber on your equipment, the sooner your food will be done. If you're using a kettle grill or a bullet smoker, your chicken wings might be done in an hour. If you're using a bigger rig or a genuine smoker, they might take 1½ hours.

3 lbs	chicken wings, tips removed	1.5 kg
¾ cup	barbecue seasoning mix (store-bought or see recipes, pages 27–34)	175 mL
1 cup	barbecue sauce (store-bought or see recipes, pages 50–65)	250 mL

1. Rinse wings under cold running water and pat dry with paper towels. Place in a large disposable aluminum pan. Sprinkle with seasoning mix and toss to coat. Pour barbecue sauce over wings and toss to coat. Let stand at room temperature for about 15 minutes, or until surface of wings is tacky. Meanwhile, prepare a fire in your smoker. *(For instructions, see pages 8–11.)*

2. Place pan on the smoker rack, add wood to the coals and close the lid. Smoke at 225°F to 250°F (110°C to 120°C) for 1 to 1½ hours, or until juices run clear when chicken is pierced.

Italian Sausage

So easy, so good.

SERVES 4

Recommended wood: cherry, pecan or hickory

TIPS

You can also smoke other kinds of fresh sausages — from salmon, turkey and chicken sausages to Polish sausage and bratwurst.

• • •

If you want to make Italian Sausage & Artichoke Soup (see recipe, page 269), put thawed frozen or drained canned artichoke hearts in a disposable aluminum pan and smoke with the sausage for the same amount of time.

| 1 lb | Italian sausage links, any variety | 500 g |

1. Prepare a fire in your smoker. *(For instructions, see pages 8–11.)*

2. Add wood to the coals and wait until smoke is fragrant, 5 to 10 minutes. Place sausage directly on the smoker rack (or smoke in a disposable aluminum pan) and close the lid. Smoke at 225°F to 250°F (110°C to 120°C) for 45 to 60 minutes, or until no longer pink inside. Let stand for 15 minutes before slicing.

Baby Back Ribs

Baby back ribs are naturally more tender than large spare ribs, so they're great for beginning barbecuers. In this recipe, you get to practice all the steps to perfect smoked ribs, from marinating to glazing. Marinating ribs before smoking adds a sweet flavor and helps keep the ribs moist during cooking. Sprinkling with a rub adds flavor and a dark "bark." Glazing with barbecue sauce at the end gives ribs an attractive sheen.

SERVES 4 TO 8	**Recommended wood:** a combination of apple and cherry	

TIPS

Peeling the membrane from ribs is easier to do when the ribs are cold, right out of the refrigerator.

• • •

Place clear fruit juices (such as apple and pineapple) in a large, clean, plastic spray bottle, usually available at hardware or home improvement stores. To spray foods during smoking, simply open the lid of the smoker, spray the meat, then close the lid quickly to keep the temperature steady.

4	full racks pork baby back ribs	4
4 cups	apple juice	1 L
¾ cup	Flower of the Flames Rib Rub (see recipe, page 32)	175 mL
	Additional apple juice for spraying	
	Clover or other amber liquid honey for brushing	
3 cups	Flower of the Flames Raspberry Barbecue Sauce (see recipe, page 50)	750 mL

1. Rinse ribs under cold running water and, using a paring knife and your fingers or needle-nose pliers, peel the membrane from the underside. Discard membrane. Place ribs in a large sealable plastic bag or in a large disposable aluminum pan and pour in apple juice. Seal or cover and refrigerate for at least 4 hours or for up to 6 hours.

2. Remove ribs from apple juice, but do not pat dry. Discard juice. Place ribs on a baking sheet and sprinkle with rib rub, coating evenly. Let stand at room temperature for about 15 minutes, or until surface of ribs is tacky. Meanwhile, prepare a fire in your smoker. *(For instructions, see pages 8–11.)*

Keep barbecue sauces
or glazes in a metal bowl
or pan near the smoker
so they stay warm and
can be easily brushed
on meat.

3. Place ribs directly on the smoker rack, add wood to the coals and close the lid. Smoke at 225°F to 250°F (110°C to 120°C), spraying with apple juice every hour, for 2 hours. Brush ribs with honey, close the lid and smoke for 30 minutes. Brush with barbecue sauce, close the lid and smoke for 30 to 60 minutes, or until meat pulls away from the ends of the bones.

4. Serve with any remaining sauce or another sauce of your choice.

In Memphis, Tennessee, barbecue restaurants offer smoked ribs two ways. "Dry" means they have a dry rub on them but are not sauced. "Wet" means the sauce has been brushed on.

Pork Tenderloin

Pork tenderloin is usually associated with grilling or other methods of fast cooking because it's tender. But it's also delicious smoked. Because this recipe is easy and doesn't take a long time, try it before you attempt a pork shoulder blade so you can practice regulating the temperature on your smoker.

SERVES 4	**Recommended wood:** fruit wood (apple, cherry, pear, peach, etc.)	

TIPS

For a darker color on the exterior of your smoked pork tenderloin, grill it over a hot fire first, just for a minute or so, until you get good grill marks. Then put it on the indirect side of your grill and finish cooking as above. Using this method, your pork tenderloin should be completely smoked in 75 minutes or less.

• • •

Be aware that, due to carry-over cooking, the internal temperature of pork tenderloins will rise a few degrees between the time they are removed from the smoker and the time they are sliced. To ensure that your pork is not overcooked, remove it from the oven a few minutes before the internal temperature registers the desired degree of doneness.

4	pork tenderloins	4
	Olive oil for brushing	
	Kosher salt and freshly ground black pepper	
1 cup	tomato-based barbecue sauce (store-bought or see recipes, pages 50, 52–58 and 62–63)	250 mL
½ cup	seedless raspberry preserves	125 mL

1. Prepare a fire in your smoker. *(For instructions, see pages 8–11.)*

2. Brush pork with olive oil, then season to taste with salt and pepper.

3. In a small bowl, combine barbecue sauce and raspberry preserves.

4. Place pork directly on the smoker rack, add wood to the coals and close the lid. Smoke at 225°F to 250°F (110°C to 120°C) for 1 hour. Brush with half of the barbecue sauce mixture, close the lid and smoke for 40 to 75 minutes, or until a meat thermometer inserted in the thickest part of a tenderloin registers 160°F (70°C).

5. Serve with the remainder of the sauce.

Pork Chops

This recipe uses a slather, a mustard-based mixture used to seal in moisture and turn the dry rub into a kind of "bark" on the exterior of the chops. You can also practice glazing the chops at the end of cooking with a sweet and sassy barbecue sauce.

SERVES 4	**Recommended wood:** a combination of apple and hickory

TIPS

For the most succulent result, you'll want thick-cut, bone-in pork chops.

• • •

The smaller the smoking chamber on your equipment, the sooner your food will be done. If you're using a kettle grill or a bullet smoker, your pork chops might be done in 3½ hours. If you're using a bigger rig or a genuine smoker, they might take 4 hours.

4	bone-in center-cut pork chops, each about 2 inches (5 cm) thick	4
½ cup	Dijon mustard	125 mL
½ cup	mayonnaise	125 mL
½ cup	Honey & Spice Rub (see recipe, page 31)	125 mL
1¼ cups	Mustard & Marmalade Barbecue Sauce (see recipe, page 60)	300 mL

1. Rinse pork chops under cold running water and pat dry.

2. In a bowl, combine mustard and mayonnaise. Spread over pork chops, then sprinkle on dry rub. Let stand at room temperature for 15 to 20 minutes, or until surface of chops is tacky. Meanwhile, prepare a fire in your smoker. *(For instructions, see pages 8–11.)*

3. Place pork chops directly on the smoker rack, add wood to the coals and close the lid. Smoke at 225°F to 250°F (110°C to 120°C) for 3 hours. Brush with barbecue sauce, close the lid and smoke for 30 minutes, or until a meat thermometer inserted in the center of a chop registers 160°F (70°C).

4. Serve with any remaining sauce.

Pork Shoulder Blade

Tough, muscular pork shoulder blade — also known as pork butt or Boston butt — becomes fall-apart tender after slow-cooking on your smoker. It's a rewarding dish that is well worth the 9 to 10 hours' cooking time. Just sprinkle the meat with dry rub, spray with a tart, clear fruit juice throughout the smoking process, then glaze with a little barbecue sauce during the last hour. Mmmmm. Most barbecuers will do several pork butts at a time, then wrap and freeze some for later use, as this meat makes wonderful pulled pork sandwiches any time of year.

SERVES 10 TO 12	Recommended wood: a combination of hickory and apple or cherry	

TIPS

Place clear fruit juices (such as apple and pineapple) in a large, clean, plastic spray bottle, usually available at hardware, home improvement or kitchenware stores. To spray foods during smoking, simply open the lid of the smoker, spray the meat, then close the lid quickly to keep the temperature steady.

* * *

Pork shoulder blade is done when you can stick a meat fork into the pork, give it a twist and pull the meat apart easily.

3½ cups	barbecue seasoning mix (store-bought or see recipes, pages 27–34)	875 mL
1	boneless pork shoulder blade roast (6 to 8 lbs/3 to 4 kg)	1
1 cup	fruit juice (such as apple or pineapple) for spraying	250 mL
2 cups	barbecue sauce (store-bought or see recipes, pages 50–65)	500 mL

1. Sprinkle seasoning mix over the surface of the pork, coating evenly. Let stand at room temperature for about 15 minutes, or until surface of pork is tacky. Meanwhile, prepare a fire in your smoker. *(For instructions, see pages 8–11.)*

2. Place pork directly on the smoker rack, add wood to the coals and close the lid. Smoke at 225°F to 250°F (110°C to 120°C), spraying with fruit juice every hour, for 7 hours. Place butt in a disposable aluminum pan. Pour 1 cup (250 mL) of the barbecue sauce over the meat, cover with aluminum foil and place pan on the smoker rack. Close the lid and smoke for 2 hours, or until pork is fork-tender (see tip, at left). Let stand, covered, for 20 minutes. Remove from pan and discard juice.

3. To serve, remove strings if necessary and pull pork apart with two forks. If you wish, combine pulled pork with the remaining barbecue sauce, or simply pass the sauce at the table.

At some North American barbecue contests, judges prefer pork shoulder blade sliced thickly rather than shredded.

Beef Brisket Flat

This is a good starter recipe, to give you a feel for how long it takes to tenderize and smoke, before you tackle a larger whole brisket.

SERVES 10 TO 12	Recommended wood: a combination of hickory and apple or cherry	

TIP

A brisket flat is, just as the term implies, the smaller or flatter part of the whole beef brisket. Have your butcher cut it for you.

	Onion salt	
	Granulated garlic (see tip, opposite)	
	Freshly ground black pepper	
1	boneless beef brisket flat (5 to 7 lbs/2.5 to 3.5 kg)	1
2½ cups	Rich & Delicious Brisket Mop (see recipe, page 45)	625 mL
3 cups	Honey Mustard Barbecue Sauce (see recipe, page 61) or sauce of your choice	750 mL

1. Sprinkle a heavy coating of the onion salt, granulated garlic and pepper onto the brisket. Massage brisket for 5 minutes to work the rub into the meat. Set aside.

2. Prepare a fire in your smoker. *(For instructions, see pages 8–11.)*

3. Place brisket directly on the smoker rack, add wood to the coals and close the lid. Smoke at 225°F to 250°F (110°C to 120°C) for 2 hours. Brush brisket with mop and continue smoking, mopping once every hour, for 5 hours. Remove brisket from smoker and place in a disposable aluminum pan. Slather brisket with barbecue sauce, wrap with foil and place pan on the smoker rack. Smoke for 1½ hours, until tender.

Standing Rib Roast

You will never roast a standing rib again after you try this recipe. You'll get the same crusty exterior and juicy interior that you do in roasting, but the beef will take on a deeper, smokier flavor that is better than prime rib served at the finest restaurant.

SERVES 8 TO 10

Recommended wood: hickory with a little mesquite

TIPS

You can find granulated garlic at well-stocked supermarkets or online (see the Source Guide, page 356).

• • •

If you want to make traditional Yorkshire Pudding to go with this dish, trim off some of the fat before putting the beef in the smoker.

1	standing beef rib roast (4 to 6 lbs/2 to 3 kg), at room temperature	1
¼ cup	olive oil	50 mL
½ cup	cracked peppercorns	125 mL
1 tbsp	granulated garlic (see tip, at left)	15 mL

1. Trim all but ½ inch (1 cm) of the white fat from the roast and discard (or save for Yorkshire Pudding). Rub with olive oil and press peppercorns and granulated garlic into the surface of the meat. Insert a meat thermometer in the center of the roast, away from the bone.

2. Prepare a fire in your smoker. *(For instructions, see pages 8–11.)*

3. Place roast, fat side up, directly on the smoker rack, add wood to the coals and close the lid. Smoke at 225°F to 250°F (110°C to 120°C) until meat thermometer registers 140°F (60°C) for rare, about 3 to 3½ hours, or to desired doneness. Remove from smoker, remove meat thermometer and wrap roast tightly in plastic wrap. Let stand for 15 to 20 minutes. Unwrap, slice and serve.

Leg of Lamb

This lamb is delicious served with a Hollandaise sauce to which chopped fresh herbs such as rosemary, parsley and thyme have been added.

SERVES 8 TO 10	Recommended wood: a combination of hickory and apple

TIPS

Have your butcher butterfly the leg of lamb for you.

• • •

If the lamb is tied into a roast, remove strings before marinating.

• • •

The smaller the smoking chamber on your equipment, the sooner your food will be done. If you're using a kettle grill or a bullet smoker, your leg of lamb might be done in 2 hours. If you're using a bigger rig or a genuine smoker, it might take 3 hours.

1	boneless leg of lamb (4 to 5 lbs/ 2 to 2.5 kg), butterflied	1
2½ cups	Mediterranean Marinade (see recipe, page 42)	625 mL
	Olive oil for brushing	
	Kosher salt and freshly ground black pepper	

1. Place lamb in a large non-metallic baking dish. Pour marinade over lamb. Cover and refrigerate for at least 2 hours or for up to 8 hours.

2. Remove lamb from marinade and pat dry. Discard marinade. Brush lamb with olive oil and season to taste with salt and pepper. Set aside.

3. Prepare a fire in your smoker. *(For instructions, see pages 8–11.)*

4. Place lamb flat on the smoker rack, add wood to the coals and close the lid. Smoke at 225°F to 250°F (110°C to 120°C) until a meat thermometer inserted in the thickest part of the lamb registers 145°F (63°C) for medium-rare, about 2 to 3 hours, or to desired doneness.

Salmon Fillet

This easy recipe makes for a great presentation at a family gathering or party. Line a platter with sturdy lettuce leaves and arrange the smoked salmon fillet on them. Overlap thin slices of lemon around the perimeter of the platter.

SERVES 8	**Recommended wood:** a combination of hickory, apple and oak

TIPS

A vinaigrette has less acid than a marinade, so it's safe to marinate fish for longer.

◦ ◦ ◦

The smaller the smoking chamber on your equipment, the sooner your food will be done. If you're using a kettle grill or a bullet smoker, your salmon fillet might be done in an hour. If you're using a bigger rig or a genuine smoker, it might take 1½ hours.

1	whole salmon fillet (skin on)	1
1½ cups	bottled Italian vinaigrette	375 mL
	Mediterranean or Cajun seasoning blend	

1. Place salmon skin side down in a non-metallic baking dish. Pour vinaigrette over fish. Cover and refrigerate for 2 hours.

2. Remove salmon from vinaigrette and pat dry. Discard vinaigrette. Sprinkle salmon with seasoning and set aside.

3. Prepare a fire in your smoker. *(For instructions, see pages 8–11.)*

4. Add wood to the coals and wait until smoke is fragrant, 5 to 10 minutes. Place salmon, skin side down, directly on the smoker rack and close the lid. Smoke at 225°F to 250°F (110°C to 120°C) for 1 hour, until fish flakes easily in the thickest part of the fillet when tested with a fork.

Tuna Steak

Meaty tuna almost tastes like a beef steak when you smoke it. Try it this way, served with a Middle Eastern–style sauce, then try the cold-smoked Tuna in Fresh Orange & White Balsamic Marinade on page 187. You'll be hooked.

SERVES 4	Recommended wood: hickory or mesquite

TIPS

For more color in this dish, add a sprinkle of smoked paprika or sprigs of fresh herbs right before serving.

• • •

If you smoke a tuna steak to rare, medium-rare or medium doneness, it will be moister and more flavorful than if you smoke it longer.

4	tuna steaks, cut 1 inch (2.5 cm) thick	4
	Olive oil for brushing	
	Kosher salt and freshly ground black pepper	

Hummus-Tahini Sauce

2	cloves garlic, minced	2
1 cup	hummus	250 mL
¼ cup	tahini	50 mL
	Freshly squeezed lemon juice	

1. Prepare a fire in your smoker. *(For instructions, see pages 8–11.)*

2. Brush tuna steaks with olive oil, then season to taste with salt and pepper.

3. Add wood to the coals and wait until smoke is fragrant, 5 to 10 minutes. Place tuna steaks directly on the smoker rack and close the lid. Smoke at 225°F to 250°F (110°C to 120°C) until the tuna is medium-rare, about 30 to 45 minutes, or to desired doneness.

4. *Prepare the Hummus-Tahini Sauce:* In a bowl, whisk together garlic, hummus and tahini. Whisk in lemon juice to taste.

5. Serve each tuna steak with a dollop of sauce.

Whole Trout

Deliciously easy! The one that didn't get away will make for succulent eating.

SERVES 4 TO 6	**Recommended wood:** alder, maple, hickory or pecan		

TIPS

One medium lemon yields about 3 tbsp (45 mL) juice.

• • •

The smaller the smoking chamber on your equipment, the sooner your food will be done. If you're using a kettle grill or a bullet smoker, your trout might be done in 1½ hours. If you're using a bigger rig or a genuine smoker, it might take 2 hours.

6	sprigs fresh herbs (such as tarragon, dill, chives or Italian parsley)	6
6	thin slices fresh lemon	6
1	whole trout (3 to 4 lbs/1.5 to 2 kg), cleaned and scaled	1
½ cup	dry white wine	125 mL
¼ cup	freshly squeezed lemon juice	50 mL
¼ cup	unsalted butter, melted	50 mL
	Kosher salt and freshly ground black pepper	

1. Place herb sprigs and lemon slices in the cavity of the fish.

2. In a disposable aluminum pan, combine wine, lemon juice and butter. Place fish in the pan and spoon some of the basting liquid over it. Sprinkle with salt and pepper to taste. Set aside.

3. Prepare a fire in your smoker. *(For instructions, see pages 8–11.)*

4. Place pan on the smoker rack, add wood to the coals and close the lid. Smoke at 225°F to 250°F (110°C to 120°C) for 1½ to 2 hours, or until fish is opaque and flakes easily when tested with a fork. Discard cooking liquid.

Scallops

Smoked scallops take on a burnished appearance and a smoky flavor, yet remain succulent and meaty.

SERVES 4	Recommended wood: oak, pecan or hickory

TIPS

For the best results, use larger scallops.

• • •

The smaller the smoking chamber on your equipment, the sooner your food will be done. If you're using a kettle grill or a bullet smoker, your scallops might be done in 45 minutes. If you're using a bigger rig or a genuine smoker, they might take an hour.

1 lb	large sea scallops	500 g
	Olive oil for drizzling	
	Kosher salt and freshly ground black pepper	

1. Rinse scallops under cold running water and pat dry. Place in a single layer in a disposable aluminum pan, drizzle with olive oil and season to taste with salt and pepper.

2. Prepare a fire in your smoker. *(For instructions, see pages 8–11.)*

3. Add wood to the coals and wait until smoke is fragrant, 5 to 10 minutes. Place pan on the smoker rack and close the lid. Smoke at 225°F to 250°F (110°C to 120°C) for 45 to 60 minutes, or until scallops are opaque and somewhat firm to the touch.

Shrimp

When you serve these shrimp at a party, perhaps adding a little liquid smoke flavoring to your favorite cocktail sauce, your guests will think you've worked all day to make something this good. Don't tell them otherwise.

SERVES 4	Recommended wood: oak, pecan or hickory

TIP

If you wish, thread shrimp on skewers and smoke directly on the rack. There's no need to soak the skewers in water first, as the temperature in your smoker should stay below 250°F (120°C). Do not crowd shrimp on the skewers, or they will take longer to cook through.

1 lb	large shrimp	500 g
	Olive oil for drizzling	
	Kosher salt and freshly ground black pepper	

1. Peel shrimp, leaving tail shell intact, and devein. Rinse under cold running water and pat dry. Place in a single layer in a disposable aluminum pan, drizzle with olive oil and season to taste with salt and pepper.

2. Prepare a fire in your smoker. *(For instructions, see pages 8–11.)*

3. Add wood to the coals and wait until smoke is fragrant, 5 to 10 minutes. Place pan on the smoker rack and close the lid. Smoke at 225°F to 250°F (110°C to 120°C) for 45 minutes, or until shrimp are pink and opaque and somewhat firm to the touch.

Vegetables, Fruits, Cheese and Nuts

WHEN PEOPLE TALK about traditional barbecue or slow-smoked foods, they usually mean meats such as pork ribs or beef brisket. But vegetables, fruits, cheeses and nuts also benefit from time in the smoker. When cold-smoked, they take on a smoky aroma, but their appearance, texture and color remain virtually unchanged. After a spell in the hot smoker, these foods have a softer appearance, a "cooked" texture and a burnished look, as well as a smoky aroma.

I like to use cold-smoked vegetables and fruits in relishes and side dishes where their colors stand out. I use hot-smoked vegetables and fruits for stand-alone appetizers and side dishes that have a more rustic appearance. Cold-smoked cheeses can usually be sliced to add to an appetizer tray, while hot-smoked cheeses have softened enough for spreading on bread or crackers. Whole almonds, pecans, walnuts and other nuts taste wonderful smoked and can be made even crisper by spreading them evenly on a baking sheet after smoking and letting them toast in a 350°F (180°C) oven for about 15 minutes.

Whether you want a light, medium or heavy smoke flavor on your foods comes down to preference. That's where my advice of "practice makes perfect" comes in. Slow-smoking is a technique, so keep practicing to come up with your own signature smoke flavors.

If you like, season vegetables, fruits, cheeses and nuts with a dry rub of your choice before smoking for an even greater savory flavor.

VEGETABLE, FRUIT, CHEESE AND NUT RECIPES

COLD-SMOKED

Cold-Smoked Vegetables 98
Artichoke & Red Onion Relish. . . . 99
Asparagus on Skewers 100
Coleslaw in Pineapple
    Soy Dressing 101
Red Onion & Tomato Salsa 102
Fiesta Pepper Salsa 103
Potato Salad. 104
Potato Salad with Celery
    & Pickles. 105
Cold-Smoked Fruit. 106
Fresh Fruit Salsa. 107
Cold-Smoked Cheese 108
Cheese, Vegetable &
    Pepperoni Skewers 109
Gouda with Onion, Jalapeño
    Pepper & Artichoke Relish. . . 110
Brie with Brown Sugar
    & Pecans 111

HOT-SMOKED

Hot-Smoked Vegetables 112
Oak-Smoked Brussels Sprouts
    with Lime & Brown Sugar. . . 113
Brown Sugar & Maple
    Cabbage 114
Corn in the Husk 115
Corn Relish. 116
Stuffed Eggplant with
    Bacon, Garlic & Cream 117
Wheat Berry & Olive
    Tapenade. 118
Onion & Charred Pepper
    Salsa. 119

Sausage-Stuffed Mushrooms . . . 120
Stuffed Portobello
    Mushrooms 121
Portobello Mushrooms
    with Brandied Cream 122
Spicy Acorn Squash 123
Stuffed Tomatoes. 124
Tomato Guacamole 125
Three-Bean Barbecue
    Casserole 126
French Canadian
    Barbecued Beans. 127
Horseradish Potatoes. 128
Sweet Potatoes 128
Potato Casserole 129
Pecan-Smoked Vegetable
    Skewers 130
Ratatouille 131
Fettuccine with Garlic,
    Tomato & Basil. 132
Vegetable Chowder 133
Hot-Smoked Fruit. 134
Apple-Smoked Apples. 135
Hot-Smoked Cheese 136
Salad Caprese with Mozzarella,
    Basil & Tomatoes 137
Goat Cheese–Stuffed
    Tomatoes 138
Goat Cheese & Chipotle Dip . . . 139
Marinated Tofu. 140
Smoky Deviled Eggs 141
Smoked Peanuts 142
Spicy Nuts 143
Rosemary Almonds 144
Smokehouse Almonds 145

Cold-Smoked Vegetables

With cold-smoking — that is, smoking at a temperature under 200°F (100°C) — vegetables take on a smoky flavor but do not change color as with hot-smoking. Cabbage stays a spring green, tomatoes a vivid red, yellow bell peppers a bright yellow. That makes cold-smoked vegetables ideal for relishes, salsas and slaws, in which their bright colors and bold flavors are shown to their fullest.

Because cold-smoking requires a special type of smoker with the firebox far away from the food, I do lots of different vegetables at the same time. I like to use peach wood, which gives a unique and sweet smoke flavor, but any wood (other than, perhaps, the very strong mesquite) will work. Try any or all of the vegetables here!

Recommended wood: peach or other fruit wood

TIPS

Use cold-smoked vegetables in salsas, slaws, soups, salads and appetizers.

• • •

You can also cold-smoke canned artichokes and tomatoes: Just drain off excess liquid, then pour the vegetables out onto the wire rack.

• • •

Make ahead

Place cold-smoked vegetables in an airtight container and store in the refrigerator for up to 1 week.

Canned artichokes, drained, or frozen artichokes, thawed

Roma (plum) tomatoes, halved lengthwise

Red or yellow onions, halved

Jalapeño peppers, halved lengthwise

Yellow, red and/or green bell peppers, halved lengthwise and seeded

Zucchini, halved lengthwise

Yellow summer squash (such as yellow zucchini), halved lengthwise

Asparagus, trimmed

Mushrooms, stemmed

Cloves of garlic, threaded onto bamboo skewers

Eggplant, halved lengthwise (skin on)

Cabbage, quartered

1. Prepare a fire in your cold smoker, using 3 oz (90 g) of wood. Set temperature to 200°F (100°C) until wood starts to smoke. Turn temperature dial to Off and place a pan of ice on top of the cold plate. Then set temperature to 100°F (40°C).

2. Place vegetables on a wire rack, place in the smoker and close the lid or door. For a light smoke flavor, smoke for 75 minutes; medium smoke, 80 minutes; heavy smoke, 105 minutes.

Artichoke & Red Onion Relish

Serve this colorful relish with scallops, red snapper or other fish or shellfish — it's a great accompaniment for all smoked seafood.

MAKES ABOUT 2 CUPS (500 ML)

TIP

See opposite for instructions on cold-smoking garlic, artichokes and red onion.

• • •

Make ahead

Spoon into an airtight container and store in the refrigerator for up to 1 week.

3	cloves garlic, cold-smoked and minced	3
1	can (14 oz/398 mL) artichokes, cold-smoked	1
½ cup	diced cold-smoked red onion	125 mL
½ cup	diced green onions	125 mL
½ cup	chopped fresh cilantro	125 mL
3 tbsp	olive oil	45 mL
2 tbsp	drained capers	25 mL
2 tbsp	freshly squeezed lemon juice	25 mL
1 tbsp	minced seeded jalapeño pepper	15 mL
1 tsp	chopped fresh mint	5 mL
1 tsp	kosher salt	5 mL
½ tsp	coarsely ground black pepper	2 mL

1. In a blender or food processor, process garlic, artichokes, red onion, green onions, cilantro, oil, capers, lemon juice, jalapeño pepper, mint, salt and pepper until chunky.

Asparagus on Skewers

This delicious appetizer or side dish goes well with smoked fish, pork or chicken. The asparagus stays green during cold-smoking, and threading it onto skewers ensures that you don't lose any stalks in the smoker.

SERVES 4

Recommended wood: cherry

TIP

One lemon will yield about 3 tbsp (45 mL) juice.

- Eight 6-inch (15 cm) bamboo skewers

1½ lbs	asparagus, trimmed	750 g
3 tbsp	freshly squeezed lemon juice	45 mL
2 tbsp	freshly squeezed orange juice	25 mL
2 tbsp	extra-virgin olive oil	25 mL
	Kosher salt	

1. Soak skewers in warm water for 10 minutes.
2. Place asparagus on a baking sheet and drizzle with lemon juice, orange juice and oil. Sprinkle with salt to taste. Thread several stalks onto each skewer and set aside.
3. Prepare a fire in your cold smoker, using 3 oz (90 g) of wood. Set temperature to 200°F (100°C) until wood starts to smoke. Turn temperature dial to Off and place a pan of ice on top of the cold plate. Then set temperature to 140°F (60°C).
4. Place skewers on a wire rack, place in the smoker and close the lid or door. Smoke for 1½ hours, or until asparagus is tender–crisp. Serve immediately.

Coleslaw in Pineapple Soy Dressing

Who says slaw has to be ho-hum? Make a batch of this version for a gathering and watch it disappear. Cold-smoking gives the cabbage a pleasant, smoky flavor but doesn't change its color.

SERVES 8

TIPS

I like to use cylindrical-shaped napa cabbage in this recipe because of its ruffled leaves. If you prefer, you could use 1 large head of round cabbage.

● ● ●

See page 98 for instructions on cold-smoking cabbage.

2	heads napa cabbage, quartered and cold-smoked	2

Pineapple Soy Dressing

¼ cup	soy sauce	50 mL
¼ cup	olive oil	50 mL
¼ cup	pineapple juice	50 mL
2 tbsp	freshly squeezed lime juice	25 mL

1. With a sharp knife, cut cabbage into fine shreds and place in a large bowl.

2. *Prepare the dressing:* In a small bowl, whisk together soy sauce, olive oil, pineapple juice and lime juice. Pour over cabbage and toss to blend. Serve immediately.

Red Onion & Tomato Salsa

You'll love this vivid salsa with smoked brisket, flank steak or chicken. It's great with leftovers too — try spooning it on a brisket or smoked chicken sandwich.

MAKES ABOUT 4 CUPS (1 L)

TIP

See page 98 for instructions on cold-smoking tomatoes, garlic, jalapeño pepper and red onion.

● ● ●

Make ahead

Cover and store in the refrigerator for up to 1 week.

3	large Roma (plum) tomatoes, cold-smoked	3
2	cloves garlic, cold-smoked	2
1	jalapeño pepper, cold-smoked, stemmed and seeded	1
¼ cup	coarsely chopped cold-smoked red onion	50 mL
1	can (12 oz/375 mL) tomato sauce	1
	Juice of 2 large limes	
1 tsp	chili powder	5 mL
1 tsp	ground cumin	5 mL
½ tsp	kosher salt	2 mL
¼ tsp	freshly ground black pepper	1 mL
3 tbsp	minced fresh cilantro	45 mL

1. In a blender or food processor, process tomatoes, garlic, jalapeño pepper, red onion, tomato sauce, lime juice, chili powder, cumin, salt and pepper until chunky.

2. Transfer to a bowl and stir in cilantro.

Fiesta Pepper Salsa

This salsa is great with a wheel of baked or smoked Brie or other smoked cheese.

MAKES ABOUT 2 CUPS (500 ML)

TIP

See page 98 for instructions on cold-smoking tomatoes, garlic and yellow and red bell peppers.

• • •

Make ahead

Cover and store in the refrigerator for up to 1 week.

3	Roma tomatoes, cold-smoked, seeded and diced	3
2	cloves garlic, cold-smoked	2
½ cup	diced cold-smoked yellow bell pepper	125 mL
½ cup	diced cold-smoked red bell pepper	125 mL
6	green onions, diced, white parts and some of the green	6
1 tbsp	olive oil	15 mL
1 tsp	minced fresh basil	5 mL
1 tsp	minced fresh cilantro	5 mL
½ tsp	kosher salt	2 mL
½ tsp	chili powder	2 mL

1. In a bowl, stir together tomatoes, garlic, yellow pepper, red pepper, green onions, oil, basil, cilantro, salt and chili powder until well blended.

Potato Salad

This is a very unusual recipe, but also very delicious.

Recommended wood: peach or other fruit wood

TIP

You can find granulated garlic at well-stocked supermarkets or online (see the Source Guide, page 356).

• • •

Make ahead

Store in the refrigerator for up to 3 days.

1 lb	new or waxy potatoes	500 g
2	hard-boiled eggs, finely chopped	2
2	green onions, chopped	2
¾ cup	sour cream	175 mL
¼ cup	shredded Cheddar cheese	50 mL
3 tbsp	diced red bell peppers	45 mL
3 tbsp	freshly squeezed lime juice	45 mL
2 tbsp	minced fresh cilantro	25 mL
¼ tsp	kosher salt	1 mL
¼ tsp	chili powder	1 mL
Pinch	granulated garlic (see tip, at left)	Pinch

1. In a saucepan, cover potatoes with cold water. Bring to a boil over high heat. Reduce heat and boil gently for about 15 minutes, or until fork-tender. Drain and let cool slightly. Peel and halve potatoes lengthwise.

2. Meanwhile, prepare a fire in your cold smoker, using 3 oz (90 g) of wood. Set temperature to 200°F (100°C) until wood starts to smoke. Reduce temperature to 140°F (60°C) and place a pan of ice on top of the cold plate.

3. Place potatoes on a wire rack, place in the smoker and close the lid or door. Smoke for 1 hour, or until fragrant with smoke.

4. Dice potatoes and place in a large bowl. Add eggs, green onions, sour cream, cheese, red peppers, lime juice, cilantro, salt, chili powder and garlic; mix well. Cover and refrigerate for at least 3 hours before serving.

Potato Salad with Celery & Pickles

This recipe yields a sweet/sour potato salad with a hint of smoke.

SERVES 4 TO 6

Recommended wood: apple

Make ahead

Store in the refrigerator for up to 3 days.

1 lb	potatoes	500 g
2	hard-boiled eggs, finely chopped	2
¼ cup	diced onion	50 mL
¼ cup	mayonnaise	50 mL
3 tbsp	diced celery	45 mL
3 tbsp	coarsely chopped dill pickles	45 mL
3 tbsp	cider vinegar	45 mL
2 tbsp	olive oil	25 mL
1 tbsp	barbecue seasoning mix (store-bought or see recipes, pages 27–34)	15 mL
2 tsp	packed light brown sugar	10 mL

1. In a saucepan, cover potatoes with cold water. Bring to a boil over high heat. Reduce heat and boil gently for about 15 minutes, or until fork-tender. Drain and let cool slightly. Peel and halve potatoes lengthwise.

2. Prepare a fire in your cold smoker, using 3 oz (90 g) of wood. Set temperature to 200°F (100°C) until wood starts to smoke. Reduce temperature to 140°F (60°C) and place a pan of ice on top of the cold plate.

3. Place potatoes on a wire rack, place in the smoker and close the lid or door. Smoke for 1 hour, or until fragrant with smoke.

4. Dice potatoes and place in a large bowl. Add eggs, onions, mayonnaise, celery, pickles, vinegar, oil, seasoning mix and brown sugar; mix well. Serve warm or cover and refrigerate until ready to serve.

Cold-Smoked Fruit

Why cold-smoke fruit? You still get a vibrant color, but you add a hint of wood smoke for a counterpoint to the natural fruit flavor.

Recommended wood: peach or pecan

3	pears, halved	3
3	oranges, halved	3
1	pineapple, peeled, cored and quartered lengthwise	1
1 lb	red or green grapes	500 g

1. Prepare a fire in your cold smoker, using 3 oz (90 g) of wood. Set temperature to 200°F (100°C) until wood starts to smoke. Turn temperature dial to Off and place a pan of ice on top of the cold plate. Then set temperature to 100°F (40°C).

2. Place fruit on a wire rack, place in the smoker and close the lid or door. For a light smoke flavor, smoke for 75 minutes; medium smoke, 80 minutes; heavy smoke, 105 minutes.

Fresh Fruit Salsa

Serve this colorful and flavorful take on traditional salsa with smoked shrimp for a delicious hot-weather meal.

MAKES ABOUT 3 CUPS (750 ML)

TIP

See page 98 for instructions on cold-smoking garlic, red bell pepper and red onion. See opposite for instructions on cold-smoking pineapple, pear and orange.

• • •

Make ahead

Store in the refrigerator for up to 3 days.

1	clove garlic, cold-smoked	1
¾ cup	diced peeled cold-smoked pineapple	175 mL
½ cup	diced cold-smoked red bell pepper	125 mL
½ cup	diced cold-smoked pear	125 mL
½ cup	diced cold-smoked orange (peel on)	125 mL
¼ cup	diced cold-smoked red onion	50 mL
1	serrano chili pepper, seeded and diced	1
2 tbsp	olive oil	25 mL
1 tbsp	minced fresh mint	15 mL
1 tbsp	minced fresh chives	15 mL
1 tbsp	freshly squeezed lime juice	15 mL
1 tsp	minced fresh basil	5 mL
1 tsp	kosher salt	5 mL

1. In a bowl, combine garlic, pineapple, red pepper, pears, oranges, red onion, serrano pepper, oil, mint, chives, lime juice, basil and salt. Cover and refrigerate for at least 1 hour before serving.

Cold-Smoked Cheese

If you have the right equipment, it's easy to cold-smoke your own slicing cheese to enjoy as a snack or in a recipe. Use any or all of these cheeses.

TIPS

Cold-smoked cheese is great as an appetizer or on sandwiches.

• • •

To smoke semi-soft cheese, see recipe, page 74.

• • •

Make ahead

Place in an airtight container and store in the refrigerator for up to 1 week. If you have a vacuum packaging machine, you can extend the life of your cold-smoked cheese up to 1 month.

Recommended wood: apple, cherry or maple

8 oz	firm cheese (see list of possibilities, below)	250 g

- Cheddar (medium, sharp or extra-sharp)
- Monterey Jack
- Swiss or baby Swiss
- Gouda
- Colby
- Mozzarella
- Provolone

1. Prepare a fire in your cold smoker, using 4 oz (125 g) of wood. Set temperature to 200°F (100°C) until wood starts to smoke. Turn temperature dial to Off and place a pan of ice on top of the cold plate. Then set temperature to 60°F (20°C).

2. Place cheese on a wire rack, place in the smoker and close the lid or door. For a light smoke flavor, smoke for 75 minutes; medium smoke, 80 minutes; heavy smoke, 105 minutes.

Cheese, Vegetable & Pepperoni Skewers

This fun and unusual way to serve antipasto has a hint of smoky flavor.

SERVES 6	**Recommended wood:** grape or other fruit wood

TIP

Vary this recipe by using your favorite antipasto foods. Try small balls of fresh mozzarella, other Italian cured meats, roasted red bell pepper and large pitted black olives.

- Twelve 12-inch (30 cm) bamboo skewers

1 cup	olive oil	250 mL
½ cup	champagne vinegar or white wine vinegar	125 mL
1 tsp	chopped fresh cilantro	5 mL
1 tsp	chopped fresh basil	5 mL
12	cubes salami	12
12	cubes Swiss cheese	12
1	zucchini, cut into 1-inch (2.5 cm) slices	1
12	cubes pepperoni	12
1	red bell pepper, cut into large pieces	1
1	jar (16 oz/450 mL) marinated artichoke hearts, drained	1

1. Soak skewers in water for 30 minutes.

2. In a small bowl, combine oil, vinegar, cilantro and basil. Set aside.

3. Onto each skewer, thread a salami cube, cheese cube, zucchini slice, pepperoni cube, red pepper piece and artichoke heart. Place skewers on a baking sheet and drizzle with oil mixture. Set aside.

4. Prepare a fire in your cold smoker, using 3 oz (90 g) of wood. Set temperature to 200°F (100°C) until wood starts to smoke. Reduce temperature to 140°F (60°C) and place a pan of ice on top of the cold plate.

5. Place skewers on a wire rack, place in the smoker and close the lid or door. Smoke for 1 hour, or until fragrant with smoke.

Gouda with Onion, Jalapeño Pepper & Artichoke Relish

When you make this appetizer, everyone will ask for the recipe. Serve with slices of French bread or crackers.

SERVES 8	Recommended wood: hickory or pecan		

TIP

The hickory wood gives a slightly more pronounced smoke flavor than the pecan.

2	jalapeño peppers, seeded and diced	2
1	red onion, diced	1
1 cup	drained canned artichoke hearts	250 mL
1 cup	chopped drained canned tomatoes	250 mL
¼ cup	chopped fresh cilantro	50 mL
2 tbsp	olive oil	25 mL
1 lb	Gouda cheese	500 g

1. Prepare a fire in your cold smoker, using 4 oz (125 g) of wood. Set temperature to 200°F (100°C) until wood starts to smoke. Turn temperature dial to Off and place a pan of ice on top of the cold plate. Then set temperature to 60°F (20°C).

2. In a disposable aluminum pan, combine jalapeño peppers, red onion, artichoke hearts, tomatoes and cilantro. Drizzle with oil and toss to coat. Place cheese and pan of vegetables on a wire rack, place in the smoker and close the lid or door. For a light smoke flavor, smoke for 75 minutes; medium smoke, 80 minutes; heavy smoke, 105 minutes.

3. To serve, place cheese in the middle of a platter and surround with relish.

Brie with Brown Sugar & Pecans

Serve your guests this scrumptious appetizer and they'll beg for more. Brie is a very soft cheese and will melt in the smoker. Serve with a sliced baguette.

SERVES 4

TIPS

To toast pecans, arrange them in a single layer on a baking sheet and toast in a 350°F (180°C) oven for 15 minutes or until fragrant.

• • •

For cold-smoking, I like to use an electric smoker, set as low as possible. You can also use a wood pellet grill, set on Low. You want to aim for 50°F to 60°F (10°C to 20°C) for this dish.

• 4 oz (125 g) cherry and apple wood chips		
¼ cup	packed brown sugar	50 mL
¼ cup	butter, melted	50 mL
1	8-oz (250 g) round Brie cheese	1
2 oz	toasted pecans (see tip, at left), coarsely chopped	60 g

1. In a bowl of water, soak wood chips for at least 30 minutes. Drain.

2. In a small bowl, combine brown sugar and butter.

3. Place Brie in a shallow disposable aluminum pie plate. Dot with butter mixture.

4. Prepare a fire in your cold smoker, using soaked wood chips. Set temperature to 200°F (100°C) until wood starts to smoke. Turn temperature dial to Off and place a pan of ice on top of the cold plate. Then set temperature to 60°F (20°C).

5. Place pie plate on a wire rack, place in the smoker and close the lid or door. For a light smoke flavor, smoke for 75 minutes; medium smoke, 80 minutes; heavy smoke, 105 minutes.

6. Sprinkle cheese with pecans and place a cocktail spreader in the cheese.

Hot-Smoked Vegetables

Hot-smoked vegetables take on a burnished color and actually cook through when they smoke, so more vegetables can be hot-smoked than cold-smoked. Soft, tender, juicy vegetables such as tomatoes, bell peppers, zucchini and summer squash will take about 1 hour to smoke. Harder, denser vegetables such as potatoes and squash can take up to 3 hours to cook through.

Recommended wood: apple or other fruit wood

Make ahead

Place hot-smoked vegetables in an airtight container and store in the refrigerator for up to 1 week or in the freezer for up to 3 months.

Canned artichokes, drained, or frozen artichokes, thawed

Roma (plum) tomatoes, halved lengthwise

Red or yellow onions, halved

Jalapeño peppers, halved

Yellow, red and/or green bell peppers, halved lengthwise and seeded

Zucchini, halved lengthwise

Yellow summer squash (such as yellow zucchini), halved lengthwise

Mushrooms, stemmed

Cloves of garlic, threaded onto bamboo skewers

Ears of corn, in the husk

Potatoes, pricked all over with a knife

Sweet potatoes, pricked all over with a knife

Winter squash, halved

1. Prepare a fire in your smoker. *(For instructions, see pages 8–11.)*

2. Place vegetables on the smoker rack, add wood to the coals and close the lid. Smoke tender vegetables at 225°F to 250°F (110°C to 120°C) for 1 hour. Smoke potatoes and winter squash at 225°F to 250°F (110°C to 120°C) for 2 to 3 hours, or until tender.

Oak-Smoked Brussels Sprouts with Lime & Brown Sugar

If you're smoking a turkey for a holiday dinner, why not smoke sprouts as well? Once you taste these, you'll banish any thought of sprouts another way.

SERVES 8

Recommended wood: oak, especially whispering oak

TIP

One lime will yield 1 to 2 tbsp (15 to 25 mL) juice.

1½ lbs	Brussels sprouts	750 g
3 tbsp	butter	45 mL
1 tbsp	freshly squeezed lime juice	15 mL
3 tbsp	pure maple syrup	45 mL

1. Trim outer leaves from Brussels sprouts, rinse sprouts carefully and place in a disposable aluminum pan.

2. In a small saucepan, melt butter over medium heat. Stir in lime juice. Pour butter mixture over sprouts and drizzle with maple syrup. Set aside.

3. Prepare a fire in your smoker. *(For instructions, see pages 8–11.)*

4. Place pan on the smoker rack, add wood to the coals and close the lid. Smoke at 225°F to 250°F (110°C to 120°C) for 1½ hours, or until sprouts are tender.

Brown Sugar & Maple Cabbage

So simple, yet so good! The cabbage takes on a sweet and smoky flavor.

SERVES 4

Recommended wood: apple or other fruit wood

TIP

Put cabbage on to smoke when you're already smoking something else, like a pork or chicken dish.

1	head cabbage	1
1 cup	packed light brown sugar	250 mL
3 tbsp	butter	45 mL
¼ cup	pure maple syrup	50 mL

1. Cut out the core of the cabbage to make a hole. Make a large foil cup to hold the head of cabbage, bringing the foil at least a quarter of the way up the cabbage, with the hole facing up. Pack brown sugar into the cabbage, dot with butter and drizzle with maple syrup. Set aside.

2. Prepare a fire in your smoker. *(For instructions, see pages 8–11.)*

3. Place cabbage on the smoker rack, add wood to the coals and close the lid. Smoke at 225°F to 250°F (110°C to 120°C) for 3 hours. Wrap cabbage completely in foil and smoke for 1 hour, or until tender.

Corn in the Husk

So easy, so delicious! Put corn on to smoke when you're smoking a pork tenderloin or chicken, timing it so they get done around the same time.

SERVES 6	Recommended wood: pear or other fruit wood

TIPS

Ancho-Herb Dry Rub (see recipe, page 30) tastes mighty fine on this corn, but you choose your own flavoring.

● ● ●

The smaller the smoking chamber on your equipment, the sooner your food will be done. If you're using a kettle grill or a bullet smoker, your corn might be done in 45 minutes. If you're using a bigger rig or a genuine smoker, it might take an hour.

6	ears corn, in the husk	6
½ cup	butter, softened	125 mL
⅓ cup	barbecue seasoning mix (store-bought or see recipes, pages 27–34)	75 mL
1 tbsp	pure maple syrup	15 mL

1. Peel back corn husks and remove the silk, leaving just a few layers of husk on each ear. Spread butter over each cob, sprinkle with seasoning mix and drizzle with maple syrup. Fold husks back over corn. Set aside.

2. Prepare a fire in your smoker. *(For instructions, see pages 8–11.)*

3. Add wood to the coals and wait until smoke is fragrant, 5 to 10 minutes. Place corn on the smoker rack and close the lid. Smoke at 225°F to 250°F (110°C to 120°C) for 1 hour, or until tender.

Corn Relish

Homemade corn relish has been a staple on farmhouse tables for generations. Here, the blend of corn, peppers and onions gets a smoky twist, for an updated and irresistible version of the original. Put the vegetables on while you're smoking something else, or fire up your smoker to make lots of this relish.

MAKES ABOUT 6 CUPS (1.5 L)

Recommended wood: hickory

● Three to four 12-inch (30 cm) bamboo skewers

4	cloves garlic	4
2	small jalapeño peppers, cut in half lengthwise and seeded	2
1	large red onion, cut into 1-inch (2.5 cm) thick slices	1
5 to 6	ears corn, in the husk	5 to 6
1½ cups	white wine vinegar	375 mL
½ cup	granulated sugar	125 mL
½ cup	olive oil	125 mL
2 tbsp	hot pepper flakes	25 mL
2 tbsp	dried thyme	25 mL
2 tbsp	chopped fresh parsley	25 mL
	Kosher salt and freshly ground black pepper	

1. Soak skewers in water for 30 minutes.

2. Meanwhile, prepare a fire in your smoker. *(For instructions, see pages 8–11.)*

3. Add wood to the coals and wait until smoke is fragrant, 5 to 10 minutes. Thread garlic, jalapeño peppers and onion onto skewers. Place skewers and corn on the smoker rack and close the lid. Smoke at 225°F to 250°F (110°C to 120°F) for 1 hour, or until corn is tender.

4. When corn is cool enough to handle, remove husks and, using a paring knife, cut off kernels into a large bowl. Chop vegetables and stir into corn.

5. In a medium bowl, whisk together vinegar, sugar, oil, hot pepper flakes, thyme, parsley, salt and pepper. Pour over vegetables and toss to blend.

Stuffed Eggplant with Bacon, Garlic & Cream

Place this show-stopping dish on the smoker when you're smoking a turkey, brisket, whole chicken or beef tenderloin. You might as well do several things at once, when you can.

SERVES 4	Recommended wood: apple or other fruit wood	

TIP

Choose a firm eggplant with smooth skin that feels heavy for its size, and avoid those with soft or brown spots. Use within a day or two of purchase. The flesh discolors quickly, so cut into cubes just before sautéing.

1	eggplant	1
¼ cup	butter	50 mL
1	clove garlic, minced	1
1 cup	sliced mushrooms	250 mL
¼ cup	diced onion	50 mL
½ cup	crumbled crispy bacon (about 8 strips)	125 mL
¼ cup	whipping (35%) cream	50 mL
3 tbsp	freshly grated Parmesan cheese	45 mL
3 tbsp	dry bread crumbs	45 mL

1. Prepare a fire in your smoker. *(For instructions, see pages 8–11.)*

2. Slice eggplant in half lengthwise. Using a paring or serrated knife, remove as much of the flesh as you can without cutting into the skin. Set shell aside and cut flesh into cubes.

3. In a skillet, melt butter over medium-high heat. Add garlic, mushrooms and onion; sauté for 3 to 5 minutes, or until softened. Add the flesh of the eggplant and sauté for 5 minutes, or until tender. Add bacon, whipping cream, Parmesan and bread crumbs; mix well. Fill shell with eggplant mixture.

4. Place shell on the smoker rack, add wood to the coals and close the lid. Smoke at 225°F to 250°F (110°C to 120°C) for 1½ hours, or until eggplant is warmed through and fragrant with smoke. Let cool for 15 minutes before serving. To serve, slice or spoon onto plates.

Wheat Berry & Olive Tapenade

This smoky blend of cooked whole wheat kernels and kalamata olives is delicious on crusty bread.

MAKES ABOUT 2 CUPS (500 ML)

TIPS

Serve in a crock with country-style bread.

• • •

Smoked olives are also delicious in casseroles, chicken salad and dips.

• • •

Make ahead

Spoon into an airtight container and store in the refrigerator for up to 1 week.

Recommended wood: apple or hickory

¾ cup	wheat berries (whole wheat kernels)	175 mL
1 cup	pitted kalamata olives	250 mL
1	clove garlic, minced	1
¼ cup	olive oil	50 mL
1 tsp	Dijon mustard	5 mL

1. In a medium saucepan, combine wheat berries and 2¼ cups (550 mL) water; bring to a boil over medium–high heat. Reduce heat and simmer for about 1 hour, or until tender. Drain.

2. Meanwhile, prepare a fire in your smoker. *(For instructions, see pages 8–11.)*

3. Add wood to the coals and wait until smoke is fragrant, 5 to 10 minutes. Place olives in a small disposable aluminum pan and place on the smoker rack. Close the lid. Smoke at 225°F to 250°F (110°C to 120°C) for 1 hour, or until fragrant with smoke.

4. In a food processor, process wheat kernels, smoked olives, garlic, oil and mustard until a paste forms.

Onion & Charred Pepper Salsa

This salsa carries a smoky flavor from the onion. If you wish, you can smoke the red bell pepper and serrano chili too. Serve with Sea Bass Skewers Lemonada (see recipe, page 162) or other smoked fish or shellfish.

(see recipe, page 162)

SERVES 4 TO 6

TIPS

See page 112 for instructions on hot-smoking red onion.

• • •

Be careful when working with hot peppers such as the serrano. Always wear rubber gloves, as the oils in the pepper could irritate your skin.

• • •

Make ahead

Cover and store in the refrigerator for up to 1 week

- Preheat oven to 450°F (230°C)
- Baking sheet

1	large red bell pepper	1
½	red onion, hot-smoked and chopped	½
12	large basil leaves, chopped	12
4	oil-packed sun-dried tomatoes, drained and chopped	4
2	large tomatoes, seeded and diced	2
1	large clove garlic, minced	1
1	serrano chili pepper, stemmed, seeded and finely chopped	1
¼ cup	olive oil	50 mL
3 tbsp	chopped black olives	45 mL
1 tbsp	champagne vinegar or white wine vinegar	15 mL
1 tbsp	raspberry vinegar	15 mL
	Kosher salt	
	Freshly ground black pepper	

1. Place red pepper on baking sheet and roast in preheated oven for 15 to 20 minutes, turning once, or until pepper is charred on all sides. Wrap pepper tightly in plastic wrap and let stand for 15 minutes. Remove plastic wrap. When cool enough to handle, remove stem, core and seeds, then cut pepper into a medium dice.

2. In a medium bowl, combine red pepper, onion, basil, sun-dried tomatoes, tomatoes, garlic, serrano pepper, oil, olives, champagne vinegar, raspberry vinegar and salt and pepper to taste; mix well.

Sausage-Stuffed Mushrooms

Put these delicious appetizers on to smoke when you're smoking something that takes more time, such as a pork butt, ribs or a brisket. You'll have something to nibble as you tend the fire.

SERVES 3 TO 6		

Recommended wood: pecan

TIP

If bulk sausage is not available, remove casings from sausages and crumble into skillet.

8 oz	bulk pork breakfast-type sausage	250 g
1	large bunch (12 oz/375 g) spinach, rinsed and stemmed	1
5 oz	blue cheese	150 g
3 oz	cream cheese	90 g
1 tbsp	freshly grated Parmesan cheese	15 mL
6	jumbo mushrooms, stemmed and cleaned	6
	Additional freshly grated Parmesan cheese for sprinkling	

1. In a skillet, over medium heat, cook sausage, breaking up with a spoon, until no longer pink inside. Transfer to a plate, reserving fat in pan.

2. In the same skillet, add the spinach and stir until it begins to wilt. Remove from heat and let cool.

3. In a food processor, pulse sausage, spinach, blue cheese, cream cheese and Parmesan until almost smooth. Fill each mushroom with spinach mixture and sprinkle with additional Parmesan. Set aside.

4. Prepare a fire in your smoker. *(For instructions, see pages 8–11.)*

5. Add wood to the coals and wait until smoke is fragrant, 5 to 10 minutes. Place mushrooms on the smoker rack and close the lid. Smoke at 225°F (110°C) for 30 minutes, or until fragrant with smoke.

Stuffed Portobello Mushrooms

Colorful with summer vegetables and fragrant with smoke, these portobellos make a great first course or a vegetarian main course.

SERVES 6	Recommended wood: a combination of apple and cherry	

TIP
This vegetable and cream cheese stuffing is also delicious smoked in a seeded and halved (lengthwise) eggplant, yellow summer squash or zucchini.

6	portobello mushrooms, stem and gills removed	6
2 tbsp	olive oil	25 mL
½ cup	cream cheese, softened	125 mL
¼ cup	oil-packed sun-dried tomatoes, puréed	50 mL
½ cup	shredded yellow summer squash (such as yellow zucchini)	125 mL
¼ cup	shredded zucchini	50 mL
¼ cup	julienned red bell pepper	50 mL
6	slices provolone cheese	6
	Balsamic vinegar for drizzling	

1. Rub mushrooms with olive oil. Place gill side up on a disposable aluminum baking sheet.

2. In a bowl, using a fork, combine cream cheese and tomato purée; set aside.

3. In another bowl, combine squash, zucchini and red pepper.

4. Spread mushrooms with cream cheese mixture, sprinkle with vegetables and top with a slice of cheese. Set aside.

5. Prepare a fire in your smoker. *(For instructions, see pages 8–11.)*

6. Add wood to the coals and wait until smoke is fragrant, 5 to 10 minutes. Place baking sheet on the smoker rack and close the lid. Smoke at 200°F (100°C) for 1 hour, or until mushrooms have softened and cheese has melted.

7. Serve hot, drizzled with balsamic vinegar.

Portobello Mushrooms with Brandied Cream

Serve these mushrooms as rustic appetizers, a hearty side dish or a vegetarian main course.

SERVES 8 AS AN APPETIZER OR SIDE DISH, 4 AS A MAIN COURSE

Recommended wood: hickory or apple

8	large portobello mushrooms, stems removed	8
	Olive oil for brushing	
	Kosher salt and coarsely ground black pepper	
½ cup	whipping (35%) cream	125 mL
⅓ cup	brandy	75 mL
½ tsp	dried thyme	2 mL

TIPS

Brandied cream is also delicious on smoked onions.

• • •

The smaller the smoking chamber on your equipment, the sooner your food will be done. If you're using a kettle grill or a bullet smoker, your mushrooms might be done in an hour. If you're using a bigger rig or a genuine smoker, they might take 1½ hours.

1. Prepare a fire in your smoker. *(For instructions, see pages 8–11.)*

2. Brush mushrooms evenly with olive oil and season with salt and pepper. Place stem side up on the smoker rack, add wood to the coals and close the lid. Smoke at 225°F to 250°F (110°C to 120°C) for 1½ hours, or until bubbling and fragrant with smoke. During the last 30 minutes of smoking, combine whipping cream, brandy and thyme in a bowl. Drizzle mushrooms with half the mixture.

3. To serve, drizzle mushrooms with the remaining brandied cream.

Spicy Acorn Squash

Put the squash on when you're smoking a pork loin or tenderloin — or even a turkey — that is also sprinkled with Honey & Spice Rub. Then, for a dazzling finish, drizzle everything with Buttery Brown Sugar and Lime Basting Sauce.

SERVES 8	Recommended wood: apple or hickory	

Variation

This recipe also works for butternut and other types of squash. Slice squash so that the most flesh is exposed to the smoke, and adjust timing according to the size of the squash.

2	acorn squash, halved and seeded	2
¼ cup	butter, melted	50 mL
½ cup	Honey & Spice Rub (see recipe, page 31)	125 mL
⅔ cup	Buttery Brown Sugar & Lime Basting Sauce (see recipe, page 48)	150 mL

1. Brush the flesh of each squash half with melted butter and sprinkle with dry rub. Set aside.

2. Prepare a fire in your smoker. *(For instructions, see pages 8–11.)*

3. Place squash halves cut side up on the smoker rack, add wood to the coals and close the lid. Smoke at 225°F to 250°F (110°C to 120°C) for 2 hours, or until tender. During the last 15 minutes of smoking, brush squash flesh with some of the basting sauce.

4. Serve in the half shell with the remaining basting sauce and butter.

Stuffed Tomatoes

Try this recipe for a wonderful summer side dish.

SERVES 8

Recommended wood: pecan or hickory

TIP

To make your own dry bread crumbs, toast bread until dry and lightly browned. Let cool, then process in a food processor or blender to fine crumbs. Each slice of toast will make about ⅓ cup (75 mL) crumbs. You can store dry bread crumbs in the freezer for up to 3 months.

8	large beefsteak tomatoes	8
¼ cup	butter	50 mL
1	clove garlic, minced	1
1 cup	finely chopped mushrooms	250 mL
¼ cup	diced onion	50 mL
½ cup	crumbled crispy bacon (about 8 strips)	125 mL
¼ cup	whipping (35%) cream	50 mL
3 tbsp	freshly grated Parmesan cheese	45 mL
3 tbsp	dry bread crumbs	45 mL

1. Prepare a fire in your smoker. *(For instructions, see pages 8–11.)*

2. Using a serrated knife, carve out the core of each tomato. Scrape out about 2 to 3 inches (5 to 7.5 cm) of the tomato flesh, without cutting into the skin. Place tomato shells in a disposable aluminum pan. Seed and chop tomato flesh.

3. In a skillet, melt butter over medium-high heat. Add garlic, mushrooms and onion; sauté for 3 to 5 minutes, or until softened. Add tomato flesh and sauté for 5 minutes, or until tender. Add bacon, cream, Parmesan and bread crumbs; mix well. Stuff tomatoes with the mixture.

4. Place pan on the smoker rack, add wood to the coals and close the lid. Smoke at 225°F to 250°F (110°C to 120°C) for 1½ hours, or until warmed through and fragrant with smoke. Let cool for 15 minutes before serving. To serve, slice or place a whole tomato onto each plate.

Tomato Guacamole

Lightly smoked tomatoes add resonance to traditional guacamole. I wouldn't fire up my cooker just to do these tomatoes, but they're great to add to the pit when you're smoking meats.

SERVES 8	Recommended wood: apple or hickory	

Make ahead

Store in the refrigerator for up to 2 days. Like any guacamole, the longer this sits, the more discolored it will get.

2	large beefsteak tomatoes, cored	2
3	large ripe avocados, pitted	3
1/2 cup	chopped green onions	125 mL
1/2 cup	chopped fresh cilantro	125 mL
1/2 cup	freshly squeezed lime juice	125 mL
	Kosher salt and freshly ground black pepper	

1. Prepare a fire in your smoker. *(For instructions, see pages 8–11.)*

2. Add wood to the coals and wait until smoke is fragrant, 5 to 10 minutes. Place tomatoes in a disposable aluminum pan and place on the smoker rack. Close the lid. Smoke at 225°F to 250°F (110°C to 120°C) for 30 minutes, or until tomatoes are still firm but are fragrant with smoke.

3. Peel and chop tomatoes and place in a medium bowl. Using a fork, mix in avocados, green onions, cilantro, lime juice and salt and pepper to taste, mashing until avocados are chunky. Serve right away, or cover and refrigerate before serving.

Three-Bean Barbecue Casserole

When you put ribs, chicken or brisket on the smoker, leave room for this dish. Use a disposable aluminum pan, or a dish you don't mind getting that burnished look from sitting in the smoker.

Recommended wood: fruit, alder, hickory, oak or pecan

TIP

This casserole can also be baked in a 350°F (180°C) oven for 30 minutes, or until bubbly, but you won't get that smoky flavor or taste.

3 tbsp	vegetable oil	45 mL
3	large cloves garlic, minced	3
2	mild green chili peppers, stemmed, seeded and diced	2
1	large red onion, diced	1
1 cup	sour cream	250 mL
1	can (14 to 19 oz/398 to 540 mL) pinto beans, drained and rinsed	1
1	can (14 to 19 oz/398 to 540 mL) black beans, drained and rinsed	1
1	can (14 to 19 oz/398 to 540 mL) red kidney beans, drained and rinsed	1
½ cup	chopped fresh cilantro	125 mL
	Kosher salt and coarsely ground black pepper	
1 cup	shredded sharp Cheddar or pepperjack cheese	250 mL

1. Prepare a fire in your smoker. *(For instructions, see pages 8–11.)*

2. In a large skillet, heat oil over medium-high heat. Add garlic, chili peppers and onion; sauté until vegetables have softened, about 8 minutes. Stir in sour cream, pinto, black and red kidney beans, cilantro and salt and pepper to taste. Transfer to a large disposable aluminum pan and sprinkle with cheese.

3. Place pan on the smoker rack, add wood to the coals and close the lid. Smoke at 225°F to 250°F (110°C to 120°C) for 1½ hours, or until casserole is bubbling and fragrant with smoke.

French Canadian Barbecued Beans

When you put a large pan of these beans on the smoker, they'll slow-cook and take on the flavor of the hearth, probably tasting like a pot of beans did in Quebec three centuries ago.

SERVES 8	Recommended wood: maple, oak or hickory	

TIPS

Put these beans on to smoke when you're smoking a pork butt, pork loin, brisket or any meat that takes a longer time.

• • •

This casserole can also be baked in a 350°F (180°C) oven for 30 minutes, or until bubbly, but you won't get that smoky flavor or taste.

2 lbs	dry white pea (navy) beans, soaked for 8 hours or overnight	1 kg
4	stalks celery, chopped	4
2	onions, chopped	2
1 cup	packed brown sugar	250 mL
¾ cup	ketchup	175 mL
⅓ cup	fancy molasses or pure maple syrup	75 mL
1 tsp	dry mustard	5 mL
	Kosher salt and freshly ground black pepper	
	Chopped smoked pork or sausage	

1. Drain beans and place beans in a large pot with enough fresh water to cover. Bring to a boil over high heat. Reduce heat, cover and simmer until tender, about 45 minutes. Drain and transfer to a large disposable aluminum pan. Stir in celery, onions, brown sugar, ketchup, molasses, mustard, salt and pepper to taste and pork to taste. Add enough water to cover. Set aside.

2. Prepare a fire in your smoker. *(For instructions, see pages 8–11.)*

3. Put pan on the smoker rack, add wood to the coals and close the lid. Smoke at 225°F to 250°F (110°C to 120°C) for 5 to 6 hours, or until beans are bubbling and fragrant with smoke.

Horseradish Potatoes

Because you mash the potatoes for this casserole, it's best made with warm potatoes from the smoker. Dress it up by adding crumbled crispy bacon, or down by substituting grated Cheddar cheese and chopped green onions for the horseradish. It's wonderful served with a smoked beef roast or brisket.

SERVES 8		
8	large russet potatoes, hot-smoked and peeled	8
1 cup	whipping (35%) cream	250 mL
¼ cup	butter, melted	50 mL
1 tbsp	prepared horseradish	15 mL
	Kosher salt and freshly ground black pepper	

TIPS
See page 112 for instructions on hot-smoking potatoes.

• • •

Place potatoes on the smoker about 2½ to 3 hours before your beef roast or brisket is done, so they'll be done at the same time.

1. In a large bowl, mash potatoes with cream, butter and horseradish. Season to taste with salt and pepper. Serve immediately.

Sweet Potatoes

If you have a Thanksgiving turkey on the smoker, why not add sweet potatoes too? If you like them baked, you'll love them smoked. These are wonderful served with whipped honey butter or simply with butter, salt and pepper.

SERVES 8	Recommended wood: hickory or apple	
8	sweet potatoes	8
	Vegetable oil	

TIP
You can also smoke-roast these potatoes. Smoke them for 1 hour, then transfer to a 350°F (180°C) oven and roast for 45 minutes, or until tender.

1. Using a paring knife, prick sweet potatoes in several places. Brush with vegetable oil and set aside.

2. Prepare a fire in your smoker. *(For instructions, see pages 8–11.)*

3. Place sweet potatoes on the smoker rack, add wood to the coals and close the lid. Smoke at 225°F to 250°F (110°C to 120°C) for 2 hours, or until tender.

Potato Casserole

With potato casseroles, you have the option of baking them in the oven or smoking them on your pit. For a little extra time but a whole lot of flavor, why not do the latter? These potatoes are decadent, but oh so good!

SERVES 8	Recommended wood: apple or cherry	

TIP
You can also bake this casserole in a 250°F (120°C) oven for 3 to 3½ hours, but you won't have that smoky aroma and flavor.

1	package (24 oz/750 g) frozen hash-brown potatoes	1
1 tsp	garlic powder	5 mL
	Kosher salt and freshly ground black pepper	
¼ cup	melted butter	50 mL
¾ cup	whipping (35%) cream	175 mL
2 tbsp	snipped fresh chives (optional)	25 mL

1. Thaw hash browns enough that you are able to flake them with a fork. In a greased 8-cup (2 L) disposable aluminum pan, layer a third each of the flaked potatoes, garlic powder, salt, pepper and butter. Repeat layers twice. Pour cream over the potatoes. Set aside.

2. Prepare a fire in your smoker. *(For instructions, see pages 8–11.)*

3. Place pan on the smoker rack, add wood to the coals and close the lid. Smoke at 225°F to 250°F (110°C to 120°C) for 3 to 3½ hours, or until potatoes are bubbling, golden and fragrant with smoke. Garnish with chives, if desired. Serve hot.

Pecan-Smoked Vegetable Skewers

Colorful and delicious, these vegetable skewers are a wonderful side dish with smoked ribs, brisket or Brined & Basted Sirloin Roast (see recipe, page 274). Pecan adds a medium smoke flavor that is just slightly sweet.

SERVES 8	Recommended wood: pecan

TIP

Keep a disposable aluminum pan as close to the heat of your smoker as possible, and place your herb butter inside. That way, your herb butter stays warm and is within easy reach. The aluminum pan ensures that, if you spill any herb butter, you won't have a mess.

- Eight 12-inch (30 cm) bamboo skewers

6	canned artichoke bottoms or hearts	6
1	zucchini, cut into 2-inch (5 cm) chunks	1
1	yellow summer squash (such as yellow zucchini), cut into 2-inch (5 cm) chunks	1
1	red bell pepper, cut into 2-inch (5 cm) chunks	1
1	red onion, cut into wedges	1
8 oz	mushrooms	250 g
½ cup	butter, melted	125 mL
2 tbsp	minced fresh basil	25 mL
1 tbsp	minced fresh mint	15 mL

1. Soak skewers in water for 30 minutes.

2. Thread artichokes, zucchini, squash, red pepper, onion and mushrooms onto skewers, then place on a baking sheet.

3. In a bowl, combine butter, basil and mint. Brush vegetables with half of the herb butter. Set aside. Reserve the remaining herb butter and keep warm by the smoker.

4. Prepare a fire in your smoker. *(For instructions, see pages 8–11.)*

5. Place skewers on the smoker rack, add wood to the coals and close the lid. Smoke at 225°F to 250°F (110°C to 120°C), basting occasionally with herb butter, for 1 hour, or until vegetables are tender and fragrant with smoke.

Ratatouille

In the Provençal tradition, ratatouille, a combination of summer vegetables, is baked in a wood-burning village oven. By smoking it, you'll come close to achieving the authentic flavor of the dish.

SERVES 8	Recommended wood: apple	

TIP

Put a pan of ratatouille on to smoke when you're smoking a leg of lamb, whole chickens or a beef roast.

3	cloves garlic, minced	3
2	zucchini, diced	2
2	eggplants, diced	2
2	plum tomatoes, chopped	2
1	red onion, chopped	1
½ cup	olive oil	125 mL
¼ cup	freshly grated Parmesan cheese	50 mL
¼ cup	dry red wine	50 mL
2 tsp	packed brown sugar	10 mL
1 tsp	kosher salt	5 mL

1. In a disposable aluminum pan, combine garlic, zucchini, eggplants, tomatoes, red onion, oil, cheese, wine, brown sugar and salt; toss well. Set aside.

2. Prepare a fire in your smoker. *(For instructions, see pages 8–11.)*

3. Place pan on the smoker rack, add wood to the coals and close the lid. Smoke at 225°F to 250°F (110°C to 120°C) for 1½ hours, or until vegetables are tender.

Fettuccine with Garlic, Tomato & Basil

It's well worth smoking lots of garlic and tomatoes so you'll have them on hand as flavorings for dishes such as this one.

SERVES 6 TO 8	Recommended wood: hickory

1	bulb garlic	1
3	large tomatoes, cored	3
½ cup	olive oil, divided	125 mL
2 lbs	fettuccine pasta	1 kg
¼ cup	shredded fresh basil	50 mL
	Kosher salt and freshly ground black pepper	

1. Cut about ½ inch (1 cm) from the top of the garlic so that the cloves are exposed. Score the tops of the tomatoes. Place garlic and tomatoes on a disposable baking sheet and drizzle with half of the olive oil. Set aside.

2. Prepare a fire in your smoker. *(For instructions, see pages 8–11.)*

3. Add wood to the coals and wait until smoke is fragrant, 5 to 10 minutes. Place baking sheet on the smoker rack and close the lid. Smoke at 225°F to 250°F (110°C to 120°C) for 1 hour, or until garlic and tomatoes are tender and fragrant with smoke.

4. Cook fettuccine according to package directions.

5. Meanwhile, squeeze the garlic from the bulb. Peel, seed and chop tomatoes. Place garlic and tomatoes in a bowl. Add the remaining olive oil and blend well.

6. Drain pasta and toss with the garlic and tomato mixture. Sprinkle with shredded basil and season to taste with salt and pepper.

Vegetable Chowder

In this vegetarian recipe, you get the flavor of bacon in the chowder without the meat, especially if you've used hickory or apple to smoke the vegetables. Delicious!

SERVES 8

TIPS
See page 112 for instructions on hot-smoking potatoes, jalapeño peppers, red and green peppers and corn.

· · ·

When you fire up your smoker, especially in the summer, add some vegetables when you have room. When they've smoked, peel, seed and chop them — or, in the case of corn, scrape off the kernels — put them in freezer bags and store in the freezer for up to 3 months. Then you'll have them on hand as "frozen assets" for recipes like this one.

4	large potatoes, hot-smoked, peeled and chopped	4
2	jalapeño peppers, hot-smoked, seeded and chopped	1
1	red bell pepper, hot-smoked and chopped	1
1	green bell pepper, hot-smoked and chopped	1
6 cups	hot-smoked corn kernels	1.5 L
2 tbsp	butter	25 mL
1	large onion, finely chopped	1
3 cups	half-and-half (10%) or light (5%) cream	750 mL
	Kosher salt and freshly ground black pepper	

1. In a large saucepan, melt butter over medium–high heat. Add onion and sauté until transparent, about 7 minutes. Add potatoes, jalapeño peppers, red pepper, green pepper, corn and enough water to cover. Reduce heat, cover and simmer for 1 hour, until vegetables are tender and flavors have blended. Stir in cream and bring back to a simmer. Season to taste with salt and pepper. Serve hot or cold.

Hot-Smoked Fruit

Why hot-smoke fruit? You get the flavor of the hearth and a great side dish or garnish to serve with slow-smoked meats. Unlike the technique for cold-smoking fruit, you need to brush fruit destined for the hot smoker with melted butter and lemon juice to keep the fruit from browning and forming a skin.

Recommended wood: apple or pecan

Make ahead

Place hot-smoked fruit in an airtight container and store in the refrigerator for up to 1 week.

¼ cup	butter, melted	50 mL
¼ cup	freshly squeezed lemon juice	50 mL
6	apples, cored	6
3	oranges, halved	3
1	pineapple, quartered lengthwise	1
1 lb	red and/or green grapes on the stem	500 g

1. In a bowl, combine butter and lemon juice.

2. Place fruit on a disposable aluminum baking sheet and brush with butter mixture. Set aside.

3. Prepare a fire in your smoker. *(For instructions, see pages 8–11.)*

4. Add wood to the coals and wait until smoke is fragrant, 5 to 10 minutes. Place baking sheet on the smoker rack and close the lid. Smoke at 225°F to 250°F (110°C to 120°C) for 45 to 60 minutes, or until fruit has softened and bronzed and is fragrant with smoke.

Apple-Smoked Apples

For a wonderful accompaniment to an autumn meal, put these on to smoke when you're already doing a pork roast, ribs or chicken. I especially like to use red-skinned apples like Jonathan, Red Delicious or McIntosh.

SERVES 6

Recommended wood: apple

TIP

If you can't find hot pepper jelly, melt 1 tbsp (15 mL) red hot cinnamon candies in ¼ cup (50 mL) apple jelly over low heat.

6	apples, cored	6
2 tbsp	butter, melted	25 mL
¼ cup	pure maple syrup	50 mL
¼ cup	hot pepper jelly	50 mL
¼ cup	packed brown sugar	50 mL

1. Place apples on a disposal aluminum baking sheet and drizzle with butter. Set aside.

2. In a small saucepan, over medium heat, combine maple syrup, pepper jelly and brown sugar. Cook until jelly has melted, about 8 minutes. Stir to blend. Set aside.

3. Prepare a fire in your smoker. *(For instructions, see pages 8–11.)*

4. Place baking sheet on the smoker rack, add wood to the coals and close the lid. Smoke at 225°F to 250°F (110°F to 120°C) for 1 hour. Pour syrup mixture over apples, close the lid and smoke for 15 minutes. Baste with syrup mixture, close the lid and smoke for about 15 minutes, or until apples are tender.

Hot-Smoked Cheese

It's easy to hot-smoke your own cheese, using any type of equipment. Hot-smoked cheese will be much softer and more melted than cold-smoked. Use any or all of these cheeses.

Recommended wood: apple, cherry or maple

TIPS

Hot-smoked cheese is great in dips, on pizza and in casseroles.

* * *

To smoke semi-soft cheese, see recipe, page 74.

* * *

Make ahead

Place in an airtight container and store in the refrigerator for up to 1 month. Cheese will lose its smoky aroma over time.

8 oz	firm cheese (see list of possibilities, below)	250 g

Olive oil

- Cheddar cheese (medium, sharp or extra-sharp)
- Monterey Jack
- Swiss or baby Swiss
- Gouda
- Colby
- Mozzarella
- Provolone

1. Prepare a fire in your smoker. *(For instructions, see pages 8–11.)*

2. Place cheese in a disposable aluminum pan and brush or spray with olive oil.

3. Add wood to the coals and wait until smoke is fragrant, 5 to 10 minutes. Place pan on the smoker rack and close the lid. Smoke at 200°F (100°C) for 45 to 60 minutes, or until cheese is bronzed and fragrant with smoke.

Salad Caprese with Mozzarella, Basil & Tomatoes

Try this twist on the traditional summer salad of fresh tomatoes and fresh mozzarella. You'll like the smoky contrast between the tomatoes and cheese and the fresh basil.

SERVES 4	**Recommended wood:** hickory or maple

TIP

If you can find fresh rounds of mozzarella still in liquid, use that. If not, any large piece will work well.

1 lb	cherry tomatoes (about 2 cups/500 mL)	500 g
1 lb	mozzarella cheese	500 mL
½ cup	bottled Italian vinaigrette, divided	125 mL
16	fresh basil leaves	16

1. Place cherry tomatoes and mozzarella in a disposable aluminum pan. Drizzle with half of the vinaigrette. Set aside.

2. Prepare a fire in your smoker. *(For instructions, see pages 8–11.)*

3. Add wood to the coals and wait until smoke is fragrant, 5 to 10 minutes. Place pan on the smoker rack and close the lid. Smoke at 225°F to 250°F (110°C to 120°C) for 45 minutes, or until tomatoes have split their skins and mozzarella is bronzed and fragrant with smoke. Let cool slightly.

4. To serve, slice mozzarella and arrange with cherry tomatoes on 4 plates. Drizzle with the remaining vinaigrette and garnish each salad with 4 fresh basil leaves.

Goat Cheese–Stuffed Tomatoes

Put this easy side dish on the smoker while you're smoking something else.

Variation

Use large beefsteak tomatoes, cut into thick slices, and put a pat of goat cheese on each slice before smoking.

8	tomatoes, cored	8
8 oz	fresh chèvre (goat) cheese	250 g
	Olive oil for spraying	
	Chopped fresh herbs (such as Italian parsley, basil and chives) for sprinkling	

1. Using a serrated knife, carve out the core of each tomato. Scrape out about 2 to 3 inches (5 to 7.5 cm) of the tomato flesh, without cutting into the skin. Place tomato shells in a disposable aluminum pan. Pack the cavities with cheese. Spray tops with olive oil and sprinkle with herbs. Set aside.

2. Prepare a fire in your smoker. *(For instructions, see pages 8–11.)*

3. Add wood to the coals and wait until smoke is fragrant, 5 to 10 minutes. Place pan on the smoker rack and close the lid. Smoke at 225°F to 250°F (110°C to 120°C) for 1 hour, or until tops are bronzed and tomatoes are fragrant with smoke.

Goat Cheese & Chipotle Dip

Serve this easy dip with a big flavor with corn tortilla chips or toasted French or artisan bread.

SERVES 4	**Recommended wood:** hickory or pecan

TIP

If you don't spray the top of the mixture with olive oil, it will develop a skin.

2	canned chipotle peppers, minced	2
8 oz	fresh chèvre (goat) cheese	250 g
¼ cup	minced fresh cilantro	50 mL
	Olive oil for spraying	

1. In a medium bowl, combine chipotle peppers, cheese and cilantro. Spoon into a disposable aluminum pan. Spray with olive oil and set aside.

2. Prepare a fire in your smoker. *(For instructions, see pages 8–11.)*

3. Add wood to the coals and wait until smoke is fragrant, 5 to 10 minutes. Place pan on the smoker rack and close the lid. Smoke at 225°F to 250°F (110°C to 120°C) for 1 hour, or until the top is bronzed and dip is fragrant with smoke. Serve immediately.

Marinated Tofu

You can please your vegetarian friends at a barbecue by smoking tofu. In this recipe, the marinade helps keep the tofu moist.

SERVES 8	**Recommended wood:** hickory, pecan or maple

TIP

You can buy jalapeño pepper powder and ancho chili powder at better herb and spice emporiums, by mail order or online (see the Source Guide, page 356).

2	cloves garlic, minced	2
2 lbs	extra-firm tofu, well drained and cut into ¼-inch (0.5 cm) cubes	1 kg
1 cup	rice vinegar	250 mL
2 tbsp	granulated sugar	25 mL
1 tbsp	ancho chili powder (see tip, at left)	15 mL
2 tsp	kosher salt	10 mL
½ tsp	jalapeño pepper powder (see tip, at left)	2 mL

1. In a large bowl, combine garlic, tofu, vinegar, sugar, chili powder, salt and jalapeño powder, tossing gently with a rubber spatula to coat. Transfer to a disposable aluminum pan and spread out in a single layer. Set aside.

2. Prepare a fire in your smoker. *(For instructions, see pages 8–11.)*

3. Add wood to the coals and wait until smoke is fragrant, 5 to 10 minutes. Place pan on the smoker rack and close the lid. Smoke at 225°F to 250°F (110°C to 120°C), tossing the tofu in the marinade once or twice, for 1 hour, or until tofu is fragrant with smoke.

Smoky Deviled Eggs

Although I wouldn't fire up my cooker just to smoke these eggs, they're great when you're already doing something else, especially if you want a wonderful deviled egg side dish.

SERVES 12	Recommended wood: any wood you're already using

Make ahead

Place in an airtight container and store in the refrigerator for up to 3 days.

6	hard-boiled eggs, shelled	6
¼ cup	mayonnaise	50 mL
2 tbsp	finely chopped celery and celery leaves	10 mL
1 tbsp	prepared horseradish	15 mL
1 tsp	Worcestershire sauce	5 mL
½ tsp	hot pepper sauce (or to taste)	2 mL

1. Prepare a fire in your smoker. *(For instructions, see pages 8–11.)*

2. Add wood to the coals and wait until smoke is fragrant, 5 to 10 minutes. Place eggs in a disposable aluminum pan and place on the smoker rack. Close the lid. Smoke at 225°F to 250°F (110°C to 120°C) for 1 hour, or until eggs are a light golden color and are fragrant with smoke.

3. Cut eggs in half lengthwise and scoop yolks into a bowl. Using a fork, mix in mayonnaise, celery and leaves, horseradish, Worcestershire sauce and hot pepper sauce until a smooth paste forms.

4. Using a spoon, stuff the cavity of each egg half with yolk mixture. Serve warm or chilled.

Smoked Peanuts

This is a great way to take the common peanut to higher realms of appetizer glory.

SERVES 8	Recommended wood: cherry

TIPS

I prefer to use Spanish peanuts, but any raw peanut will taste good.

• • •

Vegetable and garlic spray is a nonstick cooking spray in a garlic flavor. You could also spray the peanuts with garlic-flavored olive oil.

• • •

For a crisper texture after smoking, spread peanuts in a single layer on a baking sheet and toast in a 350°F (180°C) oven for 15 minutes.

• • •

Make ahead

Place in an airtight container and store at room temperature for up to 1 month.

1 lb	raw peanuts, shelled	500 g
	Vegetable and garlic spray (see tip, at left)	
2 tbsp	fine kosher or sea salt	25 mL

1. Place peanuts in a disposable aluminum pan, spray with vegetable garlic spray and sprinkle with salt. Set aside.

2. Prepare a fire in your smoker. *(For instructions, see pages 8–11.)*

3. Place pan on the smoker rack, add wood to the coals and close the lid. Smoke at 225°F to 250°F (110°C to 120°C) for 2 hours, or until peanuts are fragrant with smoke. Serve warm or at room temperature.

Spicy Nuts

Great party fare! Smoke several batches of nuts and keep them on hand for easy entertaining.

SERVES 8	Recommended wood: cherry

Make ahead

Let cool, place in an airtight container and store at room temperature for up to 1 month.

1 lb	mixed salted and roasted nuts	500 g
	Vegetable and garlic spray (see tip, opposite)	
1 cup	Honey & Spice Rub (see recipe, page 31)	250 mL

1. Place nuts in a disposable aluminum pan and spray with vegetable garlic spray. Sprinkle on dry rub and toss to coat. Set aside.

2. Prepare a fire in your smoker. *(For instructions, see pages 8–11.)*

3. Place pan on the smoker rack, add wood to the coals and close the lid. Smoke at 225°F to 250°F (110°C to 120°C) for 2 hours, or until nuts are fragrant with smoke. Serve warm or at room temperature.

Rosemary Almonds

These almonds are delicious with a glass of wine before dinner.

SERVES 8

Recommended wood: cherry, hickory or pecan

Variation

Substitute walnuts for the almonds.

• • •

Make ahead

Let cool, place in an airtight container and store at room temperature for up to 1 month.

2	cloves garlic, finely chopped	2
1	sprig fresh rosemary, chopped	1
2 cups	blanched almonds	500 mL
2 tbsp	olive oil	25 mL
1½ tsp	kosher salt	7 mL

1. In a bowl, combine garlic, rosemary, almonds and oil until almonds are completely coated. Season with salt. Spread evenly in a disposable aluminum pan. Set aside.

2. Prepare a fire in your smoker. *(For instructions, see pages 8–11.)*

3. Add wood to the coals and wait until smoke is fragrant, 5 to 10 minutes. Place pan on the smoker rack and close the lid. Smoke at 225°F to 250°F (110°C to 120°C) for 45 to 60 minutes, or until almonds are fragrant with smoke. Serve warm.

Smokehouse Almonds

Give almonds a deep, smoky taste with mesquite or hickory, or a combination of the two. A spicy rub also helps bring out their flavor.

SERVES 8

Recommended wood: mesquite or hickory

TIP

If you want crisper almonds, after smoking spread them in a single layer on a baking sheet and toast in a 350°F oven (180°C) for 15 minutes.

● ● ●

Make ahead

Let cool, place in an airtight container and store at room temperature for up to 1 month.

1 lb	almonds (skin on)	500 g
	Vegetable and garlic spray (see tip, page 142)	
	Honey & Spice Rub (see recipe, page 31)	

1. Place nuts in a disposable aluminum pan and spray with vegetable garlic spray. Sprinkle on dry rub and toss to coat. Set aside.

2. Prepare a fire in your smoker. *(For instructions, see pages 8–11.)*

3. Place pan on the smoker rack, add wood to the coals and close the lid. Smoke at 225°F to 250°F (110°C to 120°C) for 2 hours, or until almonds are fragrant with smoke. Serve warm or at room temperature.

Fish and Shellfish

WHOLE FISH, FILLETS, FISH STEAKS and shellfish all benefit from low and slow smoking over aromatic wood.

If you've never smoked fish yourself, or enjoyed hot-smoked fish and shellfish, you're in for a treat. Hot-smoking adds another flavor level and is especially good with oilier fish such as salmon and mackerel, but it's also delicious with freshwater fish such as trout and walleye pike, and saltwater fish such as haddock or monkfish. You can even hot-smoke oysters, lobster, shrimp and scallops.

You'll want to make sure fish and shellfish stay moist during smoking, with a marinade, a baste or a simple brush of olive oil. Hot-smoked fish and shellfish take on a burnished appearance and are cooked all the way through, but not preserved.

I recommend you start with hot-smoking before venturing into cold-smoking. Strictly speaking, commercial cold-smoking is done at temperatures way below 100°F (60°C), which is the lower limit on my SmokinTex®, so I can't do "real" cold-smoked salmon or scallops. But I can still produce cold-smoked fish and shellfish that are more translucent than when they're hot-smoked, and they're still delicious. They just aren't preserved, as they would be with commercial equipment. But once you've tried the Scallop Martinis (page 191), I think you'll agree that cold-smoking has its virtues!

With fish and shellfish, I think alder is the best wood smoke flavor. But fruit woods and a little bit of a deeper-flavored wood such as pecan, oak or hickory can also be delicious.

FISH AND SHELLFISH RECIPES

HOT-SMOKED

Garden Catfish 148

Soy & Green Onion
    Catfish Fillets 149

Haddock Fillets in White Wine,
    Ginger & Horseradish 150

Alder-Smoked Halibut Steaks
    in Orange, Soy & Lime
    Marinade 151

Alder-Smoked Red Snapper
    with Citrus Spray 152

Salmon with White Wine
    & Pesto 153

Salmon with Sweet
    Orange Baste 154

Hickory-Smoked Salmon
    with Buttery Brown Sugar
    & Lime Baste 155

Apple-Smoked Salmon
    with Green Grape Sauce . . . 156

Salmon "Candy" 158

Mediterranean-Style Tilapia 159

Margarita-Style Sea Bass 160

Sea Bass Skewers Lemonada . . . 162

Shark Steaks in Orange
    & Soy Marinade 164

Alder-Smoked Shark Steaks 165

Three P's Shark Skewers 166

Butter-Basted Whole Trout 167

Crab-Stuffed Whole Trout 168

Trout in Lavender Butter 170

Whitefish in Cumin-Cilantro
    Marinade 171

Maple-Smoked Whitefish 172

Lobster in Savory Sauce 173

Lobster Tail Kabobs in White
    Balsamic Vinaigrette 174

Flower of the Flames Oysters . . 175

Barbecued Oysters 176

Scallops in Sesame Marinade . . 177

Lemon-Herb Scallops 178

Lime & Ginger Prawns 179

Alder-Smoked Shrimp 180

Shrimp in Lime & Lager
    Marinade 181

Honey-Basted Shrimp 182

COLD-SMOKED

Red Snapper & Vegetables 183

Salmon in Bay Brine 184

Salmon in Maple Brine 185

Herb-Brined Salmon 186

Tuna in Fresh Orange &
    White Balsamic Marinade . . 187

Mussels in Apple-Garlic
    Marinade 188

Hickory-Smoked Mussels
    in Passionberry Wine 189

Scallops 190

Scallop Martinis 191

Garden Catfish

Farm-raised catfish is great year-round on the smoker, as it is raised in ponds, feeds from the top on special food and goes from being harvested in a net to an almost-frozen fillet in 30 minutes. Catfish farmers have the processing down to a science.

SERVES 4	Recommended wood: a combination of alder and apple	

TIPS

You'll need 2 lemons to make ⅓ cup (75 mL) juice.

• • •

Feel free to substitute other medium-firm white fish, such as halibut or trout.

½ cup	olive oil	125 mL
1	clove garlic, minced	1
⅓ cup	freshly squeezed lemon juice	75 mL
¼ cup	diced carrots	50 mL
¼ cup	diced celery	50 mL
¼ cup	diced green onions	50 mL
2 tbsp	chopped fresh parsley	25 mL
1 tbsp	minced fresh thyme	15 mL
2 tsp	kosher salt	10 mL
1 tsp	freshly ground black pepper	5 mL
4	catfish fillets (each about 6 oz/175 g)	4
	Limes, thinly sliced	
	Apple juice for spraying	

1. In a skillet, heat oil over medium-high heat. Cook garlic, lemon juice, carrots, celery, onions, parsley, thyme, salt and pepper for 2 minutes, until vegetables soften. Remove from heat and let cool slightly.

2. Rinse fish under cold running water and pat dry. Place in a disposable aluminum pan. Ladle vegetable mixture evenly over the fillets and top with lime slices. Cover and refrigerate while smoker is heating.

3. Prepare a fire in your smoker. *(For instructions, see pages 8–11.)*

4. Place foil or pan on the smoker rack, add wood to the coals and close the lid. Smoke at 200°F (100°C), spraying every 30 minutes with apple juice, for 1½ hours, or until fish flakes easily in the thickest part of a fillet when tested with a fork.

Soy & Green Onion Catfish Fillets

Because farm-raised catfish, which mature in freshwater ponds along the Mississippi Delta, feed from the top of the water, they have a fresher flavor and firmer texture than fish from the wild. Plus, they're usually available at grocery store seafood departments.

SERVES 6 TO 8

Recommended wood: a combination of grape (or other fruit wood) and alder

TIPS

Farm-raised catfish is a great fish on which the beginning barbecuer can practice, as it's relatively inexpensive and is available all year long (fresh or frozen, then thawed).

* * *

Make sure to look for dark sesame oil. The lighter version will not be toasted and will not have the same flavor.

* * *

If you prefer, you can marinate the fish in a shallow dish instead of a bag.

Marinade

½ cup	sake	125 mL
¼ cup	granulated sugar	50 mL
¼ cup	soy sauce	50 mL
¼ cup	vegetable oil	50 mL
3 tbsp	toasted sesame oil (see tip, at left)	45 mL
3 tbsp	minced garlic	45 mL
2 tbsp	minced green onions	25 mL
½ tsp	hot pepper flakes	2 mL
6 to 8	catfish fillets (each about 6 oz/175g)	6 to 8

1. *Prepare the marinade:* In a small bowl, combine sake, sugar, soy sauce, vegetable oil, sesame oil, garlic, green onions and hot pepper flakes.

2. Rinse fish under cold running water and pat dry. Place in a large sealable plastic bag and pour in marinade. Seal bag, toss lightly to coat and refrigerate overnight.

3. Prepare a fire in your smoker. *(For instructions, see pages 8–11.)*

4. Remove fish from marinade and discard marinade. Place fish directly on the smoker rack, add wood to the coals and close the lid. Smoke at 200°F (100°C) for 1½ hours, or until fish flakes easily in the thickest part of a fillet when tested with a fork.

Haddock Fillets in White Wine, Ginger & Horseradish

When you smoke haddock this way, you get moist and tender fillets with a smoky flavor in a tangy, aromatic sauce.

SERVES 12	Recommended wood: grape or other fruit wood

TIPS

If you prefer, you can marinate the fish in a shallow dish instead of a bag.

● ● ●

Use any leftovers to make a smoked fish salad, dressed with mayonnaise, or a kedgeree for brunch.

Marinade

1 cup	dry white wine	250 mL
¼ cup	minced onion	50 mL
¼ cup	vegetable oil	50 mL
¼ cup	soy sauce	50 mL
1 tbsp	minced gingerroot	15 mL
1½ tsp	prepared horseradish	7 mL
1 tsp	minced garlic	5 mL
12	haddock fillets (each about 5 oz/150 g)	12

1. *Prepare the marinade:* In a small bowl, combine wine, onion, oil, soy sauce, ginger, horseradish and garlic.

2. Rinse fish under cold running water and pat dry. Place in a large sealable plastic bag and pour in marinade. Seal bag, toss lightly to coat and refrigerate for 3 hours.

3. Prepare a fire in your smoker. *(For instructions, see pages 8–11.)*

4. Transfer fish to disposable aluminum pans and pour marinade over fish. Place pans on the smoker rack, add wood to the coals and close the lid. Smoke at 200°F (100°C) for 1½ hours, or until fish flakes easily in the thickest part of a fillet when tested with a fork.

Alder-Smoked Halibut Steaks in Orange, Soy & Lime Marinade

The trick in this recipe is not to let the halibut marinate for long, as the acidic content in the marinade could "cook" the fish into ceviche. Delicious, but not what you want here.

SERVES 4	Recommended wood: alder

TIPS
You'll need 1 to 2 limes to make 2 tbsp (25 mL) juice.

• • •

The smaller the smoking chamber on your equipment, the sooner your food will be done. If you're using a kettle grill or a bullet smoker, your halibut might be done in 45 minutes. If you're using a bigger rig or a genuine smoker, it might take an hour.

Orange, Soy & Lime Marinade

1	clove garlic, minced	1
½ cup	freshly squeezed orange juice	125 mL
½ cup	soy sauce	125 mL
2 tbsp	olive oil	25 mL
2 tbsp	minced fresh parsley	25 mL
2 tbsp	freshly squeezed lime juice	25 mL
1 tsp	minced fresh basil	5 mL
1 tsp	minced fresh mint	5 mL
¼ tsp	freshly ground black pepper	1 mL
4	halibut steaks (each about 6 oz/175 g)	4

1. *Prepare the marinade:* In a small bowl, combine garlic, orange juice, soy sauce, oil, parsley, lime juice, basil, mint and pepper.

2. Rinse fish under cold running water and pat dry. Place in a shallow disposable aluminum pan and pour in marinade. Cover and refrigerate for 30 minutes.

3. Meanwhile, prepare a fire in your smoker. *(For instructions, see pages 8–11.)*

4. Add wood to the coals and wait until smoke is fragrant, 5 to 10 minutes. Place pan on the smoker rack and close the lid. Smoke at 225°F to 250°F (110°C to 120°C) for 1 hour, or until fish flakes easily in the thickest part of a steak when tested with a fork.

Alder-Smoked Red Snapper with Citrus Spray

For a tasty treat, serve this dish with a colorful slaw.

SERVES 4	Recommended wood: alder	

TIP

A citrus spray is simply orange, tangerine or another citrus juice poured into a spray bottle. Use it to mist fish and shellfish on your smoker for a moist and delicious result.

4	red snapper fillets (each about 6 oz/175 g)	4
⅓ cup	Fresh Garlic & Herb Paste (see recipe, page 35)	75 mL
	Orange juice for spraying	

1. Rinse fish under cold running water and pat dry. Place in a disposable aluminum pan and brush top with Fresh Garlic and Herb Paste. Cover and refrigerate while smoker is heating.

2. Prepare a fire in your smoker. *(For instructions, see pages 8–11.)*

3. Add wood to the coals and wait until smoke is fragrant, 5 to 10 minutes. Place pan on the smoker rack and close the lid. Smoke at 225°F to 250°F (110°C to 120°C), spraying every 15 minutes with orange juice, for 1 hour, or until fish flakes easily in the thickest part of a fillet when tested with a fork.

Salmon with White Wine & Pesto

Here's a simply wonderful way to make hot-smoked salmon.

SERVES 6 TO 8

Recommended wood: alder

2 lbs	salmon fillets	1 kg
½ cup	dry white wine, divided	125 mL
	Kosher salt and freshly ground black pepper	
1½ cups	prepared pesto	375 mL

TIPS

Make sure all bones are removed from the fish by running your fingers over the flesh. Use needle-nose or special fish pliers to pull out any bones that remain.

• • •

Sometimes a large fish fillet, like salmon, just won't fit in a disposable aluminum pan. That's when it's a good idea to make your own foil container. Just use a double thickness of heavy-duty aluminum foil and crimp the edges so that the liquid stays in the foil "pan."

• • •

The leftovers are delicious in a Pesto Salmon Salad — just flake the salmon and add a little bit of olive oil or mayonnaise to bind the mixture together.

1. Rinse salmon under cold running water and pat dry. Remove as many bones as possible. Place skin side down on a double thickness of aluminum foil, folding up the edges to make a 2-inch (5 cm) rim. Pour half of the wine over the salmon and sprinkle with salt and pepper to taste. Cover and refrigerate while smoker is heating.

2. Prepare a fire in your smoker. *(For instructions, see pages 8–11.)*

3. Add wood to the coals and wait until smoke is fragrant, 5 to 10 minutes. Spread a thick layer of pesto on top of the fish. Place foil on the smoker rack and close the lid. Smoke at 225°F to 250°F (110°C to 120°C) for 1 hour, or until fish flakes easily in the thickest part of a fillet when tested with a fork.

4. To serve, pour the remaining wine over the salmon.

Salmon with Sweet Orange Baste

The combination of salmon and fresh orange is absolutely delicious. In this recipe, the salmon is flavored with orange twice: in the marinade and in a baste.

SERVES 6	Recommended wood: hickory	

TIPS

Make sure all bones are removed from the fish by running your fingers over the flesh. Use needle-nose or special fish pliers to pull out any bones that remain.

• • •

If you prefer, you can marinate the fish in a shallow dish instead of a bag.

6	salmon fillets (each about 8 oz/250 g)	6
1 cup	Fresh Orange & White Balsamic Marinade (see recipe, page 39)	250 mL
1¼ cups	Sweet Orange Baste (see recipe, page 46)	300 mL

1. Rinse salmon under cold running water and pat dry. Remove as many bones as possible. Place in a large sealable plastic bag and pour in marinade. Seal bag, toss lightly to coat and refrigerate for 2 hours.

2. Prepare a fire in your smoker. *(For instructions, see pages 8–11.)*

3. Remove salmon from marinade, but do not pat dry. Discard marinade. Place salmon skin side down on a double thickness of heavy-duty aluminum foil, folding up the edges to make a 2-inch (5 cm) rim.

4. Add wood to the coals and wait until smoke is fragrant, 5 to 10 minutes. Place foil on the smoker rack and close the lid. Smoke at 225°F to 250°F (110°C to 120°C) for 15 minutes. Pour baste over salmon, close the lid and smoke for 45 minutes, or until fish flakes easily in the thickest part of a fillet when tested with a fork.

Hickory-Smoked Salmon with Buttery Brown Sugar & Lime Baste

The flavor builds in this recipe, from the savory marinade to the fragrant hickory smoke to the buttery basting sauce. Yum!

SERVES 6	Recommended wood: hickory

TIPS

Make sure all bones are removed from the fish by running your fingers over the flesh. Use needle-nose or special fish pliers to pull out any bones that remain.

• • •

If you prefer, you can marinate the fish in a shallow dish instead of a bag.

6	salmon fillets (each about 8 oz/250 mL)	6
1/3 cup	Soy-Sherry Marinade (see recipe, page 37)	75 mL
1/2 cup	Buttery Brown Sugar & Lime Basting Sauce (see recipe, page 48)	125 mL

1. Rinse salmon under cold running water and pat dry. Remove as many bones as possible. Place in a large sealable plastic bag and pour in marinade. Seal bag, toss lightly to coat and refrigerate for 2 hours.

2. Prepare a fire in your smoker. *(For instructions, see pages 8–11.)*

3. Remove salmon from marinade, but do not pat dry. Discard marinade. Place salmon, skin side down, on a double thickness of heavy-duty aluminum foil, folding up the edges to make a 2-inch (5 cm) rim.

4. Add wood to the coals and wait until smoke is fragrant, 5 to 10 minutes. Place foil on the smoker rack and close the lid. Smoke at 225°F to 250°F (110°C to 120°C) for 15 minutes. Pour basting sauce over salmon, close the lid and smoke for 45 minutes, or until fish flakes easily in the thickest part of a fillet when tested with a fork.

Apple-Smoked Salmon with Green Grape Sauce

The contrast of the coral-colored salmon with the green grapes is wonderful.

SERVES 4

Recommended wood: apple

TIPS

Make sure all bones are removed from the fish by running your fingers over the flesh. Use needle-nose or special fish pliers to pull out any bones that remain.

• • •

Achieving a low, low temperature, as in this recipe, can be difficult for the novice barbecuer. But here's a good way to do it. If you have a charcoal grill, prepare a hot fire, then brush the coals to one side and let them die down. When you can hold your hand 5 inches (13 cm) above the coals for 5 seconds, your coals are ready for very low and slow smoking. Simply place the wood on the coals, then your food on the grill grate across from the coals, cover and smoke.

1 tsp	dry mustard	5 mL
1 tsp	kosher salt	5 mL
1 tsp	crushed fresh thyme	5 mL
1 tsp	chopped fresh mint	5 mL
½ tsp	freshly ground black pepper	2 mL
½ tsp	minced garlic	2 mL
4	salmon fillets (each 6 to 8 oz/175 to 250 g)	4
2 tbsp	pure maple syrup	25 mL

Green Grape Sauce

1½ tsp	butter	7 mL
2 cups	seedless green grapes, halved	500 mL
½ tsp	minced garlic	2 mL
½ cup	dry red wine	125 mL
¼ cup	granulated sugar	50 mL
Pinch	kosher salt	Pinch
	Additional salt and freshly ground black pepper (optional)	

1. In a small bowl, combine mustard, salt, thyme, mint, pepper and garlic.

2. Rinse salmon under cold running water and pat dry. Remove as many bones as possible. Place skin side down on a double thickness of heavy-duty aluminum foil, folding up the edges to make a 2-inch (5 cm) rim. Rub both sides of salmon with maple syrup; sprinkle both sides with seasoning mixture. Cover and refrigerate while smoker is heating. Reserve any remaining seasoning mixture for the grape sauce.

3. Prepare a fire in your smoker. *(For instructions, see pages 8–11.)*

4. Add wood to the coals and wait until smoke is fragrant, 5 to 10 minutes. Place foil on the smoker rack and close the lid. Smoke at 175°F (85°C) for 1 hour, or until fish flakes easily in the thickest part of a fillet when tested with a fork.

5. *Prepare the sauce:* In a skillet, melt butter over medium-high heat. Sauté grapes and garlic until garlic is transparent, about 2 to 3 minutes. Add wine, sugar and salt. Bring to a boil and cook, stirring occasionally, until sauce is reduced by half. Season to taste with any remaining seasoning mixture or with salt and pepper.

6. Place fish on a serving platter and cover with sauce.

Salmon "Candy"

In Vancouver and other parts of British Columbia, you'll see strips of sugary-crusted smoked salmon jerky known as salmon "candy." This dish is delicious as a snack or casual appetizer, and it's a great way to use up scraps of salmon when you trim a fillet. The sweetness of the syrup helps temper the smoky flavor from the long cooking process.

SERVES 4 AS AN APPETIZER

TIP
Make sure all bones are removed from the fish by running your fingers over the flesh. Use needle-nose or special fish pliers to pull out any bones that remain.

Recommended wood: alder, cherry or maple

4	salmon fillets (each about 4 oz/125 g), skinned (or 1 lb/500 g skinless salmon scraps)	4
1¼ cups	pure maple syrup, divided	300 mL
¼ cup	kosher salt	50 mL

1. Rinse salmon under cold running water and pat dry. Remove as many bones as possible. Place skin side down in a deep glass or other non-metallic dish large enough to hold the fillets.

2. In a small bowl, combine ¼ cup (50 mL) of the maple syrup, salt and ¼ cup (50 mL) water into a slushy mixture. Pour over salmon, covering fish completely. (If necessary, add more water.) Cover and refrigerate for 12 hours.

3. Prepare a fire in your smoker. *(For instructions, see pages 8–11.)*

4. Remove fish from brine, but do not pat dry. Discard brine. Pour the remaining 1 cup (250 mL) maple syrup into a wide bowl. Cut fish into 2-inch (5 cm) wide slices and dip quickly into syrup. Discard any excess syrup.

5. Place fish pieces directly on the smoker rack, add wood to the coals and close the lid. Smoke at 225°F to 250°F (110°C to 120°C) for 2 hours, or until fish is very firm to the touch and burnished in appearance.

Mediterranean-Style Tilapia

Tilapia is a delicious farmed freshwater fish that does not take long to smoke. Here, I've given it a Mediterranean treatment that tastes great and is good for you too.

SERVES 4	Recommended wood: a combination of alder and cherry	

TIP

When tilapia is not available, substitute farm-raised freshwater catfish.

4	tilapia fillets (each about 6 oz/175 g)	4
4	cloves garlic, crushed	4
3 tbsp	olive oil	45 mL
1	onion, chopped	1
1	small tomato, chopped	1
1	small green bell pepper, chopped	1

1. Rinse fish under cold running water and pat dry. Rub with crushed garlic, then place on a double thickness of heavy-duty aluminum foil, folding up the edges to make a 2-inch (5 cm) rim. Place foil on a baking sheet. Spoon olive oil over fish, coating evenly. Sprinkle with onion, tomato and green pepper. Cover and refrigerate for at least 1 hour or overnight.

2. Prepare a fire in your smoker. *(For instructions, see pages 8–11.)*

3. Add wood to the coals and wait until smoke is fragrant, 5 to 10 minutes. Place foil on the smoker rack and close the lid. Smoke at 225°F to 250°F (110°C to 120°C) for 30 minutes, or until fish flakes easily in the thickest part of a fillet when tested with a fork.

Margarita-Style Sea Bass

Arriba! *Make a batch of margaritas to sip while you tend the smoker, then celebrate your own fiesta of flavors with this dish.*

SERVES 4	Recommended wood: grape or other fruit wood	

Lime and Lager Marinade (see recipe, page 38) would also be good with sea bass.

TIPS

You'll need 3 to 4 medium limes to make ¼ cup (50 mL) juice.

• • •

If you prefer, you can marinate the fish in a shallow dish instead of a bag.

• • •

Marinade

3	cloves garlic	3
¼ cup	freshly squeezed lime juice	50 mL
¼ cup	tequila	50 mL
¼ cup	orange-flavored liqueur	50 mL
¼ cup	olive oil	50 mL
1 tsp	kosher salt	5 mL
4	sea bass fillets (each about 6 oz/175 g)	4
1 tbsp	olive oil	15 mL
	Freshly ground black pepper	

Salsa

3	tomatoes, diced	3
1	onion, chopped	1
1	small serrano chili peppers, seeded and minced	1
¼ cup	chopped fresh parsley	50 mL
¼ cup	minced fresh cilantro	50 mL
2 tbsp	pure maple syrup	25 mL
	Kosher salt	

1. *Prepare the marinade:* In a large bowl, combine garlic, lime juice, tequila, orange-flavored liqueur, olive oil and salt.

2. Rinse fish under cold running water and pat dry. Place in a large sealable plastic bag and pour in marinade. Seal bag, toss lightly to coat and refrigerate for 30 minutes.

3. Meanwhile, prepare a fire in your smoker. *(For instructions, see pages 8–11.)*

4. Remove fillets from marinade and pat dry. Transfer marinade to a saucepan. Brush fillets with oil and sprinkle with pepper.

5. Add wood to the coals and wait until smoke is fragrant, 5 to 10 minutes. Place fillets directly on the smoker rack and close the lid. Smoke at 225°F (110°C) for 45 minutes, or until fish flakes easily in the thickest part of a fillet when tested with a fork.

6. Meanwhile, bring marinade to a boil over medium-high heat and boil for 3 minutes. Remove from heat and strain out garlic cloves.

7. *Prepare the salsa:* In a medium bowl, toss together tomatoes, onion, serrano peppers, parsley, cilantro and maple syrup. Season to taste with salt.

8. To serve, spoon salsa over fish and drizzle with marinade.

Sea Bass Skewers Lemonada

This Italian fusion barbecue dish makes a colorful presentation.

SERVES 4 TO 6	Recommended wood: alder

TIP
Doctor up prepared salsa by adding smoky flavor. Start with 1 tsp (5 mL) of bottled chipotle sauce, liquid smoke or smoked paprika. Stir, then taste and go from there.

• Eight 12-inch (30 cm) bamboo skewers

Marinade

1	clove garlic, minced	1
¾ cup	olive oil	175 mL
2 tbsp	freshly squeezed lemon juice	25 mL
2 tbsp	minced fresh parsley	25 mL
1 tbsp	minced fresh thyme	15 mL
	Freshly ground black pepper	
4 to 6	sea bass fillets (each 6 oz/175 g), skin removed and cut into 1½-inch (4 cm) cubes	4 to 6
1	lemon, cut into 8 wedges, then halved to make 16 pieces	1
1	red bell pepper, cut into 1½-inch (4 cm) squares	1
1	recipe Onion & Charred Pepper Salsa (page 119)	1

1. Soak skewers in water for a least 1 hour or for up to 2 hours.

2. *Prepare the marinade:* In a small bowl, combine garlic, olive oil, lemon juice, parsley, thyme and pepper to taste.

TIP

The smaller the smoking chamber on your equipment, the sooner your food will be done. If you're using a kettle grill or a bullet smoker, your sea bass skewers might be done in 30 minutes. If you're using a bigger rig or a genuine smoker, they might take 45 minutes.

3. Rinse fish under cold running water and pat dry. Place in a large sealable plastic bag and pour in marinade. Seal bag, toss lightly to coat and refrigerate for 30 minutes.

4. Meanwhile, prepare a fire in your smoker. *(For instructions, see pages 8–11.)*

5. Remove fish from marinade, but do not pat dry. Discard marinade. Thread fish onto skewers alternately with lemon and red pepper pieces.

6. Add wood to the coals and wait until smoke is fragrant, 5 to 10 minutes. Place skewers on the smoker rack and close the lid. Smoke at 225°F to 250°F (110°C to 120°C) for 30 to 45 minutes, or until fish is barely opaque.

7. To serve, spoon salsa onto a serving platter and arrange skewers on top.

Shark Steaks in Orange & Soy Marinade

Simply delicious. In this recipe, the marinade is also used as a basting mixture.

SERVES 6

Recommended wood: a combination of grape and a little apple

TIP

Shark is a very firm fish with a moderate flavor. When it's not available, you can substitute fish with similar characteristics, such as cobia, drum, salmon, skate, swordfish or yellowfin tuna.

| 6 | shark steaks (each about 6 oz/175 g) | 6 |
| 2 cups | Orange & Soy Marinade (see recipe, page 39) | 500 mL |

1. Rinse fish under cold running water and pat dry. Place in a large sealable plastic bag and pour in half of the marinade. Seal bag, toss to coat and refrigerate for 2 hours. Reserve the remaining marinade in the refrigerator.

2. Prepare a fire in your smoker. *(For instructions, see pages 8–11.)*

3. Remove fish from marinade, but do not pat dry. Discard marinade. Place fish directly on the smoker rack, add wood to the coals and close the lid. Smoke at 225°F to 250°F (110°C to 120°C), basting with the remaining marinade every 30 minutes, for 1½ hours, or until fish is opaque and flakes easily in the thickest part of a steak when tested with a fork.

Alder-Smoked Shark Steaks

Shark is a firm-textured fish with a moderate flavor that does very well on the smoker. I like to use a marinade with shark, then serve it with a fresh salsa to finish.

SERVES 4 TO 6	Recommended wood: alder

Variation

Instead of shark, try black drum, cobia or swordfish.

Marinade

1	clove garlic, minced	1
2 tbsp	minced green onions	25 mL
2 tbsp	chopped fresh parsley	25 mL
2 tbsp	soy sauce	25 mL
2 tbsp	rice vinegar	25 mL
2 tbsp	freshly squeezed lime juice	25 mL
2 tbsp	olive oil	25 mL
2 tsp	chopped fresh mint	10 mL
½ tsp	freshly ground black pepper	2 mL
4 to 6	shark steaks (each about 6 oz/175 g)	4 to 6

1. *Prepare the marinade:* In a small bowl, combine garlic, green onions, parsley, soy sauce, vinegar, lime juice, oil, mint and pepper.

2. Rinse fish under cold running water and pat dry. Place in a large sealable plastic bag and pour in marinade. Seal bag, toss to coat and refrigerate for 30 minutes, turning at least once.

3. Meanwhile, prepare a fire in your smoker. *(For instructions, see pages 8–11.)*

4. Remove fish from marinade, but do not pat dry. Discard marinade. Place fish directly on the smoker rack, add wood to the coals and close the lid. Smoke at 225°F to 250°F (110°C to 120°C) for 1½ hours, or until fish is opaque and flakes easily in the thickest part of a steak when tested with a fork.

Three P's Shark Skewers

"Three P's" means bell pepper, pineapple and pear in these colorful and flavorful skewers. Peeling is optional for the fruit.

SERVES 4	Recommended wood: grape or other fruit wood

TIP

Unpeeled fruit on skewers provides an interesting and rustic appearance.

● ● ●

Variation

If you can't find shark, use another firm-textured fish steak such as monkfish, salmon or swordfish.

● Eight 12-inch (30 cm) bamboo skewers

4	shark steaks (each about 6 oz/175 g), cut into 1-inch (2.5 cm) cubes	4
2	pears, cored and cut into 1-inch (2.5 cm) slices	2
1	yellow or green bell pepper, cut into chunks	1
1	small pineapple, cored and cut into 1½-inch (4 cm) slices and then into triangles	1
3 tbsp	butter, melted	45 mL
2 tbsp	chopped fresh mint	25 mL
1 tbsp	grated lemon zest	15 mL
2 tbsp	freshly squeezed lemon juice	25 mL

1. Soak skewers in water for 30 minutes.

2. Rinse fish under cold running water and pat dry. Thread shark, pears, pepper and pineapple onto skewers. Place on a baking sheet.

3. In a small bowl, combine butter, mint, lemon zest and lemon juice. Brush skewers with half of the butter mixture. Cover and refrigerate while smoker is heating. Reserve the remaining butter mixture and keep warm by the smoker.

4. Prepare a fire in your smoker. *(For instructions, see pages 8–11.)*

5. Add wood to the coals and wait until smoke is fragrant, 5 to 10 minutes. Place skewers on the smoker rack and close the lid. Smoke at 225°F to 250°F (110°C to 120°C), basting occasionally with the remaining butter mixture, for 30 minutes, or until fish is opaque and flakes easily when tested with a fork.

Butter-Basted Whole Trout

When you serve their catch this way, the anglers in your family will feel that their time spent in chilly streams has been amply rewarded. You can, of course, also use fresh trout "caught" at the grocery store.

SERVES 4	Recommended wood: oak or pecan

TIP
One lemon will yield 2 to 3 tsp (10 to 15 mL) zest and 3 tbsp (45 mL) juice.

½ cup	melted butter	125 mL
1 tsp	grated lemon zest	5 mL
¼ cup	freshly squeezed lemon juice	50 mL
	Freshly ground white pepper	
2	whole rainbow trout (each about 12 oz/375 g), scaled and cut open	2

1. In a small bowl, combine butter, lemon zest, lemon juice and white pepper.

2. Rinse trout under cold running water and pat dry. Place cut side up in a disposable aluminum pan. Brush the cavity of each trout with butter mixture. Cover and refrigerate while smoker is heating.

3. Prepare a fire in your smoker. *(For instructions, see pages 8–11.)*

4. Place pan on the smoker rack, add wood to the coals and close the lid. Smoke at 225°F to 250°F (110°C to 120°C), basting with butter mixture every 30 minutes, for 1 to 1½ hours, or until fish flakes easily in the thickest part when tested with a fork.

5. Serve drizzled with any remaining butter mixture.

Crab-Stuffed Whole Trout

When I say this recipe is a winner, I mean it! This dish won the Grand Championship at the Kansas State Barbecue Contest a few years ago. It looks great and tastes even better!

SERVES 6 TO 8

Recommended wood: cherry

TIPS

If you can't find fresh crab meat, you can use thawed frozen crab meat. Just make sure to use real crab and not imitation.

• • •

If you prefer, you could use the stuffing from Stuffed Eggplant with Bacon, Garlic & Cream (see recipe, page 117) instead of this stuffing.

½ tsp	kosher salt	2 mL
½ tsp	freshly ground white pepper	2 mL
¼ tsp	hot pepper flakes	1 mL
¼ tsp	dried basil	1 mL
Pinch	dried thyme	Pinch
½ cup	butter	125 mL
2	cloves garlic, minced	2
½ cup	diced onion	125 mL
¼ cup	diced celery	50 mL
¼ cup	diced green bell pepper	50 mL
1 lb	fresh crab meat (see tip, at left), picked over	500 g
1	egg, beaten	1
1 cup	fine dry bread crumbs	250 mL
3 tbsp	freshly grated Parmesan cheese	45 mL
6	trout (each about 12 oz/375 g), scaled, boned and split open	6

1. Combine salt, white pepper, hot pepper flakes, basil and thyme and mix well.

2. In a nonstick skillet, melt butter over medium-high heat. Sauté garlic, onion, celery, green pepper and seasoning mixture for 2 minutes, until translucent. Add crab and sauté for 5 minutes to let flavors blend. Stir in egg, bread crumbs and cheese. Remove from heat and let cool slightly.

TIP

The smaller the smoking chamber on your equipment, the sooner your food will be done. If you're using a kettle grill or a bullet smoker, your trout might be done in 1½ hours. If you're using a bigger rig or a genuine smoker, they might take 2 hours.

3. Rinse trout under cold running water and pat dry. Place cut side up on a disposable aluminum baking sheet. Fill the cavity of each fish with crab stuffing. Cover and refrigerate while smoker is heating.

4. Prepare a fire in your smoker. *(For instructions, see pages 8–11.)*

5. Place pan on the smoker rack, add wood to the coals and close the lid. Smoke at 225°F to 250°F (110°C to 120°C) for 1½ hours, or until fish flakes easily in the thickest part when tested with a fork.

Trout in Lavender Butter

Think of lavender as an herb with an aromatic flavor like thyme, and this recipe won't seem so unusual.

SERVES 4	Recommended wood: alder

TIP

You can buy organic dried lavender buds at health food stores or through mail-order spice emporiums (see the Source Guide, page 356). If you garden, or have a friend who does, you can harvest, dry and keep your own lavender buds in a clean, dry jar.

Marinade

4	green onions, chopped	4
1/4 cup	freshly squeezed lemon juice	50 mL
2 tbsp	melted butter	25 mL
2 tbsp	olive oil	25 mL
2 tbsp	chopped fresh parsley	25 mL
2 tbsp	dried lavender buds (preferably organic, see tip, at left)	25 mL
1 tbsp	hot pepper sauce	15 mL
1/2 tsp	ground ginger	2 mL
1/2 tsp	kosher salt	2 mL
4	trout (each about 1 lb/500 g), scaled and cut open	4

1. *Prepare the marinade:* In a small bowl, combine green onions, lemon juice, butter, oil, parsley, lavender, hot pepper sauce, ginger and salt; mix well. Place half of the marinade in a large, shallow dish. Reserve the remaining marinade in the refrigerator.

2. Rinse trout under cold running water and pat dry. Pierce the skin of the fish in several places with the tines of a fork. Roll fish in the marinade in the dish, coating inside and out. Cover and refrigerate for 1 hour, turning occasionally.

3. Prepare a fire in your smoker. *(For instructions, see pages 8–11.)*

4. Remove fish from marinade, but do not pat dry. Discard marinade. Place fish directly on the smoker rack, add wood to the coals and close the lid. Smoke at 200°F (100°C), brushing with reserved marinade every 30 minutes, for 1 to 1 1/2 hours, or until fish flakes easily in the thickest part when tested with a fork.

Whitefish in Cumin-Cilantro Marinade

Here's another great way to vary the flavor of smoked freshwater fish.

SERVES 4 TO 6	Recommended wood: alder or maple

TIP

If a fish fillet is very thin, place it in a disposable aluminum pan, then on the smoker rack, so it won't fall through the grates.

• • •

Variation

Instead of whitefish, try trout, salmon, monkfish, haddock or walleye pike.

Marinade

1	clove garlic, minced	1
2 tbsp	olive oil	25 mL
1 tbsp	minced fresh cilantro	15 mL
1 tsp	grated lime zest	5 mL
1 tbsp	freshly squeezed lime juice	15 mL
1 tsp	ground cumin	5 mL
4 to 6	whitefish fillets (each about 6 oz/175 g)	4 to 6

1. *Prepare the marinade:* In a small bowl, combine garlic, oil, cilantro, lime zest, lime juice and cumin.

2. Rinse fish under cold running water and pat dry. Place in a large sealable plastic bag and pour in marinade. Seal bag, toss to coat and refrigerate for at least 2 hours or overnight.

3. Prepare a fire in your smoker. *(For instructions, see pages 8–11.)*

4. Add wood to the coals and wait until smoke is fragrant, 5 to 10 minutes. Remove fish from marinade, but do not pat dry. Discard marinade. Place fish, skin side down, directly on the smoker rack and close the lid. Smoke at 200°F (100°C) for 1 hour, or until fish flakes easily in the thickest part of a fillet when tested with a fork.

Maple-Smoked Whitefish

All around the Great Lakes region, you'll find lake fish — whole chubs, lake trout and whitefish fillets — locally smoked with maple wood. The smokehouse technique is to liberally salt the fish down to draw out moisture, then lay them on racks in the smokehouse to cold-smoke (because the fish are far away from the heat of the fire) for hours. At home, it's easier to hot-smoke these beauties. If you brine them first, you'll get even better flavor.

SERVES 8	Recommended wood: maple

TIP

Turn leftover smoked fish into delectable pâtés, cocktail spreads or dips by flaking it into a bowl and combining it with softened cream cheese and the flavorings of your choice.

• • •

Variation

Try this recipe with trout, haddock or monkfish.

8	whitefish fillets (each about 8 oz/250 g)	8
4 cups	Maple Mustard Brine (see recipe, page 21)	1 L

1. Rinse fish under cold running water and pat dry. Place in a large sealable plastic bag and pour in brine. Seal bag, toss to coat and refrigerate for at least 1 hour or for up to 2 hours.

2. Prepare a fire in your smoker. *(For instructions, see pages 8–11.)*

3. Add wood to the coals and wait until smoke is fragrant, 5 to 10 minutes. Remove fish from brine and pat dry. Discard brine. Place fish, skin side down, directly on the smoker rack and close the lid. Smoke at 225°F to 250°F (110°C to 120°C) for 1 hour, or until fish flakes easily in the thickest part of a fillet when tested with a fork.

Lobster in Savory Sauce

A succulent smoked lobster dipped into a buttery sauce flavored with garlic, herbs and a touch of seafood seasoning is my idea of heaven.

SERVES 4	Recommended wood: grape or other fruit wood	

TIPS

Either have your fishmonger kill the lobsters right before you want to smoke them (hurry home!), or do it yourself by sticking a paring knife between their eyes.

• • •

It's much more economical to make your own seasoning mixes. Use the freshest dried seasonings you can find (the color and aroma of the dried ingredients will be more vivid) and make up small batches of your own special blends.

- Four 12-inch (30 cm) bamboo or metal skewers

4	lobsters (each about 1 lb/500 g)	4
2	lemons, seeds removed and sliced	2
2	cloves garlic, minced	2
1 cup	butter	250 mL
¼ cup	Worcestershire sauce	50 mL
¼ cup	soy sauce	50 mL
2 tbsp	ketchup	25 mL
1 tbsp	cracked black pepper	15 mL
½ tbsp	chopped fresh parsley	7 mL
1 tsp	minced fresh basil	5 mL
1 tsp	minced fresh dill	5 mL
½ tsp	seafood seasoning mix	2 mL

1. Soak bamboo skewers in water for 30 minutes.

2. Thread a skewer through the center of each lobster to keep tails from curling while cooking. Cover and refrigerate while smoker is heating.

3. Prepare a fire in your smoker. *(For instructions, see pages 8–11.)*

4. Place lobster skewers on the smoker rack, add wood to the coals and close the lid. Smoke at 225°F to 250°F (110°C to 120°C) for 45 minutes, or until lobsters have turned a bright red.

5. Meanwhile, in a medium saucepan, combine lemon slices, garlic, butter, Worcestershire sauce, soy sauce, ketchup, pepper, parsley, basil, dill and seafood seasoning mix. Bring to a boil over high heat; reduce heat and simmer for 15 minutes to let flavors blend. Pour into a small bowl and keep warm.

6. To serve, cut lobsters into pieces with a chef's knife or cleaver and serve with dipping sauce.

Lobster Tail Kabobs in White Balsamic Vinaigrette

Serve these colorful and delicious kabobs as a sophisticated appetizer or a tantalizing main course.

TIP
One lemon will yield about 3 tbsp (45 mL) juice.

Recommended wood: peach

- Eight 12-inch (30 cm) bamboo skewers

4	ears fresh sweet corn, shucked and halved crosswise	4
1	large red bell pepper, stemmed, seeded and quartered lengthwise	1
4	rock lobster tails (each about 8 oz/250 g), halved lengthwise	4
1	red onion, quartered	1
3 tbsp	freshly squeezed lemon juice	45 mL
2 tbsp	white balsamic vinegar	25 mL
2 tbsp	extra-virgin olive oil	25 mL
	Kosher salt and freshly ground black pepper	

1. Soak skewers in water for 30 minutes.

2. Thread each skewer with half a corn cob, a red pepper quarter, half a lobster tail and a red onion quarter. Place on a baking sheet and drizzle with lemon juice, vinegar and oil. Season to taste with salt and pepper. Cover and refrigerate while smoker is heating.

3. Prepare a fire in your smoker. *(For instructions, see pages 8–11.)*

4. Add wood to the coals and wait until smoke is fragrant, 5 to 10 minutes. Place skewers on the smoker rack and close the lid. Smoke at 225°F to 250°F (110°C to 120°C) for 1 hour, or until lobster and corn are tender.

Flower of the Flames Oysters

Depending on how much you like oysters, this can serve 6 people or just 1! Of course, the recipe can be doubled or tripled if you want to serve a wonderful appetizer at a party.

SERVES 2	Recommended wood: alder

TIP

One lemon will yield about 3 tbsp (45 mL) juice, so you'll likely need 2 lemons for this recipe.

1 tsp	olive oil	5 mL
12 oz	fresh spinach (1 bunch), stemmed and coarsely chopped	375 g
1	clove garlic, minced	1
¼ cup	freshly squeezed lemon juice	50 mL
1 tsp	kosher salt	5 mL
½ tsp	hot pepper sauce	2 mL
6	select oysters on the half shell	6

1. In a small skillet, heat oil over medium-high heat. Sauté spinach, garlic, lemon juice, salt and hot pepper sauce until spinach begins to wilt, about 2 minutes. Remove from heat and let cool.

2. Meanwhile, prepare a fire in your smoker. *(For instructions, see pages 8–11.)*

3. Add wood to the coals and wait until smoke is fragrant, 5 to 10 minutes. Top each oyster with spinach mixture. Place oysters in their half shells on the smoker rack and close the lid. Smoke at 225°F to 250°F (110°C to 120°C) for 15 to 20 minutes, or until oysters are somewhat firm.

Barbecued Oysters

Simply delicious! Again, this recipe can be doubled or tripled to serve at a gathering as an appetizer.

SERVES 2	Recommended wood: apple or other fruit wood

TIP

They used to say that you shouldn't buy oysters in months without an "r" in the name (so not in May, June, July or August). However, oysters are now farm-raised in cold waters and are perfectly good at any time of year.

6	select oysters on the half shell	6
½ cup	hot and spicy prepared barbecue sauce	125 mL
3 tbsp	shredded sharp Cheddar cheese	45 mL

1. Prepare a fire in your smoker. *(For instructions, see pages 8–11.)*

2. Add wood to the coals and wait until smoke is fragrant, 5 to 10 minutes. Top each oyster with barbecue sauce and sprinkle with cheese. Place oysters in their half shells on the smoker rack and close the lid. Smoke at 225°F to 250°F (110°C to 120°C) for 15 to 20 minutes, or until oysters are somewhat firm.

Salmon with White Wine & Pesto (page 153)

Apricot Chicken Quarters (page 199)
with Red Onion & Tomato Salsa (page 102)

Buffalo-Style Hot Wings (page 207)

Various Brines, Rubs, Marinades,
Bastes and Sauces (pages 21–71)

Stuffed Cornish Game Hens with
Apricot Mustard Sauce (page 220)

Pork Shoulder Blade with Peachy
Barbecue Sauce (page 228)

Cold-Smoked Vegetables (page 98)

Pork Loin Roast with
Hot Pepper Jelly Glaze (page 245)

World Championship Ribs (page 251)

Red Snapper & Vegetables (page 183)

Flank Steak Skewers
in Lime Cola Marinade (page 283)

The Ultimate Slow-Smoked Burger (page 300)

Grand Champion Rack of Lamb (page 314)

Scallops in Sesame Marinade

The larger the scallop, the more luscious the dish.

Recommended wood: oak, pecan or hickory

1 lb	large scallops	500 g
2 cups	Sesame Marinade (see recipe, page 43)	500 mL

1. Rinse scallops under cold running water and pat dry. Place in a large sealable plastic bag and pour in half of the marinade. Seal bag, toss to coat and refrigerate for 30 minutes.

2. Meanwhile, prepare a fire in your smoker. *(For instructions, see pages 8–11.)*

3. Add wood to the coals and wait until smoke is fragrant, 5 to 10 minutes. Remove scallops from marinade, but do not pat dry. Discard marinade. Place scallops in a disposable aluminum pan. Place pan on the smoker rack and close the lid. Smoke at 225°F to 250°F (110°C to 120°C) for 45 to 60 minutes, or until scallops are opaque and somewhat firm to the touch.

4. Serve scallops, drizzled with the remaining marinade, in a bowl or on a platter.

TIP

The smaller the smoking chamber on your equipment, the sooner your food will be done. If you're using a kettle grill or a bullet smoker, your scallops might be done in 45 minutes. If you're using a bigger rig or a genuine smoker, they might take an hour.

• • •

Variation

This recipe also works well with shrimp.

Lemon-Herb Scallops

Sweet, tender scallops get a buttery, herby, smoky treatment in this recipe. Fruit wood enhances the essential sweetness of the shellfish.

TIP

By threading shrimp or scallops onto skewers, you allow the smoke to envelop the maximum surface area of the shellfish, without losing any through the grates. Leave a little space in between each piece.

Recommended wood: grape or other fruit wood

- Eight 12-inch (30 cm) bamboo skewers

Marinade

2½ tbsp	olive oil	32 mL
¼ cup	butter, melted	50 mL
3	cloves garlic, minced	3
½ cup	minced fresh basil	125 mL
⅓ cup	freshly squeezed lemon juice	75 mL
3 tbsp	minced fresh oregano	45 mL
3 tbsp	minced fresh mint	45 mL
3 tbsp	spicy prepared mustard	45 mL
	Kosher salt	
3 lbs	large scallops	1.5 kg

1. Soak skewers in water for 30 minutes.

2. *Prepare the marinade:* In a medium bowl, combine oil and butter. Stir in garlic, basil, lemon juice, oregano, mint and mustard. Season to taste with salt.

3. Rinse scallops under cold running water and pat dry. Place in a large sealable plastic bag and pour in marinade. Seal bag, toss to coat and refrigerate for 1 hour.

4. Prepare a fire in your smoker. *(For instructions, see pages 8–11.)*

5. Add wood to the coals and wait until smoke is fragrant, 5 to 10 minutes. Remove scallops from marinade, but do not pat dry. Discard marinade. Thread scallops onto skewers. Place skewers on the smoker rack and close the lid. Smoke at 225°F to 250°F (110°C to 120°C) for 45 to 60 minutes, or until scallops are opaque and somewhat firm to the touch.

Lime & Ginger Prawns

Aromatic from the lime zest and pungent from the ginger, this is a great way to change the taste of basic smoked shrimp.

SERVES 8 AS AN APPETIZER, 4 AS A MAIN COURSE

TIPS

You'll need 3 to 4 medium limes to make 1 tbsp (15 mL) zest and ¼ cup (50 mL) juice.

• • •

If you prefer, you can marinate the prawns in a shallow dish instead of a bag.

Recommended wood: sassafras, alder or other light wood

• Eight 12-inch (30 cm) bamboo skewers

Marinade

4	green chili peppers, seeded and chopped	4
4	cloves garlic, crushed	4
1	2-inch (5 cm) piece gingerroot, chopped	1
1	onion, coarsely chopped	1
1 tbsp	grated lime zest	15 mL
¼ cup	freshly squeezed lime juice	50 mL
2 tbsp	olive oil	25 mL
24	jumbo tiger prawns (shrimp), peeled and deveined	24

1. Soak skewers in water for 30 minutes.

2. *Prepare the marinade:* In a food processor, process chili peppers, garlic, ginger, onion, lime zest, lime juice and oil until smooth.

3. Rinse prawns under cold running water and pat dry. Place in a large sealable plastic bag and pour in marinade. Seal bag, toss to coat and refrigerate for 4 hours.

4. Prepare a fire in your smoker. *(For instructions, see pages 8–11.)*

5. Add wood to the coals and wait until smoke is fragrant, 5 to 10 minutes. Remove prawns from marinade, but do not pat dry. Discard marinade. Thread prawns onto skewers, piercing each first through the tail, then through the head end. Place skewers on the smoker rack and close the lid. Smoke at 225°F to 250°F (110°C to 120°C) for 1 hour, or until shrimp are pink and opaque.

Alder-Smoked Shrimp

Hot-smoked shrimp are delicious as an appetizer or as a main course, your choice.

SERVES 16 AS AN APPETIZER, 8 AS A MAIN COURSE

Recommended wood: alder

4 lbs	large shrimp, peeled and deveined	2 kg
½ cup	freshly squeezed lemon juice	125 mL
⅓ cup	roasted garlic (see tip, at left)	75 mL
¼ cup	olive oil	50 mL
1 tsp	kosher salt	5 mL
1 tsp	freshly ground black pepper	5 mL

TIPS

Roasted garlic is a delicious addition to marinades. To roast garlic, cut about ½ inch (1 cm) off the pointed end of a garlic bulb, place it in a small pan and drizzle with olive oil. Roast in a 350°F (180°C) oven for 30 to 45 minutes, or until cloves are fork-tender when you squeeze. When cool, squeeze garlic from individual cloves into a bowl. Use right away, or cover and store in the refrigerator for up to 2 weeks or in the freezer for up to 3 months.

• • •

To make a smoky cocktail sauce, add a few drops of liquid smoke to your favorite combination of chili sauce and prepared horseradish.

1. Rinse shrimp under cold running water and pat dry. Place in a shallow disposable aluminum pan.

2. In a small bowl, combine lemon juice, garlic, oil, salt and pepper. Pour over shrimp. Cover and refrigerate for 2 hours.

3. Prepare a fire in your smoker. *(For instructions, see pages 8–11.)*

4. Add wood to the coals and wait until smoke is fragrant, 5 to 10 minutes. Place pan on the smoker rack and close the lid. Smoke at 225°F to 250°F (110°C to 120°C) for 45 to 60 minutes, or until shrimp are pink and opaque.

5. Serve hot, at room temperature or chilled.

Shrimp in Lime & Lager Marinade

So easy, yet so good! This is another great appetizer for a casual gathering.

TIP

Only marinate the shrimp for about 30 minutes, as the acidic ingredients in the marinade could "cook" the shrimp to ceviche — not what you want here.

Recommended wood: oak, pecan or hickory

1 lb	large shrimp with their tails on, peeled and deveined	500 g
2½ cups	Lime & Lager Marinade (see recipe, page 38)	625 mL

1. Rinse shrimp under cold running water and pat dry. Place in a large sealable plastic bag and pour in half of the marinade. Seal bag, toss to coat and refrigerate for 30 minutes. Reserve the remaining marinade.

2. Meanwhile, prepare a fire in your smoker. *(For instructions, see pages 8–11.)*

3. Add wood to the coals and wait until smoke is fragrant, 5 to 10 minutes. Remove shrimp from marinade, but do not pat dry. Discard marinade. Place shrimp in a disposable aluminum pan. Place pan on the smoker rack and close the lid. Smoke at 225°F to 250°F (110°C to 120°C) for 45 to 60 minutes, or until shrimp are pink and opaque.

4. Serve shrimp, drizzled with the reserved marinade, in a bowl or on a platter.

Honey-Basted Shrimp

Tender smoked shrimp come out of the smoker bronzed and delicious, and even more so when you baste them with a simple honey, olive oil and Worcestershire mixture.

SERVES 4	Recommended wood: grape or other fruit wood

TIPS

If you prefer, you could thread these shrimp onto eight 12-inch (30 cm) bamboo skewers and smoke them that way.

• • •

Keep a disposable aluminum pan as close to the heat of your smoker as possible, and place your baste inside. That way, your baste stays warm and it's within easy reach. The aluminum pan ensures that, if you spill any baste, you won't have a mess.

Marinade

1 cup	Worcestershire sauce	250 mL
2 tbsp	dry white wine	25 mL
2 tbsp	bottled Italian vinaigrette	25 mL
½ tsp	garlic powder	2 mL
Pinch	freshly ground black pepper	Pinch
1 lb	large shrimp with their tails on, peeled and deveined	500 g

Honey Baste

¼ cup	amber liquid honey	50 mL
¼ cup	olive oil	50 mL
2 tbsp	Worcestershire sauce	25 mL

1. *Prepare the marinade:* In a small bowl, combine Worcestershire sauce, wine, vinaigrette, garlic powder and pepper.

2. Rinse shrimp under cold running water and pat dry. Place in a large sealable plastic bag and pour in marinade. Seal bag, toss to coat and refrigerate for 1 hour.

3. Prepare a fire in your smoker. *(For instructions, see pages 8–11.)*

4. *Meanwhile, prepare the baste:* In a small bowl, combine honey, oil and Worcestershire sauce.

5. Add wood to the coals and wait until smoke is fragrant, 5 to 10 minutes. Remove shrimp from marinade, but do not pat dry. Discard marinade. Place shrimp in a disposable aluminum pan. Place pan on the smoker rack and close the lid. Smoke at 225°F to 250°F (110°C to 120°C), basting every 15 minutes, for 1 hour, or until shrimp are pink and opaque.

Red Snapper & Vegetables

When you cold-smoke snapper and vegetables, the food stays its natural fresh color while still taking on the smoky flavor.

SERVES 6 TO 8	Recommended wood: alder	

TIP

If you don't want to get teary, try freezing onions for 20 minutes before slicing or chopping.

	Vegetable oil	
6 to 8	red snapper fillets (each about 6 oz/175 g)	6 to 8
3	Roma (plum) tomatoes, sliced	3
2	cloves garlic, minced	2
1	onion, thinly sliced	1
½	green bell pepper, thinly sliced	½
½ cup	dry white wine	125 mL
2 tbsp	minced fresh parsley	25 mL
2 tbsp	minced fresh basil	25 mL

1. Rinse snapper under cold running water and pat dry. Spray or brush a shallow disposable aluminum pan with vegetable oil and place fillets in the pan. Top each fillet with tomatoes, garlic, onion and pepper. Drizzle with wine and sprinkle with parsley and basil. Cover and refrigerate while smoker is heating.

2. Prepare a fire in your cold smoker, using 3 oz (90 g) of wood. Set temperature to 200°F (100°C) until wood starts to smoke. Reduce temperature to 170°F (75°C) and place a pan of ice on top of the cold plate.

3. Place pan on the smoker rack and close the lid or door. Smoke for 2 hours, or until fish is firm to the touch, slightly burnished and translucent all the way through.

Salmon in Bay Brine

A luscious way to get the translucent appearance, silken texture and smoky/briny flavor of the best smoked salmon.

SERVES 12	**Recommended wood:** alder or oak

TIP

Most barbecuers who specialize in cold-smoked fish have their own way of smoking salmon. Smoking salmon at 225°F to 250°F (110°C to 120°C) will be more convenient for the hobbyist or backyarder. However, if you want the truest, most translucent and slightly smoky salmon, slow-smoke it at temperatures as low as 60°F (16°C) for a longer period of time.

• • •

Make ahead

Place in an airtight container and store in the refrigerator for up to 1 week or in the freezer for up to 3 months.

Bay & Brown Sugar Brine

2	bay leaves	2
2 cups	soy sauce	500 mL
1 cup	dry white wine	250 mL
1/3 cup	packed brown sugar	75 mL
1/4 cup	kosher salt	50 mL
1 1/2 tsp	dried mint	7 mL
1 1/2 tsp	minced fresh parsley	7 mL
1 1/2 tsp	garlic powder	7 mL
1 1/2 tsp	freshly ground black pepper	7 mL
4 lbs	salmon fillets	2 kg

1. *Prepare the brine:* In a medium bowl, combine bay leaves, soy sauce, 1 cup (250 mL) water, wine, brown sugar, salt, mint, parsley, garlic powder and pepper.

2. Rinse salmon under cold running water and pat dry. Remove as many bones as possible. Place skin side down in a deep glass or other non-metallic dish large enough to hold the fillets. Spoon brine over fish, covering fish completely. (If necessary, add more water.) Cover and refrigerate for at least 8 hours or for up to 12 hours.

3. Prepare a fire in your cold smoker, using 3 oz (90 g) of wood. Set temperature to 200°F (100°C) until wood starts to smoke. Reduce temperature to 140°F (60°C) and place a pan of ice on top of the cold plate.

4. Remove salmon from brine and pat dry. Discard brine. Place salmon directly on the smoker rack and close the lid or door. Smoke for 4 to 5 hours, or until fish is firm to the touch, slightly burnished and translucent all the way through.

5. Serve at room temperature or chilled.

Salmon in Maple Brine

If you're going to cold-smoke fish, I suggest you use some kind of a brine first. Brining imbues the fish with great flavor and texture before the long, slow process of cold-smoking.

SERVES 16

Recommended wood: alder, cherry or maple

TIP

For better flavor and color, use the dark amber, or Grade B, variety of maple syrup, if available.

• • •

Make ahead

Place in an airtight container and store in the refrigerator for up to 1 week or in the freezer for up to 6 months.

1 cup	kosher salt	250 mL
1 cup	pure maple syrup (see tip, at left)	250 mL
4 lbs	salmon fillets	2 kg

1. In a medium bowl, combine salt, maple syrup and 1 cup (250 mL) water into a slushy mixture.

2. Rinse salmon under cold running water and pat dry. Remove as many bones as possible. Place skin side down in a deep glass or other non-metallic dish large enough to hold the fillets. Spoon slushy mixture over fish, covering fish completely. (If necessary, add more water.) Cover and refrigerate for 12 hours.

3. Prepare a fire in your cold smoker, using 3 oz (90 g) of wood. Set temperature to 200°F (100°C) until wood starts to smoke. Reduce temperature to 100°F (40°C) and place a pan of ice on top of the cold plate.

4. Remove salmon from brine, but do not pat dry. Discard brine. Place salmon directly on the smoker rack and close the lid or door. Smoke at 100°F to 120°F (40°C to 50°C) for 12 to 14 hours, or until fish is firm to the touch, slightly burnished and translucent all the way through.

5. Serve warm, at room temperature or chilled.

Herb-Brined Salmon

Brining removes extra liquid from the salmon, then infuses it with flavor.

SERVES 16	Recommended wood: alder

TIP

This salmon is cold-smoked, but at a higher temperature than Salmon in Maple Brine (see recipe, page 185), so it gets done faster. If you want to cold-smoke this at 100°F to 120°F (40°C to 50°C), it will take 12 to 14 hours.

• • •

Make ahead

Place in an airtight container and store in the refrigerator for up to 1 week or in the freezer for up to 3 months.

Herb Brine

2	bay leaves	2
2 cups	soy sauce	500 mL
1 cup	dry white wine	250 mL
1/3 cup	packed brown sugar	75 mL
1/4 cup	kosher salt	50 mL
1/2 tsp	dried mint	2 mL
1/2 tsp	dried parsley	2 mL
1/2 tsp	garlic powder	2 mL
1/2 tsp	freshly ground black pepper	2 mL
4 lbs	salmon fillets, skinned	2 kg

1. *Prepare the brine:* In a deep glass or other non-metallic dish large enough to hold the salmon fillets, combine bay leaves, soy sauce, 1 cup (250 mL) water, wine, brown sugar, salt, mint, parsley, garlic powder and pepper.

2. Rinse salmon under cold running water and pat dry. Remove as many bones as possible. Place salmon in the dish. Spoon brine over fish, covering fish completely. (If necessary, add more water.) Cover and refrigerate for at least 8 hours or for up to 12 hours.

3. Prepare a fire in your cold smoker, using 3 oz (90 g) of wood. Set temperature to 200°F (100°C) until wood starts to smoke. Reduce temperature to 140°F (60°C) and place a pan of ice on top of the cold plate.

4. Remove salmon from brine, but do not pat dry. Discard brine. Place salmon directly on the smoker rack and close the lid or door. Smoke for about 4 hours, or until fish is firm to the touch, slightly burnished and translucent all the way through.

5. Serve warm, at room temperature or chilled.

Tuna in Fresh Orange & White Balsamic Marinade

This flavorful but less acidic marinade is fine to use on fish for longer than the usual recommended 30 minutes. The orange zest really gives it extra flavor.

SERVES 4	Recommended wood: alder	

| 4 | tuna steaks (each about 6 oz/175 g) | 4 |
| 1 cup | Fresh Orange & White Balsamic Marinade (see recipe, page 39) | 250 mL |

TIP

Make an orange mayonnaise to go with this dish by mixing together good-quality prepared mayonnaise with orange zest and orange juice to taste.

• • •

Variation

Salmon steaks are also good prepared this way.

1. Rinse tuna under cold running water and pat dry. Place in a large sealable plastic bag and pour in marinade. Seal bag, toss to coat and refrigerate for at least 2 hours or for up to 6 hours.

2. Prepare a fire in your cold smoker, using 3 oz (90 g) of wood. Set temperature to 200°F (100°C) until wood starts to smoke. Reduce temperature to 190°F (90°C) and place a pan of ice on top of the cold plate.

3. Remove tuna from marinade, but do not pat dry. Discard marinade. Place tuna directly on the smoker rack and close the lid. Smoke for 45 minutes for medium-rare, or until desired doneness. (Should be served medium-rare to medium.)

Mussels in Apple-Garlic Marinade

This recipe is borderline between cold- and hot-smoking. Many barbecuers consider cold-smoking to be any temperature under 200°F (100°C) because it's so difficult to maintain a very low fire using regular smoking equipment. However, smokers like the SmokinTex®, which I use, can smoke at very low or very high temperatures.

SERVES 4	**Recommended wood:** any fruit wood

TIP

Apple wine is available from some apple orchards or fruit wineries. If you can't find it, substitute 2 cups (500 mL) dry white wine and 2 cups (500 mL) apple juice.

• • •

Variation

These mussels can also be hot-smoked at 225°F to 250°F (110°C to 120°C) for 35 to 45 minutes, or until mussels open.

4	cloves garlic, chopped	4
2 lbs	mussels, scrubbed (discard any that do not close when tapped)	1 kg
4 cups	apple wine	1 L
½ cup	chopped onion	125 mL
¼ cup	snipped chives	50 mL
2 tbsp	kosher salt	25 mL

1. Place garlic, mussels, wine, onions, chives and salt in a large sealable plastic bag. Seal, toss to coat and refrigerate overnight.

2. Prepare a fire in your cold smoker, using 3 oz (90 g) of wood. Set temperature to 200°F (100°C) until wood starts to smoke. Reduce temperature to 180°F (82°C) and place a pan of ice on top of the cold plate.

3. Remove mussels from marinade. Discard marinade and any mussels that do not close when tapped. Place mussels directly on the smoker rack and close the lid. Smoke for about 1 hour, or until mussels open. Discard any mussels that do not open.

Hickory-Smoked Mussels in Passionberry Wine

This smoked mussels recipe offers a different constellation of flavors.

SERVES 4

Recommended wood: hickory

8	cloves garlic, chopped	8
6	stems fresh thyme	6
6	serrano chili peppers, split	6
2 lbs	mussels, scrubbed (discard any that do not close when tapped)	1 kg
3 cups	passionberry or other berry fruit wine (see tip, at left)	750 mL
½ cup	chopped onion	125 mL
2 tbsp	kosher salt	25 mL

1. Place garlic, thyme, serrano peppers, mussels, wine, onion and salt in a large sealable plastic bag. Seal, toss to coat and refrigerate overnight.

2. Prepare a fire in your cold smoker, using 3 oz (90 g) of wood. Set temperature to 200°F (100°C) until wood starts to smoke. Reduce temperature to 180°F (82°C) and place a pan of ice on top of the cold plate.

3. Remove mussels from marinade. Discard marinade and any mussels that do not close when tapped. Place mussels directly on the smoker rack and close the lid. Smoke for about 1 hour, or until mussels open. Discard any mussels that do not open.

TIP

"Passionberry" is a marketing name for a combination of passion fruit and berry. Passionberry wine is available from some fruit wineries. If you can't find it, or any berry fruit wine, substitute 2 cups (500 mL) apple wine and 1 cup (250 mL) cranberry or cran-raspberry juice.

● ● ●

Variation

These mussels can also be hot-smoked at 225°F to 250°F (110°C to 120°C) for 35 to 45 minutes, or until mussels open.

Scallops

Although you can cold-smoke small bay scallops as well as the large Digby or diver-harvested scallops, I think it's easier and more impressive to go with the larger shellfish. It's easier to tell when they're done, and it's more impressive to the friends and family who devour them.

SERVES 8	Recommended wood: alder or cherry

TIP

Since smoking is a time-consuming process, why not do lots of scallops, or scallops and salmon, all at the same time? Use as many racks as your smoker will allow.

● ● ●

Make ahead

Place in an airtight container and store in the refrigerator for up to 1 week or in the freezer for up to 6 months.

4 lbs	large scallops	2 kg

1. Cover two cold-smoker racks with cheesecloth. Rinse scallops under cold running water and pat dry. Arrange evenly over covered racks. Place racks in the highest positions in your cold smoker.

2. Prepare a fire in your cold smoker, using 3 oz (90 g) of wood. Set temperature to 200°F (100°C) until wood starts to smoke. Reduce temperature to 100°F (40°C) and place a pan of ice on top of the cold plate.

3. Close the lid and smoke at 100°F to 120°F (40°C to 50°C) for 10 hours, or until scallops are pale and translucent, but somewhat firm to the touch.

Scallop Martinis

Here's a fun way to serve your cold-smoked scallops. For a party, you can increase this recipe to accommodate however many guests — or smoked scallops — you have.

SERVES 4 AS AN
APPETIZER

TIP

See opposite for instructions on cold-smoking scallops.

16	large scallops (about 1 lb/500 g), cold-smoked	16
4 tsp	vodka	20 mL
1 tsp	dry white vermouth	5 mL
	Large green olives	

1. Place 4 scallops in each of 4 chilled martini glasses. Drizzle 1 tsp (5 mL) vodka and ¼ tsp (1 mL) vermouth over the scallops in each glass. Garnish with olives.

Poultry

WHEN CHICKEN, TURKEY and other types of poultry come off the smoker, they're bronzed on the outside and an opaque pale pink on the inside. They stay moist and tender during the long, slow cooking process and take on a wonderful sweet smoke flavor.

Whole chickens and turkeys, as well as bone-in parts, benefit the most from smoking. I'm very partial to smoked chicken wings as an appetizer, so I have several recipes for those. Dark meat turkey, often unappreciated, gets a new lease on life when you smoke it. Of course, you could smoke a boneless skinless chicken breast if you wanted to, but by the time it got done, it wouldn't have much smoke flavor. A bone-in breast stays moister and simply tastes better off the smoker.

Poultry can be especially juicy if you brine it before smoking. Simply make up a batch of any of the brines in this book, immerse the bird in the brine, cover and refrigerate for at least 8 hours or overnight. Then remove the bird from the brine, discard the brine and rinse the poultry under cold running water.

Marinades are also great on poultry, as they help hold moisture and flavor in the somewhat delicate flesh of the bird. You could also use a dry rub, then baste the bird as it smokes.

Because poultry is so sweet, I don't like to use a strong wood such as hickory or mesquite to smoke it, unless the hickory or mesquite is in combination with other milder woods. My favorite hard wood for chicken is apple; for turkey, pecan. But experiment with wood smoke flavors yourself and see what you like.

POULTRY RECIPES

Aromatic Whole Chicken 194
Whole Chicken in Orange, Garlic
   & Brown Sugar Brine 195
Whole Chicken with Orange
   & Tarragon 196
Here a Chick, There a Chick. . . . 197
Chick, Chick, Chick. 198
Apricot Chicken Quarters 199
Easy Barbecued Chicken 200
Raspberry Chicken Breasts. 201
Santa Fe Chicken Breasts
   in Coffee Lime Marinade . . . 202
Apricot Chicken Skewers 203
Pecan-Glazed Chicken Thighs . . 204
Sassy, Spicy Chicken Wings 205
Sweet Wings 206
Buffalo-Style Hot Wings. 207
Cherry Chipotle Wings. 208

Pecan-Smoked Apricot
   Chicken Wings. 209
Sesame Turkey 210
Sweet & Smoky Turkey Breasts . . 211
Mango & Chipotle
   Turkey Breast 212
Pineapple-Soy Turkey
   Tenderloins 214
Southwestern-Style
   Turkey Thighs. 215
Honey-Chipotle Turkey
   Drumsticks 216
Smoky, Spicy Turkey Wings 217
Soy & Garlic Duck Breast 218
Five-Spice Duck Breast 219
Stuffed Cornish Game Hens with
   Apricot Mustard Sauce 220
Cornish Game Hens with
   Honey Spice Glaze. 222

Aromatic Whole Chicken

Here's an easy smoked chicken recipe for the barbecue beginner.

SERVES 8	Recommended wood: a combination of apple and hickory		

TIPS

You can use either sweetened or unsweetened apple juice — it's up to you!

• • •

Depending on the size of the plastic bags you use, two whole chickens might not fit in one bag (keep in mind that the bag has to be able to seal when you are judging whether you will need a second bag). If that's the case, use two bags and pour half of the Italian dressing into each bag.

• • •

Place any leftovers in an airtight container and store in the refrigerator for up to 1 week.

2	whole chickens (each about 4 lbs/2 kg)	2
1	bottle (16 oz/500 mL) Italian vinaigrette	1
½ cup	Aromatic Poultry Rub (see recipe, page 29)	125 mL
	Apple juice for spraying	

1. Rinse chickens inside and out under cold running water and pat dry. Place in a large sealable plastic bag (or bags) and pour in Italian dressing. Seal bag, toss to coat and refrigerate for at least 8 hours or for up to 24 hours.

2. Remove chickens from marinade, but do not pat dry. Discard marinade. Sprinkle chickens with dry rub. Set aside.

3. Prepare a fire in your smoker. *(For instructions, see pages 8–11.)*

4. Place chickens, breast side up, directly on the smoker rack, add wood to the coals and close the lid. Smoke at 225°F to 250°F (110°C to 120°C), spraying with apple juice every 30 minutes, for 4 to 5 hours, or until a meat thermometer inserted in the thickest part of a thigh registers 180°F (82°C). Let chicken rest for 15 minutes before carving.

Whole Chicken in Orange, Garlic & Brown Sugar Brine

Brining a chicken before smoking will produce juicy, tender results. When you finish the chicken with an aromatic orange baste, it's a match made in heaven.

SERVES 8	Recommended wood: apple, cherry or other fruit wood	
2	whole chickens (each about 4 lbs/2 kg)	2
6 cups	Orange, Garlic & Brown Sugar Brine (see recipe, page 22)	1.5 L
1¼ cups	Sweet Orange Baste (see recipe, page 46)	300 mL

TIP

Depending on the size of the plastic bags you use, two whole chickens might not fit in one bag (keep in mind that the bag has to be able to seal when you are judging whether you will need a second bag). If that's the case, use two bags and pour half of the brine into each bag.

1. Rinse chickens inside and out under cold running water and pat dry. Place in a large sealable plastic bag (or bags) and pour in brine. Seal bag, toss to coat and refrigerate for at least 8 hours or for up to 24 hours.

2. Remove chickens from brine and discard brine. Rinse chickens inside and out under cold running water, but do not pat dry. Set aside.

3. Prepare a fire in your smoker. *(For instructions, see pages 8–11.)*

4. Place chickens, breast side up, directly on the smoker rack, add wood to the coals and close the lid. Smoke at 225°F to 250°F (110°C to 120°C), basting with Sweet Orange Baste every 30 minutes, for 4 to 5 hours, or until a meat thermometer inserted in the thickest part of a thigh registers 180°F (82°C). Let chicken rest for 15 minutes before carving.

Whole Chicken with Orange & Tarragon

Here's a simply delicious way to smoke a whole chicken. Remember to remove anything you find in the cavity of the chicken.

SERVES 4	Recommended wood: any fruit wood

TIP

When food is cold, it takes longer to smoke it. For the recipes in this book, you want to bring your food to room temperature before smoking.

• • •

Variation

Instead of the orange and tarragon flavoring paste, try 1½ cups (375 mL) of Fresh Herb & Spice Paste or Fresh Garlic & Herb Paste (see recipes, page 35).

Flavoring Paste

¼ cup	minced fresh parsley	50 mL
¼ cup	minced fresh tarragon	50 mL
¼ cup	minced fresh mint	50 mL
¼ cup	olive oil	50 mL
	Juice of 1 orange	
1	whole frying chicken (about 3 lbs/1.5 kg)	1
	Kosher salt and freshly ground black pepper	

1. *Prepare the flavoring paste:* In a small bowl, combine parsley, tarragon, mint, oil and orange juice.

2. Rinse chicken inside and out under cold running water and pat dry. Rub flavoring paste evenly onto chicken, inside and out, then season to taste with salt and pepper. Set aside.

3. Prepare a fire in your smoker. *(For instructions, see pages 8–11.)*

4. Place chicken, breast side up, directly on the smoker rack, add wood to the coals and close the lid. Smoke at 225°F to 250°F (110°C to 120°C) for 4 to 5 hours, or until a meat thermometer inserted into the thickest part of the thigh registers 180°F (82°C).

Here a Chick, There a Chick

You'll get two smoked chickens from this recipe, and it's easy for beginning barbecuers.

SERVES 8	Recommended wood: any fruit wood

TIPS

To crush brown mustard seeds, use a mortar and pestle or place seeds in a shallow dish and crush with the bottom of a heavy pot.

* * *

Depending on the size of the plastic bags you use, two whole chickens might not fit in one bag (keep in mind that the bag has to be able to seal when you are judging whether you will need a second bag). If that's the case, use two bags and pour half of the marinade into each bag.

Marinade

2 cups	apple juice	500 mL
1 cup	rice vinegar	250 mL
½ cup	minced garlic	125 mL
¼ cup	brown mustard seeds, crushed	50 mL
¼ cup	red wine vinegar	50 mL
2 tbsp	freshly ground black pepper	25 mL
2 tbsp	Hungarian sweet paprika	25 mL
2 tbsp	Worcestershire sauce	25 mL
2 tbsp	soy sauce	25 mL
2	whole chickens (each about 4 lbs/2 kg)	2

1. *Prepare the marinade:* In a large bowl, combine apple juice, rice vinegar, garlic, mustard seeds, red wine vinegar, pepper, paprika, Worcestershire sauce and soy sauce.

2. Rinse chickens inside and out under cold running water and pat dry. Place in a large sealable plastic bag (or bags) and pour in marinade. Seal bag, toss to coat and refrigerate for 2 hours.

3. Remove chickens from marinade, but do not pat dry. Set aside. Discard marinade.

4. Prepare a fire in your smoker. *(For instructions, see pages 8–11.)*

5. Place chickens, breast side up, directly on the smoker rack, add wood to the coals and close the lid. Smoke at 225°F to 250°F (110°C to 120°C) for 4 to 5 hours, or until a meat thermometer inserted into the thickest part of a thigh registers 180°F (82°C).

Chick, Chick, Chick

If you're going to smoke one whole chicken, why not three, if you've got the room on your smoker? Invite friends and family over, or smoke for leftovers to use in sandwiches, salads, casseroles or other dishes.

SERVES 12	Recommended wood: a combination of apple and hickory

TIPS

You can buy jalapeño pepper powder at better herb and spice emporiums, by mail order or online (see the Source Guide, page 356). If jalapeño pepper powder is not available, you can use a spice grinder to grind dried jalapeño pieces to a fine powder. Just be careful of the dust when opening the grinder, avoiding breathing it or getting it in your eyes. Clean the grinder well by grinding (and discarding) several small batches of white rice. This helps clean out the crevices in the grinder.

• • •

You can find granulated garlic and onion at well-stocked supermarkets or online (see the Source Guide, page 356).

• • •

Place any leftovers in an airtight container and store in the refrigerator for up to 1 week.

Seasoning Mix

1 tbsp	jalapeño pepper powder (see tip, at left)	15 mL
1 tbsp	freshly ground black pepper	15 mL
1 tbsp	granulated garlic (see tip, at left)	15 mL
1 tbsp	granulated onion (see tip, at left)	15 mL
1 tbsp	dry rubbed sage	15 mL
½ tbsp	dried dillweed	7 mL
1 tbsp	dried mint	15 mL
3	whole frying chickens (each about 3 lbs/1.5 kg)	3

1. *Prepare the seasoning mix:* In a small bowl, combine jalapeño pepper powder, pepper, garlic, onions, sage, dill and mint.

2. Rinse chickens inside and out under cold running water and pat dry. Sprinkle seasoning mix evenly over chickens, inside and out. Set aside.

3. Prepare a fire in your smoker. *(For instructions, see pages 8–11.)*

4. Place chickens, breast side up, directly on the smoker rack, add wood to the coals and close the lid. Smoke at 225°F to 250°F (110°C to 120°C) for 4 to 5 hours, or until a meat thermometer inserted in the thickest part of the chicken registers 180°F (82°C).

Apricot Chicken Quarters

A tasty recipe for the beginning barbecuer. The chicken smokes in a pan for the first 2½ hours, while you baste with the sauce in the pan. Then you place the chicken directly on the smoker rack, and the sauce on the chicken cooks to a beautiful sheen.

SERVES 4	**Recommended wood:** a combination of hickory, apple and peach

TIP

If your grocery store doesn't sell chicken cut into four pieces, use a frying chicken cut into breasts, wings, thighs, etc. Your smoking time after placing the chicken directly on the rack will be about 30 minutes less.

1	whole frying chicken (about 3 lbs/1.5 kg), quartered	1
1 cup	Apricot, Apricot, Apricot Barbecue Sauce (see recipe, page 65)	250 mL
¼ cup	pure maple syrup	50 mL
2 tsp	Southwestern-style seasoning mix	10 mL
1 tsp	kosher salt	5 mL
1 tsp	freshly ground black pepper	5 mL

1. Rinse chicken under cold running water and pat dry.

2. In a large disposable aluminum pan, combine barbecue sauce, maple syrup, seasoning mix, salt and pepper. Add chicken, toss to coat and let stand at room temperature for 30 minutes. Meanwhile, prepare a fire in your smoker. *(For instructions, see pages 8–11.)*

3. Place pan on the smoker rack, add wood to the coals and close the lid. Smoke at 225°F to 250°F (110°C to 120°C), basting every 30 minutes, for 2½ hours. Remove chicken from pan and place skin side up directly on the smoker rack. Close the lid and smoke for 45 minutes, or until a meat thermometer inserted in the thickest part of the chicken registers 170°F (75°C).

Easy Barbecued Chicken

This is another great dish for beginners — you get a tender and tasty reward in less than 3 hours for practicing your barbecue technique.

SERVES 6	Recommended wood: a combination of cherry and oak

TIPS

Use four chunks of cherry and two chunks of oak.

• • •

I use Old Bay® seasoning in this recipe, but feel free to use whatever seafood seasoning mix you like.

2 cups	barbecue sauce (store-bought or see recipes, pages 50–65)	500 mL
4 tsp	seafood seasoning mix, divided	20 mL
3½ lbs	bone-in chicken pieces	1.75 kg
¼ cup	olive oil	50 mL

1. In a small saucepan, over medium-low heat, combine barbecue sauce and 2 tsp (10 mL) of the seafood seasoning mix. Simmer for 10 minutes. Remove from heat and keep warm by the smoker.

2. Rinse chicken under cold running water and pat dry. Lightly brush with oil, then sprinkle with the remaining seafood seasoning mix. Set aside.

3. Prepare a fire in your smoker. *(For instructions, see pages 8–11.)*

4. Place chicken, skin side up, directly on the smoker rack, add wood to the coals and close the lid. Smoke at 225°F to 250°F (110°C to 120°C) for 2 hours. Brush chicken with barbecue sauce mixture, close the lid and smoke for 30 minutes, or until a meat thermometer inserted in the thickest part of the chicken registers 170°F (75°C).

5. Serve with any remaining barbecue sauce on the side.

Raspberry Chicken Breasts

In just 1½ hours — a short time on a smoker — you can have absolutely luscious chicken breasts with the tang of raspberry. These are delicious straight from the smoker, but are also good as leftovers on a salad with raspberry vinaigrette.

SERVES 4	Recommended wood: pecan

TIPS

If Montreal chicken seasoning is not available, you can substitute Montreal steak seasoning or your favorite dry rub.

● ● ●

Place any leftovers in an airtight container and store in the refrigerator for up to 1 week.

Marinade

½ cup	seedless raspberry preserves	125 mL
⅓ cup	raspberry vinegar	75 mL
2 tbsp	Montreal chicken seasoning (see tip, at left)	25 mL
4	boneless skinless chicken breasts (each about 8 oz/250 g)	4

1. *Prepare the marinade:* In a small saucepan, over medium heat, combine raspberry preserves, vinegar, ¼ cup (50 mL) water and chicken seasoning. Simmer, stirring constantly, until preserves melt, 5 to 7 minutes. Remove from heat and let cool completely.

2. Rinse chicken under cold running water and pat dry. Place in a sealable plastic bag and pour in two-thirds of the marinade. Seal bag, toss to coat and refrigerate for 2 hours. Reserve the remaining marinade in the refrigerator.

3. Remove chicken from marinade, but do not pat dry. Set aside. Discard marinade.

4. Prepare a fire in your smoker. *(For instructions, see pages 8–11.)*

5. Place chicken directly on the smoker rack, add wood to the coals and close the lid. Smoke at 225°F to 250°F (110°C to 120°C), basting with the reserved marinade every 30 minutes, for 1½ hours, or until a meat thermometer inserted in the thickest part of a breast registers 170°F (75°C).

Santa Fe Chicken Breasts in Coffee Lime Marinade

Using pecan wood for the smoke flavoring gives this dish a taste similar to smoky beans or the famous Hatch green chilies you find in Santa Fe, New Mexico. This chicken is wonderful served with a fruit relish or chutney.

SERVES 6	**Recommended wood:** pecan with, perhaps, a little cherry

TIP

Smoke chicken breasts with the skin on for added moisture. Then, if you prefer, remove the skin before serving.

6	bone-in chicken breasts (each about 6 to 8 oz/175 to 250 g)	6
1⅓ cups	Coffee Lime Marinade (see recipe, page 41)	325 mL

1. Rinse chicken under cold running water and pat dry. Place in a large sealable plastic bag and pour in marinade. Seal bag, toss to coat and refrigerate for at least 3 hours or for up to 6 hours.

2. Remove chicken from marinade, but do not pat dry. Set aside. Discard marinade.

3. Prepare a fire in your smoker. *(For instructions, see pages 8–11.)*

4. Place chicken, skin side up, directly on the smoker rack, add wood to the coals and close the lid. Smoke at 225°F to 250°F (110°C to 120°C) for 3½ to 4 hours, or until a meat thermometer inserted in the thickest part of a breast registers 170°F (75°C).

Apricot Chicken Skewers

If you're tending a smoker for long hours, you'll enjoy snacking on these speedier morsels while you prepare the main event. If you can bring yourself to share, they make great appetizers.

SERVES 4 AS AN APPETIZER

TIPS

Look for apricot syrup where syrups for pancakes or ice creams are shelved at the grocery store.

• • •

One medium orange yields ⅓ to ½ cup (75 to 125 mL) juice. If you prefer, you can use store-bought orange juice in this recipe.

• • •

Serve these skewers with Apricot, Apricot, Apricot Barbecue Sauce (see recipe, page 65).

Recommended wood: pecan

• Four 12-inch (30 cm) bamboo skewers

Marinade

1	jar (10 oz/300 mL) apricot preserves	1
¼ cup	apricot syrup (see tip, at left)	50 mL
¼ cup	orange juice	50 mL
¼ cup	butter	50 mL
4	boneless skinless chicken breasts (each about 4 oz/125 g)	4
2	red bell peppers, cut in large cubes	2

1. Soak skewers in water for 30 minutes.

2. *Prepare the marinade:* In a medium saucepan, over medium-low heat, stir together apricot preserves, apricot syrup, orange juice and butter. Simmer until butter has melted, 5 to 7 minutes.

3. Rinse chicken under cold running water and pat dry. Cut into 1-inch (2.5 cm) cubes. Place in a sealable plastic bag and pour in ¾ cup (175 mL) of the marinade. Seal bag, toss to coat and refrigerate for at least 30 minutes or for up to 8 hours. Reserve the remaining marinade in the refrigerator.

4. Remove chicken from marinade, but do not pat dry. Discard marinade. Thread chicken and peppers onto skewers and place on a baking sheet for transport to the smoker. Set aside.

5. Prepare a fire in your smoker. *(For instructions, see pages 8–11.)*

6. Place skewers directly on the smoker rack, add wood to the coals and close the lid. Smoke at 225°F to 250°F (110°C to 120°C), basting occasionally with the reserved marinade, for 1 hour, or until juices run clear when chicken is pierced.

Pecan-Glazed Chicken Thighs

From the spicy dry rub to the mellow barbecue glaze and Pecan Honey finish, this smoked chicken recipe is a winner.

SERVES 8	Recommended wood: a combination of apple and cherry

TIPS

Smoke chicken thighs with the skin on for added moisture. Then, if you prefer, remove the skin before serving.

• • •

Pecan Honey is a wonderful finishing glaze for smoked pork and game too. It's also a great way to rescue foods that have taken on a very bitter flavor from over-smoking.

8	bone-in chicken thighs (each about 4 oz/125 g)	8
¼ cup	Every-Flavor Spice Rub (see recipe, page 30)	50 mL

Pecan Honey

½ cup	pecan halves	125 mL
¼ cup	amber liquid honey	50 mL
3 cups	Barbecue Glaze (see recipe, page 67)	750 mL

1. Rinse chicken under cold running water and pat dry. Sprinkle both sides of chicken evenly with dry rub. Set aside.

2. *Prepare the Pecan Honey:* In a large bowl, combine pecans and honey. Set aside.

3. Prepare a fire in your smoker. *(For instructions, see pages 8–11.)*

4. Place chicken directly on the smoker rack, add wood to the coals and close the lid. Smoke at 225°F to 250°F (110°C to 120°C) for 1 hour. Transfer chicken to a disposable aluminum pan and pour in Barbecue Glaze. Place pan on the smoker rack and close the lid. Smoke for 1 hour. Pour Pecan Honey over chicken and close the lid. Smoke for 20 minutes, or until a meat thermometer inserted in the thickest part of a thigh registers 170°F (75°C).

Sassy, Spicy Chicken Wings

This is a great recipe for beginners to the world of smoke and spice, as chicken wings are inexpensive and will smoke in about 1½ hours. These wings are delicious as an appetizer or as a finger-lickin' entrée.

SERVES 12 AS AN APPETIZER OR 6 AS A MAIN COURSE

TIPS

If desired, remove wing tips before sprinkling wings with dry rub.

• • •

Chicken wings are easy to smoke and can take on just about any flavoring. Try them dusted with a rub such as All-Purpose Barbecue Rub (see recipe, page 27), then glazed with a sauce such as Cherry Chipotle Barbecue Sauce (see recipe, page 63) or Honey Mustard Barbecue Sauce (see recipe, page 61) during the last hour of smoking.

Recommended wood: a combination of sugar maple and cherry

3 lbs	chicken wings	1.5 kg
⅔ cup	Sassy, Spicy Pork Rub (see recipe, page 34)	150 mL
1 cup	Mustard & Marmalade Barbecue Sauce (see recipe, page 60)	250 mL

1. Rinse wings under cold running water and pat dry. Place in a large disposable aluminum pan, sprinkle with dry rub and toss to coat. Pour in barbecue sauce and toss to coat. Let stand at room temperature for about 15 minutes, or until surface is tacky. Meanwhile, prepare a fire in your smoker. *(For instructions, see pages 8–11.)*

2. Place pan on the smoker rack, add wood to the coals and close the lid. Smoke at 225°F to 250°F (110°C to 120°C) for 1 to 1½ hours, or until juices run clear when chicken is pierced.

Sweet Wings

Here's another easy recipe that's wonderful as a casual appetizer. The marinade is also good on a whole chicken.

Recommended wood: pecan, oak or hickory

TIPS

If desired, remove wing tips before placing wings in the plastic bag(s).

• • • •

Depending on the size of the plastic bags you use, 5 lbs (2.5 kg) of wings might not fit in one bag (keep in mind that the bag has to be able to seal when you are judging whether you will need a second bag). If that's the case, use two bags and pour half of the marinade into each bag.

Honeyed Worcestershire Marinade

4 cups	Worcestershire sauce	1 L
¾ cup	amber liquid honey	175 mL
1 tbsp	minced garlic	15 mL
5 lbs	chicken wings	2.5 kg

1. *Prepare the marinade:* In a large bowl, combine Worcestershire sauce, honey and garlic.

2. Rinse wings under cold running water and pat dry. Place in a large sealable plastic bag (or bags) and pour in marinade. Seal bag, toss to coat and refrigerate for 2 hours.

3. Remove wings from marinade, but do not pat dry. Discard marinade. Place wings in a single layer in disposable aluminum pans and set aside.

4. Prepare a fire in your smoker. *(For instructions, see pages 8–11.)*

5. Place pans on the smoker rack, add wood to the coals and close the lid. Smoke at 225°F to 250°F (110°C to 120°C) for 2 hours, or until juices run clear when chicken is pierced.

Buffalo-Style Hot Wings

These are HOT! As with true Buffalo chicken wings, serve these with blue cheese dressing and celery sticks to help cut the heat. The combination can be addictive. It's great party food, especially when you're watching the big game.

SERVES 8	Recommended wood: oak, apple or pecan

TIPS

If desired, remove wing tips before placing wings in the plastic bag(s).

• • •

Depending on the size of the plastic bags you use, 5 lbs (2.5 kg) of wings might not fit in one bag (keep in mind that the bag has to be able to seal when you are judging whether you will need a second bag). If that's the case, use two bags and pour half of the marinade into each bag.

Marinade

4 cups	hot sauce, such as Frank's RedHot®	1 L
1½ cups	amber liquid honey	375 mL
¼ cup	butter, melted	50 mL
5 lbs	chicken wings	2.5 kg

1. *Prepare the marinade:* In a large bowl, combine hot pepper sauce, honey and butter.

2. Rinse wings under cold running water and pat dry. Place in a large sealable plastic bag (or bags) and pour in marinade. Seal bag, toss to coat and refrigerate for at least 2 hours or for up to 6 hours.

3. Remove wings from marinade, but do not pat dry. Discard marinade. Place wings in a single layer in disposable aluminum pans and set aside.

4. Prepare a fire in your smoker. *(For instructions, see pages 8–11.)*

5. Place pans on the smoker rack, add wood to the coals and close the lid. Smoke at 225°F to 250°F (110°C to 120°C) for 2 hours, or until juices run clear when chicken is pierced.

Cherry Chipotle Wings

Here's a great example of how to layer flavor: marinate with Chipotle Marinade, smoke over cherry wood and finish with Cherry Chipotle Barbecue Sauce. Delicious!

SERVES 8

Recommended wood: cherry or other fruit wood

TIPS

If desired, remove wing tips before placing wings in the plastic bag(s).

• • •

Depending on the size of the plastic bags you use, 5 lbs (2.5 kg) of wings might not fit in one bag (keep in mind that the bag has to be able to seal when you are judging whether you will need a second bag). If that's the case, use two bags and pour half of the marinade into each bag.

5 lbs	chicken wings	2.5 kg
1½ cups	Chipotle Marinade (see recipe, page 36)	375 mL
5 cups	Cherry Chipotle Barbecue Sauce (see recipe, page 63)	1.25 L

1. Rinse wings under cold running water and pat dry. Place in a large sealable plastic bag (or bags) and pour in marinade. Seal bag, toss to coat and refrigerate for 2 hours.

2. Remove wings from marinade, but do not pat dry. Discard marinade. Place wings in a single layer in disposable aluminum pans and set aside.

3. Prepare a fire in your smoker. *(For instructions, see pages 8–11.)*

4. Place pans on the smoker rack, add wood to the coals and close the lid. Smoke at 225°F to 250°F (110°C to 120°C) for 1 hour. Brush wings with barbecue sauce and close the lid. Smoke for 1 hour, or until juices run clear when chicken is pierced.

5. Serve wings with any remaining sauce on the side.

> Cherry wood is a favorite in Michigan and Ontario, where both sweet and sour cherries benefit from the Great Lakes climate.

Pecan-Smoked Apricot Chicken Wings

The sweetness of fruit such as apricots marries well with the slightly bitter flavor you get from smoke. Serve these delectable wings at your next backyard barbecue.

SERVES 6 TO 8	**Recommended wood:** pecan

TIPS

If desired, remove wing tips before brushing wings with sauce.

• • •

The smaller the smoking chamber on your equipment, the sooner your food will be done. If you're using a kettle grill or a bullet smoker, your chicken wings might be done in 2 hours. If you're using a bigger rig or a genuine smoker, they might take 2½ hours.

Apricot Sauce

2	cloves garlic	2
1	can (15 oz/425 mL) apricots, drained	1
2 tbsp	ketchup	25 mL
2 tbsp	olive oil	25 mL
2 tbsp	rice vinegar	25 mL
2 tbsp	orange juice	25 mL
½ tsp	hot pepper sauce	2 mL
¼ tsp	kosher salt	1 mL
3 lbs	chicken wings	1.5 kg

1. *Prepare the sauce:* In a blender, process garlic, apricots, ketchup, oil, vinegar, orange juice, hot pepper sauce and salt until smooth.

2. Rinse wings under cold running water and pat dry. Place in a large disposable aluminum pan and brush with some of the sauce. Set aside.

3. Prepare a fire in your smoker. *(For instructions, see pages 8–11.)*

4. Place pan on the smoker rack, add wood to the coals and close the lid. Smoke at 225°F to 250°F (110°C to 120°C), basting with the remaining apricot sauce every 30 minutes, for 2 to 2½ hours, or until juices run clear when chicken is pierced.

Sesame Turkey

A new twist on the traditional Thanksgiving bird, this smoked turkey is delicious any time of year! A smoked turkey has a dark, bronzed exterior and a juicy, opaque, pale pink (from the smoke) interior.

SERVES 10 TO 12	**Recommended wood:** a combination of pecan and apple, cherry or other fruit wood

TIPS

You can use either sweetened or unsweetened apple juice — it's up to you!

• • •

The smaller the smoking chamber on your equipment, the sooner your food will be done. If you're using a kettle grill or a bullet smoker, your turkey might be done in 5 hours. If you're using a bigger rig or a genuine smoker, it might take 6 hours.

1	turkey (about 10 lbs/5 kg)	1
3 cups	Sesame Marinade (see recipe, page 43)	750 mL
	Apple juice for spraying	

1. Rinse turkey inside and out under cold running water and pat dry. Place in a large sealable plastic bag or a deep pan. Pour in marinade, making sure the turkey is covered by the marinade as much as possible, and seal or cover. Refrigerate for at least 8 hours or for up to 12 hours, turning turkey several times.

2. Remove turkey from marinade, but do not pat dry. Discard marinade. Wrap turkey in cheesecloth and set aside.

3. Prepare a fire in your smoker. *(For instructions, see pages 8–11.)*

4. Place turkey, breast side up, directly on the smoker rack, spray cheesecloth with apple juice, add wood to the coals and close the lid. Smoke at 225°F to 250°F (110°C to 120°C), spraying cheesecloth with apple juice every 30 minutes, for 6 hours, or until a meat thermometer inserted in the thickest part of the turkey registers 180°F (82°C). Let turkey rest for 15 minutes before unwrapping and carving.

Sweet & Smoky Turkey Breasts

If you love white meat, this is a great way to do a holiday bird.

Recommended wood: pecan

TIPS

This recipe also works for bone-in turkey breasts, but they will take about 30 to 60 minutes longer.

• • •

Smoke turkey breasts with the skin on for added moisture. Then, if you prefer, remove the skin before serving.

• • •

If you have room, smoke some winter squash or sweet potatoes at the same time (see page 112 for instructions).

Marinade

¼ cup	olive oil	50 mL
¼ cup	soy sauce	50 mL
2 tbsp	packed brown sugar	25 mL
2 tbsp	freshly squeezed lime juice	25 mL
1 tbsp	pure maple syrup	15 mL
2	cloves garlic, minced	2
1 tbsp	finely chopped fresh basil	15 mL
½ tsp	dried oregano	2 mL
2	boneless turkey breast halves (each about 3 lbs/1.5 kg)	2

1. *Prepare the marinade:* In a small bowl, combine olive oil, soy sauce, brown sugar, lime juice and maple syrup. Set aside.

2. In a small bowl, combine garlic, basil and oregano.

3. Rinse turkey under cold running water and pat dry. Rub garlic mixture over turkey. Place turkey in a large sealable plastic bag and pour in marinade. Seal bag, toss to coat and refrigerate for at least 6 hours or for up to 12 hours, turning several times.

4. Remove turkey from marinade, but do not pat dry. Set aside. Discard marinade.

5. Prepare a fire in your smoker. *(For instructions, see pages 8–11.)*

6. Place turkey directly on the smoker rack, add wood to the coals and close the lid. Smoke at 225°F to 250°F (110°C to 120°C) for 2 hours, or until a meat thermometer inserted in the thickest part of a breast registers 170°F (75°C). Let turkey rest for 15 minutes before carving.

Mango & Chipotle Turkey Breasts

Marinated in a mango and chipotle mixture, this turkey breast takes on an even more exotic flavor from smoking over grape and pear wood.

SERVES 6 TO 8 | **Recommended wood:** a combination of grape and pear

TIPS

If you can't find grape or pear, turn to another fruit wood such as apple or cherry.

• • •

Depending on the size of the plastic bags you use, two turkey breast halves might not fit in one bag (keep in mind that the bag has to be able to seal when you are judging whether you will need a second bag). If that's the case, use two bags and pour one-third of the marinade into each bag.

Marinade

1 cup	ketchup	250 mL
½ cup	mango juice	125 mL
3 tbsp	packed brown sugar	45 mL
2 tbsp	finely minced green onions	25 mL
2 tbsp	puréed chipotle pepper in adobo sauce	25 mL
1 tsp	ground cumin	5 mL
1 tsp	minced fresh basil	5 mL
1 tsp	minced fresh mint	5 mL
½ tsp	kosher salt	2 mL
2	turkey breast halves (each about 2 lbs/1 kg)	2
	Additional mango juice for spraying	

1. *Prepare the marinade:* In a medium bowl, combine ketchup, mango juice, brown sugar, green onions, chipotle, cumin, basil, mint and salt.

2. Rinse turkey under cold running water and pat dry. Place in a large sealable plastic bag (or bags) and pour in two-thirds of the marinade. Seal bag, toss to coat and refrigerate for at least 2 hours or for up to 24 hours. Reserve the remaining marinade in the refrigerator.

TIP

The smaller the
smoking chamber on
your equipment, the
sooner your food will
be done. If you're using
a kettle grill or a bullet
smoker, your turkey
breasts might be done
in 3 hours. If you're
using a bigger rig or a
genuine smoker, they
might take 4 hours.

3. Remove turkey from marinade, but do not pat dry. Set aside. Discard marinade.

4. Prepare a fire in your smoker. *(For instructions, see pages 8–11.)*

5. Place turkey directly on the smoker rack, add wood to the coals and close the lid. Smoke at 225°F to 250°F (110°C to 120°C), basting with the reserved marinade and spraying with mango juice every 30 minutes, for 4 hours, or until a meat thermometer inserted in the thickest part of a breast registers 170°F (75°C). Let turkey rest for 15 minutes before carving.

Pineapple-Soy Turkey Tenderloins

In this recipe, the turkey stays tender and juicy, and the flavor is terrific!

Recommended wood: apple

TIPS

You can use either sweetened or unsweetened pineapple juice — it's up to you!

• • •

For 2 tbsp (25 mL) lime juice, you'll need 1 to 2 medium limes.

Marinade

¼ cup	soy sauce	50 mL
¼ cup	olive oil	50 mL
¼ cup	pineapple juice	50 mL
2 tbsp	freshly squeezed lime juice	25 mL
Pinch	ground ginger	Pinch
4	turkey tenderloins (each about 8 oz/250g)	4
½ cup	unsalted butter, melted	125 mL

1. *Prepare the marinade:* In a small bowl, combine soy sauce, oil, pineapple juice, lime juice and ginger.

2. Rinse turkey under cold running water and pat dry. Place turkey in a large sealable plastic bag and pour in marinade. Seal bag, toss to coat and refrigerate for at least 2 hours or for up to 8 hours.

3. Remove turkey from marinade, but do not pat dry. Set aside. Discard marinade.

4. Prepare a fire in your smoker. *(For instructions, see pages 8–11.)*

5. Place turkey directly on the smoker rack, add wood to the coals and close the lid. Smoke at 225°F to 250°F (110°C to 120°C), basting with butter every 30 minutes, for 1½ to 2 hours, or until a meat thermometer inserted in the thickest part of a tenderloin registers 170°F (75°C). Let turkey rest for 15 minutes before serving.

Southwestern-Style Turkey Thighs

When turkey goes on sale, experiment with smoking turkey thighs.

SERVES 4	Recommended wood: peach or other fruit wood

TIPS

You can often find fajita seasoning mix in individual seasoning packages. If you can't find it, use a Southwestern-style seasoning mix that includes ground cumin.

• • •

Look for peach and apricot nectar in bottles or cartons in the fruit juice section of well-stocked supermarkets and health food stores.

• • •

Sometimes, the parts can be more than the whole. Try smoking turkey parts — thighs, legs and breasts — instead of a whole turkey. Breast meat tends to get done faster than the darker leg and thigh meat, and you'll achieve succulent results if you give each part its correct timing.

Marinade

1 cup	barbecue sauce (store-bought or see recipes, pages 50–65)	250 mL
2 tsp	Southwestern-style seasoning mix	10 mL
1 tsp	kosher salt	5 mL
1 tsp	freshly ground black pepper	5 mL
1 tsp	fajita seasoning mix (see tip, at left)	5 mL
4	turkey thighs (each about 8 oz/250 g)	4
	Peach or apricot nectar (see tip, at left) for spraying	

1. *Prepare the marinade:* In a small bowl, combine barbecue sauce, Southwestern-style seasoning mix, salt, pepper and fajita seasoning mix.

2. Rinse turkey under cold running water and pat dry. Place in a large sealable plastic bag and pour in three-quarters of the marinade. Seal bag, toss to coat and refrigerate for 30 minutes. Reserve the remaining marinade in the refrigerator.

3. Remove turkey from marinade, but do not pat dry. Set aside. Discard marinade.

4. Prepare a fire in your smoker. *(For instructions, see pages 8–11.)*

5. Place turkey directly on the smoker rack, add wood to the coals and close the lid. Smoke at 225°F to 250°F (110°C to 120°C), spraying with peach nectar every 30 minutes, for 3 hours. Baste with the reserved marinade and close the lid. Smoke for 1 hour, or until a meat thermometer inserted in the thickest part of a thigh registers 170°F (75°C). Let turkey rest for 15 minutes before serving.

Honey-Chipotle Turkey Drumsticks

This easy dish has a wonderful symphony of flavors, and it's perfect for the beginner practicing barbecue techniques.

SERVES 4	Recommended wood: peach or other fruit wood	

TIPS

You can buy chipotle chili powder at better herb and spice emporiums, by mail order or online (see the Source Guide, page 356).

• • •

You can use either sweetened or unsweetened pineapple juice — it's up to you!

Baste

1	clove garlic, minced	1
3 tbsp	amber liquid honey	45 mL
1 tbsp	tomato sauce	15 mL
1 tbsp	soy sauce	15 mL
½ tsp	ground cinnamon	2 mL
½ tsp	chipotle chili powder (see tip, at left)	2 mL
4	small turkey drumsticks (each about 1 lb/500 g)	4
	Pineapple juice for spraying	

1. *Prepare the baste:* In a small bowl, combine garlic, honey, tomato sauce, soy, cinnamon and chipotle chili powder.

2. Rinse turkey under cold running water and pat dry. Brush with baste. Set aside. Reserve the remaining baste.

3. Prepare a fire in your smoker. *(For instructions, see pages 8–11.)*

4. Place turkey directly on the smoker rack, add wood to the coals and close the lid. Smoke at 225°F to 250°F (110°C to 120°C), basting with the reserved baste and spraying with pineapple juice every 30 minutes, for 3 hours, or until a meat thermometer inserted in the thickest part of a drumstick registers 170°F (75°C). Let turkey rest for 15 minutes before serving.

Smoky, Spicy Turkey Wings

Serve turkey wings hot off the smoker or freeze them to add a smoky depth to a pot of soup.

SERVES 4 TO 6

Recommended wood: pecan

TIPS

Jalapeño pepper powder is available from better spice emporiums or online (see the Source Guide, page 356). If you can't find it, substitute about 1 tsp (5 mL) hot pepper sauce.

• • •

Make sure to trim off the wing tips, as they have very little meat.

• • •

Depending on the size of the plastic bags you use, 12 turkey wings might not fit in one bag (keep in mind that the bag has to be able to seal when you are judging whether you will need a second bag). If that's the case, use two bags and pour half of the marinade into each bag.

• • •

Make ahead

Place smoked wings in freezer bags and store in the freezer for up to 3 months.

Marinade

4	green onions, chopped	4
4	cloves garlic, crushed	4
1 cup	pear juice	250 mL
½ cup	packed brown sugar	125 mL
1 tbsp	olive oil	15 mL
1 tbsp	raspberry vinegar	15 mL
½ tsp	ground allspice	2 mL
½ tsp	jalapeño pepper powder (see tip, at left)	2 mL
	Kosher salt and freshly ground black pepper	
12	turkey wings, tips removed	12

1. *Prepare the marinade:* In a food processor or blender, process green onions, garlic, pear juice, brown sugar, olive oil, vinegar, allspice, jalapeño pepper powder and salt and pepper to taste until well blended.

2. Rinse wings under cold running water and pat dry. Place in a large sealable plastic bag (or bags) and pour in marinade. Seal bag, toss to coat and refrigerate for 3 hours.

3. Remove wings from marinade, but do not pat dry. Set aside. Transfer marinade to a medium saucepan and bring to a boil over medium-high heat; cook for 3 to 5 minutes, or until heated through. Set aside.

4. Prepare a fire in your smoker. *(For instructions, see pages 8–11.)*

5. Place wings directly on the smoker rack, add wood to the coals and close the lid. Smoke at 225°F to 250°F (110°C to 120°C), basting with cooked marinade every 30 minutes, for 2 to 2½ hours, or until juices run clear when turkey is pierced.

Soy & Garlic Duck Breast

If you have any leftovers (fat chance!), make a smoked duck salad by slicing and fanning the duck over an assortment of greens, then drizzling with an Asian-style dressing.

SERVES 6	Recommended wood: a combination of pecan and sugar maple

TIP

The type of duck you choose will determine the timing in this recipe. Smaller Long Island duck breasts will be a juicy medium-rare in 1½ hours; the larger and meatier Muscovy duck breasts will take at least 30 minutes longer. A good instant-read or meat thermometer is your guide. Position one in the thickest part of the largest duck breast. When the internal temperature reaches 150°F (65°C), pull the duck breasts off the smoker to achieve medium-rare. They'll continue to cook for a few moments.

Marinade

3	cloves garlic, minced	3
¾ cup	dry red wine	175 mL
2 tbsp	soy sauce	25 mL
1 tbsp	Worcestershire sauce	15 mL
½ tsp	onion powder	2 mL
½ tsp	dried thyme	2 mL
½ tsp	minced fresh mint	2 mL
½ tsp	dry mustard	2 mL
6	boneless skinless duck breasts (each about 6 oz/175 g)	6
	Butter, melted	

1. *Prepare the marinade:* In a small bowl, combine garlic, wine, soy sauce, Worcestershire sauce, onion powder, thyme, mint and mustard.

2. Rinse duck under cold running water and pat dry. Place in a large sealable plastic bag and pour in marinade. Seal, toss to coat and refrigerate for at least 4 hours or overnight.

3. Remove duck from marinade, but do not pat dry. Set aside. Discard marinade.

4. Prepare a fire in your smoker. *(For instructions, see pages 8–11.)*

5. Place duck directly on the smoker rack, add wood to the coals and close the lid. Smoke at 225°F to 250°F (110°C to 120°C), spraying with margarine every 30 minutes, for 1½ to 2 hours, or until a meat thermometer inserted in the thickest part of a breast registers 150°F (65°C) for medium-rare, or until desired doneness.

Five-Spice Duck Breast

For this recipe, I've doctored up my All-Purpose Barbecue Rub with ground ginger, dry mustard and five-spice powder and added the Apricot Maple Glaze for a truly spectacular result.

SERVES 4	**Recommended wood:** apple or cherry	

TIP

Five-spice powder is available at well-stocked supermarkets, gourmet shops and herb and spice stores.

● ● ●

Variation

The time it takes to smoke duck breasts depends on the type you use. Very small wild duck breasts will take about 1 hour; Long Island duck breasts, as here, will take 1½ hours; large Muscovy duck breasts will take 2 hours or more.

¼ cup	All-Purpose Barbecue Rub (see recipe, page 27)	50 mL
1 tsp	ground ginger	5 mL
1 tsp	dry mustard	5 mL
1 tsp	five-spice powder (see tip, at left)	5 mL
4	boneless Long Island duck breasts (each about 6 oz/175 g)	4
1½ cups	Apricot Maple Glaze (see recipe, page 66)	375 mL

1. In a small bowl, combine barbecue rub, ginger, mustard and five-spice powder.

2. Rinse duck under cold running water and pat dry. With a sharp knife, score the fatty skin of each duck breast with four horizontal slashes. Sprinkle both sides of duck breasts with dry rub. Set aside.

3. Prepare a fire in your smoker. *(For instructions, see pages 8–11.)*

4. Place duck, skin side up, directly on the smoker rack, add wood to the coals and close the lid. Smoke at 225°F to 250°F (110°C to 120°C) for 1 hour. Baste with glaze and close lid. Smoke for 30 minutes, until a meat thermometer inserted in the thickest part of a breast registers 150°F (65°C) for medium-rare, or until desired doneness.

Stuffed Cornish Game Hens with Apricot Mustard Sauce

A luscious way to serve Cornish game hens or pheasant. The Apricot Mustard Sauce stirs together in seconds, and is also delicious with turkey, chicken and pork.

SERVES 4

TIP

Look for apricot syrup where syrups for pancakes or ice creams are shelved at the grocery store.

Recommended wood: a combination of pecan and sugar maple

2	cloves garlic, minced	2
6 tbsp	unsalted butter, at room temperature	90 mL
1/3 cup	crumbled crispy bacon (about 5 strips)	75 mL
2 tbsp	chopped fresh rosemary	25 mL
1 tbsp	minced fresh mint	15 mL
2 tsp	fresh thyme leaves	10 mL
Pinch	kosher salt	Pinch
Pinch	freshly ground black pepper	Pinch
4	Cornish game hens (each about 8 oz/250 g)	4
	Additional kosher salt and freshly ground black pepper	

Apricot Mustard Sauce

3 tbsp	apricot preserves	45 mL
2½ tsp	Dijonnaise (or equal parts Dijon mustard and mayonnaise)	12 mL
2 tsp	apricot syrup (see tip, at left)	10 mL

1. In a bowl, combine garlic, butter, bacon, rosemary, mint, thyme, salt and pepper.

2. Rinse hens inside and out under cold running water and pat dry. Using your fingers, smear some of the butter mixture under the breast skin of each game hen, loosening the skin from meat. Place some of the butter mixture in the cavity of each hen. Sprinkle hens inside and out with salt and pepper. Set aside.

3. *Prepare the sauce:* In a small bowl, combine apricot preserves, Dijonnaise and apricot syrup. Set aside.

4. Prepare a fire in your smoker. *(For instructions, see pages 8–11.)*

5. Place hens, breast side up, directly on the smoker rack, add wood to the coals and close the lid. Smoke at 225°F to 250°F (110°C to 120°C) for 3 hours, or until a meat thermometer inserted in the thickest part of a hen registers 170°F (75°C).

6. Serve hens with sauce on the side.

Cornish Game Hens with Honey Spice Glaze

So simple, yet so good. Serve with a wild rice dish or a smoked potato casserole and a green vegetable.

SERVES 8	**Recommended wood:** a combination of cherry and pecan

TIP

Why amber honey? Most honey you buy at the grocery store, such as clover honey, will be an amber color, which indicates a medium flavor and sweetness. Light honeys made from blossoms have a more flowery, sugary flavor; darker honeys such as sunflower have a deep, almost sulphurous flavor. For barbecuing purposes, stick with amber.

Honey Spice Glaze

2	cloves garlic, minced	2
¾ cup	amber liquid honey	175 mL
½ cup	olive oil	125 mL
¼ cup	rice vinegar	50 mL
¼ cup	dry sherry	50 mL
1 tbsp	ground cumin	15 mL
1 tbsp	minced fresh mint	15 mL
1½ tsp	anise seed	7 mL
¾ tsp	ground allspice	3 mL
8	Cornish game hens (each about 8 oz/250 g)	8
	Kosher salt and freshly ground black pepper	

1. *Prepare the glaze:* In a small saucepan, over medium-low heat, combine garlic, honey, oil, vinegar, sherry, cumin, mint, anise and allspice. Simmer until mixture thickens slightly, about 3 minutes. Remove from heat and let cool.

2. Rinse hens inside and out under cold running water and pat dry. Brush with glaze and sprinkle generously with salt and pepper. Set aside.

3. Prepare a fire in your smoker. *(For instructions, see pages 8–11.)*

4. Place hens, breast side up, directly on the smoker rack, add wood to the coals and close the lid. Smoke at 225°F to 250°F (110°C to 120°C), basting with glaze every 30 minutes, for 3 hours, or until a meat thermometer inserted in the thickest part of a hen registers 170°F (75°C).

5. Serve with any additional glaze on the side.

Pork

BARBECUED PORK IS probably the slow-smoked meat that is best known around the world. From ancient China to modern-day Memphis or Vancouver, you can find great examples of slow-smoked pork in restaurants, barbecue contests and backyards.

Traditionally, tougher cuts such as ribs and boneless pork shoulder blade (also known as pork butt or Boston butt) were given a simple rub of salt and pepper, then slow-smoked over whatever hard wood was plentiful: apple, hickory, oak, pecan or maple. These cuts also benefit from long, slow cooking over fragrant wood, such as traditional hickory, but also apple, cherry, maple, oak and pecan.

Today, you can slow-smoke any cut of pork, and it will taste wonderful. I put everything from pork tenderloin to chops, steak and roast on the smoker to slow-cook to perfection. By using a variety of brines, marinades, dry rubs, bastes and sauces, your pork can taste a little different every time.

In Kansas City, where I live, I can find just about any cut of ribs, from the larger St. Louis–style spareribs (which contain skirt meat) to the smaller and more naturally tender baby backs. Use whatever pork is available in your area — if you tend it carefully on the smoker, you'll have fabulous results.

My preferred woods for pork are fruit woods such as apple and cherry, sometimes with a little hickory or maple thrown in for depth of flavor. Many contest barbecuers use a combination of apple, hickory and oak to slow-smoke pork. But, again, use whatever wood is available in your area, and you'll be happy with the pork you've barbecued.

PORK RECIPES

Ancho-Herb Pork
   Shoulder Blade 226
Pork Shoulder Blade with
   Sassy Raspberry Vinegar
   Baste 227
Pork Shoulder Blade with
   Peachy Barbecue Sauce. . . . 228
Pork Shoulder Blade in
   Pineapple-Soy Marinade . . . 230
Orange & Maple–Glazed
   Pork Shoulder Blade 232
Pecan-Smoked Pork Tenderloin
   with Fresh Garlic &
   Herb Paste 233
Spicy Pork Tenderloin. 234
Pork Tenderloin in White Wine
   Marinade 235
Pork Loin Roast with
   Raspberry-Mustard Glaze. . . 236
Maple-Smoked Pork Loin Roast
   with Cranberry Glaze 237
Pork Loin Roast with
   Cranberry Glaze. 238
Cilantro Coconut Pork Loin
   Roast 240
Peach-Smoked Apricot
   Pork Loin Roast 241
Sugar Maple–Smoked
   Pork Loin Roast in
   Lime Cola Marinade. 242
Apple & Hickory–Smoked
   Pork Loin Roast with
   Ancho-Herb Dry Rub 243
Pork Loin Roast in Maple
   Mustard Brine 244

Pork Loin Roast with Hot
   Pepper Jelly Glaze. 245
Creole-Style Pork Steak 246
Apple-Cranberry Pork Loin
   Chops. 247
Tennessee Bourbon–Brined
   Pork Chops 248
Brandied Pineapple &
   Mango Pork Chops 249
Apple & Cherry–Smoked
   Baby Back Ribs. 250
World Championship Ribs 251
Plum Good Ribs. 252
Low- & Slow-Smoked
   Baby Back Ribs with
   Apricot Glaze. 253
Spicy Cola Baby Back Ribs. 254
New Mexico–Style Ribs 256
Brown Sugar–Rubbed Ribs 257
Apple & Hickory–Smoked Ribs
   in Red Wine Marinade 258
Adam & Eve Ribs 260
Country-Style Ribs with
   Asian Plum Sauce. 261
Rum & Cola Country-Style Ribs. . 262
Orange & Raspberry
   Country-Style Ribs 263
Hoisin Pork Skewers. 264
Italian Antipasto Skewers. 265
Cherry-Smoked Fresh Pork
   Sausage 266
Pineapple-Glazed Hot Italian
   Sausage 268
Italian Sausage & Artichoke
   Soup. 269

Ancho-Herb
Pork Shoulder Blade

Tough, muscular pork shoulder blade becomes fall-apart tender after low and slow cooking on your smoker. It's a rewarding dish that is well worth the 9 to 10 hours of tending your smoker. Just sprinkle the meat with dry rub, spray with pineapple juice throughout the smoking process, and glaze with a little maple syrup and barbecue sauce during the last hour. Mmmmm. This meat makes wonderful pulled pork sandwiches, and many barbecuers smoke several pork butts at a time, then wrap and freeze the meat for later use.

SERVES 10 TO 12	Recommended wood: cherry

TIPS

Your pork shoulder blade is done when you can stick a meat fork into the pork, give it a twist and pull the meat apart easily.

• • •

Place any leftovers in an airtight container and store in the refrigerator for up to 1 week or in the freezer for up to 3 months.

At some North American barbecue contests, judges prefer pork shoulder blade thickly sliced rather than shredded.

1	bone-in pork shoulder blade roast (6 to 8 lbs/3 to 4 kg)	1
3½ cups	Ancho-Herb Dry Rub (see recipe, page 30)	875 mL
1 cup	pineapple juice for spraying	250 mL
½ cup	pure maple syrup	125 mL
2 cups	barbecue sauce (store-bought or see recipes, pages 50–65)	500 mL

1. Trim fat and remove large veins from pork shoulder blade, if necessary. Rinse under cold running water and pat dry. Sprinkle dry rub over the surface of the meat, coating evenly. Let stand at room temperature for about 15 minutes, or until surface is tacky.

2. Meanwhile, prepare a fire in your smoker. *(For instructions, see pages 8–11.)*

3. Place pork directly on the smoker rack, add wood to the coals and close the lid. Smoke at 225°F to 250°F (110°C to 120°C), spraying with pineapple juice every 30 minutes, for 7 hours. Place pork in a disposable aluminum pan. Pour in maple syrup, then 1 cup (250 mL) of the barbecue sauce and cover with aluminum foil. Smoke for 2 hours, or until pork is fork-tender. Let rest, covered, for 20 minutes. Remove from pan and discard juice.

4. To serve, pull pork apart with two forks. If you wish, combine pulled pork with the remaining barbecue sauce, or simply pass the sauce at the table.

Pork Shoulder Blade with Sassy Raspberry Vinegar Baste

Because pork shoulder blade is fatty, you need a tart and tangy basting sauce as a complementary flavor. To get the "bark," or dark exterior on the meat, you need a good dry rub. And to achieve the most tender texture, you need long, slow smoking.

SERVES 10 TO 12

Recommended wood: maple

TIPS

The smaller the smoking chamber on your equipment, the sooner your food will be done. If you're using a kettle grill or a bullet smoker, your pork shoulder blade might be done in 8 hours. If you're using a bigger rig or a genuine smoker, your pork might take 10 hours.

• • •

Place any leftovers in an airtight container and store in the refrigerator for up to 1 week or in the freezer for up to 3 months.

1	boneless pork shoulder blade roast (about 5 to 6 lbs/2.5 to 3 kg), tied	1
1 cup	dry rub, such as Sassy, Spicy Pork Rub (see recipe, page 34)	250 mL

Sassy Raspberry Vinegar Baste

¾ cup	kosher salt	175 mL
¾ cup	granulated sugar	175 mL
¾ cup	raspberry vinegar	175 mL

1. Rinse pork under cold running water and pat dry. Sprinkle dry rub over the surface of the meat, coating evenly. Let stand at room temperature for about 15 minutes, or until surface is tacky.

2. *Prepare the baste:* In a medium bowl, combine salt, sugar, vinegar and ¾ cup (175 mL) water. Set aside.

3. Prepare a fire in your smoker. *(For instructions, see pages 8–11.)*

4. Place pork directly on the smoker rack, add wood to the coals and close the lid. Smoke at 225°F to 250°F (110°C to 120°C), basting every hour, for 8 to 10 hours, or until pork is fork-tender. Let rest for 15 minutes.

5. To serve, cut off strings and pull pork apart with two forks.

Pork Shoulder Blade with Peachy Barbecue Sauce

This recipe uses a blend of maple and hickory for smoking. If you want a sweeter smoke flavor, use more maple; if you want a heavier smoke flavor, use more hickory. Here, you start out at a hotter 350°F (180°C), then reduce the heat and slow-cook to a tender finish.

SERVES 10 TO 12	Recommended wood: a combination of maple and hickory	

TIPS

This recipe uses a dual-temperature method to get more of a "bark," or dark exterior, on the pork. You can also try this method with pork loin roast or beef brisket.

• • •

Place any leftovers in an airtight container and store in the refrigerator for up to 1 week or in the freezer for up to 3 months.

Dry Rub

2 cups	packed brown sugar	500 mL
1/3 cup	kosher salt	75 mL
1/4 cup	sweet Hungarian paprika	50 mL
1/4 cup	chili powder	50 mL
1/4 cup	onion powder	50 mL
1/4 cup	garlic powder	50 mL
1 tsp	dried basil	5 mL
1 tsp	dried thyme	5 mL
1	bone-in pork shoulder blade roast (about 8 lbs/4 kg)	1
2 cups	pineapple juice, divided	500 mL
8 cups	Peachy Barbecue Sauce (see recipe, page 64)	2 L

1. *Prepare the dry rub:* In a medium bowl, combine brown sugar, salt, paprika, chili powder, onion powder, garlic powder, basil and thyme.

2. Trim fat and remove large veins from pork shoulder blade, if necessary. Rinse under cold running water and pat dry. Moisten with 1 cup (250 mL) of the pineapple juice, then liberally apply dry rub to the surface of the meat, coating evenly. Cover and refrigerate for 1½ hours. Remove from refrigerator and let warm to room temperature while smoker is heating.

3. Meanwhile, prepare a fire in your smoker. *(For instructions, see pages 8–11.)*

4. Place pork directly on the smoker rack, add wood to the coals and close the lid. Smoke at 350°F (180°C) for 2 hours, spraying with pineapple juice every hour. Reduce heat to 225°F (110°C) and smoke for 3 hours, spraying with pineapple juice every hour. Place pork in a disposable aluminum pan, pour in 2 cups (500 mL) of the barbecue sauce and cover with aluminum foil. Smoke, lifting the foil and spraying with pineapple juice every hour, for 2 hours, or until pork is fork-tender. Let rest, covered, for 20 minutes. Remove from pan and discard juice.

5. To serve, pull pork apart with two forks. If you wish, combine pulled pork with the remaining barbecue sauce, or simply pass the sauce at the table.

Pork Shoulder Blade in Pineapple-Soy Marinade

Pork shoulder blade, a tough cut, takes its own sweet time to get tender on the smoker, but it's worth every minute. The one-two punch of the Pineapple-Soy Marinade and the Honey & Spice Rub produce a pork butt you just won't be able to stop eating.

SERVES 8	Recommended wood: cherry

TIPS

You can find granulated garlic at well-stocked supermarkets or online (see the Source Guide, page 365).

• • •

I use a large injector to inject marinade deep into the meat. You can buy these at some specialty kitchen shops. You could also use a large veterinary syringe, available at veterinary supply houses, instead of the injector.

• • •

Place any leftovers in an airtight container and store in the refrigerator for up to 1 week or in the freezer for up to 2 months.

Pineapple-Soy Marinade

1 cup	pineapple juice	250 mL
1 cup	soy sauce	250 mL
1 cup	Worcestershire sauce	250 mL
¼ cup	rice vinegar	50 mL
1 tbsp	granulated garlic (see tip, at left)	15 mL
1	boneless pork shoulder blade roast (6 to 8 lbs/3 to 4 kg), tied	1
¾ cup	Honey & Spice Rub (see recipe, page 31)	175 mL
1 cup	clover or other amber liquid honey	250 mL
1 cup	barbecue sauce (store-bought or see recipes, pages 50–65)	250 mL

1. *Prepare the marinade:* In a medium bowl, combine pineapple juice, soy sauce, Worcestershire sauce, vinegar and garlic. Place in a container with a pouring spout.

2. Rinse pork under cold running water and pat dry. Fill a large veterinary syringe or injector (see tip, at left) with some of the marinade and inject the pork. Do this several times, all over the meat, until you have used 1 cup (250 mL) of the marinade. Pour ¼ cup (50 mL) of the marinade over the pork butt to moisten, then liberally apply dry rub to the surface of the meat, coating evenly. Let stand at room temperature for about 15 minutes, or until surface is tacky. Pour the remaining marinade into a spray bottle.

The smaller the smoking chamber on your equipment, the sooner your food will be done. If you're using a kettle grill or a bullet smoker, your pork might be done in 9 hours. If you're using a bigger rig or a genuine smoker, it might take 10 hours.

3. Meanwhile, prepare a fire in your smoker. *(For instructions, see pages 8–11.)*

4. Place pork directly on the smoker rack, add wood to the coals and close the lid. Smoke at 225°F to 250°F (110°C to 120°C), spraying with marinade every 30 minutes, for 7 hours. Place pork in a disposable aluminum pan, pour in honey and cover with aluminum foil. Smoke, spraying with marinade every 30 minutes, for 2 to 3 hours, or until pork is fork-tender. Let rest, covered, for 20 minutes.

5. To serve, cut off strings and pull pork apart with two forks. If you wish, combine pulled pork with barbecue sauce, or simply pass the sauce at the table.

Orange & Maple–Glazed Pork Shoulder Blade

With a tart and tangy glaze, this pork shoulder blade will slow-smoke to pull-apart tenderness. Double the recipe, so you have leftovers to freeze.

SERVES 6	Recommended wood: maple

TIPS

Look for pear nectar in bottles or cartons in the fruit juice section of well-stocked supermarkets and health food stores.

• • •

Place any leftovers in an airtight container and store in the refrigerator for up to 1 week or in the freezer for up to 3 months.

Glaze

2	cloves garlic, minced	2
½ cup	orange marmalade	125 mL
¼ cup	pure maple syrup	50 mL
2 tsp	prepared mustard	10 mL
½ tsp	ground cloves	2 mL
Pinch	cracked black pepper	Pinch
1	boneless pork shoulder blade roast (about 3½ lbs/1.75 kg), tied	1
	Pear nectar (see tip, at left) or apple juice for spraying	

1. *Prepare the glaze:* In a small bowl, combine garlic, marmalade, maple syrup, mustard, cloves and pepper.

2. Rinse pork under cold running water and pat dry. Rub with three-quarters of the glaze and set aside. Reserve the remaining glaze.

3. Prepare a fire in your smoker. *(For instructions, see pages 8–11.)*

4. Place pork directly on the smoker rack, add wood to the coals and close the lid. Smoke at 225°F to 250°F (110°C to 120°C), spraying with pear nectar every hour, for 4 hours. Brush with the reserved glaze, close the lid and smoke for 1 to 2 hours, or until pork is fork-tender. Let rest for 15 minutes before slicing or shredding.

Pecan-Smoked Pork Tenderloin with Fresh Garlic & Herb Paste

Pecan adds a mellow smoke flavor that pairs well with the sweetness the garlic and herb paste gets as it cooks over time. I love smoked pork tenderloin sliced as an appetizer or served as an entrée.

SERVES 6 TO 8	Recommended wood: pecan	

TIPS

The smaller the smoking chamber on your equipment, the sooner your food will be done. If you're using a kettle grill or a bullet smoker, your pork tenderloin might be done about 30 minutes sooner.

• • •

Place any leftovers in an airtight container and store in the refrigerator for up to 1 week or in the freezer for up to 3 months.

| 3 lbs | pork tenderloin (about 3 or 4), trimmed | 1.5 kg |
| ⅓ cup | Fresh Garlic & Herb Paste (see recipe, page 35) | 75 mL |

1. Rinse pork under cold running water and pat dry. Place on a baking sheet and brush with paste. Let stand at room temperature for 30 minutes.

2. Meanwhile, prepare a fire in your smoker. *(For instructions, see pages 8–11.)*

3. Place pork directly on the smoker rack, tucking thin end of tenderloins under, add wood to the coals and close the lid. Smoke at 225°F to 250°F (110°C to 120°C) for 1¾ to 2¼ hours, until a meat thermometer inserted in the thickest part of the pork registers 160°F (70°C) for medium-well, or until desired doneness (see tip, page 236). Let rest for 15 minutes before slicing.

Spicy Pork Tenderloin

If beginning barbecuers can keep the fire at an even temperature and add the right amount of wood at the right time, this recipe will reward them with "advanced" flavor.

SERVES 6 TO 8 | **Recommended wood:** a combination of apple and cherry

TIPS

If you want to use a marinade as a basting sauce too, there are two ways to go about it with food safety in mind. The first is to make a double batch of the marinade. Use one batch to marinate, the other batch to baste. The second is to boil any marinade that has touched raw meat, poultry, fish or shellfish for at least 3 minutes. Let the cooked marinade cool, then use it to baste.

• • •

One medium orange yields ⅓ to ½ cup (75 to 125 mL) juice. If you prefer, you can use store-bought orange juice in this recipe.

• • •

Place any leftovers in an airtight container and store in the refrigerator for up to 1 week or in the freezer for up to 3 months.

Marinade

1	clove garlic, minced	1
½ cup	minced green onions	125 mL
¼ cup	orange juice	50 mL
1 tbsp	minced gingerroot	15 mL
1 tbsp	minced serrano chili pepper	15 mL
1 tbsp	freshly squeezed lime juice	15 mL
1 tbsp	soy sauce	15 mL
1 tsp	ground allspice	5 mL
¼ tsp	ground cinnamon	1 mL
3 lbs	pork tenderloin (3 or 4), trimmed	1.5 kg

1. *Prepare the marinade:* In a small bowl, combine garlic, green onions, orange juice, ginger, serrano pepper, lime juice, soy sauce, allspice and cinnamon.

2. Rinse pork under cold running water and pat dry. Place in a large sealable plastic bag and pour in marinade. Seal bag, toss to coat and refrigerate for 4 hours.

3. Remove pork from marinade, but do not pat dry. Set aside. Transfer marinade to a small saucepan and bring to a boil over high heat; boil for 3 minutes. Remove from heat and let cool.

4. Prepare a fire in your smoker *(see pages 8–11)*.

5. Place pork directly on the smoker rack, tucking thin end of tenderloins under, add wood to the coals and close the lid. Smoke at 225°F to 250°F (110°C to 120°C), basting with cooked marinade every 30 minutes, for 1¾ to 2¼ hours, until a meat thermometer inserted in the thickest part of the pork registers 160°F (70°C) for medium-well, or until desired doneness (see tip, page 236). Let rest for 15 minutes before slicing.

Pork Tenderloin in White Wine Marinade

This sophisticated recipe is well worth serving to dinner guests.

SERVES 6 TO 8	**Recommended wood:** a combination of hickory and cherry

TIPS

For great flavor, I sometimes like to smoke pork tenderloin at a lower temperature, as in this recipe.

• • •

While the pork tenderloin is on the smoker, why not also smoke potatoes or squash to accompany it? See page 112 for instructions on hot-smoking vegetables, but keep in mind that they'll take a bit longer at this lower temperature.

• • •

Place any leftovers in an airtight container and store in the refrigerator for up to 1 week or in the freezer for up to 3 months.

White Wine Marinade

¼ cup	dry white wine	50 mL
1½ tbsp	olive oil	22 mL
½ tsp	minced shallots	2 mL
¼ tsp	freshly squeezed lemon juice	1 mL
¼ tsp	each minced garlic and dried rosemary	1 mL
Pinch	each sugar, celery salt, kosher salt and freshly ground black pepper	Pinch
3 lbs	pork tenderloin (3 or 4), trimmed	1.5 kg
	Pineapple juice for spraying	

1. *Prepare the marinade:* In a small bowl, whisk together wine, oil, shallots, lemon juice, garlic, rosemary, sugar, celery salt, kosher salt and pepper.

2. Rinse pork under cold running water and pat dry. Place in a large sealable plastic bag and pour in marinade. Seal bag, toss to coat and refrigerate for at least 2 hours or overnight.

3. Remove pork from marinade, but do not pat dry. Set aside. Discard marinade.

4. Prepare a fire in your smoker. *(For instructions, see pages 8–11.)*

5. Place pork directly on the smoker rack, tucking thin ends of tenderloins under, add wood to the coals and close the lid. Smoke at 200°F (100°C), spraying with pineapple juice every 30 minutes, for 2 to 2½ hours, or until a meat thermometer inserted in the thickest part of the pork registers 160°F (70°C) for medium-well, or until desired doneness (see tip, page 236). Let rest for 15 minutes before slicing. .

Pork Loin Roast with Raspberry-Mustard Glaze

This roast is delicious with smoked acorn squash. Simply brush squash halves with olive oil and place them cut side up on the smoker to smoke along with the pork loin. Glaze both dishes with the Raspberry-Mustard Glaze during the last hour of smoking.

SERVES 6 TO 8

Recommended wood: apple or cherry

TIPS

If you like your pork well done, smoke until the thermometer registers 170°F (75°C).

Place any leftovers in an airtight container and store in the refrigerator for up to 1 week or in the freezer for up to 3 months.

Be aware that, due to carry-over cooking, the internal temperature of a large pork roast will rise a few degrees between the time it is removed from the smoker and the time it is sliced. To ensure that your roast is not overcooked, remove it from the oven a few minutes before the internal temperature registers the desired degree of doneness.

Raspberry-Mustard Glaze

1 cup	seedless raspberry preserves	250 mL
¼ cup	packed brown sugar	50 mL
¼ cup	pure maple syrup	50 mL
3 tbsp	cider vinegar	45 mL
2 tbsp	dry mustard	25 mL
1	boneless pork loin roast (about 3 lbs/1.5 kg), trimmed	1
¾ cup	Savory Brown Sugar Rub (see recipe, page 28)	175 mL

1. *Prepare the glaze:* In a small bowl, combine raspberry preserves, brown sugar, maple syrup, vinegar and mustard. Set aside.

2. Rinse pork under cold running water and pat dry. Sprinkle with dry rub and let stand at room temperature for about 15 minutes, or until surface is tacky.

3. Meanwhile, prepare a fire in your smoker. *(For instructions, see pages 8–11.)*

4. Place pork directly on the smoker rack, add wood to the coals and close the lid. Smoke at 225°F to 250°F (110°C to 120°C) for 2 hours. Brush with glaze, close the lid and smoke for 1 to 2 hours, or until a meat thermometer inserted in the thickest part of the pork registers 160°F (70°C) for medium-well, or until desired doneness (see tip, at left). Let rest for 15 minutes before slicing. Pass any remaining glaze at the table.

Maple-Smoked Pork Loin Roast with Cranberry Glaze

This dish is scrumptious, especially when there's a little nip in the air. If you're looking for an alternative to Thanksgiving turkey, this is it.

SERVES 12

Recommended wood: a combination of maple and cherry or apple

TIPS

Pass Cherry Chipotle Barbecue Sauce (see recipe, page 63) or Red Currant Sauce (see recipe, page 67) at the table; either would be delicious with this roast.

• • •

Place any leftovers in an airtight container and store in the refrigerator for up to 1 week or in the freezer for up to 3 months.

• • •

Be aware that, due to carry-over cooking, the internal temperature of a large pork roast will rise a few degrees between the time it is removed from the smoker and the time it is sliced. To ensure that your roast is not overcooked, remove it from the oven a few minutes before the internal temperature registers the desired degree of doneness.

1	boneless pork loin roast (about 6 lbs/3 kg)	1
1½ tsp	kosher salt	7 mL
½ tsp	freshly ground black pepper	2 mL

Cranberry Glaze

1	can (16 oz/454 mL) whole-berry cranberry sauce	1
½ tsp	grated orange zest	2 mL
¼ cup	freshly squeezed orange juice	50 mL
¼ cup	dry sherry	50 mL
¼ tsp	ground cinnamon	1 mL

1. Rinse pork under cold running water and pat dry. Season with salt and pepper. Set aside.

2. *Prepare the glaze:* In a medium bowl, combine cranberry sauce, orange zest, orange juice, sherry and cinnamon. Set aside.

3. Prepare a fire in your smoker. *(For instructions, see pages 8–11.)*

4. Place pork directly on the smoker rack, add wood to the coals and close the lid. Smoke at 200°F (100°C), basting with glaze every 30 minutes, for 6 to 7 hours, until a meat thermometer inserted in the thickest part of the pork registers 160°F (70°C) for medium-well, or until desired doneness (see tip, at left). Let rest for 15 minutes before slicing. Pass any remaining glaze at the table.

Pork Loin Roast with Cranberry Glaze

The sweet/tart cranberry in the marinade, spray and glaze gives this dish a festive flavor. The triple cranberry treatment also works well for pork chops, chicken, turkey and game hens.

SERVES 10 TO 12	**Recommended wood:** a combination of apple and peach

TIPS

Why amber honey? Most honey you buy at the grocery store, such as clover honey, will be an amber color, which indicates a medium flavor and sweetness. Light honeys made from blossoms have a more flowery, sugary flavor; darker honeys such as sunflower have a deep, almost sulphurous flavor. For barbecuing purposes, stick with amber.

• • •

Be aware that, due to carry-over cooking, the internal temperature of a large pork roast will rise a few degrees between the time it is removed from the smoker and the time it is sliced. To ensure that your roast is not overcooked, remove it from the oven a few minutes before the internal temperature registers the desired degree of doneness.

Cranberry Vinaigrette

1	can (16 oz/454 mL) whole-berry cranberry sauce	1
1/4 cup	amber liquid honey	50 mL
1/2 tsp	grated orange zest	2 mL
3 tbsp	freshly squeezed orange juice	45 mL
3 tbsp	dry sherry	45 mL
1/4 tsp	ground cinnamon	1 mL
1/4 tsp	kosher salt	1 mL
1	boneless pork loin roast (about 7 lbs/3.5 kg), trimmed	1
	Cranberry juice for spraying	

Cranberry Glaze

1 cup	cranberry juice	250 mL
1/4 cup	granulated sugar	50 mL
1/4 cup	amber liquid honey	50 mL
1/4 cup	lemon-lime soda	50 mL

1. *Prepare the vinaigrette:* In a medium saucepan, combine cranberry sauce, honey, orange zest, orange juice, sherry, cinnamon and salt; bring to a boil over medium heat. Reduce heat and simmer for 10 minutes. Remove from heat and let cool.

TIPS

The smaller the smoking chamber on your equipment, the sooner your food will be done. If you're using a kettle grill or a bullet smoker, your pork loin roast might be done about an hour sooner.

* * *

Place any leftovers in an airtight container and store in the refrigerator for up to 1 week or in the freezer for up to 3 months.

2. Rinse pork under cold running water and pat dry. Place in a large sealable plastic bag and pour in vinaigrette. Seal bag, toss to coat and refrigerate for 4 hours.

3. Remove pork from vinaigrette, but do not pat dry. Set aside. Discard vinaigrette.

4. Prepare a fire in your smoker. *(For instructions, see pages 8–11.)*

5. Place pork directly on the smoker rack, add wood to the coals and close the lid. Smoke at 225°F to 250°F (110°C to 120°C), spraying with cranberry juice every 30 minutes, for 5 to 6 hours.

6. *Meanwhile, prepare the glaze:* In a small bowl, combine cranberry juice, sugar, honey and soda.

7. Brush pork with glaze, close the lid and smoke, brushing with glaze every 30 minutes, for 1 hour, or until a meat thermometer inserted in the thickest part of the pork registers 160°F (70°C) for medium-well, or until desired doneness (see tip, opposite). Let rest for 15 minutes before slicing.

Cilantro Coconut Pork Loin Roast

You can take a basic smoke flavor in just about any direction. In this recipe, spraying with coconut milk adds a Caribbean finish to the dish.

SERVES 6 TO 8	Recommended wood: maple	

3	cloves garlic, minced	3
3	small serrano chili peppers, seeded	3
2 cups	loosely packed fresh cilantro sprigs	500 mL
2 tbsp	granulated sugar	25 mL
1 tsp	ground turmeric	5 mL
1 tsp	curry powder	5 mL
Pinch	kosher salt	Pinch
3 tbsp	fish sauce (see tip, at left)	45 mL
1	boneless pork loin roast (about 3 lbs/1.5 kg)	1
1 cup	coconut milk	250 mL

1. In a food processor, process garlic, serrano peppers, cilantro, sugar, turmeric, curry powder and salt to a coarse paste. Add fish sauce and process until smooth.

2. Rinse pork under cold running water and pat dry. Place in a large, shallow dish and rub with paste, coating evenly. Cover and refrigerate for at least 3 hours or overnight.

3. Prepare a fire in your smoker. *(For instructions, see pages 8–11.)*

4. Place pork directly on the smoker rack, add wood to the coals and close the lid. Smoke at 225°F to 250°F (110°C to 120°C), basting with coconut milk every 30 minutes, for 3 to 4 hours, or until a meat thermometer inserted in the thickest part of the pork registers 160°F (70°C) for medium-well, or until desired doneness (see tip, at left). Let rest for 15 minutes before slicing.

Peach-Smoked Apricot Pork Loin Roast

Pork loin, cooked over low heat and slathered with a yummy apricot sauce, stays moist and juicy on the smoker.

SERVES 6 TO 8	Recommended wood: peach or other fruit wood

TIPS

The smaller the smoking chamber on your equipment, the sooner your food will be done. If you're using a kettle grill or a bullet smoker, your pork loin roast might be done about an hour sooner.

. . .

Place any leftovers in an airtight container and store in the refrigerator for up to 1 week or in the freezer for up to 3 months.

. . .

Be aware that, due to carry-over cooking, the internal temperature of a large pork roast will rise a few degrees between the time it is removed from the smoker and the time it is sliced. To ensure that your roast is not overcooked, remove it from the oven a few minutes before the internal temperature registers the desired degree of doneness.

Sauce

1	can (17 oz/484 g) apricot halves, drained	1
2 tbsp	ketchup	25 mL
2 tbsp	olive oil	25 mL
1 tbsp	freshly squeezed lemon juice	15 mL
½ tsp	kosher salt	2 mL
1	boneless pork loin roast (about 3 lbs/1.5 kg)	1

1. *Prepare the sauce:* In a blender or food processor, process apricots, ketchup, oil, lemon juice and salt until smooth. Set aside.

2. Rinse pork under cold running water and pat dry. Set aside.

3. Prepare a fire in your smoker. *(For instructions, see pages 8–11.)*

4. Place pork directly on the smoker rack, add wood to the coals and close the lid. Smoke at 225°F to 250°F (110°C to 120°C) for 2 hours. Brush with sauce, close the lid and smoke, brushing with sauce every 15 minutes, for 1 to 2 hours, until a meat thermometer inserted in the thickest part of the pork registers 160°F (70°C) for medium–well, or until desired doneness (see tip, at left). Let rest for 15 minutes before slicing. Pass any remaining sauce at the table.

Sugar Maple–Smoked Pork Loin Roast in Lime Cola Marinade

Here's an easy way to smoke a succulent pork loin. While you're at it, smoke the decadent Potato Casserole (see recipe, page 129) to accompany this dish.

SERVES 6 TO 8	**Recommended wood:** sugar maple

TIPS

The smaller the smoking chamber on your equipment, the sooner your food will be done. If you're using a kettle grill or a bullet smoker, your pork loin roast might be done in 3 hours. If you're using a bigger rig or a genuine smoker, your pork might take 4 hours.

• • •

Place any leftovers in an airtight container and store in the refrigerator for up to 1 week or in the freezer for up to 3 months.

| 1 | boneless pork loin roast (about 3 lbs/1.5 kg) | 1 |
| 4 cups | Lime Cola Marinade (see recipe, page 37) | 1 L |

1. Rinse pork under cold running water and pat dry. Place in a large, shallow dish and pour in marinade. Cover and refrigerate for at least 3 hours or overnight.

2. Remove pork from marinade, but do not pat dry. Set aside. Discard marinade.

3. Prepare a fire in your smoker. *(For instructions, see pages 8–11.)*

4. Place pork directly on the smoker rack, add wood to the coals and close the lid. Smoke at 225°F to 250°F (110°C to 120°C) for 3 to 4 hours, or until a meat thermometer inserted in the thickest part of the pork registers 160°F (70°C) for medium-well, or until desired doneness (see tip, page 241). Let rest for 15 minutes before slicing.

Apple & Hickory–Smoked Pork Loin Roast with Ancho-Herb Dry Rub

To echo the "kick" from the ancho chili in the rub, smoke a pan of Horseradish Potatoes (see recipe, page 128) alongside the pork loin.

SERVES 6 TO 8	**Recommended wood:** a combination of apple and hickory

TIPS

The smaller the smoking chamber on your equipment, the sooner your food will be done. If you're using a kettle grill or a bullet smoker, your pork loin roast might be done in 3 hours. If you're using a bigger rig or a genuine smoker, your pork might take 4 hours.

• • •

Place any leftovers in an airtight container and store in the refrigerator for up to 1 week or in the freezer for up to 3 months.

| 1 | boneless pork loin roast (about 3 lbs/1.5 kg) | 1 |
| ½ cup | Ancho-Herb Dry Rub (see recipe, page 30) | 125 mL |

1. Rinse pork under cold running water and pat dry. Sprinkle with dry rub and let stand at room temperature for about 15 minutes, or until surface is tacky.

2. Meanwhile, prepare a fire in your smoker. *(For instructions, see pages 8–11.)*

3. Place pork directly on the smoker rack, add wood to the coals and close the lid. Smoke at 225°F to 250°F (110°C to 120°C) for 3 to 4 hours, or until a meat thermometer inserted in the thickest part of the pork registers 160°F (70°C) for medium–well, or until desired doneness (see tip, page 241). Let rest for 15 minutes before slicing.

Pork Loin Roast in Maple Mustard Brine

Brining helps give the pork loin a buttery texture. To really round out the flavor, glaze with Apricot Maple Glaze during the last hour of smoking.

SERVES 6 TO 8	Recommended wood: maple

TIPS
The smaller the smoking chamber on your equipment, the sooner your food will be done. If you're using a kettle grill or a bullet smoker, your pork loin roast might be done in 3 hours. If you're using a bigger rig or a genuine smoker, your pork might take 4 hours.

• • •

Place any leftovers in an airtight container and store in the refrigerator for up to 1 week or in the freezer for up to 3 months.

1	boneless pork loin roast (about 3 lbs/1.5 kg)	1
8 cups	Maple Mustard Brine (see recipe, page 21)	2 L
1½ cups	Apricot Maple Glaze (see recipe, page 66)	375 mL

1. Rinse pork under cold running water and pat dry. Place in a deep pan and pour in brine until pork is covered (add water, if necessary). Cover and refrigerate for at least 3 hours or overnight.

2. Remove pork from brine, rinse under cold running water and pat dry. Set aside. Discard brine.

3. Prepare a fire in your smoker. *(For instructions, see pages 8–11.)*

4. Place pork directly on the smoker rack, add wood to the coals and close the lid. Smoke at 225°F to 250°F (110°C to 120°C) for 2 hours. Brush with glaze, close the lid and smoke for 1 to 2 hours, or until a meat thermometer inserted in the thickest part of the pork registers 160°F (70°C) for medium-well, or until desired doneness (see tip, page 241). Let rest for 15 minutes before slicing. Pass any remaining glaze at the table.

Pork Loin Roast with Hot Pepper Jelly Glaze

A lusciously easy way to serve a traditional pork roast, but with a smoky twist. If you like, smoke a few potatoes along with the roast (see page 112 for instructions), then mash them for a deliciously comforting side dish.

SERVES 4 TO 6	Recommended wood: hickory	

TIPS

The smaller the smoking chamber on your equipment, the sooner your food will be done. If you're using a kettle grill or a bullet smoker, your pork loin roast might be done in 3 hours. If you're using a bigger rig or a genuine smoker, your pork might take 4 hours.

• • •

Place any leftovers in an airtight container and store in the refrigerator for up to 1 week or in the freezer for up to 3 months.

1	boneless pork loin roast (about 2 lbs/1 kg)	1
4 cups	apple juice	1 L
½ cup	Brown Sugar Rib Rub (see recipe, page 33)	125 mL
1 cup	hot pepper jelly	250 mL
	Additional apple juice for spraying	

1. Rinse pork under cold running water and pat dry. Place in a large sealable plastic bag and pour in apple juice. Seal bag and refrigerate for at least 8 hours or for up to 12 hours.

2. Remove pork from marinade and pat dry. Discard marinade. Sprinkle dry rub over the surface of the meat, coating evenly. Set aside.

3. Prepare a fire in your smoker. *(For instructions, see pages 8–11.)*

4. Meanwhile, in a small saucepan, melt hot pepper jelly over medium-low heat. Keep warm by the smoker.

5. Place pork directly on the smoker rack, add wood to the coals and close the lid. Smoke at 225°F to 250°F (110°C to 120°C), spraying with apple juice every 30 minutes, for 2 hours. Brush with hot pepper jelly, close the lid and smoke, spraying with apple juice every 30 minutes, for 1 to 1½ hours, or until a meat thermometer inserted in the thickest part of the pork registers 160°F (70°C) for medium-well, or until desired doneness (see tip, page 241). Let rest for 15 minutes before slicing.

Creole-Style Pork Steak

Barbecued pork steak is a big favorite with folks in the St. Louis, Missouri, area, nestled right along the Mississippi River. Riverboat traffic to and from New Orleans enhanced a French flair in this city, so a Creole seasoning with pork steak is not only delicious, but authentic, too.

SERVES 4 TO 6	Recommended wood: peach or other fruit wood

TIPS

Creole-style seasoning is a dry blend of sweet herbs and hot and spicy chili peppers.

• • •

Place any leftovers in an airtight container and store in the refrigerator for up to 1 week or in the freezer for up to 3 months.

Marinade

1 cup	dry sherry	250 mL
½ cup	soy sauce	125 mL
¼ cup	packed brown sugar	50 mL
2 tbsp	Creole-style seasoning (see tip, at left)	25 mL
2 tbsp	minced garlic	25 mL
2 tbsp	tomato purée	25 mL
1 tsp	freshly ground black pepper	5 mL
2 lbs	pork leg or shoulder steak	1 kg

1. *Prepare the marinade:* In a medium bowl, combine sherry, soy sauce, brown sugar, Creole-style seasoning, garlic, tomato purée and pepper.

2. Rinse pork under cold running water and pat dry. Place in a large, sealable plastic bag and pour in marinade. Seal bag, toss to coat and refrigerate for at least 4 hours or for up to 24 hours.

3. Remove pork from marinade and pat dry. Set aside. Transfer marinade to a small saucepan and bring to a boil over high heat. Reduce heat to medium-low and simmer until slightly thickened, about 15 minutes. Remove from heat and set aside.

4. Meanwhile, prepare a fire in your smoker. *(For instructions, see pages 8–11.)*

5. Place pork directly on the smoker rack, add wood to the coals and close the lid. Smoke at 225°F to 250°F (110°C to 120°C) for 1 hour, or until juices run clear when pork is pierced with a knife. Let rest for 10 minutes, then slice thinly across the grain. Pass the cooked marinade at the table.

Apple-Cranberry Pork Loin Chops

A great dish for fall. The pork chops take on a rosy appearance, and the apples take on the flavor of the autumn hearth to make a smoky apple glaze — a perfect combination.

SERVES 6	Recommended wood: apple	

1 cup	cranberry–apple juice	250 mL
½ cup	pure maple syrup	125 mL
2 tbsp	raspberry vinegar	25 mL
6	bone-in pork rib or center loin chops, about 1 inch (2.5 cm) thick	6
2	red apples, such as Jonathan or Red Delicious	2

1. In a small bowl, combine cranberry–apple juice, maple syrup and vinegar.

2. Rinse pork under cold running water and pat dry. Place in a large sealable plastic bag and pour in marinade. Seal bag, toss to coat and refrigerate for 8 hours or overnight.

3. Remove pork from marinade, but do not pat dry. Set aside. Transfer marinade to a skillet and set aside.

4. Prepare a fire in your smoker. *(For instructions, see pages 8–11.)*

5. Place pork directly on the smoker rack, add wood to the coals and close the lid. Smoke at 225°F to 250°F (110°C to 120°C) for 2 hours, until juices run clear when pork is pierced with a knife.

6. During the last hour of smoking, cut each apple into 3 wedges. Place in a disposable aluminum pan, place on the smoker rack and smoke for 20 minutes. Transfer apples to the marinade in the skillet; bring to a boil over medium heat. Cook, uncovered, stirring occasionally, until apples are tender and liquid is thick and syrupy, about 10 minutes. Spoon over smoked pork chops.

Tennessee Bourbon–Brined Pork Chops

Pork today is much less fatty than that of a generation ago, so brining is one way to add extra moisture to the meat. The bourbon adds a sweet, smoky flavor. If you like, serve the chops with Bourbon Barbecue Sauce (page 52).

SERVES 8

Recommended wood: apple

8	bone-in pork center loin chops, about 1 inch (2.5 cm) thick	8
1½ cups	Tennessee Bourbon Brine (see recipe, page 23)	375 mL

TIPS

The smaller the smoking chamber on your equipment, the sooner your food will be done. If you're using a kettle grill or a bullet smoker, your pork chops might be done in 1 hour. If you're using a bigger rig or a genuine smoker, your pork might take 2 hours.

＊　＊　＊

Place any leftovers in an airtight container and store in the refrigerator for up to 1 week or in the freezer for up to 3 months.

1. Rinse pork under cold running water and pat dry. Place in a deep pan and pour in brine (brine may not completely cover pork). Cover and refrigerate, turning once, for 3 hours.

2. Remove pork from brine, rinse under cold running water and pat dry. Set aside. Discard brine.

3. Prepare a fire in your smoker. *(For instructions, see pages 8–11.)*

4. Place pork directly on the smoker rack, add wood to the coals and close the lid. Smoke at 225°F to 250°F (110°C to 120°C) for about 2 hours, until juices run clear when pork is pierced with a knife.

Brandied Pineapple & Mango Pork Chops

With a marinade of brandy, pineapple and mango juices, how could this pork be anything but delicious?

SERVES 6

Recommended wood: grape or other fruit wood, such as apple or cherry

1	clove garlic, minced	1
2 cups	pineapple juice	500 mL
¼ cup	kosher salt	50 mL
¼ cup	packed brown sugar	50 mL
¼ cup	mango juice	50 mL
¼ cup	brandy	50 mL
1 tbsp	chili powder	15 mL
1 tbsp	dried sage	15 mL
6	bone-in pork center loin chops, about 2 inches (5 cm) thick	6

TIPS

Throw a few sweet potatoes, pricked all over with a fork, on the smoker with the pork chops. When the sweet potatoes feel soft when you squeeze them, they're done. Skin, then mash them with butter, salt and pepper and serve alongside the pork chops.

• • •

Place any leftovers in an airtight container and store in the refrigerator for up to 1 week or in the freezer for up to 3 months.

1. In a medium bowl, combine garlic, pineapple juice, salt, brown sugar, mango juice, brandy, chili powder and sage.

2. Rinse pork under cold running water and pat dry. Place in a large sealable plastic bag and pour in half of the marinade. Seal bag, toss to coat and refrigerate for 3 hours. Reserve the remaining marinade in the refrigerator.

3. Remove pork from marinade, but do not pat dry. Set aside. Discard marinade.

4. Prepare a fire in your smoker. *(For instructions, see pages 8–11.)*

5. Place pork directly on the smoker rack, add wood to the coals and close the lid. Smoke at 225°F to 250°F (110°C to 120°C), basting every 30 minutes with reserved marinade, for 3 to 4 hours, until a meat thermometer inserted in the thickest part of the pork registers 160°F (70°C) for medium-well, or until desired doneness (see tip, page 241).

Apple & Cherry–Smoked Baby Back Ribs

This is a great recipe for the beginner, although the flavor is certainly not elementary. Baby backs, cut from each side of the spine, are naturally tender; thus, it's easy to get a tender result.

SERVES 4	**Recommended wood:** a combination of apple and cherry

<table>
<tr><td>3 lbs</td><td>baby back ribs, trimmed and membrane removed (see tip, opposite)</td><td>1.5 kg</td></tr>
<tr><td>3 cups</td><td>apple juice</td><td>750 mL</td></tr>
<tr><td>2 tsp</td><td>kosher salt</td><td>10 mL</td></tr>
<tr><td>2 tsp</td><td>coarsely ground black pepper</td><td>10 mL</td></tr>
<tr><td></td><td>Additional apple juice for spraying</td><td></td></tr>
</table>

TIPS

Depending on the size of the plastic bags you use, 3 lbs (1.5 kg) of ribs might not fit in one bag (keep in mind that the bag has to be able to seal when you are judging whether you will need more than one). If that's the case, use as many bags as you need, and divide the apple juice evenly among them.

• • •

Serve with either Apple Ancho Barbecue Sauce (see recipe, page 62) or Cherry Chipotle Barbecue Sauce (see recipe, page 63) — or any of the other barbecue sauces in this book — for a lip-smackin' finish.

1. Rinse ribs under cold running water and pat dry. Place in a large sealable plastic bag (or bags) and pour in apple juice. Seal bag and refrigerate for 2 hours.

2. Remove ribs from apple juice, but do not pat dry. Discard apple juice. Sprinkle both sides of ribs with salt and pepper, coating evenly. Set aside.

3. Prepare a fire in your smoker. *(For instructions, see pages 8–11.)*

4. Place ribs, meaty side up, directly on the smoker rack, add wood to the coals and close the lid. Smoke at 225°F to 250°F (100°C to 120°C), spraying with apple juice every 30 minutes, for 4 to 6 hours, or until meat pulls away from the ends of the bones.

World Championship Ribs

This recipe includes every technique I can think of to make the best ribs on the planet, and includes the rub I used to win a world championship in Limerick, Ireland. Try them and judge for yourself.

SERVES 6 TO 8	Recommended wood: a combination of apple, oak and hickory	

6 lbs	baby back ribs, trimmed and membrane removed	3 kg
4 cups	apple juice	1 L
5 cups	Flower of the Flames Rib Rub (see recipe, page 32)	1.25 L
	Additional apple juice for spraying	
1	bottle (8 oz/250 mL) squeezable margarine	1
1	jar (8 oz/250 mL) amber liquid honey	1
1 cup	Flower of the Flames Raspberry Barbecue Sauce (see recipe, page 50)	250 mL

TIPS

To remove the membrane, turn ribs over and place a thin-bladed knife under the thin skin of the first ribs at either end, lifting up on the skin. Use a paper towel or needle-nose pliers to grip the skin and pull it from the ribs. Also, be sure to remove all unwanted fat.

• • •

Depending on the size of the plastic bags you use, 6 lbs (3 kg) of ribs might not fit in one bag (keep in mind that the bag has to be able to seal when you are judging whether you will need more than one). If that's the case, use as many bags as you need and divide the apple juice evenly among them.

1. Rinse ribs under cold running water and pat dry. Place in a large sealable plastic bag (or bags) and pour in apple juice. Seal bag and refrigerate for at least 8 hours or overnight.

2. Remove ribs from apple juice and pat dry. Discard apple juice. Place ribs on baking sheets and sprinkle both sides with dry rub, coating evenly. Let stand at room temperature for about 15 minutes, or until surface is tacky.

3. Meanwhile, prepare a fire in your smoker. *(For instructions, see pages 8–11.)*

4. Place ribs, meaty side up, directly on the smoker rack, add wood to the coals and close the lid. Smoke at 225°F to 250°F (110°C to 120°C), spraying with apple juice every 30 minutes, for 2½ to 3 hours. Squeeze margarine over ribs, close the lid and smoke for 30 minutes. Brush with honey, close the lid and smoke for 30 minutes. Brush with barbecue sauce, close the lid and smoke for 30 to 60 minutes, or until meat pulls away from the ends of the bones.

Plum Good Ribs

The title says it all. Bottled Chinese plum sauce provides the key flavor.

SERVES 4	Recommended wood: a combination of apple and maple

TIPS

To remove the membrane, turn ribs over and place a thin-bladed knife under the thin skin of the first ribs at either end, lifting up on the skin. Use a paper towel or needle-nose pliers to grip the skin and pull it from the ribs. Also, be sure to remove all unwanted fat.

• • •

Depending on the size of the plastic bags you use, 3½ lbs (1.75 kg) of ribs might not fit in one bag (keep in mind that the bag has to be able to seal when you are judging whether you will need more than one). If that's the case, use as many bags as you need and divide the marinade evenly among them.

Marinade

2	cloves garlic, crushed	2
⅓ cup	bottled plum sauce	75 mL
2 tbsp	grated gingerroot	25 mL
2 tbsp	orange juice	25 mL
1 tbsp	barbecue sauce (store-bought or see recipes, pages 50–65)	15 mL
1 tbsp	olive oil	15 mL
1¼ tsp	ground cumin	6 mL
3½ lbs	baby back pork ribs, trimmed and membrane removed	1.75 kg
	Apple juice for spraying	

1. *Prepare the marinade:* In a small bowl, combine garlic, plum sauce, ginger, orange juice, barbecue sauce, oil and cumin.

2. Rinse ribs under cold running water and pat dry. Place in a large sealable plastic bag (or bags) and pour in marinade. Cover and refrigerate for at least 1 hour or overnight.

3. Remove ribs from marinade, but do not pat dry. Set aside. Discard marinade.

4. Prepare a fire in your smoker. *(For instructions, see pages 8–11.)*

5. Place ribs, meaty side up, directly on the smoker rack, add wood to the coals and close the lid. Smoke at 225°F to 250°F (110°C to 120°C), spraying with apple juice every 30 minutes, for 4 to 5 hours, or until meat pulls away from the ends of the bones.

Low- & Slow-Smoked Baby Back Ribs with Apricot Glaze

When you have a little more time, try these ribs, smoked at a low 200°F (100°C), for a sweet and very tender finish.

SERVES 8	Recommended wood: a combination of apple and cherry

TIPS

To remove the membrane, turn ribs over and place a thin-bladed knife under the thin skin of the first ribs at either end, lifting up on the skin. Use a paper towel or needle-nose pliers to grip the skin and pull it from the ribs. Also, be sure to remove all unwanted fat.

• • •

Look for apricot syrup where syrups for pancakes or ice creams are shelved at the grocery store.

• • •

The smaller the smoking chamber on your equipment, the sooner your food will be done. If you're using a kettle grill or a bullet smoker, your ribs might be done in 5 hours. If you're using a bigger rig or a genuine smoker, they might take 6 hours.

8 lbs	baby back ribs, trimmed and membrane removed	4 kg
⅔ cup	Sassy, Spicy Pork Rub (see recipe, page 34)	150 mL

Apricot Glaze

1 cup	apricot preserves	250 mL
¼ cup	apricot syrup (see tip, at left)	50 mL
	Apple juice for spraying	

1. Rinse ribs under cold running water and pat dry. Sprinkle with dry rub and let stand at room temperature for 30 minutes.

2. *Prepare the glaze:* In a small saucepan, over medium heat, stir together apricot preserves and apricot syrup until well blended. Keep warm by the smoker.

3. Prepare a fire in your smoker. *(For instructions, see pages 8–11.)*

4. Place ribs, meaty side up, directly on the smoker rack, add wood to the coals and close the lid. Smoke at 200°F (100°C), spraying with apple juice every 30 minutes, for 3 hours. Brush with glaze, close the lid and smoke, brushing with glaze every 30 minutes, for 2 to 3 hours, or until meat pulls away from the ends of the bones.

Spicy Cola Baby Back Ribs

With cola as a marinade and a spicy tomato barbecue sauce as a baste, these ribs turn out tender, smoky and sweet.

| SERVES 6 TO 8 | **Recommended wood:** a combination of apple and cherry |

TIPS

To remove the membrane, turn ribs over and place a thin-bladed knife under the thin skin of the first ribs at either end, lifting up on the skin. Use a paper towel or needle-nose pliers to grip the skin and pull it from the ribs. Also, be sure to remove all unwanted fat.

* * *

You can buy ancho chili powder at better herb and spice emporiums, by mail order or online (see the Source Guide, page 356).

* * *

Depending on the size of the plastic bags you use, 6 lbs (3 kg) of ribs might not fit in one bag (keep in mind that the bag has to be able to seal when you are judging whether you will need more than one). If that's the case, use as many bags as you need and divide the cola evenly among them.

| 6 lbs | baby back ribs, trimmed and membrane removed | 3 kg |
| 1 | can (12 oz/355 mL) cola | 1 |

Barbecue Sauce

2	cloves garlic, minced	2
1	onion, minced	1
1 cup	packed dark brown sugar	250 mL
1 cup	ketchup	250 mL
1½ tsp	freshly squeezed lemon juice	7 mL
1 tsp	ancho chili powder (see tip, at left)	5 mL
½ tsp	hot pepper sauce	2 mL

1. Rinse ribs under cold running water and pat dry. Place in a large sealable plastic bag (or bags) and pour in cola. Cover and refrigerate for 2 hours.

2. *Meanwhile, prepare the barbecue sauce:* In a medium bowl, combine garlic, onion, 2 cups (500 mL) water, brown sugar, ketchup, lemon juice, chili powder and hot pepper sauce. Set aside.

3. Remove ribs from cola, but do not pat dry. Set aside. Discard cola.

TIP

The smaller the smoking chamber on your equipment, the sooner your food will be done. If you're using a kettle grill or a bullet smoker, your ribs might be done in 4 hours. If you're using a bigger rig or a genuine smoker, they might take 5 hours.

4. Prepare a fire in your smoker. *(For instructions, see pages 8–11.)*

5. Place ribs, meaty side up, directly on the smoker rack, add wood to the coals and close the lid. Smoke at 225°F to 250°F (110°C to 120°C) for 3½ hours. Brush ribs with sauce and wrap each rack of ribs in a sheet of heavy-duty aluminum foil. Smoke without adding more wood for 30 to 90 minutes, or until meat pulls away from the ends of the bones. Let rest for 15 minutes before cutting.

Ribbers and Ribfests: Throughout the summer, especially in communities around the Great Lakes area, barbecuers, or "ribbers," who are passionate about slow-smoked ribs get together to compete and have fun. A ribfest is just that: a competition and a celebration of barbecued pork ribs of all kinds. The proceeds usually benefit a charitable cause.

New Mexico–Style Ribs

Because the dry rub is somewhat bitter and the mesquite used for smoking is very strong, you need a sweet sauce to finish these ribs. Serve them with either Apple Ancho Barbecue Sauce (see recipe, page 62) or Cherry Chipotle Barbecue Sauce (see recipe, page 63).

Recommended wood: a combination of mesquite and a fruit wood, such as apple or cherry

TIPS

To remove the membrane, turn ribs over and place a thin-bladed knife under the thin skin of the first ribs at either end, lifting up on the skin. Use a paper towel or needle-nose pliers to grip the skin and pull it from the ribs. Also, be sure to remove all unwanted fat.

• • •

Depending on the size of the plastic bags you use, 3 lbs (1.5 kg) of ribs might not fit in one bag (keep in mind that the bag has to be able to seal when you are judging whether you will need more than one). If that's the case, use as many bags as you need and divide the apple juice evenly among them.

3 lbs	baby back ribs, trimmed and membrane removed	1.5 kg
3 cups	apple juice	750 mL
½ cup	New Mexico–Style Rub (see recipe, page 27)	125 mL
	Additional apple juice for spraying	

1. Rinse ribs under cold running water and pat dry. Place in a large sealable plastic bag (or bags) and pour in apple juice. Seal bag and refrigerate for 2 hours.

2. Remove ribs from apple juice, but do not pat dry. Discard apple juice. Sprinkle both sides of ribs with dry rub, coating evenly. Set aside.

3. Prepare a fire in your smoker. *(For instructions, see pages 8–11.)*

4. Place ribs, meaty side up, directly on the smoker rack, add wood to the coals and close the lid. Smoke at 225°F to 250°F (100°C to 120°C), spraying with apple juice every 30 minutes, for 4 to 6 hours, or until meat pulls away from the ends of the bones.

Brown Sugar–Rubbed Ribs

This recipe makes "dry" (unsauced) Memphis-style ribs, but if you want to glaze them with sauce during the last hour, go right ahead. You can also serve the sauce at the table. I recommend Memphis-Style Barbecue Sauce (see recipe, page 58) as the accompaniment.

SERVES 6 TO 8	Recommended wood: hickory	

TIPS

To remove the membrane, turn ribs over and place a thin-bladed knife under the thin skin of the first ribs at either end, lifting up on the skin. Use a paper towel or needle-nose pliers to grip the skin and pull it from the ribs. Also, be sure to remove all unwanted fat.

• • •

Depending on the size of the plastic bags you use, 6 lbs (3 kg) of ribs might not fit in one bag (keep in mind that the bag has to be able to seal when you are judging whether you will need more than one). If that's the case, use as many bags as you need and divide the apple juice evenly among them.

6 lbs	baby back ribs, trimmed and membrane removed	3 kg
4 cups	apple juice	1 L
3½ cups	Brown Sugar Rib Rub (see recipe, page 33)	875 mL
	Additional apple juice for spraying	

1. Rinse ribs under cold running water and pat dry. Place in a large sealable plastic bag (or bags) and pour in apple juice. Seal bag and refrigerate for at least 8 hours or overnight.

2. Remove ribs from marinade and pat dry. Discard marinade. Sprinkle both sides of ribs with dry rub, coating evenly. Let stand at room temperature for about 15 minutes, or until surface is tacky.

3. Meanwhile, prepare a fire in your smoker. *(For instructions, see pages 8–11.)*

4. Place ribs, meaty side up, directly on the smoker rack, add wood to the coals and close the lid. Smoke at 225°F to 250°F (110°C to 120°C), spraying with apple juice every 30 minutes, for 4 to 5 hours, or until meat pulls away from the ends of the bones.

Apple & Hickory–Smoked Ribs in Red Wine Marinade

Marinated in red wine, brushed with melted butter and sweetened with maple syrup, these ribs are luscious from first bite to last.

SERVES 6 TO 8	**Recommended wood:** a combination of apple and hickory

TIPS

Jalapeño pepper powder is available from better spice emporiums or online (see the Source Guide, page 356). If you can't find it, substitute about 2 tsp (10 mL) hot pepper sauce.

• • •

Spareribs (side ribs), which are a larger cut taken from the sides of the hog, take longer to cook and get more tender than baby back ribs, which come from either side of the backbone.

Red Wine Marinade

2	cloves garlic, minced	2
1 cup	dry red wine, such as burgundy	250 mL
½ cup	packed brown sugar	125 mL
¼ cup	granulated sugar	50 mL
¼ cup	Worcestershire sauce	50 mL
3 tbsp	kosher salt	45 mL
1 tbsp	chili powder	15 mL
1 tsp	jalapeño pepper powder (see tip, at left)	5 mL
8 lbs	St. Louis–style pork spare (side) ribs, trimmed and membrane removed	4 kg
	Apple juice for spraying	
	Melted butter and pure maple syrup for brushing	

1. *Prepare the marinade:* In a medium bowl, combine garlic, wine, brown sugar, granulated sugar, Worcestershire sauce, salt, chili powder and jalapeño pepper powder.

2. Rinse ribs under cold running water and pat dry. Place in a large sealable plastic bag (or bags) and pour in marinade over them. Seal bag, toss to coat and refrigerate for at least 2 hours or for up to 3 hours.

TIPS

Depending on the size of the plastic bags you use, 8 lbs (4 kg) of ribs might not fit in one bag (keep in mind that the bag has to be able to seal when you are judging whether you will need more than one). If that's the case, use as many bags as you need, and divide the marinade evenly among them.

• • •

The smaller the smoking chamber on your equipment, the sooner your food will be done. If you're using a kettle grill or a bullet smoker, your spareribs might be done in 4 hours. If you're using a bigger rig or a genuine smoker, your ribs might take 5 to 6 hours.

3. Remove ribs from marinade, but do not pat dry. Set aside. Discard marinade.

4. Prepare a fire in your smoker. *(For instructions, see pages 8–11.)*

5. Place ribs, meaty side up, directly on the smoker rack, add wood to the coals and close the lid. Smoke at 225°F to 250°F (110°C to 120°C), spraying with apple juice every 30 minutes, for 2 hours. Brush with butter and maple syrup, close the lid and smoke for 2 to 4 hours, or until meat pulls away from the ends of the bones.

Adam & Eve Ribs

Apple juice makes all the difference in this beginner's recipe. The flavor will transport you back to the Garden — or at least make your backyard seem a more delicious place to be. You also get to practice all the steps to perfect smoked ribs, from marinating to glazing. Marinating the ribs before smoking adds a sweet flavor and helps keep them moist during cooking. Glazing with barbecue sauce at the end gives the ribs a sheen that's attractive to your friends and family, as well as barbecue contest judges.

SERVES 4 TO 6	Recommended wood: a combination of apple and cherry

Recommended wood: a combination of apple and cherry

6 lbs	St. Louis–style pork spare (side) ribs, trimmed and membrane removed	3 kg
4 cups	apple juice	1 L
¾ cup	Flower of the Flames Rib Rub (see recipe, page 32)	175 mL
	Apple juice for spraying	
	Clover or other amber liquid honey for brushing	
	Flower of the Flames Raspberry Barbecue Sauce (page 50) for glazing	

TIPS

St. Louis–style ribs have the chine bone and brisket flap trimmed off.

• • •

Depending on the size of the plastic bags you use, 6 lbs (3 kg) of ribs might not fit in one bag (keep in mind that the bag has to be able to seal when you are judging whether you will need more than one). If that's the case, use as many bags as you need and divide the apple juice evenly among them.

• • •

Keep glazes and sauces warm in a disposable aluminum pan or an old saucepan set near the smoker. They brush on better when they're warm.

• • •

Serve with the sauce of your choice or more Flower of the Flames Raspberry Barbecue Sauce.

1. Rinse ribs under cold running water and pat dry. Place in a large sealable plastic bag (or bags) and pour in apple juice. Seal bag and refrigerate for at least 4 hours or overnight.

2. Remove ribs from apple juice, but do not pat dry. Discard apple juice. Sprinkle both sides of ribs with dry rub, coating evenly. Let stand at room temperature for about 15 minutes, or until surface is tacky.

3. Meanwhile, prepare a fire in your smoker. *(For instructions, see pages 8–11.)*

4. Place ribs, meaty side up, directly on the smoker rack, add wood to the coals and close the lid. Smoke at 225°F to 250°F (110°C to 120°C), spraying with apple juice every 30 minutes, for 4 to 6 hours, or until meat is just starting to pull away from the ends of the bones. Brush with honey, close the lid and smoke for 30 minutes. Brush with barbecue sauce, close the lid and smoke for 30 minutes, or until meat pulls away from the ends of the bones.

Country-Style Ribs with Asian Plum Sauce

Country-style ribs are not true ribs at all, but "fingers" of meat cut from the pork loin. When they're slow-cooked, however, they're just as tender and tasty as baby backs, especially when sauced with a sweet mixture at the end.

SERVES 8 TO 10	**Recommended wood:** apple or other fruit wood	

3 to 4 lbs	country-style pork ribs	1.5 to 2 kg
1¾ cups	Easy Asian Marinade (see recipe, page 40)	425 mL

Asian Plum Sauce

1 cup	plum jam	250 mL
¼ cup	minced green onion	50 mL
¼ cup	freshly squeezed lemon juice	50 mL
2 tbsp	hoisin sauce	25 mL
1 tbsp	grated gingerroot	15 mL
1 tsp	dry mustard	5 mL

TIPS

Depending on the size of the plastic bags you use, 3 to 4 lbs (1.5 to 2 kg) of ribs might not fit in one bag (keep in mind that the bag has to be able to seal when you are judging whether you will need more than one). If that's the case, use as many bags as you need and divide the marinade evenly among them.

• • •

Make an easy Asian-style barbecue sauce to serve with these ribs or other smoked dishes that start with an Asian-style marinade: To 1 cup (250 mL) of your favorite tomato-based barbecue sauce, stir in ½ cup (125 mL) plum jelly or jam, 1 tbsp (15 mL) soy sauce and 2 tsp (10 mL) toasted sesame oil.

1. Rinse ribs under cold running water and pat dry. Place in a large sealable plastic bag (or bags) and pour in marinade. Seal bag, toss to coat and refrigerate for at least 8 hours or for up to 12 hours.

2. Remove ribs from marinade and pat dry. Set aside. Discard marinade.

3. Prepare a fire in your smoker. *(For instructions, see pages 8–11.)*

4. *Meanwhile, prepare the plum sauce:* In a saucepan, over medium-low heat, combine plum jam, green onion, lemon juice, hoisin sauce, ginger and mustard. Cook, stirring, until well blended and heated through. Keep warm by the smoker.

5. Place ribs, meaty side up, directly on the smoker rack, add wood to the coals and close the lid. Smoke at 225°F to 250°F (110°C to 120°C) for 2 hours. Brush with plum sauce, close the lid and smoke for 1 to 2 hours, or until fork-tender.

Rum & Cola Ribs

These sweet, sticky "ribs" cut from the tough pork shoulder are made tender by slow smoking.

Recommended wood: peach or other fruit wood, such as apple or cherry

TIPS

If you can't find lime-flavored cola, simply add a little lime juice and zest to regular cola, to taste.

• • •

Jalapeño pepper powder is available from better spice emporiums or online (see the Source Guide, page 356).

• • •

Depending on the size of the plastic bags you use, 4 lbs (2 kg) of ribs might not fit in one bag (keep in mind that the bag has to be able to seal when you are judging whether you will need more than one). If that's the case, use as many bags as you need and divide the marinade evenly among them.

Marinade

3	green onions, finely chopped	3
2	cloves garlic, minced	2
2 cups	lime-flavored cola	500 mL
¼ cup	amber liquid honey	50 mL
2 tbsp	rum	25 mL
2 tbsp	olive oil	25 mL
4 lbs	country-style pork ribs	2 kg
2 tsp	jalapeño pepper powder (see tip, at left)	10 mL
2 tsp	lemon pepper	10 mL
2 tsp	kosher salt	10 mL

1. *Prepare the marinade:* In a medium bowl, combine green onions, garlic, cola, honey, rum and oil.

2. Rinse ribs under cold running water and pat dry. Place in a large sealable plastic bag (or bags) and pour in half of the marinade. Seal bag, toss to coat and refrigerate for 2 hours. Reserve the remaining marinade in the refrigerator.

3. Meanwhile, combine jalapeño pepper powder, lemon pepper and salt.

4. Remove ribs from marinade and pat dry. Discard marinade. Sprinkle both sides of ribs with seasoning mixture, coating evenly. Set aside.

5. Prepare a fire in your smoker. *(For instructions, see pages 8–11.)*

6. Place ribs, meaty side up, directly on the smoker rack, add the wood to the coals and close the lid. Smoke at 225°F to 250°F (110°C to 120°C), basting every 30 minutes with the reserved marinade, for 4 to 6 hours, or until fork-tender.

Orange & Raspberry Country-Style Ribs

Country-style ribs — finger-length cuts from the loin — really benefit from long, slow smoking and a sweet basting sauce, as in this recipe. Serve any remaining sauce at the table.

SERVES 4	Recommended wood: sugar maple

TIP

Why amber honey? Most honey you buy at the grocery store, such as clover honey, will be an amber color, which indicates a medium flavor and sweetness. Light honeys made from blossoms have a more flowery, sugary flavor; darker honeys such as sunflower have a deep, almost sulphurous flavor. For barbecuing purposes, stick with amber.

• • •

Look for apricot nectar in bottles or cartons in the fruit juice section of well-stocked supermarkets and health food stores.

Basting Sauce

1	can (6 oz/175 mL) tomato paste	1
½ cup	packed brown sugar	125 mL
¼ cup	frozen orange juice concentrate, thawed	50 mL
¼ cup	amber liquid honey	50 mL
2 tbsp	raspberry vinegar	25 mL
1 tbsp	prepared mustard	15 mL
1 tbsp	Worcestershire sauce	15 mL
	Kosher salt and freshly ground black pepper	
2 lbs	country-style pork ribs	1 kg
	Peach or apricot nectar (see tip, at left) for spraying	

1. *Prepare the basting sauce:* In a small bowl, combine tomato paste, brown sugar, orange juice concentrate, honey, vinegar, mustard, Worcestershire sauce and salt and pepper to taste. Set aside.

2. Rinse ribs under cold running water and pat dry. Set aside.

3. Prepare a fire in your smoker. *(For instructions, see pages 8–11.)*

4. Place ribs, meaty side up, directly on the smoker rack, add wood to the coals and close the lid. Smoke at 225°F to 250°F (110°C to 120°C), spraying every 30 minutes with peach nectar, for 2½ hours. Brush with basting sauce, close the lid and smoke, turning and brushing with sauce frequently, for 25 to 35 minutes, or until fork-tender.

Hoisin Pork Skewers

These Asian-style skewers are delicious as an appetizer or satisfying as an entrée. Serve with Asian Plum Sauce (from Country-Style Ribs with Asian Plum Sauce, page 261), if you like.

SERVES 6 AS A MAIN COURSE

Recommended wood: hickory or apple

TIPS
The smaller the smoking chamber on your equipment, the sooner your food will be done. If you're using a kettle grill or a bullet smoker, your pork skewers might be done about 30 minutes sooner.

• • •

If you want to serve this as an appetizer instead of a main course, divide the pork among 12 smaller skewers rather than 6.

• Six 12-inch (30 cm) bamboo skewers

3	cloves garlic, minced	3
1	2-inch (5 cm) piece gingerroot, peeled and chopped	1
⅓ cup	hoisin sauce	75 mL
2 tbsp	rice vinegar	25 mL
2 tbsp	soy sauce	25 mL
2 tbsp	dry sherry	25 mL
1 tbsp	peanut oil	15 mL
½ tsp	grated lemon zest	2 mL
1½ lbs	boneless loin pork, cut into 1-inch (2.5 cm) pieces	750 g
½ cup	chopped green onions	125 mL

1. Soak skewers in water for 30 minutes.

2. In a blender or food processor, purée garlic, ginger, hoisin sauce, vinegar, soy sauce, sherry, oil and lemon zest until smooth. Transfer half of the purée to a large bowl and add pork; toss well to coat. Cover and let stand at room temperature for 10 minutes. Reserve the remaining purée in the refrigerator.

3. Drain pork and thread onto skewers. Set aside.

4. Prepare a fire in your smoker. *(For instructions, see pages 8–11.)*

5. Place skewers directly on the smoker rack, add wood to the coals and close the lid. Smoke at 225°F to 250°F (110°C to 120°C) for 1½ hours.

6. To serve, brush with the remaining purée and sprinkle with green onions.

Italian Antipasto Skewers

Here's a fun way to get the party started, especially while you're waiting for the smoked chicken, turkey, brisket or leg of lamb to be ready.

TIP

The smaller the smoking chamber on your equipment, the sooner your food will be done. If you're using a kettle grill or a bullet smoker, your antipasto skewers might be done about 30 minutes sooner.

Recommended wood: oak, especially whispering oak

- Eight 10-inch (25 cm) wooden bamboo skewers

Marinade

3	large cloves garlic, minced	3
2	serrano chili peppers, seeded and minced	2
¼ cup	freshly squeezed lime juice	50 mL
2 tsp	granulated sugar	10 mL
	Kosher salt and freshly ground black pepper	
1 lb	eggplant, cut into 1-inch (2.5 cm) cubes	500 mL
8 oz	fresh spicy Italian sausages, cut into ¾-inch (2 cm) thick pieces	250 g
8 oz	fresh bratwurst sausages, cut into ¾-inch (2 cm) thick pieces	250 g

1. *Prepare the marinade:* In a small bowl, whisk together garlic, serrano peppers, lime juice, sugar and salt and pepper to taste. Set aside.

2. In a large pot of boiling water, blanch eggplant for 1 minute. Drain.

3. Thread 2 pieces of Italian sausage, 2 pieces of bratwurst and 4 pieces of eggplant onto each skewer. Lay skewers in a single layer in a shallow dish or on a rimmed baking sheet and pour in marinade. Cover and refrigerate for at least 2 hours or overnight.

4. Prepare a fire in your smoker. *(For instructions, see pages 8–11.)*

5. Place skewers directly on the smoker rack, add wood to the coals and close the lid. Smoke at 200°F (100°C) for 2 hours, or until juices run clear when sausages are pierced with a knife.

Cherry-Smoked Fresh Pork Sausage

When you really get into barbecue, you'll want to try making your own sausage. You'll need to order fresh hog casings from your butcher or a supply house and rinse them well before using. You'll also need equipment for stuffing the sausage, which you can usually find at old-fashioned hardware stores. (You could also use mixer attachments that grind the meat, combine the ingredients and extrude the sausage into the casings.) If you don't want to get into all that, simply form the sausage into loaves, wrap them in plastic wrap and form into links, as in this recipe. Smoke for about an hour, or until the sausage firms up, then remove the plastic wrap and return sausage to the smoker until done.

MAKES ABOUT 8 LBS (4 KG)	

Recommended wood: cherry or other fruit wood

TIPS

The plastic wrap will not melt or burn if you keep the temperature at 225°F to 250°F (110°C to 120°C). It helps keep the sausage moist and firm while the meat is taking on the smoky flavor.

• • •

If you use casings and you notice during smoking that they have become dry and tough, place sausages in a disposable aluminum pan of warm water on the smoker rack. Poaching in the smoker will tenderize the casings.

2 cups	ice water	500 mL
2	cloves garlic, minced	2
¼ cup	kosher salt	50 mL
¼ cup	whole fennel seeds	50 mL
2 tbsp	cracked black pepper	25 mL
2 tbsp	dried basil	25 mL
1 tbsp	hot pepper flakes	15 mL
1 tbsp	dried parsley	15 mL
6 lbs	lean ground pork	3 kg
1½ lbs	ground pork fat	750 g

1. Pour ice water into a large bowl. Add garlic, salt, fennel seeds, pepper, basil, hot pepper flakes and parsley; mix well. Using your hands or a fork, mix in pork and pork fat. Cover and refrigerate for at least 8 hours or overnight.

2. Place clear plastic wrap on a flat surface. Mold sausage mixture into 6 loaves, then form each loaf into a large link about 2 inches (5 cm) in diameter. Roll each link tightly in plastic wrap and tie off the ends. (Or stuff sausage mixture into 2-inch/5 cm diameter hog casings, tied off at 8-inch/20 cm intervals.) Set aside.

3. Prepare a fire in your smoker. *(For instructions, see pages 8–11.)*

4. Place plastic-wrapped sausages directly on the smoker rack, add wood to the coals and close the lid. Smoke at 200°F (100°C) for 1 hour, or until sausage has firmed up. Remove plastic wrap and return sausages to the smoker. Smoke for 1 to 2 hours, or until a meat thermometer inserted in the middle of a sausage registers 160°F (70°C).

Pineapple-Glazed Hot Italian Sausage

This easy recipe makes a mouthwatering appetizer. It's great party food!

SERVES 8 AS AN APPETIZER

Recommended wood: cherry or other fruit wood

1	jar (10 oz/300 mL) pineapple preserves	1
2 lbs	spicy Italian sausages	1 kg

1. Prepare a fire in your smoker. *(For instructions, see pages 8–11.)*

2. Meanwhile, in a small saucepan, over medium heat, warm pineapple preserves until they're spreadable. Keep warm by the smoker.

3. Place sausages directly on the smoker rack, add wood to the coals and close the lid. Smoke at 225°F to 250°F (110°C to 120°C) for 1 hour. Baste with pineapple preserves, close the lid and smoke, basting with pineapple preserves every 30 minutes, for 1½ hours, or until juices run clear when sausages are pierced with a knife. Let rest for 15 minutes.

4. Cut sausages into bite-sized portions and spear each piece with a decorative toothpick. Serve hot or at room temperature.

TIPS

The smaller the smoking chamber on your equipment, the sooner your food will be done. If you're using a kettle grill or a bullet smoker, your sausages might be done about 30 minutes sooner.

• • •

If you're new to smoking, instead of placing sausages directly on the smoker rack, place them in a disposable aluminum pan. You'll still get the smoky flavor, but with easier cleanup.

• • •

Make ahead

Place sausages in airtight containers and store in the refrigerator for up to 1 week or in the freezer for up to 3 months.

Italian Sausage
& Artichoke Soup

Here's a new take on an old favorite. Soups taste like they've been simmering on an open hearth when they have smoked ingredients — like the sausage and artichokes in this one.

SERVES 8

TIPS

If you can't find frozen artichoke hearts, use two 14-oz (398 mL) cans artichoke hearts, drained.

• • •

See page 112 for instructions on hot-smoking artichokes.

• • •

Serve warm with French bread.

1 tbsp	olive oil	15 mL
2	cloves garlic, minced	2
½ cup	chopped onion	125 mL
3	cans (each 14 oz/398 mL) Roma (plum) tomatoes, cut into bite-size pieces	3
3 cups	chicken stock	750 mL
½ tsp	dried Italian seasoning	2 mL
½ tsp	dried basil	2 mL
	Kosher salt and freshly grated black pepper	
12 oz	Italian Sausage (see recipe, page 81)	375 g
2	packages (each 9 oz/270 g) frozen artichoke hearts, thawed and smoked	2

1. In a large saucepan or a stockpot, heat olive oil over medium heat. Sauté garlic and onion until translucent, about 8 minutes. Stir in tomatoes and chicken stock. Increase heat to high and bring to a boil. Reduce heat to a simmer. Add Italian seasoning, basil and salt and pepper to taste. Cut sausage and artichokes into bite-sized pieces and add to the soup. Simmer for 20 minutes.

Beef

MANY PEOPLE THINK grilling is a very versatile cooking technique. But for me, grilling doesn't hold a smoldering briquette to slow-smoking. For example, grilled burgers and steaks are common — and totally delicious — backyard barbecue fare. However, if you tried to grill a tough, meaty beef brisket, you'd end up with one tough, stringy, almost inedible piece of meat. But try putting burgers (yes, burgers!), steaks (yes, steaks!), brisket or a big old beef roast on the smoker, and you've got something divinely inspired. Even meatloaf is great on the smoker. Beef just really takes to slow-smoking.

With lean cuts of meat, such as burgers or flank steak, I marinate first or use a baste while they're cooking. For not-too-fatty, big cuts of meat such as a sirloin or rib-eye roast, I use a long soak in a brine solution first, then maybe a dry rub on the outside. For brisket, I use a dry rub and then a tangy basting sauce or mop to cut the fat that oozes from the brisket while it smokes.

For beef, I like a sweet smoke from a fruit wood or a deeper note from a mixture of hard woods such as mesquite, hickory, maple and oak. For my taste, mesquite alone is too bitter and heavy.

To finish, try a tomato-based barbecue sauce, with perhaps just a hint of sweetness, such as Apple Ancho Barbecue Sauce (page 62) or Cherry Chipotle Barbecue Sauce (page 63).

BEEF RECIPES

Rib Roast 272

Calgary Stampede Rubbed
    Rib Roast 273

Brined & Basted Sirloin
    Roast 274

Bacon-Wrapped Beef
    Tenderloin 275

Cherry-Smoked Beef
    Tenderloin 276

Cola-Marinated Flank Steak 278

Flank Steak with Beefy
    Barbecue Mop 279

Apple & Pecan–Smoked
    Flank Steak with Garlic
    & Spice Rub 280

Orange & Soy Flank Steak 281

Cowboy Flank Steak 282

Flank Steak Skewers in
    Lime Cola Marinade 283

Rich, Beefy Brisket 284

Hickory & Maple–Smoked
    Beef Brisket 285

Beef Lover's Barbecued
    Brisket 286

Barbecued Brisket
    for a Crowd 287

Kansas City–Style Brisket 288

Apple Ancho Brisket 289

Smoky Mesquite Brisket 290

Brisket-Stuffed Artichoke
    Bottoms 292

Mesquite & Apple–Smoked
    Deviled Beef Ribs 293

Beef Ribs in Pale Ale Marinade . . 294

Chili-Raspberry Beef
    Short Ribs 296

Asian-Style Beef Short Ribs 297

Beef Short Ribs in Serrano-
    Szechuan Marinade 298

The Ultimate Slow-Smoked
    Burger 300

Antipasto Burgers 302

Barbecued Meatloaf 304

Mushroom, Garlic & Thyme
    Meatloaf 306

Caribbean-Style Barbecued
    Meatloaf with Papaya
    Relish 308

Rib Roast

You will never roast a prime rib again once you've tried it this way. If you place a sturdy meat thermometer in the center of the roast before you put in on the smoker, you'll be able to gauge when it's done, figuring 140°F (60°C) for rare.

SERVES 10 TO 12

Recommended wood: a combination of apple, cherry and peach

TIPS

The smaller the smoking chamber on your equipment, the sooner your food will be done. If you're using a kettle grill or a bullet smoker, your roast might be done in 2 hours. If you're using a bigger rig or a genuine smoker, it might take 2½ to 3 hours.

• • •

Place any leftovers in an airtight container and store in the refrigerator for up to 1 week.

1 tbsp	mustard powder	15 mL
2 tsp	kosher salt	10 mL
2 tsp	garlic salt	10 mL
2 tsp	onion salt	10 mL
2 tsp	celery salt	10 mL
¼ tsp	ground allspice	1 mL
1	boneless prime rib roast (about 5 lbs/2.5 kg)	1
4	sprigs fresh rosemary	4

1. In a small bowl, combine mustard powder, kosher salt, garlic salt, onion salt, celery salt and allspice.

2. Using a sharp knife, make several deep slits in the roast to form pockets of different depths. Rub seasoning mixture into meat and pockets. Set aside.

3. Prepare a fire in your smoker. *(For instructions, see pages 8–11.)*

4. Place roast directly on the smoker rack and lay rosemary on top. Add wood to the coals and close the lid. Smoke at 225°F to 250°F (110°C to 120°C) for 2 hours, until a meat thermometer inserted in the thickest part of the roast registers 150°F (65°C) for medium-rare, or until desired doneness. Let rest for 15 minutes before carving.

Calgary Stampede Rubbed Rib Roast

The week-long Calgary Stampede takes place in mid-July, with calf roping, horse racing and every other Wild West activity you can imagine. And, of course, the food is great, too — especially at the barbecue contest called Barbecue on the Bend. This rip-roarin' recipe is similar to one served at the Stampede, so round up all your friends and serve it up.

SERVES 12	Recommended wood: mesquite

TIP
Place any leftovers in an airtight container and store in the refrigerator for up to 1 week.

• • •

Make ahead

Prepare through Step 1, cover and refrigerate for up to 6 hours.

1	boneless prime rib roast (about 6 lbs/3 kg)	1
¼ cup	All-Purpose Barbecue Rub (see recipe, page 27)	50 mL

1. Using a sharp knife, cut off the fat "cap" from the roast in one piece. Cut just where the fat is attached to the meat, trimming off as little meat as possible. Reserve the fat cap. Rub roast with dry rub, coating evenly. Replace the fat cap and tie it back onto the roast with kitchen twine. Set aside.

2. Prepare a fire in your smoker. *(For instructions, see pages 8–11.)*

3. Place roast, fat side up, in a disposable aluminum pan filled with 1 inch (2.5 cm) water. Place pan on the smoker rack, add wood to the coals and close the lid. Smoke at 225°F to 250°F (110°C to 120°C) for 3 to 3½ hours, or until a meat thermometer inserted in the thickest part of the roast registers 150°F (65°C) for medium-rare, or until desired doneness. Let rest for 15 minutes before carving.

Brined & Basted Sirloin Roast

Triple the flavor of your roast with this treatment. Injecting brine into the fibers of the meat changes the cellular structure of the beef, giving a more juicy interior after hours of smoking; basting ensures a voluptuous exterior.

SERVES 8 TO 10	Recommended wood: hickory, oak or mesquite

TIPS

Gourmet and cooking shops sell large injectors or syringes; you can also buy them at veterinary supply houses. Just make sure the liquid you put in the syringe is free of anything that might clog the needle.

· · ·

Leftovers make delicious smoked beef sandwiches, especially when you top the meat with a smoky barbecue sauce such as Kansas City–Style Barbecue Sauce (see recipe, page 55).

· · ·

This technique also works well for a beef brisket; just adjust the smoking time to the size of your brisket (see brisket recipes, pages 284–290).

· · ·

Place any leftovers in an airtight container and store in the refrigerator for up to 1 week.

8 cups	Brine for Beef (see recipe, page 24), cooled	2 L
1	boneless sirloin roast (4 to 5 lbs/ 2 to 2.5 kg)	1
	Kosher salt and cracked black pepper	
¼ cup	granulated garlic (see tip, page 230)	50 mL
2½ cups	Rich & Delicious Brisket Mop (see recipe, page 45)	625 mL

1. Strain 1 cup (250 mL) of the brine into a bowl. Place roast in a large deep pan. Fill an injector or syringe (see tip, at left) with some of the strained brine and inject roast at intervals; repeat until you have used all of the strained brine. Pour unstrained brine over roast. Cover and refrigerate for at least 12 hours or for up to 48 hours.

2. Remove roast from brine and discard brine. Rinse roast under cold running water and pat dry. Sprinkle with salt and pepper to taste, then rub all over with granulated garlic. Set aside.

3. Prepare a fire in your smoker. *(For instructions, see pages 8–11.)*

4. Place roast directly on the smoker rack, add wood to the coals and close the lid. Smoke at 225°F to 250°F (110°C to 120°C) for 3 hours. Brush with mop, close the lid and smoke, mopping every 30 minutes, for 2 to 3 hours, or until a meat thermometer inserted into the thickest part of the roast registers 150°F (65°C) for medium-rare, or to desired doneness. Let rest for 15 minutes before carving.

Bacon-Wrapped Beef Tenderloin

A fabulous company dish with a built-in "wow" factor. If you have any leftovers at all, they will also taste great the next day.

SERVES 8	Recommended wood: a combination of oak (preferably white oak) and hickory

TIPS

Jalapeño pepper powder is available from better spice emporiums or online (see the Source Guide, page 356). If you can't find it, substitute about 1 tsp (5 mL) hot pepper sauce.

• • •

Serve with Apple Ancho Barbecue Sauce (see recipe, page 62).

• • •

Place any leftovers in an airtight container and store in the refrigerator for up to 1 week.

2	cloves garlic, crushed	2
¼ cup	olive oil	50 mL
2 tsp	ground nutmeg	10 mL
1 tsp	kosher salt	5 mL
½ tsp	dried thyme	2 mL
½ tsp	dried basil	2 mL
½ tsp	jalapeño pepper powder (see tip, at left)	2 mL
½ tsp	freshly ground black pepper	2 mL
3 lbs	beef tenderloin, trimmed	1.5 kg
6	strips bacon	6
	Apple juice for spraying	

1. In a small saucepan, bring garlic, oil, nutmeg, salt, thyme, basil, jalapeño pepper powder and black pepper to a simmer over medium heat. Remove from heat and let cool completely.

2. Rub beef with seasoning mixture, coating evenly, then wrap with bacon strips, securing with toothpicks if desired. Set aside.

3. Prepare a fire in your smoker. *(For instructions, see pages 8–11.)*

4. Place beef directly on the smoker rack, add wood to the coals and close the lid. Smoke at 225°F to 250°F (110°C to 120°C), spraying with apple juice every 30 minutes, for 1½ hours, until a meat thermometer inserted in the thickest part of the beef registers 150°F (65°C) for medium-rare, or until desired doneness. Let rest for 15 minutes, then slice across the grain to serve.

Cherry-Smoked Beef Tenderloin

When you serve this fabulous dish to your guests, you'll know you have a winner. This recipe won the grand prize in the National Beef Contest, sponsored by Farmland Foods, in 2000. The tenderloin takes about 1½ hours to smoke, but the sauce and relish can be prepared in minutes.

SERVES 6	Recommended wood: cherry or other fruit wood	

TIPS

Instead of cherry wood, you could also use the deeper flavor of hickory, oak or mesquite, or the sweetness of apple, or a combination of these woods.

• • •

Achiote paste, a coloring and flavoring paste popular in Mexican cuisine, is available at better grocery stores or Hispanic markets.

Beef Tenderloin

2	cloves garlic, minced	2
3 tbsp	achiote paste (see tip, at left)	45 mL
¼ cup	freshly squeezed lime juice	50 mL
½ tsp	kosher salt	2 mL
½ tsp	freshly ground black pepper	2 mL
2½ lbs	beef tenderloin, trimmed	1.5 kg

Citrus Demi-glace

½ cup	beef stock	125 mL
3 tbsp	freshly squeezed lime juice	45 mL
¾ cup	unsalted butter, cut into 12 cubes	175 mL

Roasted Red Pepper & Avocado Relish

2	avocados, pitted, seeded and diced	2
1	red bell pepper, roasted, peeled and diced (see tip, opposite)	1
¼ cup	freshly squeezed lemon juice	50 mL

1. *Prepare the beef tenderloin:* In a small bowl, combine garlic, achiote paste, lime juice, salt and pepper. Rub over beef, coating evenly. Cover and refrigerate for at least 30 minutes or for up to 60 minutes. Remove from refrigerator and let warm to room temperature while smoker is heating.

To roast and peel red pepper, place whole pepper on a baking sheet and roast in a 350°F (180°C) oven, turning until blackened on all sides, about 15 minutes. Using tongs, place pepper in a brown paper bag and close the bag. When cool enough to handle, slice, remove the seeds, then peel off the skin.

2. Prepare a fire in your smoker. *(For instructions, see pages 8–11.)*

3. Place beef directly on the smoker rack, add wood to the coals and close the lid. Smoke at 225°F to 250°F (110°C to 120°C) for 1½ hours, until a meat thermometer inserted in the thickest part of the beef registers 150°F (65°C) for medium-rare, or until desired doneness. Let rest for 15 minutes before slicing, then slice across the grain.

4. *Prepare the demi-glace:* In a small saucepan, bring beef stock to a boil over medium-high heat. Stir in lime juice and cook until reduced by one-third, about 7 minutes. Reduce heat to low and whisk in butter, one cube at a time, until smooth and silky. Place saucepan in a larger pan of hot water and keep warm until serving.

5. *Prepare the relish:* In a medium bowl, using two forks, lightly toss avocados, red pepper and lemon juice.

6. Serve sliced tenderloin topped with demi-glace, with relish on the side.

Cola-Marinated Flank Steak

If you like grilled flank steak, you'll love the tender, juicy and luscious results when you smoke it. To get the maximum smoke flavor and tenderness, this flank steak is smoked at a lower temperature than some of the other recipes. The cola marinade is also good on brisket or beef roast destined for the smoker.

SERVES 6 TO 8	Recommended wood: a combination of cherry and apple	

TIPS

For extra tenderness, ask your butcher to run flank steak through the cuber (a tenderizing machine used to make cubed steaks).

* * *

If you're using smaller equipment, such as a bullet smoker or a charcoal grill, this steak will be medium-rare in 4 to 5 hours.

* * *

Serve with Cherry Chipotle Barbecue Sauce (see recipe, page 63) for a taste treat.

* * *

Place any leftovers in an airtight container and store in the refrigerator for up to 1 week. Use leftovers to make a flank steak salad, with greens, fresh tomato, chunks of blue cheese and your favorite dressing.

8	cloves garlic, minced	8
4 cups	cola	1 L
1 cup	vegetable oil	250 mL
1 cup	balsamic vinegar	250 mL
¼ cup	kosher salt	50 mL
2 tbsp	freshly ground black pepper	25 mL
3 to 5 lbs	flank steak, trimmed	1.5 to 2.5 kg
	Apple juice for spraying	

1. In a large bowl, combine garlic, cola, oil, vinegar, salt and pepper. Set aside.

2. Place steak in a large sealable plastic bag and pour in marinade. Seal bag, toss to coat and refrigerate for at least 8 hours or, preferably, overnight.

3. Remove steak from marinade, but do not pat dry. Set aside. Discard marinade.

4. Prepare a fire in your smoker. *(For instructions, see pages 8–11.)*

5. Place steak directly on the smoker rack, add wood to the coals and close the lid. Smoke at 200°F (100°C), spraying with apple juice every 30 minutes, for 6 hours, or until a meat thermometer inserted in the thickest part of the steak registers 150°F (65°C) for medium-rare, or until desired doneness. Let rest for 15 minutes, then slice across the grain to serve.

Flank Steak with Beefy Barbecue Mop

In this recipe, the Beefy Barbecue Mop is both marinade and baste, carrying the flavor from start to finish. If you wish, serve this steak with a beefy barbecue sauce, such as Texas-Style Barbecue Sauce (see recipe, page 53).

SERVES 4 TO 6

Recommended wood: pecan, hickory or oak

TIPS

For extra tenderness, ask your butcher to run flank steak through the cuber (a tenderizing machine used to make cubed steaks).

• • •

To keep a flank steak from curling up as it smokes, score on both sides with a sharp knife, making shallow cuts on the diagonal no deeper than ⅛ inch (0.3 cm), about ¼ inch (0.5 cm) apart.

• • •

Variation

This steak is also delicious marinated and basted with Rich & Delicious Brisket Mop (see recipe, page 45).

| 2 lbs | flank steak, trimmed | 1 kg |
| 1⅔ cups | Beefy Barbecue Mop (see recipe, page 46), divided | 400 mL |

1. Place steak in a large sealable plastic bag and pour in half of the mop. Seal bag, toss to coat and let stand at room temperature for 30 minutes or refrigerate overnight, turning occasionally. Reserve the remaining mop in the refrigerator.

2. Remove steak from mop, but do not pat dry. Set aside. Discard mop.

3. Prepare a fire in your smoker. *(For instructions, see pages 8–11.)*

4. Place steak directly on the smoker rack, add wood to the coals and close the lid. Smoke at 225°F to 250°F (110°C to 120°C), brushing with the remaining mop every 30 minutes, for 2 hours, or until a meat thermometer inserted in the thickest part of the steak registers 150°F (65°C) for medium-rare, or until desired doneness. Let rest for 15 minutes, then slice across the grain to serve.

Apple & Pecan–Smoked Flank Steak with Garlic & Spice Rub

If you don't have time to slow-smoke a brisket, flank steak is the next best thing. Do several at a time, then slice, wrap and freeze for later.

SERVES 4 TO 6	Recommended wood: a combination of apple and pecan

TIPS

To keep a flank steak from curling up as it smokes, score on both sides with a sharp knife, making shallow cuts on the diagonal no deeper than ⅛ inch (0.3 cm), about ¼ inch (0.5 cm) apart.

• • •

This recipe would also work with other types of thin-cut, chewy-textured steaks, such as bavette, hanger, skirt or chuck.

• • •

To get the maximum smoke flavor and tenderness, this flank steak is smoked at a lower temperature than some of the other recipes.

• • •

Place any leftovers in an airtight container and store in the refrigerator for up to 1 week.

Garlic & Spice Rub

5	cloves garlic	5
3 tbsp	packed brown sugar	45 mL
1 tbsp	whole black peppercorns	15 mL
1 tbsp	whole yellow mustard seeds	15 mL
1 tbsp	whole coriander seeds	15 mL
2 lbs	flank steak, trimmed	1 kg
	Olive oil	
	Kosher salt	
2½ cups	Rich & Delicious Brisket Mop (see recipe, page 45)	625 mL

1. *Prepare the rub:* In a food processor, process garlic, brown sugar, peppercorns, mustard seeds and coriander seeds until seeds and garlic are crushed.

2. Rub steak with oil, then pat on rub, coating evenly. Season generously with salt. Set aside.

3. Prepare a fire in your smoker. *(For instructions, see pages 8–11.)*

4. Place steak directly on the smoker rack, add wood to the coals and close the lid. Smoke at 200°F (100°C) for 2 hours. Brush with mop, close the lid and smoke, mopping every hour, for 4 hours, or until a meat thermometer inserted in the thickest part of the steak registers 150°F (65°C) for medium-rare, or until desired doneness. Let rest for 15 minutes, then slice across the grain to serve.

Orange & Soy Flank Steak

Flank steak is one of my favorites on the smoker. It's easier and less time-consuming than a brisket, but you still get that beefy flavor and added tenderness.

SERVES 4 TO 6

Recommended wood: cherry or other fruit wood

TIPS

To keep a flank steak from curling up as it smokes, score on both sides with a sharp knife, making shallow cuts on the diagonal no deeper than ⅛ inch (0.3 cm), about ¼ inch (0.5 cm) apart.

• • •

Place any leftovers in an airtight container and store in the refrigerator for up to 1 week.

2	oranges	2
3	cloves garlic, finely chopped	3
3	bay leaves, crumbled	3
1	onion, finely chopped	1
1 cup	soy sauce	250 mL
½ cup	rice vinegar	125 mL
½ cup	olive oil	125 mL
1 tbsp	whole coriander seeds	15 mL
1 tsp	freshly ground black pepper	5 mL
2 lbs	flank steak, trimmed	1 kg

1. Rinse oranges, cut each in half and squeeze out the juice into a bowl. Cut the rind of 1 orange into ¼-inch (1 cm) dice and add it to the juice. Add garlic, bay leaves, onion, soy sauce, vinegar, oil, coriander seeds and pepper; mix well.

2. Place steak in a pan just large enough to hold it. Spread one-quarter of the marinade on the meat, coating evenly; turn it over and spread with another one-quarter of the marinade. Cover and refrigerate for at least 6 hours or overnight. Reserve the remaining marinade in the refrigerator.

3. Remove steak from marinade and scrape off most of the marinade. Set aside. Discard marinade.

4. Prepare a fire in your smoker *(see pages 8–11).*

5. Place steak directly on the smoker rack, add wood to the coals and close the lid. Smoke at 225°F to 250°F (110°C to 120°C) for 2 hours, until a meat thermometer inserted in the thickest part of the steak registers 150°F (65°C) for medium-rare, or until desired doneness. Let rest for 15 minutes, then slice across the grain to serve. Strain, then spoon reserved marinade over sliced steak.

Cowboy Flank Steak

With Tex-Mex seasonings of lime juice, cumin and chili powder, this smoked flank steak will have your taste buds saying "yee-haw!"

SERVES 4 TO 6	**Recommended wood:** pecan, hickory or oak

TIPS

To keep a flank steak from curling up as it smokes, score on both sides with a sharp knife, making shallow cuts on the diagonal no deeper than ⅛ inch (0.3 cm), about ¼ inch (0.5 cm) apart.

• • •

If flank steak is not available, substitute boneless sirloin, which will get tender sooner. Smoke for 2 hours, until a meat thermometer inserted in the thickest part of the steak registers 150°F (65°C) for medium-rare, or until desired doneness.

Marinade

2	cloves garlic, minced	2
¼ cup	soy sauce	50 mL
¼ cup	Worcestershire sauce	50 mL
2 tbsp	freshly squeezed lime juice	25 mL
2 tbsp	chopped fresh cilantro	25 mL
1 tbsp	minced gingerroot	15 mL
½ tsp	ground cumin	2 mL
¼ tsp	chili powder	1 mL
2 lbs	flank steak, trimmed	1 kg

1. *Prepare the marinade:* In a small bowl, combine garlic, soy sauce, Worcestershire sauce, lime juice, cilantro, ginger, cumin and chili powder.

2. Place steak in a large sealable plastic bag and pour in marinade. Seal bag, toss to coat and let stand at room temperature for 30 minutes or refrigerate overnight, turning occasionally.

3. Remove steak from marinade, but do not pat dry. Set aside. Transfer marinade to a small saucepan and bring to a boil over medium-high heat. Boil for 3 minutes. Remove from heat, cover and refrigerate.

4. Prepare a fire in your smoker *(see pages 8–11).*

5. Place steak directly on the smoker rack, add wood to the coals and close the lid. Smoke at 225°F to 250°F (110°C to 120°C) for 2 hours, until a meat thermometer inserted in the thickest part of the steak registers 150°F (65°C) for medium-rare, or until desired doneness. Let rest for 15 minutes.

6. While steak is resting, warm cooked marinade over low heat. To serve, thinly slice steak across the grain and top with cooked marinade.

Flank Steak Skewers in Lime Cola Marinade

Serve these steak skewers as an appetizer while you're smoking the entrée. They reach medium-rare in about an hour and take up very little space on the smoker.

SERVES 4 AS AN APPETIZER

Recommended wood: hickory or maple

TIP
Place any leftovers in an airtight container and store in the refrigerator for up to 1 week.

- Twelve 12-inch (30 cm) bamboo skewers

1 cup	Lime Cola Marinade (see recipe, page 37)	250 mL
¼ cup	dry red wine	50 mL
¼ cup	soy sauce	50 mL
1 tbsp	dry mustard	15 mL
1 tbsp	chopped fresh thyme	15 mL
1 tbsp	Worcestershire sauce	15 mL
1½ tsp	freshly ground black pepper	7 mL
1 lb	flank steak, cut across the grain into 1-inch (2.5 cm) strips	500 g

1. Soak skewers in water for 30 minutes.

2. In a small bowl, whisk together marinade, wine, soy sauce, mustard, thyme, Worcestershire sauce and pepper.

3. Place steak in a large sealable plastic bag and pour in marinade. Seal bag, toss to coat and refrigerate for at least 2 hours or overnight, tossing occasionally.

4. Remove steak from marinade and thread onto skewers. Set aside. Discard marinade.

5. Prepare a fire in your smoker. *(For instructions, see pages 8–11.)*

6. Add wood to the coals and wait until smoke is fragrant, 5 to 10 minutes. Place skewers on the smoker rack and close the lid. Smoke at 225°F to 250°F (110°C to 120°C) for 1 hour for medium-rare, or to desired doneness.

Rich, Beefy Brisket

This recipe produces a Texas-style brisket, slow-smoked to a very tender finish.

Recommended wood: a combination of mesquite and pecan

If you slice brisket with the grain, the meat will be chewy rather than tender. But when the brisket darkens and shrinks with smoking, the grain can be hard to find. Notching a brisket before you smoke it helps you identify the grain later on. Simply use a paring knife to cut a small triangle of meat (like the point of an arrow) to show which way the grain runs.

• • •

If you have food safety concerns, use disposable dish cloths to mop the beef, discarding the dish cloth after each mop, or use a basting brush and wash after each mop. Bring out and warm up 1 cup (250 mL) of the mop at a time and keep the rest in the refrigerator.

• • •

Place any leftovers in an airtight container and store in the refrigerator for up to 1 week.

5 lbs	beef brisket	2.5 kg
3½ cups	Onion & Garlic Dry Rub (see recipe, page 34)	875 mL
2½ cups	Rich & Delicious Brisket Mop (see recipe, page 45)	625 mL
3½ cups	Texas Spit (see recipe, page 54)	875 mL

1. Rub brisket with dry rub, coating evenly. Cover and refrigerate overnight.

2. Prepare a fire in your smoker. *(For instructions, see pages 8–11.)*

3. Place brisket directly on the smoker rack, add wood to the coals and close the lid. Smoke at 225°F to 250°F (110°C to 120°C), brushing with brisket mop every hour, for 8 to 10 hours, or until you can twist a fork inserted into the brisket. Pour half of the Texas Spit over brisket, close the lid and smoke for 1 hour, until fork-tender. Let rest for 15 minutes, then slice across the grain. Serve with the remaining Texas Spit.

Hickory & Maple–Smoked Beef Brisket

This is a great recipe for a beginner to practice the Texas style, meaning very low heat, not too much smoke and a tender, tender result. Texans slice their brisket fairly thick, as the meat is so tender. This recipe takes time: 24 hours to marinate, then 6 hours to smoke.

SERVES 8	Recommended wood: a combination of hickory and maple

TIPS

A brisket flat is, just as the term implies, the smaller, or flatter, part of the whole beef brisket. Have your butcher cut it for you.

• • •

If you slice brisket with the grain, the meat will be chewy rather than tender. But when the brisket darkens and shrinks with smoking, the grain can be hard to find. Notching a brisket before you smoke it helps you identify the grain later on. Simply use a paring knife to cut a small triangle of meat (like the point of an arrow) to show which way the grain runs.

• • •

Place any leftovers in an airtight container and store in the refrigerator for up to 1 week.

Marinade

2	cloves garlic, minced	2
1	small onion, diced	1
¼ cup	Worcestershire sauce	50 mL
2 tsp	kosher salt	10 mL
1 tsp	freshly ground black pepper	5 mL
1 tsp	chili powder	5 mL
4 lbs	beef brisket flat (see tip, at left)	2 kg
	Apple juice for spraying	

1. *Prepare the marinade:* In a small bowl, combine garlic, onion, Worcestershire sauce, salt, pepper and chili powder.

2. Place brisket in a large sealable plastic bag and pour in marinade. Seal bag, toss to coat and refrigerate for 24 hours.

3. Remove brisket from marinade, but do not pat dry. Set aside. Discard marinade.

4. Prepare a fire in your smoker. *(For instructions, see pages 8–11.)*

5. Place brisket directly on the smoker rack, add wood to the coals and close the lid. Smoke at 200°F (100°C), spraying with apple juice every hour, for 4 hours. Wrap brisket in foil, close the lid and smoke for 2 hours, until fork-tender. Let rest for 15 minutes, then slice across the grain.

Beef Lover's Barbecued Brisket

If you love slow-smoked brisket with a dark crust and a deep, beefy flavor, this is the recipe for you. The seasonings help create the crust and accentuate the smoky flavor. Leave plenty of time for this, as the beef needs to "marinate" overnight, then smokes for about 10 hours. Make sure to slice across the grain for the tenderest result.

SERVES 10 TO 12

Recommended wood: a combination of mesquite and pecan

TIPS

For an even deeper flavor, after about 5 hours of smoking, begin brushing brisket with Beefy Barbecue Mop (see recipe, page 46) every 30 minutes. Keep mopping until you pour on the barbecue sauce.

• • •

Cherry Chipotle Barbecue Sauce (see recipe, page 63) is especially good with this dish.

• • •

Place any leftovers in an airtight container and store in the refrigerator for up to 1 week.

1 tsp	celery salt	5 mL
1 tsp	onion salt	5 mL
1 tsp	garlic salt	5 mL
1 tsp	kosher salt	5 mL
1 tsp	freshly ground black pepper	5 mL
5 lbs	beef brisket	2.5 kg
	Additional kosher salt and freshly ground black pepper	
¼ cup	Worcestershire sauce	50 mL
2 cups	barbecue sauce (store-bought or see recipes, pages 50–65)	500 mL

1. Place brisket on a flat surface. Season with celery salt, onion salt, garlic salt, kosher salt and pepper. Cover and refrigerate overnight.

2. Sprinkle brisket with salt and pepper to taste, then drizzle with Worcestershire sauce. Set aside.

3. Prepare a fire in your smoker. *(For instructions, see pages 8–11.)*

4. Place brisket directly on the smoker rack, add wood to the coals and close the lid. Smoke at 225°F to 250°F (110°C to 120°C) for 8 to 10 hours, until brisket is tender. Pour barbecue sauce over brisket, close the lid and smoke for 1 hour, until fork-tender. Let rest for 15 minutes, then slice across the grain.

Barbecued Brisket for a Crowd

When you want to serve a great brisket for a lot of people, this is your recipe.

SERVES 24	Recommended wood: a combination of apple and cherry

(For instructions, see pages 8–11.)

TIPS

If you slice brisket with the grain, the meat will be chewy rather than tender. But when the brisket darkens and shrinks with smoking, the grain can be hard to find. Notching a brisket before you smoke it helps you identify the grain later on. Simply use a paring knife to cut a small triangle of meat (like the point of an arrow) to show which way the grain runs.

• • •

Place any leftovers in an airtight container and store in the refrigerator for up to 1 week.

Dry Rub

¼ cup	Spanish or sweet Hungarian paprika	50 mL
¼ cup	packed brown sugar	50 mL
3 tbsp	kosher salt	45 mL
3 tbsp	freshly ground black pepper	45 mL
2 tbsp	lemon pepper	25 mL
1	beef brisket (about 11 lbs/5.5 kg)	1
	Apple juice for spraying	

1. *Prepare the dry rub:* In a small bowl, combine paprika, brown sugar, salt, black pepper and lemon pepper.

2. Place brisket on a flat surface. Rub with dry rub, coating evenly. Set aside.

3. Prepare a fire in your smoker. *(For instructions, see pages 8–11.)*

4. Place brisket directly on the smoker rack, add wood to the coals and close the lid. Smoke at 225°F to 250°F (110°C to 120°C), spraying with apple juice every 30 minutes, for 12 to 14 hours, or until fork-tender. Let rest for 15 minutes, then slice across the grain.

Kansas City–Style Brisket

Kansas City–style barbecued brisket is blackened on the outside, redolent of smoke and tender, but with a little bit of chew, so you have to slice it thin. Of course, to go with this, you want Kansas City–Style Barbecue Sauce (see recipe, page 55).

SERVES 12 TO 16

Recommended wood: a combination of hickory and sugar maple

TIPS

If you slice brisket with the grain, the meat will be chewy rather than tender. But when the brisket darkens and shrinks with smoking, the grain can be hard to find. Notching a brisket before you smoke it helps you identify the grain later on. Simply use a paring knife to cut a small triangle of meat (like the point of an arrow) to show which way the grain runs.

• • •

Place any leftovers in an airtight container and store in the refrigerator for up to 1 week.

Dry Rub

¼ cup	Spanish or sweet Hungarian paprika	50 mL
¼ cup	granulated sugar	50 mL
1½ tbsp	kosher salt	22 mL
1½ tbsp	freshly ground black pepper	22 mL
1 tbsp	lemon pepper	15 mL
6 lbs	beef brisket	3 kg
	Apple juice for spraying	

1. *Prepare the dry rub:* In a small bowl, combine paprika, sugar, salt, black pepper and lemon pepper.

2. Place brisket on a flat surface. Rub with dry rub, coating evenly. Set aside.

3. Prepare a fire in your smoker. *(For instructions, see pages 8–11.)*

4. Place brisket directly on the smoker rack, add wood to the coals and close the lid. Smoke at 225°F to 250°F (110°C to 120°C), spraying with apple juice every hour, for 8 hours, or until fork-tender. Let rest for 15 minutes, then slice across the grain.

Apple Ancho Brisket

Three steps to beef heaven: first the rub, then the smoking, then the glazing sauce.

Recommended wood: a combination of hickory and cherry

5 lbs	beef brisket flat	2.5 kg
¾ cup	All-Purpose Barbecue Rub (see recipe, page 27)	175 mL
2½ cups	Rich & Delicious Brisket Mop (see recipe, page 45)	625 mL
1 cup	Apple Ancho Barbecue Sauce (see recipe, page 62)	250 mL

TIPS

A brisket flat is, just as the term implies, the smaller, or flatter, part of the whole beef brisket. Have your butcher cut it for you.

• • •

If you slice brisket with the grain, the meat will be chewy rather than tender. But when the brisket darkens and shrinks with smoking, the grain can be hard to find. Notching a brisket before you smoke it helps you identify the grain later on. Simply use a paring knife to cut a small triangle of meat (like the point of an arrow) to show which way the grain runs.

• • •

Place any leftovers in an airtight container and store in the refrigerator for up to 1 week.

1. Place brisket on a flat surface. Rub brisket with barbecue rub. Set aside.

2. Prepare a fire in your smoker. *(For instructions, see pages 8–11.)*

3. Place brisket directly on the smoker rack, add wood to the coals and close the lid. Smoke at 225°F to 250°F (110°C to 120°C) for 3 hours. Brush with mop and smoke, mopping every hour, for 3 hours. Remove brisket from smoker and place on a large sheet of aluminum foil. Pour 1 cup (250 mL) of the barbecue sauce over the meat and wrap tightly. Return to the smoker rack, close the lid and smoke for 1 hour, until fork-tender. Let rest for 15 minutes, then slice across the grain.

Smoky Mesquite Brisket

This brisket has a smokier flavor from the 7-hour smoking time and the use of mesquite as one of the woods. The sugary spray guarantees a well-burnished, crusty exterior. Yum!

SERVES 10 TO 12	Recommended wood: a combination of mesquite and hickory	

TIPS

You can find granulated garlic and onion at well-stocked supermarkets or online (see the Source Guide, page 356).

• • •

Worcestershire powder, available at better spice emporiums, is simply Worcestershire sauce with the liquid removed.

• • •

If you slice brisket with the grain, the meat will be chewy rather than tender. But when the brisket darkens and shrinks with smoking, the grain can be hard to find. Notching a brisket before you smoke it helps you identify the grain later on. Simply use a paring knife to cut a small triangle of meat (like the point of an arrow) to show which way the grain runs.

Dry Rub

½ cup	barbecue seasoning mix (store-bought or see recipes, pages 27–34)	125 mL
⅓ cup	kosher salt	75 mL
¼ cup	sweet Hungarian paprika	50 mL
¼ cup	packed brown sugar	50 mL
¼ cup	chili powder	50 mL
1 tbsp	jalapeño pepper powder (see tip, page 198)	15 mL
1 tbsp	granulated garlic (see tip, at left)	15 mL
1 tbsp	granulated onion (see tip, at left)	15 mL
1 tsp	Worcestershire powder (see tip, at left)	5 mL
1 tsp	dry mustard	5 mL
5 to 6 lbs	beef brisket	2.5 to 3 kg
½ cup	packed brown sugar	125 mL
½ cup	cider vinegar	125 mL

1. *Prepare the dry rub:* In a small bowl, combine seasoning mix, salt, paprika, brown sugar, chili powder, jalapeño pepper powder, garlic, onion, Worcestershire powder and dry mustard.

TIPS

The smaller the smoking chamber on your equipment, the sooner your food will be done. If you're using a kettle grill or a bullet smoker, your brisket might be done in 7 hours. If you're using a bigger rig or a genuine smoker, it might take 8 hours.

• • •

Place any leftovers in an airtight container and store in the refrigerator for up to 1 week.

2. Place brisket on a flat surface. Rub liberally with dry rub, coating evenly. Cover and refrigerate for up to 24 hours. Remove from refrigerator and let come to room temperature while smoker is heating.

3. In a small bowl, combine brown sugar, $\frac{1}{2}$ cup (125 mL) water and vinegar. Pour into a spray bottle.

4. Prepare a fire in your smoker. *(For instructions, see pages 8–11.)*

5. Place brisket directly on the smoker rack, add wood to the coals and close the lid. Smoke at 225°F to 250°F (110°C to 120°C), spraying with brown sugar mixture every hour, for 5 hours. Wrap brisket in foil, close the lid and smoke for 2 hours, until fork-tender. Let rest for 15 minutes, then slice across the grain.

Brisket-Stuffed Artichoke Bottoms

Smoked shredded brisket makes great sandwiches, the basis for a wonderful hot and cheesy dip, or an appetizer like this one. Make sure to plan for generous leftovers when you take the time to smoke a brisket, and you can make dishes like this.

SERVES 8 AS AN APPETIZER

TIPS

For instruction on smoking beef brisket, see any of the preceding recipes, on pages 284–290.

• • •

Place any leftovers in an airtight container and store in the refrigerator for up to 1 week.

• • •

Variations

Substitute smoked pulled pork (see recipes, pages 226–232) for the brisket.

• • •

Substitute large mushroom caps for the artichoke bottoms.

Recommended wood: a combination of apple and cherry

¼ cup	butter	50 mL
2	cloves garlic, minced	2
¼ cup	chopped green bell pepper	50 mL
1½ tsp	dried parsley	7 mL
½ tsp	crushed dried basil	2 mL
8 oz	smoked beef brisket, minced	250 g
1 cup	shredded sharp Cheddar cheese	250 mL
⅓ cup	dry bread crumbs	75 mL
¼ cup	freshly grated Parmesan cheese	50 mL
1 lb	canned artichoke bottoms, drained	500 g

1. In a medium saucepan, melt butter over medium heat. Sauté garlic, green pepper, parsley and basil for 5 minutes, until pepper is softened. Remove from heat and let cool.

2. In a large bowl, combine green pepper mixture, brisket, Cheddar, bread crumbs and Parmesan.

3. Place artichoke bottoms on a disposable aluminum baking sheet. Generously stuff each artichoke bottom with stuffing. Set aside.

4. Prepare a fire in your smoker. *(For instructions, see pages 8–11.)*

5. Add wood to the coals and wait until smoke is fragrant, 5 to 10 minutes. Place baking sheet on the smoker rack and close the lid. Smoke at 225°F to 250°F (110°C to 120°C) for 30 minutes, or until warmed through and smoke-flavored.

Mesquite & Apple–Smoked Deviled Beef Ribs

If you've ever had slow-cooked deviled beef ribs made savory with Dijon mustard, you'll love this version.

SERVES 8	Recommended wood: a combination of mesquite and apple	

TIPS

You can find granulated onion and garlic at well-stocked supermarkets or online (see the Source Guide, page 356).

• • •

For the large plastic bag, use a handle-tie plastic kitchen garbage bag, making sure it is approved for food use. Sit the bag in a large disposable aluminum pan in the refrigerator so nothing spills.

2	cloves garlic, minced	2
¼ cup	minced onion	50 mL
¼ cup	Dijonnaise (or equal parts Dijon mustard and mayonnaise)	50 mL
¼ cup	olive oil	50 mL
¼ cup	soy sauce	50 mL
2 tbsp	freshly squeezed lemon juice	25 mL
2 tbsp	minced fresh parsley	25 mL
4 lbs	beef short ribs, trimmed	2 kg
2 tbsp	lemon pepper	25 mL
½ tsp	granulated onion (see tip, at left)	2 mL
¼ tsp	granulated garlic (see tip, at left)	1 mL
Pinch	five-spice powder	Pinch

1. In a small bowl, combine minced garlic, minced onion, Dijonnaise, oil, soy sauce, lemon juice and parsley.

2. Place ribs in a large plastic bag (see tip, at left) and brush with marinade. Tie bag and refrigerate for 4 to 6 hours.

3. In a small bowl, combine lemon pepper, granulated onion, granulated garlic and five-spice powder.

4. Remove ribs from bag and sprinkle with spice mixture. Set aside. Discard any remaining marinade.

5. Prepare a fire in your smoker. *(For instructions, see pages 8–11.)*

6. Place ribs directly on the smoker rack, add wood to the coals and close the lid. Smoke at 225°F to 250°F (110°C to 120°C) for 3 to 4 hours, or until tender.

Beef Ribs in Pale Ale Marinade

Whole beef ribs are sometimes referred to as "dinosaur bones" because they seem so huge compared to pork ribs. One slab of beef ribs, which will feed 2 to 3 people, weighs 2½ to 3½ pounds (1.25 to 1.75 kg). However, when smoked low and slow, beef ribs take on the deep flavor that beef lovers crave. In this recipe, pale ale adds a slightly sweet, malty and yeasty flavor to the meat. Slathered with a Raspberry Molasses Sauce, these smoky beef ribs take on a sweet finish that's pleasing to the palate.

SERVES 6 TO 8

Recommended wood: a combination of oak, apple and mesquite

TIPS

For the large plastic bag, use a handle-tie plastic kitchen garbage bag, making sure it is approved for food use. Sit the bag in a large disposable aluminum pan in the refrigerator so nothing spills.

• • •

Instead of water, pour pale ale into the water pan (see "Adding Moisture During Smoking," page 14) to heighten the aroma and flavor.

Pale Ale Marinade

5	sprigs fresh thyme	5
1	bottle (12 oz/341 mL) pale ale	1
½ cup	fancy molasses	125 mL
1 tbsp	granulated sugar	15 mL
1 tbsp	kosher salt	15 mL
1 tsp	minced fresh mint	5 mL
½ tsp	dry mustard	2 mL
½ tsp	freshly ground white pepper	2 mL
6 to 8 lbs	whole beef ribs, trimmed	3 to 4 kg

Raspberry Molasses Sauce

1 tbsp	olive oil	15 mL
1	small onion, finely chopped	1
1 cup	raspberry vinegar	250 mL
2 cups	ketchup	500 mL
1 cup	fancy molasses	250 mL
½ cup	bourbon	125 mL
1½ tsp	kosher salt	7 mL
½ tsp	freshly ground white pepper	2 mL
	Leaves from 5 fresh thyme sprigs	

TIP

The smaller the smoking chamber on your equipment, the sooner your food will be done. If you're using a kettle grill or a bullet smoker, your ribs might be done in 3½ hours. If you're using a bigger rig or a genuine smoker, they might take 4 to 4½ hours.

• • •

Make ahead

Raspberry Molasses Sauce can be prepared up to 1 day ahead. Spoon into an airtight container and store in the refrigerator. Reheat before basting.

1. *Prepare the marinade:* In a heavy saucepan, bring 1 cup (250 mL) water, thyme, ale, molasses, sugar, salt, mint, mustard and white pepper to boil over high heat. Remove from heat and let cool completely.

2. Place ribs in a large plastic bag (see tip, at left) and pour in marinade. Tie bag, toss to coat and refrigerate for at least 8 hours or overnight, turning occasionally.

3. *Prepare the sauce:* In a large saucepan, heat oil over medium-high heat. Sauté onion until golden brown, about 6 minutes. Add vinegar and bring to a boil; boil until mixture is reduced by one-quarter, about 5 minutes. Remove from heat and stir in ketchup, molasses and ¼ cup (50 mL) water, then stir in bourbon. Return to medium-low heat and bring to a simmer. Stir in salt and white pepper. Simmer for 10 minutes to allow flavors to blend. Stir in thyme. Keep warm by the smoker.

4. Remove ribs from marinade, but do not pat dry. Set aside. Discard marinade.

5. Prepare a fire in your smoker. *(For instructions, see pages 8–11.)*

6. Place ribs directly on the smoker rack, add wood to the coals and close the lid. Smoke at 225°F to 250°F (110°C to 120°C) for 3½ hours. Baste with sauce, close the lid and smoke, basting frequently with sauce, for 30 minutes, or until ribs are very tender. Store any leftovers in the refrigerator for up to 1 week.

Chili-Raspberry Beef Short Ribs

Meaty, succulent short ribs, basted with a sweet chili-raspberry sauce, slow-smoke to a tender turn.

SERVES 6 TO 8

Recommended wood: pecan

TIP

You could also serve these ribs with a spicy tomato-based barbecue sauce "doctored up" with seedless raspberry preserves to taste.

3 lbs	beef short ribs, trimmed	1.5 kg
1 tsp	garlic salt	5 mL
1 tsp	freshly ground black pepper	5 mL

Chili-Raspberry Sauce

1 cup	ketchup	250 mL
½ cup	packed brown sugar	125 mL
½ cup	bottled chili sauce	125 mL
2 tbsp	raspberry vinegar	25 mL
1 tbsp	freshly squeezed lemon juice	15 mL

1. Sprinkle ribs evenly with garlic salt and pepper. Set aside.

2. *Prepare the sauce:* In a medium saucepan, over medium heat, combine ketchup, sugar, chili sauce, vinegar and lemon juice. Cook, stirring occasionally, for about 10 minutes to let flavors blend. Keep warm by the smoker.

3. Prepare a fire in your smoker. *(For instructions, see pages 8–11.)*

4. Place ribs directly on the smoker rack, add wood to the coals and close the lid. Smoke at 225°F to 250°F (110°C to 120°C) for 2 hours. Baste with sauce, close the lid and smoke, basting with sauce every 15 minutes, for 1 hour, or until ribs are tender.

5. Bring any remaining sauce to a boil; boil for 3 minutes. Serve with ribs.

Asian-Style Beef Short Ribs

Fusion barbecue at its best! A kiss of smoke and a marinade with Asian flavors make this a lip-smackin' good dish.

SERVES 8

Recommended wood: a combination of apple and cherry

TIPS

Make sure to look for dark sesame oil. The lighter version will not be toasted and will not have the same flavor.

• • •

To toast sesame seeds, sprinkle them in the bottom of a heavy skillet and toast over medium heat, stirring with a spoon so they don't burn, until fragrant and golden brown.

• • •

For the large plastic bag, use a handle-tie plastic kitchen garbage bag, making sure it is approved for food use. Sit the bag in a large disposable aluminum pan in the refrigerator so nothing spills.

Marinade

1 cup	thinly sliced green onions	250 mL
1 cup	soy sauce	250 mL
½ cup	toasted sesame oil (see tip, at left)	125 mL
¼ cup	packed brown sugar	50 mL
2 tbsp	sesame seeds, toasted (see tip, at left)	25 mL
2 tbsp	minced garlic	25 mL
1 tbsp	grated gingerroot	15 mL
8 lbs	beef short ribs, trimmed	4 kg

1. *Prepare the marinade:* In a medium bowl, combine onions, soy sauce, 1 cup (250 mL) water, sesame oil, brown sugar, sesame seeds, garlic and ginger.

2. Place ribs in a large plastic bag (see tip, at left) and pour in half of the marinade. Tie bag, toss to coat and refrigerate for at least 8 hours or overnight. Reserve the remaining marinade in the refrigerator.

3. Remove ribs from marinade, but do not pat dry. Set aside. Discard marinade.

4. Prepare a fire in your smoker. *(For instructions, see pages 8–11.)*

5. Place ribs directly on the smoker rack, add wood to the coals and close the lid. Smoke at 225°F to 250°F (110°C to 120°C) for 2 hours. Baste with the reserved marinade, close the lid and smoke, basting with marinade every hour, for 2 hours, or until ribs are tender.

Beef Short Ribs in Serrano-Szechuan Marinade

Yum, yum! Sweet, savory and smoky flavors all in one dish. Serve it with steamed rice and steamed broccoli. If you have any leftover marinade, drizzle it over the broccoli.

SERVES 4 TO 6	Recommended wood: apple or cherry	

TIPS	**Serrano-Szechuan Marinade**		
Look for mildly spicy Szechuan sauce in Asian markets or the Asian food aisle of better grocery stores.	2	cloves garlic, minced	2
	2	serrano chili peppers, seeded and minced	2
	¾ cup	low-sodium soy sauce	175 mL
	½ cup	sliced green onions	125 mL
Make sure to look for dark sesame oil. The lighter version will not be toasted and will not have the same flavor.	½ cup	bottled Szechuan sauce	125 mL
	¼ cup	toasted sesame oil (see tip, at left)	50 mL
	3 tbsp	packed dark brown sugar	45 mL
	¼ cup	toasted sesame seeds (see tip, at left)	45 mL
To toast sesame seeds, sprinkle them in the bottom of a heavy skillet and toast over medium heat, stirring with a spoon so they don't burn, until fragrant and golden brown.	¼ tsp	grated gingerroot	1 mL
	6 lbs	beef short ribs, trimmed	3 kg

1. *Prepare the marinade:* In a medium bowl, combine garlic, serrano peppers, soy sauce, green onions, Szechuan sauce, ¼ cup (50 mL) water, sesame oil, brown sugar, sesame seeds and ginger.

For the large plastic bag, use a handle-tie plastic kitchen garbage bag, making sure it is approved for food use. Sit the bag in a large disposable aluminum pan in the refrigerator so nothing spills.

TIPS

To get the maximum smoke flavor and tenderness, I like to smoke these ribs at a lower temperature than some of the other recipes.

• • •

Place any leftovers in an airtight container and store in the refrigerator for up to 1 week.

2. Place ribs in a large plastic bag (see tip, at left) and pour in half of the marinade. Tie bag, toss to coat and refrigerate for 4 hours, turning occasionally. Reserve the remaining marinade in the refrigerator.

3. Remove ribs from marinade, but do not pat dry. Set aside. Discard marinade.

4. Prepare a fire in your smoker. (For instructions, see pages 8–11.)

5. Place ribs directly on the smoker rack, add wood to the coals and close the lid. Smoke at 200°F (100°C) for 5 hours. Baste with the reserved marinade, close the lid and smoke, basting with marinade every 15 minutes, for 1 hour, or until ribs are tender. Store any leftovers in the refrigerator for up to 1 week.

The Ultimate Slow-Smoked Burger

This is everything you want a burger to be: savory, smoky, tangy, beefy, wonderful.

SERVES 6	Recommended wood: a combination of apple and cherry

TIPS

Don't use lean or extra-lean ground meat on the smoker; it will dry out too much.

• • •

To toast pine nuts, sprinkle them in the bottom of a heavy skillet and toast over medium heat, stirring with a spoon so they don't burn, until lightly browned. They burn very quickly, so keep an eye on them. Because pine nuts contain a lot of oil, they'll keep cooking after being removed from the heat, so take them off before they turn the ideal medium brown.

Balsamic Jelly

½ cup	white balsamic vinegar	125 mL
¼ cup	granulated sugar	50 mL
¼ cup	chicken stock	50 mL

Apricot Ham Relish

½ cup	thinly sliced red onion	125 mL
½ cup	sliced dried apricots	125 mL
3 tbsp	red wine vinegar	45 mL
2 tbsp	extra-virgin olive oil	25 mL
2 tbsp	granulated sugar	25 mL
¼ cup	diced capiccola ham	50 mL

Burgers

2	cloves garlic, minced	2
1½ lbs	medium ground beef	750 g
8 oz	ground pork	250 g
¼ cup	chardonnay or other dry white wine	50 mL
3 tbsp	toasted pine nuts (see tip, at left)	45 mL
1 tbsp	seasoned salt	15 mL
1 tsp	freshly ground black pepper	5 mL
6	slices Havarti cheese	6
6	kaiser buns, split	6
2 cups	stemmed fresh spinach leaves	500 mL

With a slow-smoked burger, regular burger buns just won't do. If kaiser buns are not available, these burgers could be served on ciabattini or other artisan bread rolls.

1. *Prepare the Balsamic Jelly:* In a small saucepan, bring vinegar, sugar and chicken stock to a boil over medium-high heat. Cook until reduced by half, about 5 minutes. Remove from heat and let cool.

2. *Prepare the Apricot Ham Relish:* In another small saucepan, bring red onion, apricots, vinegar, oil and sugar to a boil over medium-high heat. Cook, stirring occasionally, until no liquid remains, about 10 minutes. Remove from heat and stir in ham. Set aside.

3. *Prepare the burgers:* In a bowl, using your hands or a fork, combine garlic, ground beef, ground pork, chardonnay, pine nuts, seasoned salt and pepper. Shape into six ¾-inch (2 cm) thick patties. Set aside.

4. Prepare a fire in your smoker. *(For instructions, see pages 8–11.)*

5. Add wood to the coals and wait until smoke is fragrant, 5 to 10 minutes. Place burgers directly on the smoker rack and close the lid. Smoke at 350°F (180°C) for 15 to 20 minutes, or until a meat thermometer inserted in the center of a burger registers 160°F (70°C). Top each burger with a slice of cheese, close the lid and smoke until cheese begins to melt, about 2 minutes.

6. Spread the cut sides of each bun with Balsamic Jelly. Arrange spinach leaves on each bottom bun and top with a burger. Top each burger with a spoonful of Apricot Ham Relish and close the bun.

Antipasto Burgers

When you really want to pull out all the stops and show guests what burgers can be in the afterlife, make this recipe, which uses a higher heat than most smoking recipes. This dish looks complicated and time-consuming, but much of it can be prepared ahead of time. For this recipe, don't soak your wood before putting it on the coals.

SERVES 6	Recommended wood: cherry

TIPS

Don't use lean or extra-lean ground meat on the smoker; it will dry out too much.

• • •

With a slow-smoked burger, regular burger buns just won't do. If sourdough buns are not available, these burgers could be served on kaisers, ciabattini or other artisan bread rolls.

• • •

Make ahead

The Zinfandel Reduction and Zinfandel Sandwich Sauce can be prepared up to 1 day in advance. Cover and store in the refrigerator.

Zinfandel Reduction

1	small shallot, minced	1
1 cup	red Zinfandel wine	250 mL
2 tsp	granulated sugar	10 mL

Zinfandel Sandwich Sauce

2	cloves garlic, minced	2
½ cup	freshly squeezed lemon juice	125 mL
1 tsp	seasoned salt	5 mL
Dash	hot pepper sauce	Dash
Dash	Worcestershire sauce	Dash
½ cup	extra-virgin olive oil	125 mL
¼ cup	freshly grated Parmesan cheese	50 mL

Antipasto

18	spears fresh asparagus, trimmed and cut into 2-inch (5 cm) lengths	18
6	baby portobello mushrooms, stems removed, sliced	6
6	canned artichokes, drained and halved	6

Burgers

3	cloves garlic, minced	3
2 lbs	medium ground beef chuck	1 kg
½ cup	minced red onion	125 mL
4 tsp	steak seasoning	20 mL
1 tbsp	minced fresh mint	15 mL
1 tbsp	minced fresh basil	15 mL
1 tbsp	minced fresh thyme	15 mL
½ tsp	freshly ground black pepper	2 mL
6	thin slices prosciutto	6

6	slices fresh mozzarella cheese	6
2	cloves garlic, minced	2
⅓ cup	extra-virgin olive oil	75 mL
6	crusty sourdough buns, split	6
6	leaves butter lettuce	6

1. *Prepare the Zinfandel Reduction:* In a small saucepan, bring shallots, wine and sugar to a boil over high heat. Cook until reduced by half, about 15 minutes. Remove from heat and let cool. Divide in half, reserving half for the sauce and half for the burgers.

2. *Prepare the Zinfandel Sandwich Sauce:* In a blender or food processor, process garlic, lemon juice, half of the cooled Zinfandel Reduction, seasoned salt, hot pepper sauce and Worcestershire sauce. With motor running, through hole in top, slowly drizzle in oil; process for 1 minute, until smooth. Transfer to a bowl and stir in Parmesan.

3. *Prepare the Antipasto:* In a large bowl, toss asparagus, mushrooms and artichokes with ½ cup (125 mL) of the sandwich sauce. Remove the vegetables from the sauce and place them in a disposable aluminum pan.

4. *Prepare the burgers:* In a large bowl, using your hands or a fork, combine garlic, ground chuck, red onion, the remaining Zinfandel Reduction, steak seasoning, mint, basil, thyme and pepper. Shape into six ¾-inch (2 cm) thick patties and wrap each in 1 slice of prosciutto. Set aside.

5. Prepare a fire in your smoker *(see pages 8–11)*.

6. Place burgers and pan of vegetables on the smoker rack, add wood to the coals and close the lid. Smoke at 350°F (180°C) for 15 to 20 minutes, or until a meat thermometer inserted in the center of a burger registers 160°F (70°C). Top each burger with smoked vegetables, then with a slice of mozzarella. Close the lid and smoke until cheese melts, about 10 minutes.

7. Combine garlic and oil. Brush on the cut sides of each bun. Arrange lettuce leaves on each bottom bun and top with a burger. Top each burger with 1 tbsp (15 mL) of the remaining sandwich sauce and close the bun.

Barbecued Meatloaf

If you think baked meatloaf is a comfort food, try this version. This recipe makes 3 loaves, so you could have one for dinner, serve another for leftovers, and freeze the third. Smoked meatloaf sandwiches slathered with a great barbecue sauce — are you drooling yet?

Recommended wood: a combination of sugar maple, peach and cherry or other fruit wood

TIPS

Don't use lean or extra-lean ground meat on the smoker; it will dry out too much.

• • •

If you're new to smoking, place meatloaves in disposable aluminum pans instead of placing them directly on the smoker rack. You'll still get the smoky flavor, but with easier cleanup.

• • •

Use leftovers to make a barbecued meatloaf sandwich. Start with good-quality bread, then slather on your favorite barbecue sauce and pile on the meatloaf.

1½ tsp	vegetable oil	7 mL
¾ cup	diced onion	175 mL
½ cup	diced red bell pepper	125 mL
½ cup	diced carrots	125 mL
4	large eggs, beaten	4
2¼ lbs	medium ground beef	1.15 kg
12 oz	medium ground pork	375 g
12 oz	medium ground veal	375 g
⅔ cup	fine dry bread crumbs	150 mL
⅔ cup	diced yellow squash (zucchini)	150 mL
⅔ cup	diced zucchini	150 mL
¼ cup	old-fashioned rolled oats	50 mL
2 tbsp	Worcestershire sauce	25 mL
1 tbsp	Montreal chicken seasoning or poultry seasoning	15 mL
1 tbsp	mesquite-flavored barbecue seasoning	15 mL
1 tbsp	minced garlic	15 mL
1 tbsp	dried Italian seasoning	15 mL
	Apple juice for spraying	
½ cup	tomato-based barbecue sauce (store-bought or see recipes, pages 50, 52–58 and 62–63)	125 mL

Wrap smoked loaves in plastic wrap and store in the refrigerator for up to 1 week or in the freezer for up to 3 months. To reheat, unwrap and place loaves on a baking sheet in a 300°F (150°C) oven until warmed through.

1. In a skillet, heat oil over medium-high heat. Sauté onion, peppers and carrots until onion is translucent, about 5 minutes. Remove from heat and let cool.

2. In a large bowl, combine sautéed vegetables, eggs, beef, pork, veal, bread crumbs, squash, zucchini, oats, Worcestershire sauce, chicken seasoning, barbecue seasoning, garlic and Italian seasoning. Shape into three 9- by 5-inch (23 by 13 cm) loaves and place on a baking sheet for transport to the smoker. Set aside.

3. Prepare a fire in your smoker. *(For instructions, see pages 8–11.)*

4. Place loaves directly on the smoker rack, add wood to the coals and close the lid. Smoke at 200°F (100°C), spraying with apple juice every hour, for 3 hours. Brush the top of each loaf with barbecue sauce, close the lid and smoke for 1 hour, or until a meat thermometer inserted in the center of a loaf registers 160°F (70°C). Let rest for 15 minutes before slicing.

Mushroom, Garlic & Thyme Meatloaf

So many meatloaves, so little time. This recipe, flavored with Dijon and bacon, also makes 3 loaves.

SERVES 12	Recommended wood: a combination of sugar maple and pecan with cherry, peach or other fruit wood		

TIPS

Don't use lean or extra-lean ground meat on the smoker; it will dry out too much.

• • •

If you're new to smoking, place meatloaves in disposable aluminum pans instead of placing them directly on the smoker rack. You'll still get the smoky flavor, but with easier cleanup.

• • •

Use leftovers to make a barbecued meatloaf sandwich. Start with good-quality bread, then slather on your favorite barbecue sauce and pile on the meatloaf.

1 tbsp	olive oil	15 mL
2	cloves garlic, minced	2
1 cup	sliced mushrooms (about 4 oz/125 g)	250 mL
½ cup	diced onion	125 mL
¼ tsp	minced fresh thyme	1 mL
4	slices bacon, cooked crisp and finely crumbled	4
2	large eggs, beaten	2
2½ lbs	medium ground beef	1.25 kg
½ cup	dry bread crumbs	125 mL
½ cup	Dijon mustard	125 mL
2 tbsp	freshly grated Parmesan cheese	25 mL
2 tbsp	Worcestershire sauce	25 mL
1 tbsp	minced fresh parsley	15 mL
¼ tsp	freshly ground black pepper	1 mL
	Apple juice for spraying	

1. In a skillet, heat oil over medium-high heat. Sauté garlic, mushrooms, onion and thyme until onion is translucent, about 5 minutes. Remove from heat and let cool.

2. In a large bowl, combine sautéed vegetables, bacon, eggs, beef, bread crumbs, mustard, Parmesan, Worcestershire sauce, parsley and pepper. Shape into three 9- by 5-inch (23 by 13 cm) loaves and place on a baking sheet for transport to the smoker. Set aside.

3. Prepare a fire in your smoker. *(For instructions, see pages 8–11.)*

4. Place loaves directly on the smoker rack, add wood to the coals and close the lid. Smoke at 200°F (100°C), spraying with apple juice every hour, for 4 hours, or until a meat thermometer inserted in the center of a loaf registers 160°F (70°C). Let rest for 15 minutes before slicing.

Caribbean-Style Barbecued Meatloaf with Papaya Relish

Yum, yum, yum! Or should we say more, more, more! This meatloaf recipe, which makes 4 loaves, has a little kick to it and tastes wonderful with the fresh Papaya Relish.

SERVES 16

Recommended wood: a combination of hickory and peach or other fruit wood

TIPS
Don't use lean or extra-lean ground meat on the smoker; it will dry out too much.

• • •

Jamaican jerk seasoning typically contains habanero or Scotch bonnet chili peppers, some of the hottest chilies there are. If you prefer, substitute your favorite Mediterranean seasoning.

• • •

Look for mango nectar in bottles or cartons in the fruit juice section of well-stocked supermarkets and health food stores.

Papaya Relish

3 cups	diced peeled seeded papaya	750 mL
3 cups	fresh pineapple chunks (or drained canned)	750 mL
1¼ cups	diced cucumber	300 mL
½ cup	diced red onion	125 mL
½ cup	chopped fresh cilantro	125 mL
¼ cup	freshly squeezed lime juice	50 mL
¼ cup	olive oil	50 mL
2 tbsp	rice vinegar	25 mL
½ tsp	hot pepper flakes	2 mL
½ tsp	kosher salt	2 mL

Meatloaf

4	large eggs	4
6 lbs	medium ground beef	3 kg
2 cups	tomato sauce	500 mL
1⅓ cups	diced green bell peppers	325 mL
1⅓ cups	diced red onions	325 mL
¾ cup	fine dry bread crumbs	175 mL
¼ cup	minced garlic	50 mL
¼ cup	packed brown sugar	50 mL
¼ cup	Jamaican jerk seasoning	50 mL
	Mango nectar (see tip, at left) for spraying	

TIP

If you're new to smoking, place meatloaves in disposable aluminum pans instead of placing them directly on the smoker rack. You'll still get the smoky flavor, but with easier cleanup.

• • • •

Make ahead

Papaya relish can be prepared up to 1 day in advance.

Wrap smoked loaves in plastic wrap and store in the refrigerator for up to 1 week or in the freezer for up to 3 months. To reheat, unwrap and place loaves on a baking sheet in a 300°F (150°C) oven until warmed through.

1. *Prepare the relish:* In a large bowl, combine papaya, pineapple, cucumber, red onion, cilantro, lime juice, oil, vinegar, hot pepper flakes and salt. Cover and refrigerate until ready to serve.

2. *Prepare the meatloaf:* In another large bowl, combine eggs, beef, tomato sauce, green peppers, red onions, bread crumbs, garlic, brown sugar and jerk seasoning. Shape into four 9- by 5-inch (23 by 13 cm) loaves and place on a baking sheet for transport to the smoker. Set aside.

3. Prepare a fire in your smoker. *(For instructions, see pages 8–11.)*

4. Place loaves directly on the smoker rack, add wood to the coals and close the lid. Smoke at 200°F (100°C), spraying with mango nectar every hour, for 4 hours, or until a meat thermometer inserted in the center of a loaf registers 160°F (70°C). Let rest for 15 minutes before slicing. Serve with Papaya Relish.

Lamb

SLOW-SMOKED LAMB — or baaarbecue — is a new frontier for many people. But banish all thoughts of strong-flavored meat. If you buy spring lamb, trim off the excess fat and cook it to a rare or medium doneness, you'll have a tasty dish.

Almost every year, I compete in the National Lamb-BQ contest (held in Bonner Springs, Kansas), and I win ribbons more often than not. So I've developed a repertoire of slow-smoked lamb recipes that are really delicious, and I'm happy to share them with you.

The cuts of lamb that work well with slow smoking are leg of lamb (bone-in or boneless), lamb loin (if you can get it), rack of lamb, ribs and chops. Because lamb is already tender, you only have to worry about getting the meat done to your liking.

Flavors I like with lamb include garlic, Dijon mustard and strong herbs such as rosemary, but also tangy fruits, citrus fruits and honey.

My preferred wood smoke flavoring for lamb is fruit wood such as apple, cherry or peach. But pecan, oak and sugar maple — alone or in combination with fruit woods — give a medium smoke that will enhance but not overpower the lamb.

LAMB RECIPES

Cherry-Smoked Rack of Lamb
    with Fresh Herb Paste 312

Bourbon-Brined Rack of Lamb . . 313

Grand Champion
    Rack of Lamb 314

Asian-Style Lamb Ribs 315

Honey Mustard Lamb Ribs 316

Raspberry Zinfandel
    Lamb Ribs 317

Cherry-Smoked Lamb Chops . . . 318

Lamb Chops in Orange, Garlic
    & Brown Sugar Brine 319

Butterflied Leg of Lamb in
    Red Currant Marinade 320

Herb Garden Leg of Lamb
    with Red Currant Sauce 322

Mediterranean Lamb
    Appetizer Skewers 324

Lamb Skewers in Fresh
    Orange & White
    Balsamic Marinade 325

Lamb Skewers with
    Red Currant–Chili Sauce . . . 326

Smoky Lamb Meatballs
    in Marinara Sauce 328

Lamb Sausage with Apricot
    Maple Glaze 329

Perfect Score Lamb Sausage . . . 330

Cherry-Smoked Rack of Lamb with Fresh Herb Paste

If you like roasted rack of lamb, you'll love the added flavor smoking brings to this dish.

SERVES 4   **Recommended wood:** cherry or other fruit wood

TIPS

Smoked rack of lamb is delicious served with Flower of the Flames Raspberry Barbecue Sauce (see recipe, page 50).

· · ·

"French" the bones by scraping the bits of fat and flesh off the ends with a sharp knife (or have your butcher do this).

Fresh Herb Paste

8	cloves garlic	8
1½ cups	olive oil	375 mL
½ cup	freshly squeezed lemon juice	125 mL
⅓ cup	packed fresh thyme sprigs	75 mL
⅓ cup	packed fresh mint leaves	75 mL
¼ cup	packed fresh basil leaves	50 mL
2 tbsp	kosher salt	25 mL
2	racks of lamb, fat removed and bones frenched (see tip, at left)	2

1. *Prepare the paste:* In a food processor, process garlic, oil, lemon juice, thyme, mint, basil and salt until mixture becomes a paste. Spread paste over lamb. Set aside.

2. Prepare a fire in your smoker. *(For instructions, see pages 8–11.)*

3. Place lamb directly on the smoker rack, add wood to the coals and close the lid. Smoke at 225°F to 250°F (110°C to 120°C) for 1½ hours, until a meat thermometer inserted in the center of a rack reaches an internal temperature of 150°F (65°C) for medium-rare, or until desired doneness.

Bourbon-Brined Rack of Lamb

The sweetness in the bourbon brings out the sweetness in the lamb in this recipe. The appropriate drink to accompany this dish? Whiskey sours, of course.

SERVES 4	Recommended wood: cherry or other fruit wood	

TIPS

"French" the bones by scraping the bits of fat and flesh off the ends with a sharp knife (or have your butcher do this).

• • •

The smaller the smoking chamber on your equipment, the sooner your food will be done. If you're using a kettle grill or a bullet smoker, your lamb might be done in an hour. If you're using a bigger rig or a genuine smoker, it might take 1½ hours.

2	racks of lamb, fat removed and bones frenched (see tip, at left)	2
1½ cups	Tennessee Bourbon Brine (see recipe, page 23)	375 mL
1½ cups	Bourbon Barbecue Sauce (see recipe, page 52)	375 mL

1. Place lamb in a large sealable plastic bag and pour in brine. Seal bag, toss to coat and refrigerate for at least 8 hours or for up to 12 hours.

2. Remove lamb from brine and discard brine. Rinse lamb under cold running water and pat dry. Set aside.

3. Prepare a fire in your smoker. *(For instructions, see pages 8–11.)*

4. Place lamb directly on the smoker rack, add wood to the coals and close the lid. Smoke at 225°F to 250°F (110°C to 120°C) for 1 hour. Brush with barbecue sauce, close the lid and smoke for 30 minutes, until a meat thermometer inserted in the center of a rack reaches an internal temperature of 150°F (65°C) for medium-rare, or until desired doneness. Pass any remaining barbecue sauce at the table.

Grand Champion Rack of Lamb

This recipe took first place in its category at the Kansas State Fair barbecue contest and helped me win the Kansas State Grand Championship at the National Lamb-BQ Contest.

SERVES 8

Recommended wood: a combination of cherry and sugar maple

TIP

"French" the bones by scraping the bits of fat and flesh off the ends with a sharp knife (or have the butcher do this).

Grand Champion Herb Paste

1 cup	olive oil	250 mL
¼ cup	each packed fresh thyme, basil and mint leaves	50 mL
3 tbsp	seasoned salt	45 mL
2 tbsp	fresh rosemary needles	25 mL
2 tbsp	minced garlic	25 mL
1 tbsp	minced shallots	15 mL
4	racks of lamb, fat removed and bones frenched (see tip, at left)	4
½ cup	prepared mustard	125 mL
¼ cup	amber liquid honey	50 mL

1. *Prepare the paste:* In a food processor, process oil, thyme, basil, mint, seasoned salt, rosemary, garlic and shallots for 1 minute, or until mixture becomes a loose paste.

2. Place lamb in a large sealable plastic bag and pour in paste. Seal bag, toss to coat and refrigerate for 2 hours.

3. Remove lamb from paste and pat dry. Discard paste.

4. In a small bowl, combine mustard and honey; brush onto lamb. Set aside.

5. Prepare a fire in your smoker. *(For instructions, see pages 8–11.)*

6. Place lamb directly on the smoker rack, add wood to the coals and close the lid. Smoke at 225°F to 250°F (110°C to 120°C) for 1½ hours, until a meat thermometer inserted in the center of a rack reaches an internal temperature of 150°F (65°C) for medium-rare, or until desired doneness.

Asian-Style Lamb Ribs

Asian flavors go as well with lamb as they do with beef (see Asian-Style Beef Short Ribs, page 297). Serve these ribs with an Asian noodle salad and sliced cucumbers in a sweet-and-sour dressing.

SERVES 4 TO 6

Recommended wood: pecan

TIPS

Many barbecuers prefer "Denver cut" lamb ribs, a cut that features the middle, meatier ribs of the lamb breast.

• • •

For the large plastic bag, use a handle-tie plastic kitchen garbage bag, making sure it is approved for food use. Sit the bag in a large disposable aluminum pan in the refrigerator so nothing spills.

• • •

If you prefer your ribs cooked to medium, they will be done in about 1 hour.

Marinade

1 cup	thinly sliced green onions	250 mL
1 cup	soy sauce	250 mL
½ cup	toasted sesame oil (see tip, page 298)	125 mL
¼ cup	packed brown sugar	50 mL
2 tbsp	sesame seeds, toasted (see tip, page 298)	25 mL
2 tbsp	minced garlic	25 mL
1 tbsp	grated gingerroot	15 mL
12	racks lamb ribs, trimmed	12

1. *Prepare the marinade:* In a medium bowl, combine green onions, soy sauce, 1 cup (250 mL) water, sesame oil, brown sugar, sesame seeds, garlic and ginger.

2. Place ribs in a large plastic bag (see tip, at left) and pour in half of the marinade. Tie bag, toss to coat and refrigerate for at least 8 hours or overnight. Reserve the remaining marinade in the refrigerator.

3. Remove ribs from marinade, but do not pat dry. Set aside. Discard marinade.

4. Prepare a fire in your smoker. *(For instructions, see pages 8–11.)*

5. Place ribs directly on the smoker rack, add wood to the coals and close the lid. Smoke at 225°F to 250°F (110°C to 120°C), basting with the reserved marinade every 30 minutes, for 1½ hours, or until meat pulls away from the ends of the bones.

Honey Mustard Lamb Ribs

So tender, so sweet, these ribs are seriously good eating, especially when you serve them with Red Currant Sauce (see recipe, page 67).

SERVES 4 TO 6	Recommended wood: cherry	

TIP

If you prefer your ribs cooked to medium, they will be done in about 1 hour.

• • •

The smaller the smoking chamber on your equipment, the sooner your food will be done. If you're using a kettle grill or a bullet smoker, your lamb might be done in an hour. If you're using a bigger rig or a genuine smoker, it might take 1½ hours.

2	cloves garlic	2
3 tbsp	extra-virgin olive oil	45 mL
2½ tsp	chopped fresh rosemary	12 mL
2¼ tsp	kosher salt	11 mL
1 tsp	freshly ground black pepper	5 mL
1 tsp	lemon pepper	5 mL
12	racks lamb ribs, trimmed	12
¼ cup	prepared honey mustard	50 mL

1. In a food processor, process garlic, oil, rosemary, salt, black pepper and lemon pepper until garlic is finely chopped.

2. Arrange ribs on a baking sheet. Brush with honey mustard, then garlic mixture. Cover and refrigerate for 2 hours. Remove from refrigerator and let warm to room temperature while smoker is heating.

3. Prepare a fire in your smoker. *(For instructions, see pages 8–11.)*

4. Place ribs directly on the smoker rack, add wood to the coals and close the lid. Smoke at 225°F to 250°F (110°C to 120°C) for 1½ hours, or until meat pulls away from the ends of the bones.

Raspberry Zinfandel Lamb Ribs

Tiny, succulent lamb ribs get the star treatment in this recipe, with an alluring combination of raspberry vinegar, white Zinfandel and tarragon. Sometimes I go all out and add 1 cup (250 mL) of white Zinfandel to the water pan too.

SERVES 4 TO 6	**Recommended wood:** a fruit wood, such as apple or cherry

TIPS

For the large plastic bag, use a handle-tie plastic kitchen garbage bag, making sure it is approved for food use. Sit the bag in a large disposable aluminum pan in the refrigerator so nothing spills.

• • •

If you prefer your ribs cooked to medium, they will be done in about 1 hour.

• • •

Serve these ribs with a doctored-up raspberry barbecue sauce. Simply take your favorite tomato-based barbecue sauce and add seedless raspberry jam or preserves to taste.

Marinade

2	cloves garlic, minced	2
½ cup	olive oil	125 mL
½ cup	raspberry vinegar	125 mL
¼ cup	minced onion	50 mL
¼ cup	white Zinfandel wine	50 mL
2 tbsp	freshly squeezed lime juice	25 mL
1 tsp	dried tarragon	5 mL
1 tsp	chopped fresh parsley	5 mL
1 tsp	freshly ground black pepper	5 mL
12	racks lamb ribs, trimmed	12
	Additional olive oil for basting	

1. *Prepare the marinade:* In a medium bowl, combine garlic, oil, vinegar, onion, wine, lime juice, tarragon, parsley and pepper.

2. Place ribs in a large plastic bag (see tip, at left) and pour in marinade. Tie bag, toss to coat and refrigerate for 2 hours.

3. Remove ribs from marinade, but do not pat dry. Set aside. Discard marinade.

4. Prepare a fire in your smoker. *(For instructions, see pages 8–11.)*

5. Place ribs directly on the smoker rack, add wood to the coals and close the lid. Smoke at 225°F to 250°F (110°C to 120°C), basting with olive oil every 30 minutes, for 1½ hours, or until meat pulls away from the ends of the bones.

Lamb   **317**

Cherry-Smoked Lamb Chops

Give the traditional English combination of lamb and mint jelly a contemporary twist with this smoky, herby recipe.

SERVES 4 TO 6	Recommended wood: cherry

TIP

The smaller the smoking chamber on your equipment, the sooner your food will be done. If you're using a kettle grill or a bullet smoker, your lamb chops might be done in 45 minutes. If you're using a bigger rig or a genuine smoker, your chops might take an hour.

⅓ cup	Fresh Garlic & Herb Paste (see recipe, page 35)	75 mL
4	racks of lamb, cut into 1-inch (2.5 cm) thick chops	4
¼ cup	Herbal Balsamic Jelly (see recipe, page 70)	50 mL

1. Spread paste on both sides of lamb chops and let stand at room temperature for 30 minutes.

2. Meanwhile, prepare a fire in your smoker. *(For instructions, see pages 8–11.)*

3. Add wood to the coals and wait until smoke is fragrant, 5 to 10 minutes. Place chops directly on the smoker rack and close the lid. Smoke at 225°F to 250°F (110°C to 120°C) for 45 to 60 minutes, or until a meat thermometer inserted in the thickest part of a chop registers 160°F (70°C) for medium, or until desired doneness.

4. Serve each chop with a dollop of Herbal Balsamic Jelly.

> Every year, barbecue competitors and aficionados gather in Owensboro, Kentucky, for the International Bar-B-Q Festival, where they will consume 20 tons of barbecued mutton and 1,500 gallons of burgoo (a type of stew) in one 3-hour dinner. Owensboro is famous for its slow-smoked mutton (a year-old or older sheep). Mutton needs to be special-ordered from your butcher.

Lamb Chops in Orange, Garlic & Brown Sugar Brine

Orange might not be a flavor you automatically associate with lamb, but it works wonders! If you want a hat trick of orange flavor, serve this with Mustard & Marmalade Barbecue Sauce (see recipe, page 60).

SERVES 16	Recommended wood: apple or cherry	

TIPS

For the large plastic bag, use a handle-tie plastic kitchen garbage bag, making sure it is approved for food use. Sit the bag in a large disposable aluminum pan in the refrigerator so nothing spills.

• • •

The smaller the smoking chamber on your equipment, the sooner your food will be done. If you're using a kettle grill or a bullet smoker, your lamb chops might be done in 45 minutes. If you're using a bigger rig or a genuine smoker, your chops might take an hour.

8	racks of lamb, cut into 1-inch (2.5 cm) thick chops	8
6 cups	Orange, Garlic & Brown Sugar Brine (see recipe, page 22)	1.5 L
1¼ cups	Sweet Orange Baste (see recipe, page 46)	300 mL

1. Place chops in a large plastic bag (see tip, at left) and pour in brine. Tie bag, toss to coat and refrigerate for at least 8 hours or for up to 12 hours.

2. Remove chops from brine and discard brine. Rinse chops under cold running water and pat dry. Set aside.

3. Prepare a fire in your smoker. *(For instructions, see pages 8–11.)*

4. Add wood to the coals and wait until smoke is fragrant, 5 to 10 minutes. Place chops directly on the smoker rack and close the lid. Smoke at 225°F to 250°F (110°C to 120°C), brushing with baste every 15 minutes, for 45 to 60 minutes, or until a meat thermometer inserted in the thickest part of a chop registers 160°F (70°C) for medium, or until desired doneness.

Butterflied Leg of Lamb in Red Currant Marinade

The tart and tangy flavor of red currants goes well with lamb. When you slow-smoke a butterflied leg of lamb, which will lie thinner and flatter on the smoker rack, your lamb will be done sooner than if the leg were rolled and tied.

SERVES 8 TO 10	**Recommended wood:** a combination of peach and cherry or other fruit wood

TIPS

Melt red currant jelly in a small saucepan over low heat.

• • •

Jalapeño pepper powder is available from better spice emporiums or online (see the Source Guide, page 356). If you can't find it, substitute about 2 tsp (10 mL) hot pepper sauce.

• • •

To butterfly means to cut a thicker piece of meat so that it opens like a book. Sometimes, as with a leg of lamb, you have to remove the bone first. A butterflied piece of meat is flatter, so it smokes more quickly. It can also be spread with a stuffing or filling, then rolled, tied and smoked. Have your butcher butterfly the lamb for you.

Marinade

6	cloves garlic, minced	6
¾ cup	red currant jelly, melted (see tip, at left)	175 mL
½ cup	freshly squeezed lemon juice	125 mL
3 tbsp	olive oil	45 mL
2 tbsp	Worcestershire sauce	25 mL
2 tbsp	minced fresh mint	25 mL
2 tbsp	minced fresh parsley	25 mL
4 tsp	ground coriander	20 mL
1½ tsp	kosher salt	7 mL
1 tsp	jalapeño pepper powder (see tip, at left)	5 mL
1	boneless leg of lamb (5 to 5½ lbs/2.5 to 2.75 kg), butterflied	1

1. *Prepare the marinade:* In a medium bowl, combine garlic, red currant jelly, lemon juice, oil, Worcestershire sauce, mint, parsley, coriander, salt and jalapeño pepper powder.

For the large plastic bag, use a handle-tie plastic kitchen garbage bag, making sure it is approved for food use. Sit the bag in a large disposable aluminum pan in the refrigerator so nothing spills.

• • •

If you wish, carry the berry flavor through and serve with Red Currant Sauce (see recipe, page 67).

2. Using a sharp knife, trim fat from lamb. Rinse lamb under cold running water and pat dry. Place in a large plastic bag (see tip, at left) and pour in marinade. Tie bag, toss to coat and refrigerate for at least 4 hours or for up to 8 hours, turning several times.

3. Remove lamb from marinade, but do not pat dry. Set aside. Discard marinade.

4. Prepare a fire in your smoker. *(For instructions, see pages 8–11.)*

5. Place lamb directly on the smoker rack, add wood to the coals, and close the lid. Smoke at 225°F to 250°F (110°C to 120°C) for 1½ to 2 hours, or until a meat thermometer inserted in the thickest part of lamb reaches an internal temperature of 150°F (65°C) for medium-rare, or until desired doneness. Let rest for 15 minutes before carving, then another 15 minutes before serving.

Herb Garden Leg of Lamb with Red Currant Sauce

A contrast of colors and flavors makes this slow-smoked lamb dish great for entertaining. Prepare this dish when your herb garden or the herbs at the farmer's market are bountiful.

SERVES 8 TO 10	Recommended wood: cherry

TIPS

Lamb fat carries a strong flavor that many people don't like, so trim as much as you can from the meat before you marinate and smoke it.

• • •

For the large plastic bag, use a handle-tie plastic kitchen garbage bag, making sure it is approved for food use. Sit the bag in a large disposable aluminum pan in the refrigerator so nothing spills.

Herb Paste

8	cloves garlic	8
½ cup	packed fresh mint leaves	125 mL
½ cup	packed fresh thyme sprigs	125 mL
½ cup	packed fresh basil leaves	125 mL
½ cup	packed fresh chives	125 mL
1 cup	olive oil	250 mL
1 tbsp	seasoned salt	15 mL
1 tsp	freshly ground black pepper	5 mL
1	boneless leg of lamb (5 to 5½ lbs/2.5 to 2.75 kg)	1
	Grated zest of 2 lemons	
¼ cup	freshly squeezed lemon juice	50 mL
2 cups	Red Currant Sauce (see recipe, page 67)	500 mL

1. *Prepare the paste:* In a food processor, process garlic, mint, thyme, basil, chives, oil, seasoned salt and pepper until the mixture forms a paste.

2. Using a sharp knife, trim fat from lamb. Rinse lamb under cold running water and pat dry. Place in a large plastic bag (see tip, at left) and spoon in paste. Tie bag and refrigerate for at least 3 hours or for up to 8 hours. Remove from refrigerator and let warm to room temperature while smoker is heating.

3. Prepare a fire in your smoker. *(For instructions, see pages 8–11.)*

4. Place lamb directly on the smoker rack, add wood to the coals and close the lid. Smoke at 225°F to 250°F (110°C to 120°C) for 4 hours, or until a meat thermometer inserted in the thickest part of lamb reaches an internal temperature of 150°F (65°C) for medium-rare, or until desired doneness. Remove lamb from smoker, drizzle with lemon juice and top with lemon zest. Let rest for 15 minutes before carving.

5. Serve with Red Currant Sauce.

Mediterranean Lamb Appetizer Skewers

At your next cocktail party, serve something really fabulous: these skewers! Arrange them on a round platter around a bowl of the aioli and let your guests dig in.

Recommended wood: pecan or oak

Sixteen 12-inch (30 cm) bamboo skewers

2 lbs	boneless lamb shoulder or leg	1 kg
2½ cups	Mediterranean Marinade (see recipe, page 42)	625 mL
1 cup	Barbecuer's Aioli (see recipe, page 71)	250 mL

1. Rinse lamb under cold running water and pat dry. Cut into ¾-inch (2 cm) cubes. Place in a large sealable plastic bag and pour in marinade. Seal bag, toss to coat and refrigerate for at least 2 hours or overnight.

2. Soak skewers in water for 30 minutes.

3. Remove lamb from marinade, but do not pat dry. Discard marinade. Thread lamb onto skewers and place on a baking sheet for transport to the smoker. Set aside.

4. Prepare a fire in your smoker. *(For instructions, see pages 8–11.)*

5. Place skewers directly on the smoker rack, add wood to the coals and close the lid. Smoke at 225°F to 250°F (110°C to 120°C) for 2 hours, or until tender.

6. Serve with Barbecuer's Aioli.

Lamb Skewers in Fresh Orange & White Balsamic Marinade

A succulent and aromatic way to serve lamb, this recipe can only be topped by the fact that it's easy. Only 2 hours of tending the smoker for such tasty results. If you want to echo the orange flavor in the rest of the meal, add fresh orange segments to a salad or side dish.

SERVES 8 AS AN APPETIZER, 4 AS A MAIN COURSE

TIP

Chicken is also delicious with this treatment and will smoke in about the same time. Just check a piece of chicken in the middle of a skewer for doneness.

Recommended wood: peach or other fruit wood

Eight 12-inch (30 cm) bamboo skewers

2 lbs	boneless lamb shoulder or leg	1 kg
1 cup	Fresh Orange & White Balsamic Marinade (see recipe, page 39)	250 mL
1½ cups	Sweet Orange Baste (see recipe, page 46)	375 mL

1. Rinse lamb under cold running water and pat dry. Cut into 1-inch (2.5 cm) cubes. Place in a large sealable plastic bag and pour in marinade. Seal bag, toss to coat and refrigerate for at least 2 hours or overnight.

2. Soak skewers in water for 30 minutes.

3. Remove lamb from marinade, but do not pat dry. Discard marinade. Thread lamb onto skewers and place on a baking sheet for transport to the smoker.

4. Prepare a fire in your smoker. *(For instructions, see pages 8–11.)*

5. Place skewers directly on the smoker rack, add wood to the coals and close the lid. Smoke at 225°F to 250°F (110°C to 120°C), brushing with baste every 30 minutes, for 2 hours, or until tender.

Lamb Skewers with Red Currant–Chili Sauce

Good either as an appetizer or as a main course, these lamb skewers are delicious with a big green salad and crusty bread.

SERVES 8 AS AN APPETIZER, 4 AS A MAIN COURSE

TIPS

To save time, buy fresh pineapple that has already been cored, peeled and cut into chunks.

• • •

The smaller the smoking chamber on your equipment, the sooner your food will be done. If you're using a kettle grill or a bullet smoker, your lamb skewers might be done in 1½ hours. If you're using a bigger rig or a genuine smoker, they might take 2 hours.

Recommended wood: apple

Sixteen 12-inch (30 cm) bamboo skewers

2 lbs	boneless lamb shoulder or leg	1 kg
1	fresh pineapple, peeled, cored and cubed	1
1	green bell pepper, cut into ¾-inch (2 cm) squares	1
1	red bell pepper, cut into ¾-inch (2 cm) squares	1
1	large red onion, cut into 2-inch (5 cm) chunks	1

Red Currant–Chili Sauce

½ cup	prepared chili sauce	125 mL
½ cup	red currant jelly	125 mL
1 tsp	prepared mustard	5 mL
½ tsp	grated orange zest	2 mL
	Pear or apple juice for spraying	

1. Soak skewers in water for 30 minutes.
2. Rinse lamb under cold running water and pat dry. Cut into ¾-inch (2 cm) cubes. Thread lamb, pineapple, green pepper, red pepper and onion onto skewers. Place on a baking sheet for transport to the smoker. Set aside.

3. Prepare a fire in your smoker. *(For instructions, see pages 8–11.)*

4. *Meanwhile, prepare the sauce:* In a small bowl, combine chili sauce, red currant jelly, mustard and orange zest. Keep warm by the smoker.

5. Place skewers directly on the smoker rack, add wood to the coals and close the lid. Smoke at 225°F to 250°F (110°C to 120°C), brushing with sauce and spraying with pear juice every 30 minutes, for 2 hours, or until tender. Pass any remaining sauce at the table

Smoky Lamb Meatballs in Marinara Sauce

This recipe took second place at the National Lamb-BQ Contest. When you add marinara sauce to the meatballs and smoke them together, the sauce takes on a wonderful smoky flavor. Serve with spaghetti, if you like, or as cocktail meatballs (see tip, at left).

SERVES 8 TO 10

Recommended wood: a combination of apple and cherry

TIPS

Don't use lean or extra-lean ground meat on the smoker; it will dry out too much.

• • •

When serving these as cocktail meatballs, vary the flavor each time. Instead of the marinara sauce, try a prepared sweet-and-sour sauce or a homemade barbecue sauce such as Mustard & Marmalade Barbecue Sauce (see recipe, page 60).

• • •

Make ahead

Place in an airtight container and store in the refrigerator for up to 1 week or in the freezer for up to 3 months.

2	cloves garlic, minced	2
1	small onion, finely chopped	1
3 lbs	medium ground lamb	1.5 kg
1 lb	medium ground pork	500 g
½ cup	dry bread crumbs	125 mL
2 tsp	grated lemon zest	10 mL
¼ cup	freshly squeezed lemon juice	50 mL
3 tbsp	finely chopped fresh parsley	45 mL
3 tbsp	finely chopped fresh mint	45 mL
3 tbsp	finely chopped fresh basil	45 mL
2 tbsp	finely chopped fresh thyme	25 mL
½ tsp	kosher salt	2 mL
½ tsp	freshly ground black pepper	2 mL
	Prepared Italian marinara sauce	

1. In a large bowl, using your hands or a fork, combine garlic, onion, lamb, pork, bread crumbs, lemon zest, lemon juice, parsley, mint, basil, thyme, salt and pepper. Shape into small balls about 1½ to 2 inches (4 to 5 cm) in diameter. Place in a large disposable aluminum pan. Set aside.

2. Prepare a fire in your smoker. *(For instructions, see pages 8–11.)*

3. Place pan on the smoker rack, add wood to the coals and close the lid. Smoke at 225°F to 250°F (110°C to 120°C) for 1½ hours. Pour marinara sauce over meatballs and smoke for 45 minutes, or until juices run clear when meatballs are pierced with a knife.

Lamb Sausage with Apricot Maple Glaze

The great thing about smoking sausage is that it's already tender because the meat has been ground and seasoned. All you need to do is add your own flavorful touch with a glaze or a sauce. I like to use link sausage in this recipe, smoke it over a sweet fruit wood, then finish it with the glaze. Slice and serve smoked lamb sausage on toothpicks as an appetizer or enjoy it as a main course with steamed spinach and a potato casserole.

SERVES 8 AS AN APPETIZER, 4 AS A MAIN COURSE

TIPS

You can now find lamb sausages of all kinds, from bratwurst to Italian sausage and salami, at farmer's markets, gourmet grocers and better butcher shops.

• • •

If you're new to smoking, instead of placing sausages directly on the smoker rack, place them in disposable aluminum pans. You'll still get the smoky flavor, but with easier cleanup.

• • •

Make ahead

Place in an airtight container and store in the refrigerator for up to 1 week or in the freezer for up to 3 months.

Recommended wood: apple or cherry

1 lb	fresh lamb sausages	500 g
1½ cups	Apricot Maple Glaze (see recipe, page 66)	375 mL

1. Prepare a fire in your smoker. *(For instructions, see pages 8–11.)*

2. Place sausages directly on the smoker rack, add wood to the coals and close the lid. Smoke at 225°F to 250°F (110°C to 120°C), brushing with glaze every 30 minutes, for 1 to 1½ hours, or until sausage feels firm and a meat thermometer inserted in the center of a sausage registers 160°F (70°C). Pass any remaining glaze at the table.

Perfect Score Lamb Sausage

I achieved a perfect score at the National Lamb-BQ Contest with this recipe. Try it yourself for your own perfect score at dinner.

SERVES 12	Recommended wood: apple, cherry or other fruit wood

TIPS

Don't use lean or extra-lean ground meat on the smoker; it will dry out too much.

• • •

This basting jelly is delicious on any cut of lamb. Simply brush on every 30 minutes while lamb is smoking.

• • •

The plastic wrap will not melt or burn if you keep the temperature at 225°F to 250°F (110°C to 120°C). It helps keep the sausage moist and firm while the meat is taking on the smoky flavor.

Lamb Sausage

4	cloves garlic, minced	4
3 lbs	medium ground lamb	1.5 kg
1 lb	medium ground pork	500 g
½ cup	ice water	125 mL
⅓ cup	chopped fresh mint	75 mL
¼ cup	chopped fresh basil	50 mL
¼ cup	chopped fresh thyme	50 mL
¼ cup	freshly squeezed lemon juice	50 mL
2 tsp	chopped fresh marjoram	10 mL
¼ tsp	freshly ground black pepper	1 mL
Pinch	kosher salt	Pinch

Balsamic Herb Basting Jelly

1	jar (10 oz/300 mL) apple jelly	1
1 cup	balsamic vinegar	250 mL
½ cup	mixed chopped fresh herbs (such as basil, thyme and marjoram)	125 mL

1. *Prepare the sausage:* In a large bowl, using your hands or a fork, combine garlic, lamb, pork, ice water, mint, basil, thyme, lemon juice, marjoram, pepper and salt. Place plastic wrap on a flat surface and mold sausage mixture into 3 loaves. Form each loaf into a large link about 2 inches (5 cm) in diameter. Roll each link tightly in plastic wrap and tie off the ends. Set aside.

Make ahead

Place in an airtight container and store in the refrigerator for up to 1 week or in the freezer for up to 3 months.

2. *Prepare the basting jelly:* In a medium saucepan, over medium heat, combine apple jelly and vinegar; cook, stirring, until jelly melts and mixture comes together. Stir in fresh herbs. Set aside.

3. Prepare a fire in your smoker. *(For instructions, see pages 8–11.)*

4. Place plastic-wrapped sausages directly on the smoker rack, add wood to the coals and close the lid. Smoke at 225°F to 250°F (110°F to 120°C) for 1 hour. Remove plastic wrap and return sausages to the smoker rack. Close the lid and smoke, brushing with basting jelly every 30 minutes, for 1 hour, or until sausages are firm and a meat thermometer inserted in the center of a sausage registers 160°F (70°C). Let set for 15 minutes before slicing.

Specialty Smoking

ONCE YOU'VE EARNED a reputation for lip-smackin' barbecued foods, or you get a big rig, you'll be asked to smoke all kinds of things — large quantities of food for events, or unusual meats and wild game for friends. That's where specialty smoking comes in.

This chapter contains recipes for festival foods, such as smoked whole hog or cabrito (young goat); simply festive foods, such as smoked suckling pig; unusual meats, such as ostrich; and wild game. Hunters will want to try slow-smoking upland game birds such as pheasant or quail, or even deer or elk. These are meats you have to order ahead of time from your butcher or get from your favorite hunter or game supplier.

The same slow-smoking principles apply to these foods: flavor the food with brines, dry rubs or marinades first, slow-smoke over fragrant wood, then baste, glaze or accompany the food with a coordinating sauce.

For larger cuts of pork, you can use the same types of woods you use for ribs and pork shoulder blade: fruit woods, hickory, pecan, oak and sugar maple. For game meats with a bold flavor, such as deer or caribou, try woods with heavier smoke flavor, such as hickory and mesquite, in combination with sweeter woods such as apple, cherry and alder. The same rules hold, however: Less is more when it comes to smoke flavor.

SPECIALTY RECIPES

Apple-Smoked Pheasant
  Breast 334
Bacon-Wrapped Quail. 335
Quail in Blackberry Merlot
  Marinade 336
Cold-Smoked Ostrich with
  Garlic, Honey & Maple 337
Hot-Smoked Ostrich in
  Bay Leaf Marinade. 338
Venison Chops in Blackberry
  Merlot Marinade 339
Cold-Smoked Venison Sausage. . 340
Buffalo Flank Steak in
  Lime Cola Marinade 341
Pecan-Smoked Buffalo
  Tenderloin 342

Buffalo Kabobs with Sesame
  Marinade 343
Apple & Pecan–Smoked
  Buffalo Ribs 344
Barbecued Buffalo Meatloaf. . . . 345
Feast of Fancy Suckling Pig 346
Honey Mustard Pig Roast 347
Maple & Oak–Smoked
  Whole Hog. 348
Texas-Style Cabrito 350
Beer & Onion Cabrito Ribs 351
Honey Mustard Cabrito Ribs. . . . 352
Rabbit with Apricot
  Maple Glaze. 353
Garlic & Spice Rabbit. 354

Apple-Smoked Pheasant Breast

With a good marinade applied before cooking and a flavorful sauce after, this apple-smoked pheasant is as good as it gets.

SERVES 4	Recommended wood: apple	

(see recipe, page 42)

4	pheasant breasts or Muscovy duck breasts, skin on	4
1½ cups	Maple Honey Marinade (see recipe, page 42)	375 mL
4	large red apples	4
2½ cups	Apple Ancho Barbecue Sauce (see recipe, page 62)	625 mL

TIPS

You can buy farm-raised pheasant at better grocery stores or gourmet emporiums, or you can substitute meaty duck breasts such as Muscovy. If you get your pheasant from a hunter, it will probably be skinned, so lay a few bacon slices on the breasts while smoking to keep the meat moist.

• • •

If you prefer, smoke the apples for the last hour of the pheasant's smoking time, so they are still hot when you serve them.

• • •

Place any leftovers in an airtight container and store in the refrigerator for up to 1 week or in the freezer for up to 3 months.

1. Rinse pheasant under cold running water and pat dry. Place in a large sealable plastic bag and pour in three-quarters of the marinade. Seal bag, toss to coat and refrigerate for 2 hours. Reserve the remaining marinade in the refrigerator.

2. Remove pheasant from marinade, but do not pat dry. Set aside. Discard marinade.

3. Prepare a fire in your smoker. *(For instructions, see pages 8–11.)*

4. Using an apple corer or a small paring knife, remove cores from apples almost all the way through, leaving about ½ inch (1 cm) of bottom intact. Place in a disposable aluminum pan and fill centers with the reserved marinade.

5. Place pheasant and pan of apples on the smoker rack, add wood to the coals and close the lid. Smoke at 225°F to 250°F (110°C to 120°C) for 1 hour. Remove the apples. Close the lid and smoke pheasant for 2 to 3 hours, or until a meat thermometer inserted in the thickest part of a breast registers 170°F (75°C).

6. Slice apples and arrange on 4 plates. Slice pheasant breasts on the diagonal and arrange over apples. Top with barbecue sauce.

Bacon-Wrapped Quail

Serve this smoked quail with a fruity sauce such as Flower of the Flames Raspberry Barbecue Sauce (see recipe, page 50) or Apricot, Apricot, Apricot Barbecue Sauce (see recipe, page 65).

SERVES 4 AS AN APPETIZER, 2 AS A MAIN COURSE

TIP

Look for farm-raised quail at better butcher shops or gourmet markets, or befriend a hunter during the fall.

* * *

Variation

Substitute Cornish game hens for the quail and increase the smoking time by about 30 minutes.

Recommended wood: a combination of pecan and sugar maple

4	quail (each about 4 oz/125 g), skin removed	4
¾ cup	Honey & Spice Rub (see recipe, page 31)	175 mL
4	strips bacon	4

1. Rinse quail under cold running water and pat dry. Sprinkle dry rub on the exterior and in the cavity of each bird. Wrap each bird with a slice of bacon. Set aside.

2. Prepare a fire in your smoker. *(For instructions, see pages 8–11.)*

3. Place quail directly on the smoker rack, add wood to the coals and close the lid. Smoke at 225°F to 250°F (110°C to 120°C) for 1½ hours, or until juices run clear when quail is pierced.

Quail in Blackberry Merlot Marinade

If the hunter you know is successful, or you can find quail at your grocery store, this is a great "company's coming" dish. The marinade and sauce are also delicious with pheasant, grouse, duck and other game birds.

SERVES 12 AS AN APPETIZER, 6 AS A MAIN COURSE

TIPS

When food is cold, it takes longer to smoke it. For the recipes in this book, you want to bring your food to room temperature before smoking.

• • •

The smaller the smoking chamber on your equipment, the sooner your food will be done. If you're using a kettle grill or a bullet smoker, your quail might be done in 2 hours. If you're using a bigger rig or a genuine smoker, they might take 3 hours.

Recommended wood: sugar maple, pecan or oak

12	quail (each about 4 oz/125 g)	12
3 cups	Blackberry Merlot Marinade (see recipe, page 41)	750 mL
2 cups	Blackberry Merlot Sauce (see recipe, page 68)	500 mL

1. Rinse quail under cold running water and pat dry. Place in a large sealable plastic bag and pour in marinade. Seal bag, toss to coat and refrigerate for at least 2 hours or for up to 3 hours.

2. Remove quail from the marinade, but do not pat dry. Set aside. Discard marinade.

3. Prepare a fire in your smoker. *(For instructions, see pages 8–11.)*

4. Place quail, breast side up, directly on the smoker rack, add wood to the coals and close the lid. Smoke at 225°F to 250°F (110°C to 120°C) for 2 to 3 hours, or until juices run clear when quail is pierced.

5. Serve with Blackberry Merlot Sauce on the side.

Cold-Smoked Ostrich with Garlic, Honey & Maple

Here's another showy way to get great flavor from this specialty meat. The marinade also works well on pork, poultry and meaty game birds.

SERVES 6 TO 8	**Recommended wood:** cherry or other fruit wood

TIPS

You can also hot-smoke this ostrich at 225°F to 250°F (110°C to 120°C). The smoking time will decrease to about 2 hours.

• • •

Place any leftovers in an airtight container and store in the refrigerator for up to 1 week or in the freezer for up to 3 months.

Marinade

4	cloves garlic, minced	4
1¾ cups	Easy Asian Marinade (see recipe, page 40)	425 mL
½ cup	diced onion	125 mL
½ cup	pure maple syrup	125 mL
¼ cup	olive oil	50 mL
¼ cup	amber liquid honey	50 mL
2 tbsp	kosher salt	25 mL
¼ tsp	cracked black pepper	1 mL
3 lbs	boneless ostrich or emu	1.5 kg

1. *Prepare the marinade:* In a medium bowl, combine garlic, marinade, onion, maple syrup, oil, honey, salt and pepper.

2. Rinse ostrich under cold running water and pat dry. Place in a large sealable plastic bag and pour in marinade. Seal bag, toss to coat and refrigerate for at least 8 hours or overnight.

3. Remove ostrich from marinade, but do not pat dry. Set aside. Discard marinade.

4. Prepare a fire in your cold smoker, using 3 oz (90 g) of wood. Set temperature to 200°F (100°C) until wood starts to smoke. Reduce temperature to 170°F (75°C) and place a pan of ice on top of the cold plate.

5. Place ostrich directly on the smoker rack and close the lid. Smoke for 5 hours, or until a meat thermometer inserted in the thickest part of the ostrich registers 160°F (70°C). Let rest for 15 minutes before slicing.

Hot-Smoked Ostrich in Bay Leaf Marinade

Hot-smoked ostrich has a more opaque appearance and is delicious as an appetizer or an entrée. Substitute pork or turkey for the ostrich, if you wish, with the same smoking time and technique.

SERVES 12 TO 16 AS AN APPETIZER, 6 TO 8 AS A MAIN COURSE

TIPS

You can also cold-smoke this ostrich. Follow the cold-smoking instructions for the recipe on page 337.

• • •

Place any leftovers in an airtight container and store in the refrigerator for up to 1 week or in the freezer for up to 3 months.

Recommended wood: apple, cherry or other fruit wood

3 lbs	boneless ostrich or emu	1.5 kg
1½ cups	Bay Leaf Marinade (see recipe, page 38)	375 mL
	Apple juice for spraying	

1. Rinse ostrich under cold running water and pat dry. Place in a large sealable plastic bag and pour in marinade. Seal bag, toss to coat and refrigerate for at least 8 hours or overnight.

2. Remove ostrich from marinade, but do not pat dry. Set aside. Discard marinade.

3. Prepare a fire in your smoker. *(For instructions, see pages 8–11.)*

4. Place ostrich directly on the smoker rack, add wood to the coals and close the lid. Smoke at 225°F to 250°F (110°C to 120°C), spraying with apple juice every hour, for 2½ to 3 hours, or until a meat thermometer inserted in the thickest part registers 160°F (70°C). Let rest for 15 minutes before slicing.

Venison Chops in Blackberry Merlot Marinade

The blackberry and merlot flavors really complement the flavor of the venison, both before and after smoking.

SERVES 4	Recommended wood: grape or other fruit wood	

TIPS

The term "venison" refers to large game meats such as deer and elk.

• • •

Depending on the size of the plastic bags you use, 8 venison chops might not fit in one bag (keep in mind that the bag has to be able to seal when you are judging whether you will need more than one). If that's the case, use as many bags as you need, and divide the marinade evenly among them.

• • •

Game meats are very lean, so it's best to smoke them to medium-rare.

• • •

Variation

Substitute caribou for the venison, and let it marinate for at least 12 hours or for up to 2 days. Add 1 to 2 hours to the smoking time to let the tough meat get very tender.

8	venison chops, cut 1-inch (2.5 cm) thick (see tip, at left)	8
3 cups	Blackberry Merlot Marinade (see recipe, page 41)	750 mL
2 cups	Blackberry Merlot Sauce (see recipe, page 68)	500 mL

1. Place venison in a large sealable plastic bag (or bags) and pour in marinade. Seal bag, toss to coat and refrigerate for at least 4 hours or for up to 8 hours.

2. Remove venison from marinade, but do not pat dry. Set aside. Discard marinade.

3. Prepare a fire in your smoker. *(For instructions, see pages 8–11.)*

4. Place venison directly on the smoker rack, add wood to the coals and close the lid. Smoke at 225°F to 250°F (110°C to 120°C) for 1½ to 2 hours, or until a meat thermometer inserted in the center of a chop registers 150°F (65°C) for medium-rare.

5. Serve drizzled with Blackberry Merlot Sauce.

Cold-Smoked Venison Sausage

If you have a hunter in your family, this is a great way to enjoy venison.

MAKES 12 LBS (6 KG)	**Recommended wood:** a combination of oak and hickory

TIPS

You can use natural hog casings to make this sausage, if you prefer. You will need to order them from a sausage supply house or a full-service butcher. You'll also need sausage stuffing equipment, which is available at hardware or better kitchenware stores.

• • •

Curing spice mixtures (such as Morton's Tender Quick®) are located near canning and preserving supplies at grocery or hardware stores.

• • •

You can also hot-smoke this sausage. Smoke at 200°F (100°C) for 1 hour. Remove plastic wrap and return sausages to the smoker rack. Close the lid and smoke for 1 to 2 hours.

2	cloves garlic, minced	2
7 lbs	ground venison	3.5 kg
3 lbs	lean ground pork	1.5 kg
2 lbs	ground pork fat	1 kg
½ cup	minced fresh parsley	125 mL
½ cup	cognac	125 mL
½ cup	beer	125 mL
2 tbsp	freshly ground black pepper	25 mL
2 tbsp	granulated sugar	25 mL
2 tbsp	curing spice mixture (see tip, left)	25 mL

1. In a large bowl, using your hands or a fork, combine garlic, venison, pork, pork fat, parsley, cognac, beer, pepper, sugar and curing spice mixture. Cover and refrigerate for at least 8 hours or overnight.

2. Place plastic wrap on a flat surface and mold sausage mixture into 6 loaves. Form each loaf into a large link about 3 inches (7.5 cm) in diameter. Roll each link tightly in plastic wrap and tie off the ends. Set aside.

3. Prepare a fire in your cold smoker, using 12 oz (375 g) of wood. Set temperature to 200°F (100°C) until wood starts to smoke. Reduce temperature to 175°F (80°C) and place a pan of ice on top of the cold plate.

4. Place plastic-wrapped sausages directly on the smoker rack and close the lid. Smoke for 1 hour. Remove plastic wrap and return sausages to the smoker rack. Close the lid and smoke for 2 hours, or until sausages are firm and a meat thermometer inserted in the center of a sausage registers 170°F (75°C). Let rest for 15 minutes before slicing.

Buffalo Flank Steak in Lime Cola Marinade

This easy recipe yields lots of benefits from very few ingredients. I go light on the hickory when I smoke this dish. As with beef flank steak, it's important to slice the meat across the grain for maximum tenderness.

SERVES 8	**Recommended wood:** a combination of pecan and hickory

TIPS

The smaller the smoking chamber on your equipment, the sooner your food will be done. If you're using a charcoal grill or a bullet smoker, your steak might be done in 1½ hours. If you're using a bigger rig or a genuine smoker, it might take 2½ hours.

• • •

Buffalo and other game meats are leaner than domestic meats, and thus can dry out if overcooked. I recommend smoking game meat steaks and chops to medium-rare.

• • •

Place any leftovers in an airtight container and store in the refrigerator for up to 1 week or in the freezer for up to 3 months.

| 3 lbs | buffalo flank steak, well trimmed | 1.5 kg |
| 2 cups | Lime Cola Marinade (see recipe, page 37) | 500 mL |

1. Place steak in a large sealable plastic bag and pour in half of the marinade. Seal bag, toss to coat and refrigerate for at least 6 hours or overnight. Reserve the remaining marinade in the refrigerator.

2. Remove steak from marinade, but do not pat dry. Set aside. Discard marinade.

3. Prepare a fire in your smoker. *(For instructions, see pages 8–11.)*

4. Place steak directly on the smoker rack, add wood to the coals and close the lid. Smoke at 225°F to 250°F (110°C to 120°C), basting with the reserved marinade every 30 minutes, for 1½ to 2½ hours, or until a meat thermometer inserted in the thickest part of the steak registers 150°F (65°C) for medium-rare. Let rest for 15 minutes, then slice thinly across the grain.

Pecan-Smoked Buffalo Tenderloin

In the Prairie provinces of Canada and the Great Plains area of the United States, buffalo once more roam the grasslands. Their meat is prized for having less fat than beef, but a similar flavor. Buffalo is ideal for slow smoking, as the low heat keeps it tender. Cooking it to rare or medium-rare doneness also helps it stay tender.

SERVES 4	Recommended wood: pecan

TIPS

Buffalo and other game meats are leaner than domestic meats, and thus can dry out if overcooked. I recommend smoking game meat steaks and chops to medium-rare.

• • •

Place any leftovers in an airtight container and store in the refrigerator for up to 1 week or in the freezer for up to 3 months.

1	buffalo tenderloin (about 2 lbs/1 kg)	1
12	whole black peppercorns, crushed	12
3	cloves garlic, minced	3
1	small onion, sliced	1
1 tbsp	finely chopped fresh basil	15 mL
2 tsp	chopped fresh thyme	10 mL
2 tsp	chopped fresh chives	10 mL
1 cup	dry red wine	250 mL
2 tbsp	freshly squeezed lime juice	25 mL

1. Place buffalo in a shallow dish and sprinkle with peppercorns, garlic, onion, basil, thyme and chives. Pour in red wine and lime juice. Cover and refrigerate for up to 24 hours. Remove from the refrigerator and let warm to room temperature while the smoker is heating.

2. Prepare a fire in your smoker. *(For instructions, see pages 8–11.)*

3. Place buffalo directly on the smoker rack, add wood to the coals and close the lid. Smoke at 225°F to 250°F (110°C to 120°C) for 1½ hours, until a meat thermometer inserted in the thickest part of the tenderloin registers 150°F (65°C) for medium-rare.

> Buffalo ranchers are trying to get the meat labeled as bison.

Buffalo Kabobs with Sesame Marinade

Slightly sweet and smoky, these buffalo kabobs are delicious as a main course or as an appetizer.

SERVES 9 TO 12 AS AN APPETIZER, 6 AS A MAIN COURSE

TIPS

Buffalo would make an interesting and delicious addition to a "mixed barbecue" appetizer selection of smoked meat skewers.

• • •

Place any leftovers in an airtight container and store in the refrigerator for up to 1 week or in the freezer for up to 3 months.

Recommended wood: pecan

• Eighteen 12-inch (30 cm) bamboo skewers

2 lbs	buffalo round steak, cut into 1-inch (2.5 cm) cubes	1 kg
3 cups	Sesame Marinade (see recipe, page 43)	750 mL
18	mushroom caps	18
18	canned or fresh pineapple chunks	18
18	tiny pearl onions	18
1	green bell pepper, cut into 1-inch (2.5 cm) squares	1
1	red bell pepper, cut into 1-inch (2.5 cm) squares	1

1. Soak skewers in water for at least 30 minutes.

2. Place buffalo in a large sealable plastic bag and pour in half of the marinade. Seal bag, toss to coat and refrigerate for at least 6 hours or overnight. Reserve the remaining marinade in the refrigerator.

3. Remove buffalo from marinade, but do not pat dry. Discard marinade. Thread buffalo, mushroom caps, pineapple, pearl onions, red pepper and green pepper onto skewers. Place on a baking sheet and brush with some of the reserved marinade. Set aside.

4. Prepare a fire in your smoker. *(For instructions, see pages 8–11.)*

5. Place skewers on the smoker rack, add wood to the coals and close the lid. Smoke at 225°F to 250°F (110°C to 120°C), basting with the reserved marinade every 30 minutes, for 1½ to 2 hours, or until meat is slightly pink inside.

Apple & Pecan–Smoked Buffalo Ribs

I like to use Sesame Marinade on buffalo because it accentuates the sweet flavor of the meat during the smoking process.

SERVES 8	Recommended wood: a combination of apple and pecan

TIPS

These ribs are best cooked to rare or medium-rare. To check for doneness, slice into the meat near the center of a rib. The meat should be bright pink for rare and light pink for medium-rare.

* * *

Place any leftovers in an airtight container and store in the refrigerator for up to 1 week or in the freezer for up to 3 months.

Marinade

5	cloves garlic, minced	5
1 cup	Sesame Marinade (see recipe, page 43)	250 mL
⅓ cup	packed brown sugar	75 mL
3 tbsp	sliced green onions	45 mL
1 tsp	grated gingerroot	5 mL
1 tsp	hot pepper flakes	5 mL
1 tsp	rice vinegar	5 mL
5 lbs	meaty buffalo ribs	2.5 kg
	Pineapple juice for spraying	

1. *Prepare the marinade:* In a small bowl, combine garlic, marinade, brown sugar, green onions, ginger, hot pepper flakes and vinegar.

2. Place ribs in a large, deep pan and pour in marinade. Cover and refrigerate overnight.

3. Remove ribs from marinade, but do not pat dry. Set aside. Discard marinade.

4. Prepare a fire in your smoker. *(For instructions, see pages 8–11.)*

5. Place ribs, meaty side up, directly on the smoker rack, add wood to the coals and close the lid. Smoke at 225°F to 250°F (110°C to 120°C), spraying with pineapple juice every 30 minutes, for 3 hours, or until desired doneness.

Barbecued Buffalo Meatloaf

Made moist with milk and fresh vegetables and flavorful with seasonings, this healthy, smoky meatloaf is a winner.

SERVES 8	Recommended wood: a combination of apple and cherry	

TIPS

Try smoking your family's favorite meatloaf. Simply prepare your meatloaf as usual and smoke until the center of a loaf registers 160°F (70°C).

• • •

If Montreal chicken seasoning is not available, you can substitute Montreal steak seasoning or your favorite dry rub.

• • •

Make ahead

Place loaves in airtight containers and store in the refrigerator for up to 1 week or in the freezer for up to 3 months.

1 cup	fine dry bread crumbs	250 mL
1 tbsp	Montreal chicken seasoning (see tip, at left)	15 mL
1 tsp	kosher salt	5 mL
½ tsp	ground allspice	2 mL
¼ tsp	freshly ground black pepper	1 mL
1 cup	milk	250 mL
2 lbs	ground buffalo	1 kg
3	cloves garlic, minced	3
½ cup	shredded carrots	125 mL
½ cup	finely chopped yellow summer squash (zucchini)	125 mL
½ cup	diced celery	125 mL
½ cup	diced onion	125 mL
½ cup	barbecue sauce (store-bought or see recipes, pages 50–65)	125 mL

1. In a large bowl, combine bread crumbs, chicken seasoning, salt, allspice and pepper. Add milk and mix well. Let stand for 5 minutes. Using your hands or a fork, gradually blend in buffalo. Mix in garlic, carrots, squash, celery and onion. Shape into 2 loaves and place in disposable aluminum loaf pans. Set aside.

2. Prepare a fire in your smoker. *(For instructions, see pages 8–11.)*

3. Place pans on the smoker rack, add wood to the coals and close the lid. Smoke at 225°F to 250°F (110°C to 120°C) for 1½ hours. Spread barbecue sauce evenly on the top of each loaf, close the lid and smoke for 30 minutes, or until a meat thermometer inserted in the center of a loaf registers 160°F (70°C).

Feast of Fancy Suckling Pig

When you need to pull out all the stops for a special dinner or a Renaissance-style banquet, this is your dish. Smoked suckling pig is certainly delicious. Presentation counts here, so see the tip, below, for some ideas. The ball of plastic wrap will keep the pig's mouth open so it can hold an apple when it's done cooking.

SERVES 12	Recommended wood: a combination of cherry and apple

TIPS

Allow at least 1 week to special-order a suckling pig from your butcher.

• • •

If you don't have enough room in your fridge, marinate the pig overnight in a large cooler filled with bags of ice.

• • •

For a traditional look, place the pig on a large cutting board, place an apple in the mouth and garnish with fresh whole pineapples, apples, grapes and fresh herbs. For a more irreverent style, place an apple in the mouth, a top hat on the head and sunglasses over the eyes.

• • •

Variation

Instead of the All-Purpose Barbecue Rub, try Flower of the Flames Rib Rub (see recipe, page 32) or Brown Sugar Rib Rub (see recipe, page 33).

1	suckling pig (about 20 lbs/10 kg)	1
16 cups	pineapple juice	4 L
16 cups	apple juice	4 L
2 cups	All-Purpose Barbecue Rub (see recipe, page 27)	500 mL
	A combination of apple juice and pineapple juice for spraying	

1. Rinse the inside of the pig under cold running water and pat dry. Using a paring knife, peel all the membranes out of the cavity and trim off as much of the fat as possible. Place in a large roasting pan, plastic wash tub or other large container and pour in pineapple juice and apple juice. Cover and refrigerate overnight.

2. Remove pig from juice and pat dry. Discard juice. Pour dry rub into the cavity and rub in. Prop the pig's mouth open with a ball of plastic wrap. Set aside.

3. Prepare a fire in your smoker. *(For instructions, see pages 8–11.)*

4. Place pig, cavity down, directly on the smoker rack and spread out as much as possible. Cover with cheesecloth (to keep pig from getting too dark) and spray cheesecloth with juice. Add wood to the coals and close the lid. Smoke at 225°F to 250°F (110°C to 120°C), spraying cheesecloth with juice every 30 minutes, for 10 to 12 hours, or until a meat thermometer inserted into the thickest part of the pig registers 180°F (82°C). Remove from the smoker and let rest for 20 to 30 minutes. Remove the cheesecloth and ball of plastic wrap, then arrange pig on a platter.

Honey Mustard Pig Roast

When you want to have a real Southern pig pickin', this is the dish to serve, along with coleslaw tossed with a tangy vinegar dressing, North Carolina–Style Barbecue Sauce (see recipe, page 57) or Vinegar-Style Barbecue Sauce (see recipe, page 51) and cornbread or biscuits. Y'all come back now!

SERVES 50	Recommended wood: a combination of apple, cherry and peach		
3 cups	prepared mustard		750 mL
½ cup	amber liquid honey		125 mL
1	dressed pig (about 50 lbs/23 kg), skinned and exterior fat trimmed to ¼-inch (0.5 cm) thickness		1
3 cups	All-Purpose Barbecue Rub (see recipe, page 27)		750 mL
	Pear juice for spraying		

TIPS

You'll need to order a dressed pig from your butcher at least 1 week ahead of time. Have the butcher skin and trim the pig for you.

• • •

Whole hog is usually "picked," or cut up into small pieces, and served on a large platter.

• • •

Place any leftovers in an airtight container and store in the refrigerator for up to 1 week or in the freezer for up to 3 months.

1. In a large bowl, combine mustard and honey.

2. Using a hose or a pitcher of cold water, rinse the inside of the pig and pat dry. Using a paring knife, peel all the membranes out of the cavity and trim off as much of the fat as possible. Brush cavity with some of the honey mustard mixture, then rub with ½ cup (125 mL) of the dry rub. Turn the pig over, brush with the remaining honey mustard and sprinkle on the remaining dry rub. Let stand at room temperature for about 1 hour, or until surface is tacky.

3. Prepare a fire in your smoker *(see pages 8–11)*.

4. Place pig, cavity down, directly on the smoker rack and spread out as much as possible. Cover with cheesecloth (to keep pig from getting too dark) and spray cheesecloth with pear juice. Add wood to the coals and close the lid. Smoke at 225°F to 250°F (110°C to 120°C), spraying cheesecloth with pear juice every 30 minutes, for 6 to 8 hours, or until pig is beginning to burnish. Remove cheesecloth, close the lid and smoke, spraying with baste every 30 minutes, for 3 hours, or until a meat thermometer inserted in the thickest part of the pig registers 180°F (82°C). Let rest for at least 30 minutes before carving.

Maple & Oak–Smoked Whole Hog

There are only a few occasions when you might need to smoke a whole hog. One is a barbecue contest that has whole hog as a category, such as Memphis in May or the BarbeQlossal in Des Moines, Iowa. Another is a big event, such as a fundraiser for a church or school. As you might guess, it takes a smoker large enough to hold a 75-lb (34 kg) pig and enough strong people to handle it. To keep the meat as moist and tender as possible during the long smoking time, I prefer to keep the temperature to 225°F to 235°F (110°C to 115°C).

SERVES 75

TIPS

An easy way to make pork stock is to use a packaged flavor base, available from spice emporiums or better grocery stores. Usually, 1 tsp (5 mL) of flavor base added to 1 cup (250 mL) boiling water will make 1 cup (250 mL) of stock. Once you've opened the container, keep the flavor base in the refrigerator, where it will keep indefinitely.

• • •

Look for apricot nectar in bottles or cartons in the fruit juice section of well-stocked supermarkets and health food stores.

• • •

Look for apricot syrup where syrups for pancakes or ice creams are shelved at the grocery store.

Recommended wood: a combination of maple and oak (whispering oak, if you can find it)

2 cups	pork stock (see tip, at left) or chicken stock	500 mL
2 cups	apricot nectar (see tip, at left)	500 mL
2 cups	apricot syrup (see tip, at left)	500 mL
2 cups	apricot wine	500 mL
1 cup	grenadine	250 mL
1/2 cup	olive oil	125 mL
1/3 cup	soy sauce	75 mL
1/4 cup	ancho chili powder (see tip, opposite)	50 mL
1/4 cup	rice vinegar	50 mL
2 tbsp	onion powder	25 mL
2 tbsp	garlic powder	25 mL
2 tbsp	dry mustard	25 mL
2 tbsp	sweet Hungarian paprika	25 mL
1 tbsp	celery salt	15 mL
1 tbsp	MSG (optional)	15 mL
1/2 tsp	jalapeño pepper powder (see tip, opposite)	2 mL
1	dressed pig (about 75 lbs/34 kg), skinned and exterior fat trimmed to 1/4-inch (0.5 cm) thickness	1

Baste

2 cups	rice wine vinegar	500 mL
2 cups	pineapple juice	500 mL
1/2 cup	olive oil	125 mL

You can buy ancho chili powder and jalapeño pepper powder at better herb and spice emporiums, by mail order or online (see the Source Guide, page 356).

• • • •

You'll need to order a dressed pig from your butcher at least 1 week ahead of time. Have the butcher skin and trim the pig for you.

• • • •

I use a large injector to inject marinade deep into the meat. You can buy these at kitchen shops. You could also use a large veterinary syringe, available at veterinary supply houses, instead of the injector.

• • • •

Whole hog is usually "picked," or cut up into small pieces, and served on a large platter.

• • • •

Place any leftovers in an airtight container and store in the refrigerator for up to 1 week or in the freezer for up to 3 months.

1. In a large saucepan, over medium-low heat, combine pork stock, apricot nectar, apricot syrup, apricot wine, grenadine, oil, soy sauce, ancho chili powder, vinegar, onion powder, garlic powder, mustard, paprika, celery salt, MSG (if using) and jalapeño pepper powder. Simmer for 30 minutes to allow flavors to blend. Remove from heat, let cool and strain through a fine-mesh sieve.

2. Using a hose or a pitcher of cold water, rinse the inside of the pig and pat dry. Place pig on a large flat surface. Fill a large syringe or injector (see tip, at left) with some of the marinade and inject the pig all over, refilling the syringe or injector as necessary to use all of the marinade. Set aside.

3. Prepare a fire in your smoker. *(For instructions, see pages 8–11.)*

4. *Meanwhile, prepare the baste:* In a large bowl, combine vinegar, pineapple juice and oil. Pour into a large spray bottle.

5. Place pig, cavity down, directly on the smoker rack and spread out as much as possible. Cover with cheesecloth (to keep pig from getting too dark) and spray cheesecloth with baste. Add wood to the coals and close the lid. Smoke at 225°F to 235°F (110°C to 115°C), spraying cheesecloth with baste every 30 minutes, for 9 to 11 hours, or until pig is beginning to burnish. Remove cheesecloth, close the lid and smoke, spraying with baste every 30 minutes, for 3 hours, or until a meat thermometer inserted in the thickest part of the pig registers 180°F (82°C). Let rest for at least 30 minutes before carving.

Texas-Style Cabrito

Cabrito, or young goat, is a delicacy for Hispanic people and Muslims. In parts of Texas, you can even get barbecued cabrito tacos!

SERVES 8

Recommended wood: a combination of apple and pecan

TIPS

With advance notice, you can special-order leg of cabrito from your favorite butcher.

• • •

For a South of the Border flavor, serve cabrito with Apple Ancho Barbecue Sauce (see recipe, page 62) or Cherry Chipotle Barbecue Sauce (see recipe, page 63).

• • •

Place any leftovers in an airtight container and store in the refrigerator for up to 1 week or in the freezer for up to 3 months.

4	cloves garlic, minced	4
1	bay leaf	1
1 cup	rice vinegar	250 mL
1 cup	olive oil	250 mL
½ cup	granulated sugar	125 mL
2 tsp	kosher salt	10 mL
1 tsp	chopped fresh thyme	5 mL
1 tsp	chopped fresh rosemary	5 mL
1 tsp	ground cloves	5 mL
½ tsp	jalapeño pepper powder (see tip, page 198)	2 mL
1	leg of cabrito (about 7 lbs/3.5 kg)	1

1. In a medium bowl, combine garlic, bay leaf, vinegar, oil, sugar, salt, thyme, rosemary, cloves and jalapeño pepper powder.

2. Rinse cabrito under cold running water and pat dry. Place in a large sealable plastic bag and pour in half of the marinade. Seal bag, toss to coat and refrigerate for at least 12 hours or for up to 24 hours, turning often. Reserve the remaining marinade in the refrigerator.

3. Remove cabrito from marinade, but do not pat dry. Set aside. Discard marinade.

4. Prepare a fire in your smoker. *(For instructions, see pages 8–11.)*

5. Place cabrito directly on the smoker rack, add wood to the coals and close the lid. Smoke at 225°F to 250°F (110°C to 120°C), basting with the reserved marinade every 30 minutes, for 6 hours, or until a meat thermometer inserted in the thickest part of the cabrito registers 165°F (78°C). Let rest for 15 minutes, then pull meat apart with two forks (as for pulled pork) or carve.

Beer & Onion Cabrito Ribs

Cabrito ribs are often available from specialty butchers or halal markets. This recipe, however, also works with lamb or beef ribs.

SERVES 4		Recommended wood: a combination of oak and cherry	

TIP
Place any leftovers in an airtight container and store in the refrigerator for up to 1 week or in the freezer for up to 3 months.

3 lbs	cabrito ribs	1.5 kg
1	large onion, sliced	1
¼ cup	dry onion soup mix	50 mL
1 cup	lager beer (approx.)	250 mL

1. Place ribs in a large disposable aluminum pan. Arrange onion slices over ribs and sprinkle with onion soup mix. Pour in beer. Set aside.

2. Prepare a fire in your smoker. *(For instructions, see pages 8–11.)*

3. Place pan on the smoker rack, add wood to the coals and close the lid. Smoke at 225°F to 250°F (110°C to 120°C), basting with the beer in the pan every hour (add more beer if necessary), for 4 hours, or until meat pulls away from the ends of the bones.

> In early September, during Labor Day weekend, barbecue competitors head down to Brady, Texas, for the World Champion Barbecue Goat Cook-Off and a taste of mesquite-smoked goat for Saturday lunch.

Honey Mustard Cabrito Ribs

If you can smoke lamb ribs, you can smoke cabrito ribs. And this is a good way to do them.

SERVES 6	**Recommended wood:** a combination of oak and cherry

TIPS

Cabrito ribs are often available from specialty butchers or halal markets.

● ● ●

The smaller the smoking chamber on your equipment, the sooner your food will be done. If you're using a kettle grill or a bullet smoker, your ribs might be done in 4 hours. If you're using a bigger rig or a genuine smoker, they might take 5 hours.

¼ cup	prepared honey mustard	50 mL
3 tbsp	prepared horseradish	45 mL
3 tbsp	Worcestershire sauce	45 mL
4 lbs	cabrito ribs	2 kg
	Kosher salt and freshly ground black pepper	

1. In a small bowl, combine mustard, horseradish and Worcestershire sauce.

2. Sprinkle ribs with salt and pepper, then brush with some of the mustard mixture. Set aside.

3. Prepare a fire in your smoker. *(For instructions, see pages 8–11.)*

4. Place ribs, meaty side up, directly on the smoker rack, add wood to the coals and close the lid. Smoke at 225°F to 250°F (110°C to 120°C), basting with mustard mixture every hour, for 4 hours, or until meat pulls away from the ends of the bones.

Rabbit with Apricot Maple Glaze

Here's a delicious way to serve domestic rabbit. The bacon keeps the rabbit moist while it's smoking.

Recommended wood: apple, cherry or other fruit wood

TIP

Order domestic rabbit from a full-service butcher. Some butcher shops keep rabbit in the freezer section.

• • •

Look for apricot syrup where syrups for pancakes or ice creams are shelved at the grocery store.

• • •

Place any leftovers in an airtight container and store in the refrigerator for up to 1 week or in the freezer for up to 3 months.

Marinade

¼ cup	apricot syrup (see tip, at left)	50 mL
1 tsp	garlic powder	5 mL
1 tsp	kosher salt	5 mL
¼ tsp	freshly ground black pepper	1 mL
1	whole domestic rabbit (about 2½ lbs/1.25 kg), quartered	1
	Barbecue seasoning mix (store-bought or see recipes, pages 27–34)	
4	strips bacon	4
1½ cups	Apricot Maple Glaze (see recipe, page 66)	375 mL

1. *Prepare the marinade:* In a small bowl, combine apricot syrup, garlic powder, salt and pepper.

2. Rinse rabbit under cold running water and pat dry. Place in a large sealable plastic bag and pour in marinade. Seal bag, toss to coat and refrigerate for at least 8 hours or overnight.

3. Remove rabbit from marinade and pat dry. Discard marinade. Place rabbit in a disposable aluminum pan and sprinkle with seasoning mix to taste. Lay bacon slices over rabbit. Set aside.

4. Prepare a fire in your smoker *(see pages 8–11)*.

5. Place pan on the smoker rack, add wood to the coals and close the lid. Smoke at 225°F to 250°F (110°C to 120°C) for 1 hour. Brush with glaze, close the lid and smoke for 30 minutes, or until a meat thermometer inserted in the thickest part of a rabbit piece registers 160°F (70°C).

Garlic & Spice Rabbit

This rabbit gets a warm, spicy dry rub. Pair it with a fruity barbecue sauce such as Flower of the Flames Raspberry Barbecue Sauce (see recipe, page 50) for a sweet and spicy finish.

SERVES 2	Recommended wood: apple, cherry or other fruit wood

see recipe, page 50

TIPS

Place any leftovers in an airtight container and store in the refrigerator for up to 1 week or in the freezer for up to 3 months.

. . .

Add smoked rabbit or any other specialty smoked meat leftovers to soups or stews for a true taste of the old-fashioned pioneer hearth.

Marinade

6	whole cloves	6
2	cloves garlic, minced	2
½ cup	olive oil	125 mL
1 tsp	kosher salt	5 mL
Pinch	ground nutmeg	Pinch
1	whole domestic rabbit (about 2½ lbs/1.25 kg), quartered	1
	Kosher salt and freshly ground black pepper	

1. *Prepare the marinade:* In a small bowl, combine cloves, garlic, oil, salt and nutmeg.

2. Rinse rabbit under cold running water and pat dry. Place in a large sealable plastic bag and pour in marinade. Seal bag, toss to coat and refrigerate overnight.

3. Remove rabbit from marinade, but do not pat dry. Discard marinade. Place rabbit in a disposable aluminum pan and season to taste with salt and pepper. Set aside.

4. Prepare a fire in your smoker. *(For instructions, see pages 8–11.)*

5. Place pan on the smoker rack, add wood to the coals and close the lid. Smoke at 225°F to 250°F (110°C to 120°C) for 1½ hours, or until a meat thermometer inserted in the thickest part of a rabbit piece registers 160°F (70°C).

Glossary

Ingredients

Ancho chili powder: You can buy ancho chili powder at better herb and spice emporiums, by mail order or online (see the Source Guide, page 356). If you can't find it, substitute the same amount of chili powder.

Apple juice: Whether to use sweetened or unsweetened apple juice is a matter of taste. Either will work well in the recipes in this book.

Applesauce: Whether to use sweetened or unsweetened applesauce is a matter of taste. Either will work well in the recipes in this book.

Carrot powder: Look for carrot powder at better spice emporiums or online (see the Source Guide, page 356). If you can't find it, substitute the same amount of paprika.

Creole-style seasoning: A dry blend of sweet herbs and hot and spicy chili peppers. You can find Creole-style seasoning at well-stocked supermarkets or online (see the Source Guide, page 356).

Granulated garlic: Dried garlic in a larger granule than garlic powder. Granulated garlic keeps its flavor longer without going bitter (important when you're smoking something for hours), as garlic powder can sometimes do. You can find it at well-stocked supermarkets or online (see the Source Guide, page 356).

Honey: Most honey you buy at the grocery store, such as clover honey, will be an amber color, which indicates a medium flavor and sweetness. Light honeys made from blossoms have a more flowery, sugary flavor; darker honeys such as sunflower have a deep, almost sulphurous flavor. For barbecuing purposes, stick with amber.

Honey powder: You can find honey powder at better spice emporiums or online (see the Source Guide, page 356).

Jalapeño pepper powder: You can buy jalapeño pepper powder at better herb and spice emporiums, by mail order or online (see the Source Guide, page 356). If you can't find it, substitute hot pepper sauce (unless you are making a dry rub, in which case just omit it). As a rule, you'll use about twice as much hot pepper sauce as the amount of jalapeño pepper powder called for.

MSG: Monosodium glutamate (MSG) provides that fifth basic flavor, sometimes called umami, that helps bring all the other flavors (sweet, salt, sour and bitter) together. Some people have an allergic reaction to MSG, so be careful when you use it.

Granulated onion: Dried onion in a larger granule than onion powder. Granulated onion keeps its flavor longer without going bitter (important when you're smoking something for hours), as onion powder can sometimes do. You can find it at well-stocked supermarkets or online (see the Source Guide, page 356).

Paprika: There are two main types of paprika, a spice ground from dried red peppers. Spanish paprika has a sharp, pungent flavor. Sweet Hungarian paprika has a sweeter, but still pungent flavor.

Pineapple juice: Whether to use sweetened or unsweetened pineapple juice is a matter of taste. Either will work well in the recipes in this book.

Salt: Kosher salt and sea salt have a truer flavor than table salt, so they're better for use in barbecuing.

Seafood seasoning: An herb and spice blend that complements fish and shellfish. These blends usually contain herbs such as tarragon, dill and thyme, and perhaps dried lemon powder for a citrus taste. You can buy seafood seasoning blends at the grocery store or make one yourself, using dried tarragon, dill, thyme, lemon pepper and kosher salt or sea salt.

Steak sauce: Any sauce served as a condiment with steak. Look for sauces that include Worcestershire sauce and garlic.

Worcestershire powder: Available at better spice emporiums, Worcestershire powder is simply Worcestershire sauce with the liquid removed.

Equipment

Basting/mopping brushes: Use new, disposable paint brushes or special metal basting brushes with silicon tips that can take the heat.

Marinade injector: These syringes have large tubes for holding marinades. They are available at gourmet and barbecue shops.

Microplane zester: Modeled from a hasp used in carpentry, these long metal graters do a great job of grating and zesting everything from cheese to citrus fruits and gingerroot.

Source Guide

Grills and Smokers

Barbeques Galore
15041 Bake Parkway, Suite A
Irvine, California 92618
(949) 597-2400
www.bbqgalore.com
Grill manufacturers with a retail
division of over 60 stores that also
carry barbecue utensils, accessories,
books, woods, charcoal, etc.

Big Green Egg
3414 Clairmont Road
Atlanta, Georgia 30319
(800) 939-3447
www.biggreenegg.com
Manufactures an egg-shaped ceramic
Kamado-style combination smoker/grill
that smokes foods at a higher
temperature than traditional cookers.

Brinkman Corporation
4215 McEwen Road
Dallas, Texas 75244
(972) 770-8521
Manufactures bullet-shaped charcoal
and electric smokers and grills.

Traeger Industries, Inc.
P.O. Box 829
Mt. Angel, Oregon 97362
(503) 845-9234
www.traegerindustries.com
Makers of the original electric-
powered wood pellet grill/smokers.
Wood pellets are automatically fed
into the firebox and provide both
fuel and flavor.

SmokinTex
P.O. Box 250243
Plano, Texas 75025
(972) 509-4814
www.smokintex.com
Manufactures electric smokers in
stainless steel cases. Just put dry wood
chips in the smoker box, set the
temperature gauge, and you're
smoking at 250°F (120°C) and under.

Tucker Cooker Co.
122 West Carolina Avenue
Memphis, Tennessee 38103-4612
(901) 578-3221
www.tuckercooker.com
Manufactures a towable smoker that
I use for barbecue contests and at
home. Their smoker is very efficient.
You'll use a lot less charcoal with it,
but still get great results. This cooker
has an easily adjustable charcoal rack
and many other features that make it
easy to use, clean, move and tow.

Weber-Stephen Products Co.
200 East Daniels Rd.
Palatine, Illinois 60067-6266
(800) 446-1071
www.weberbbq.com
Made the first Weber grill in 1951. The
company manufactures grills, smokers,
the Weber Smokey Mountain Cooker,
charcoal chimney starters, the Weber
Rib Rack and lots of accessories.

Cobb Canada
9-8207 Swenson Way
Delta, British Columbia V4G 1J5
(604) 584-2622
e-mail: info@cobbcanada.ca

Supplies

Allied Kenco Sales

26 Lyerly St.
Houston, Texas 77022
(800) 356-5189 or (713) 691-2935
www.alliedkenco.com
"Supplying everything but the meat" is this company's motto. If you want to make sausage or jerky, this is the source for sausage casings, spices, sausage-making starter kits, Morton Tender Quick® curing salts and more.

Penzeys Spices

P.O. Box 933
Muskego, Wisconsin 53150
(800) 741-7787 or (414) 679-7207
www.penzeys.com
Wonderful spices, herbs and seasonings such as horseradish powder. Their catalog is very informative.

Zach's Spice Company

www.zachsspice.com
Check out their online catalog for unusual seasonings such as Worcestershire powder and quality ingredients for dry rubs.

Woods

Check out "big box" home improvement stores, hardware or barbecue shops in your area. Alder, apple, cherry, oak and pecan chunks can be purchased at specialty stores such as Barbeques Galore (see opposite) and from suppliers such as the following:

American BBQ Wood Products

9540 Riggs
Overland Park, Kansas 66212
(800) 223-9046 or (913) 648-7993
This company sells a variety of woods — mesquite, pecan, hickory, grape, oak, apple, cherry, sassafras, peach and alder — in logs, slabs, chunks and chips.

BBQr's Delight

P.O. Box 8727
Pine Bluff, Arkansas 71611
(877) 275-9591
www.bbqrsdelight.com
Wood pellets for fuel and smoke in 12 different flavors, including hickory, mesquite, pecan, apple, cherry, oak, black walnut and sugar maple.

Chigger Creek Products

Leon and Sarah Turner
4200 Highway D
Syracuse, Missouri 65354
(660) 298-3188
A variety of woods — hickory, apple, cherry, pecan, grape, sugar maple, alder, oak, mesquite, peach, sassafras, persimmon, pear, and apple/hickory and cherry/oak blends — in chips, chunks and logs.

Fairlane Bar-BQ Wood

12520 Third Street
Grandview, Missouri 64030
(816) 761-1350
This company specializes in mesquite, pecan, hickory, oak, apple, cherry and sassafras woods sold in bags of chunks.

Library and Archives Canada Cataloguing in Publication

Putman, Karen
    Championship BBQ secrets for real smoked food / Karen Putman.

Includes index.
ISBN-13: 978-0-7788-0138-2 (bound)
ISBN-13: 978-0-7788-0130-6 (pbk.)
ISBN-10: 0-7788-0138-1 (bound)
ISBN-10: 0-7788-0130-6 (pbk.)

1. Barbecue cookery. I. Title.

TX609.P87 2006   641.5'784   C2005-906163-4

Index

A

Adam & Eve Ribs, 260
Alder-Smoked Halibut Steaks in Orange, Soy & Lime Marinade, 151
Alder-Smoked Red Snapper with Citrus Spray, 152
Alder-Smoked Shark Steaks, 165
Alder-Smoked Shrimp, 180
All-Purpose Barbecue Rub, 27
All-Purpose Mop, 44
Ancho-Herb Dry Rub, 30
Ancho-Herb Pork Shoulder Blade, 226
antipasto, 109
Antipasto Burgers, 302
apple
 Adam & Eve Ribs, 260
 Apple & Cherry–Smoked Baby Back Ribs, 250
 Apple Ancho Barbecue Sauce, 62
 Apple Ancho Brisket, 289
 Apple-Cranberry Pork Loin Chops, 247
 Apple-Smoked Apples, 135
 Apple-Smoked Pheasant Breast, 334
 Baby Back Ribs, 82
 Brown Sugar–Rubbed Ribs, 257
 Feast of Fancy Suckling Pig, 346
 Here a Chick, There a Chick, 197
 Hot-Smoked Fruit, 134
 Mussels in Apple-Garlic Marinade, 188
 Mustard & Marmalade Barbecue Sauce, 60
 New Mexico–Style Ribs, 256
 Perfect Score Lamb Sausage, 330
 Pork Loin Roast with Hot Pepper Jelly Glaze, 245
 Rich & Delicious Brisket Mop, 45
 World Championship Ribs, 251
Apple & Cherry–Smoked Baby Back Ribs, 250
Apple & Hickory–Smoked Pork Loin Roast with Ancho-Herb Dry Rub, 243
Apple & Hickory–Smoked Ribs in Red Wine Marinade, 258
Apple & Pecan–Smoked Buffalo Ribs, 344
Apple & Pecan–Smoked Flank Steak with Garlic & Spice Rub, 280

Apple-Smoked Salmon with Green Grape Sauce, 156
apricot
 Apricot, Apricot, Apricot Barbecue Sauce, 65
 Apricot Barbecue Glaze, Easy, 66
 Apricot Chicken Quarters, 199
 Apricot Chicken Skewers, 203
 Apricot Ham Relish, 300
 Apricot Maple Glaze, 66
 Apricot Sauce, 209
 Low- and Slow-Smoked Baby Back Ribs with Apricot Glaze, 253
 Maple & Oak–Smoked Whole Hog, 348
 Orange & Raspberry Country-Style Ribs, 263
 Peach-Smoked Apricot Pork Loin Roast, 241
 Pecan-Smoked Chicken Wings, 209
 Rabbit with Apricot Maple Glaze, 353
 Southwestern-Style Turkey Thighs, 215
 Stuffed Cornish Game Hens with Apricot Mustard Sauce, 220
 The Ultimate Slow-Smoked Burger, 300
Aromatic Poultry Rub, 29
Aromatic Whole Chicken, 194
artichokes
 Antipasto Burgers, 302
 Artichoke & Red Onion Relish, 99
 Brisket-Stuffed Artichoke Bottoms, 292
 Cheese, Vegetable & Pepperoni Skewers, 109
 Cold-Smoked Vegetables, 98
 Gouda with Onion, Jalapeño Pepper & Artichoke Relish, 110
 Hot-Smoked Vegetables, 112
 Italian Sausage & Artichoke Soup, 269
 Pecan-Smoked Vegetable Skewers, 130
Asian Marinade, Easy, 40
Asian Plum Sauce, 261
Asian-Style Beef Short Ribs, 297
Asian-Style Lamb Ribs, 315
asparagus
 Antipasto Burgers, 302
 Asparagus on Skewers, 100

Cold-Smoked Vegetables, 98
avocado
 Cherry-Smoked Beef Tenderloin, 276
 Tomato Guacamole, 125

B

Baby Back Ribs, 82
bacon
 Bacon-Wrapped Beef Tenderloin, 275
 Bacon-Wrapped Quail, 335
 Mushroom, Garlic & Thyme Meatloaf, 306
 Rabbit with Apricot Maple Glaze, 353
 Stuffed Cornish Game Hens with Apricot Mustard Sauce, 220
 Stuffed Eggplant with Bacon, Garlic & Cream, 117
 Stuffed Tomatoes, 124
Balsamic Herb Basting Jelly, 330
Balsamic Jelly, 300
barbecue associations, 72
Barbecue Glaze, 67
Barbecue Sauce, 254
barbecue sauces, 49–65, 254
Barbecued Beans, 75
Barbecued Brisket for a Crowd, 287
Barbecued Buffalo Meatloaf, 345
Barbecued Meatloaf, 304
Barbecued Oysters, 176
Barbecuer's Aioli, 71
bastes, 18, 44–48, 54, 330
 for beef, 45–46
 for fish and seafood, 46, 48, 182
 for pork, 46–47, 227, 263, 348
 for poultry, 46, 216
Bay & Brown Sugar Brine, 184
Bay Leaf Marinade, 38
beans
 Barbecued Beans, 75
 French Canadian Barbecued Beans, 127
 Three-Bean Barbecue Casserole, 126
beef. See also specific cuts (below)
 bastes for, 45–46
 brines for, 24–25
 marinades for, 36, 37, 282, 285, 294, 297
 rubs and pastes for, 34–35, 280, 287–88, 290
 sauces for, 54–55, 68, 70, 294, 296, 302

beef, ground
Antipasto Burgers, 302
Barbecued Meatloaf, 304
Caribbean-Style Barbecued
Meatloaf with Papaya Relish,
308
Mushroom, Garlic & Thyme
Meatloaf, 306
The Ultimate Slow-Smoked
Burger, 300
beef brisket
Apple Ancho Brisket, 289
Barbecued Beans, 75
Barbecued Brisket for a Crowd,
287
Beef Brisket Flat, 88
Beef Lover's Barbecued Brisket,
286
Brisket-Stuffed Artichoke
Bottoms, 292
Hickory & Maple–Smoked Beef
Brisket, 285
Kansas City–Style Brisket, 288
Rich Beefy Brisket, 284
Smoky Mesquite Brisket, 290
beef flank steak
Apple & Pecan–Smoked Flank
Steak with Garlic and& Spice
Rub, 280
Cola-Marinated Flank Steak,
278
Cowboy Flank Steak, 282
Flank Steak Skewers in Lime
Cola Marinade, 283
Flank Steak with Beefy Barbecue
Mop, 279
Orange & Soy Flank Steak, 281
beef ribs
Beef Ribs in Pale Ale Marinade,
294
Beef Short Ribs in Serrano–
Szechuan Marinade, 298
beef roast
Brined & Basted Sirloin Roast,
274
Calgary Stampede Rubbed Rib
Roast, 273
Rib Roast, 272
Standing Rib Roast, 89
beef tenderloin
Bacon-Wrapped Beef
Tenderloin, 275
Cherry-Smoked Beef
Tenderloin, 276
Beefy Barbecue Mop, 46
beer
Beef Ribs in Pale Ale Marinade,
294
Beer & Brown Sugar Brine, 25
Beer & Onion Cabrito Ribs, 351

Cold-Smoked Venison Sausage,
340
Lime & Lager Marinade, 38
beginners' recipes
Adam & Eve Ribs, 260
Apple & Cherry–Smoked Baby
Back Ribs, 250
Apricot Chicken Quarters, 199
Aromatic Whole Chicken, 194
Baby Back Ribs, 82
Barbecued Beans, 75
Beef Brisket Flat, 88
Chicken Breasts, 79
Chicken Wings, 80
Easy Barbecued Chicken, 200
Garden Catfish, 148
Here a Chick, There a Chick,
197
Hickory & Maple–Smoked Beef
Brisket, 285
Honey-Chipotle Turkey
Drumsticks, 216
Italian Sausage, 81
Leg of Lamb, 90
Pork Chops, 85
Pork Shoulder Blade, 86
Pork Tenderloin, 84
Potatoes, 77
Salmon Fillet, 91
Sassy, Spicy Chicken Wings, 205
Scallops, 94
Shrimp, 95
Soft Cheese, 74
Soy & Green Onion Catfish
Fillets, 149
Spicy Pork Tenderloin, 234
Standing Rib Roast, 89
Stuffed Mushrooms, 76
Tomatoes, 78
Tuna Steak, 92
Whole Trout, 93
Blackberry Merlot Marinade, 41
Blackberry Merlot Sauce, 68
bourbon
Beef Ribs in Pale Ale Marinade,
294
Bourbon Barbecue Sauce, 52
Bourbon-Brined Rack of Lamb,
313
Tennessee Bourbon Brine, 23
brandy and cognac
Brandied Pineapple & Mango
Pork Chops, 249
Cold-Smoked Venison Sausage,
340
Portobello Mushrooms with
Brandied Cream, 122
Brie with Brown Sugar & Pecans,
111
Brine for Beef, 24

Brined & Basted Sirloin Roast, 274
brines, 18, 19–25
for fish, 21–23, 25, 184–85
brisket. *See* beef brisket
Brisket Mop, Rich & Delicious, 45
Brown Sugar & Maple Cabbage,
114
Brown Sugar Rib Rub, 33
Brown Sugar–Rubbed Ribs, 257
Brussels Sprouts with Lime & Brown
Sugar, Oak-Smoked, 113
buffalo
Apple & Pecan–Smoked Buffalo
Ribs, 344
Barbecued Buffalo Meatloaf, 345
Buffalo Flank Steak in Lime
Cola Marinade, 341
Buffalo Kabobs with Sesame
Marinade, 343
Pecan-Smoked Buffalo
Tenderloin, 342
Buffalo-Style Hot Wings, 207
bullet smokers, 9–10, 13, 15
burgers, 300–303
Butter-Basted Whole Trout, 167
Butterflied Leg of Lamb in Red
Currant Marinade, 320
Buttery Brown Sugar & Lime
Basting Sauce, 48

C

cabbage
Brown Sugar & Maple Cabbage,
114
Cold-Smoked Vegetables, 98
Coleslaw in Pineapple Soy
Dressing, 101
cabrito. *See* goat
Calgary Stampede Rubbed Rib
Roast, 273
Canadian Barbecue Association, 72
Caribbean-Style Barbecued
Meatloaf with Papaya Relish,
308
catfish
Garden Catfish, 148
Mediterranean-Style Tilapia (tip),
159
Soy & Green Onion Catfish
Fillets, 149
charcoal, 8–10, 13, 14, 15
cheese. *See also specific types of cheese
(below)*
Brie with Brown Sugar & Pecans,
111
Cheese, Vegetable & Pepperoni
Skewers, 109
Cold-Smoked Cheese, 108
Gouda with Onion, Jalapeño
Pepper & Artichoke Relish, 110

Hot-Smoked Cheese, 136
Sausage-Stuffed Mushrooms, 120
Stuffed Mushrooms, 76
Stuffed Portobello Mushrooms, 121
The Ultimate Slow-Smoked Burger, 300
cheese, Cheddar
    Barbecued Oysters, 176
    Brisket-Stuffed Artichoke Bottoms, 292
    Cold-Smoked Cheese, 108
    Hot-Smoked Cheese, 136
    Potato Salad, 104
    Three-Bean Barbecue Casserole, 126
cheese, cream
    Maple-Smoked Whitefish (tip), 172
    Sausage-Stuffed Mushrooms, 120
    Soft Cheese, 74
    Stuffed Mushrooms, 76
    Stuffed Portobello Mushrooms, 121
cheese, goat
    Goat Cheese & Chipotle Dip, 139
    Goat Cheese–Stuffed Tomatoes, 138
    Soft Cheese, 74
cheese, mozzarella
    Cold-Smoked Cheese, 108
    Hot-Smoked Cheese, 136
    Salad Caprese with Mozzarella, Basil & Tomatoes, 137
    Soft Cheese, 74
cheese, Parmesan
    Antipasto Burgers, 302
    Brisket-Stuffed Artichoke Bottoms, 292
    Crab-Stuffed Whole Trout, 168
    Mushroom, Garlic & Thyme Meatloaf, 306
    Ratatouille, 131
    Sausage-Stuffed Mushrooms, 120
    Stuffed Eggplant with Bacon, Garlic & Cream, 117
    Stuffed Mushrooms, 76
    Stuffed Tomatoes, 124
Cherry Chipotle Barbecue Sauce, 63
Cherry Chipotle Wings, 208
Cherry-Smoked Beef Tenderloin, 276
Cherry-Smoked Fresh Pork Sausage, 266
Cherry-Smoked Lamb Chops, 318
Cherry-Smoked Rack of Lamb with Fresh Herb Paste, 312

chicken
    Apricot Chicken Quarters, 199
    Apricot Chicken Skewers, 203
    Aromatic Whole Chicken, 194
    Buffalo-Style Hot Wings, 207
    Cherry Chipotle Wings, 208
    Chick, Chick, Chick, 198
    Chicken Breasts, 79
    Chicken Wings, 80
    Easy Barbecued Chicken, 200
    Here a Chick, There a Chick, 197
    Lamb Skewers in Fresh Orange & White Balsamic Marinade (tip), 325
    Pecan-Glazed Chicken Thighs, 204
    Pecan-Smoked Chicken Wings, 209
    Raspberry Chicken Breasts, 201
    Santa Fe Chicken Breasts in Coffee Lime Marinade, 202
    Sassy, Spicy Chicken Wings, 205
    Sweet Wings, 206
    Whole Chicken in Orange, Garlic & Brown Sugar Brine, 195
    Whole Chicken with Orange & Tarragon, 196
Chili-Raspberry Beef Short Ribs, 296
Chipotle Marinade, 36
Cilantro Coconut Pork Loin Roast, 240
Citrus Demi-glace, 68
Coffee Lime Marinade, 41
cola
    Cola-Marinated Flank Steak, 278
    Lime Cola Marinade, 37
    Rum & Cola Ribs, 262
    Spicy Cola Baby Back Ribs, 254
Cold-Smoked Cheese, 108
Cold-Smoked Fruit, 106
Cold-Smoked Ostrich with Garlic, Honey & Maple, 337
Cold-Smoked Vegetables, 98
Cold-Smoked Venison Sausage, 340
cold-smoking, 16–17, 98–111, 146, 183–91
Coleslaw in Pineapple Soy Dressing, 101
corn
    Corn in the Husk, 115
    Corn Relish, 116
    Hot-Smoked Vegetables, 112
    Lobster Tail Kabobs in White Balsamic Vinaigrette, 174
    Vegetable Chowder, 133
Cornish game hen
    Cornish Game Hens with Honey Spice Glaze, 222

Stuffed Cornish Game Hens with Apricot Mustard Sauce, 220
Country-Style Ribs with Asian Plum Sauce, 261
Cowboy Flank Steak, 282
Crab-Stuffed Whole Trout, 168
cranberry
    Apple-Cranberry Pork Loin Chops, 247
    Cranberry Vinaigrette, 238
    Hickory-Smoked Mussels in Passionberry Wine (tip), 189
    Maple-Smoked Pork Loin Roast with Cranberry Glaze, 237
    Pork Loin Roast with Cranberry Glaze, 238
Creole-Style Pork Steak, 246

D
dips and spreads, 118, 139, 172
duck
    Five-Spice Duck Breast, 219
    Soy & Garlic Duck Breast, 218

E
Easy Apricot Barbecue Glaze, 66
Easy Asian Marinade, 40
Easy Barbecued Chicken, 200
eggplant
    Cold-Smoked Vegetables, 98
    Italian Antipasto Skewers, 265
    Ratatouille, 131
    Stuffed Eggplant with Bacon, Garlic & Cream, 117
eggs
    Barbecued Meatloaf, 304
    Caribbean-Style Barbecued Meatloaf with Papaya Relish, 308
    Mushroom, Garlic & Thyme Meatloaf, 306
    Potato Salad, 104
    Potato Salad with Celery & Pickles, 105
    Smoky Deviled Eggs, 141
Every-Flavor Spice Rub, 30

F
Feast of Fancy Suckling Pig, 346
Fettuccine with Garlic, Tomato & Basil, 132
Fiesta Pepper Salsa, 103
finishing sauces, 49, 54, 66–71, 156, 220
fish. See also specific types of fish; seafood
    bastes for, 46, 48
    brines for, 21–23, 25, 184–85

fish (continued)
marinades for, 36–37, 39–40, 43,
149–51, 160, 162, 170–71
rubs and pastes for, 33, 35
sauces for, 60, 71, 92, 156
Five-Spice Duck Breast, 219
flank steak. See beef flank steak
Flank Steak Skewers in Lime Cola
Marinade, 283
Flank Steak with Beefy Barbecue
Mop, 279
Flower of the Flames Oysters, 175
Flower of the Flames Raspberry
Barbecue Sauce, 50
Flower of the Flames Rib Rub, 32
French Canadian Barbecued Beans,
127
Fresh Blueberry & Ginger Sauce, 69
Fresh Fruit Salsa, 107
Fresh Garlic & Herb Paste, 35
Fresh Herb & Spice Paste, 35
Fresh Orange & White Balsamic
Marinade, 39
fruit. See also specific fruits
Apple-Smoked Salmon with
Green Grape Sauce, 156
Blackberry Merlot Sauce, 68
Caribbean-Style Barbecued
Meatloaf with Papaya Relish,
308
Cold-Smoked Fruit, 106
Fresh Blueberry & Ginger Sauce,
69
Hot-Smoked Fruit, 134

G
game. See also buffalo; game birds;
rabbit; venison
brines for, 25
glazes for, 66
marinades for, 41–42, 344, 353,
354
pastes for, 35
sauces for, 64–65, 68
game birds. See also Cornish game
hen; duck; ostrich; pheasant;
quail
glazes for, 66, 222
marinades for, 38, 218
rubs for, 29–30
sauces for, 52, 65, 68, 69
Garden Catfish, 148
garlic
Alder-Smoked Shrimp, 180
Antipasto Burgers, 302
Apple & Pecan–Smoked Buffalo
Ribs, 344
Apple & Pecan–Smoked Flank
Steak with Garlic & Spice
Rub, 280

Barbecuer's Aioli, 71
Bay Leaf Marinade, 38
Blackberry Merlot Marinade, 41
Butterflied Leg of Lamb in Red
Currant Marinade, 320
Cherry-Smoked Rack of Lamb
with Fresh Herb Paste, 312
Cola-Marinated Flank Steak,
278
Cold-Smoked Ostrich with
Garlic, Honey & Maple, 337
Cold-Smoked Vegetables, 98
Corn Relish, 116
Fettuccine with Garlic, Tomato
& Basil, 132
Fresh Garlic & Herb Paste, 35
Garlic & Spice Rabbit, 354
Herb Garden Leg of Lamb with
Red Currant Sauce, 322
Herbal Balsamic Jelly, 70
Hickory-Smoked Mussels in
Passionberry Wine, 189
Hot-Smoked Vegetables, 112
Lime & Ginger Prawns, 179
Lime & Lager Marinade, 38
Lime Cola Marinade, 37
Maple Honey Marinade, 42
Mediterranean Marinade, 42
Mediterranean-Style Tilapia,
159
Mushroom, Garlic & Thyme
Meatloaf, 306
Mussels in Apple-Garlic
Marinade, 188
Perfect Score Lamb Sausage,
330
Smoky, Spicy Turkey Wings, 217
Soy & Garlic Duck Breast, 218
Texas-Style Cabrito, 350
glazes, 54, 66–67, 222
for pork, 66, 232, 236–38, 253
goat
Beer & Onion Cabrito Ribs, 351
Honey Mustard Cabrito Ribs,
352
Texas-Style Cabrito, 350
Goat Cheese & Chipotle Dip, 139
Goat Cheese–Stuffed Tomatoes,
138
Gouda with Onion, Jalapeño
Pepper & Artichoke Relish,
110
Grand Champion Rack of Lamb,
314
grills. See also smokers
ceramic, 9, 15
charcoal, 8–9, 13, 15
gas, 10, 13–14, 15
Kamado-style, 9
wood pellet, 10, 14, 15

H
haddock
Haddock Fillets in White Wine,
Ginger & Horseradish, 150
Maple-Smoked Whitefish
(variation), 172
Whitefish in Cumin-Cilantro
Marinade (variation), 171
Halibut Steaks in Orange, Soy &
Lime Marinade, Alder-Smoked,
151
ham and prosciutto
Antipasto Burgers, 302
The Ultimate Slow-Smoked
Burger, 300
Herb-Brined Salmon, 186
Herb Garden Leg of Lamb with
Red Currant Sauce, 322
Herbal Balsamic Jelly, 70
Here a Chick, There a Chick, 197
Hickory & Maple–Smoked Beef
Brisket, 285
Hickory-Smoked Mussels in
Passionberry Wine, 189
Hickory-Smoked Salmon with
Buttery Brown Sugar & Lime
Baste, 155
Hoisin Pork Skewers, 264
honey
Adam & Eve Ribs, 260
Bourbon Barbecue Sauce, 52
Buffalo-Style Hot Wings, 207
Cold-Smoked Ostrich with
Garlic, Honey & Maple, 337
Cornish Game Hens with
Honey Spice Glaze, 222
Grand Champion Rack of Lamb,
314
Honey & Spice Rub, 31
Honey-Basted Shrimp, 182
Honey-Chipotle Turkey
Drumsticks, 216
Honey Mustard Barbecue Sauce,
61
Honey Mustard Pig Roast, 347
Honeyed Worcestershire
Marinade, 206
Mustard & Marmalade Barbecue
Sauce, 60
Orange & Raspberry Country-
Style Ribs, 263
Pecan-Glazed Chicken Thighs,
204
Pork Loin Roast with Cranberry
Glaze, 238
Pork Shoulder Blade in
Pineapple-Soy Marinade,
230
Sweet Orange Baste, 46

Sweet Wings, 206
World Championship Ribs, 251
Honey Mustard Cabrito Ribs, 352
Honey Mustard Lamb Ribs, 316
Horseradish Potatoes, 128
Hot-Smoked Cheese, 136
Hot-Smoked Fruit, 134
Hot-Smoked Ostrich in Bay Leaf
  Marinade, 338
Hot-Smoked Vegetables, 112
hot-smoking, 7–16, 112–45,
  148–82
  adding moisture, 14, 15
  adding wood, 12–14, 15–16
  fire preparation, 8–12
  techniques, 15–16
  temperature control, 14–15
  timing, 16
Hummus-Tahini Sauce, 92

I

International Barbeque Cookers
  Association, 72
Italian Antipasto Skewers, 265
Italian Sausage, 81
Italian Sausage & Artichoke Soup,
  269

K

Kansas City Barbeque Society, 72
Kansas City–Style Barbecue Sauce,
  55, 72
Kansas City–Style Brisket, 288
ketchup
  Apple Ancho Barbecue Sauce, 62
  Beef Ribs in Pale Ale Marinade,
    294
  Cherry Chipotle Barbecue
    Sauce, 63
  Chili-Raspberry Beef Short
    Ribs, 296
  Flower of the Flames Raspberry
    Barbecue Sauce, 50
  French Canadian Barbecued
    Beans, 127
  Fresh Blueberry & Ginger Sauce,
    69
  Kansas City–Style Barbecue
    Sauce, 55
  Lobster in Savory Sauce, 173
  Mango & Chipotle Turkey
    Breasts, 212
  Memphis-Style Barbecue Sauce,
    58
  North Carolina–Style Barbecue
    Sauce, 57
  Red Currant Sauce, 67
  Spicy Cola Baby Back Ribs, 254
  Texas-Style Barbecue Sauce, 53

L

lamb. *See also specific cuts (below)*
  glazes for, 66
  marinades for, 42, 315, 317, 320
  pastes for, 314, 322
  sauces for, 64, 67, 70, 326
lamb, leg of
  Butterflied Leg of Lamb in Red
    Currant Marinade, 320
  Herb Garden Leg of Lamb with
    Red Currant Sauce, 322
  Lamb Skewers in Fresh Orange
    & White Balsamic Marinade,
    325
  Lamb Skewers with Red
    Currant–Chili Sauce, 326
  Leg of Lamb, 90
  Mediterranean Lamb Appetizer
    Skewers, 324
lamb, rack of
  Bourbon-Brined Rack of Lamb,
    313
  Cherry-Smoked Rack of Lamb
    with Fresh Herb Paste, 312
  Grand Champion Rack of Lamb,
    314
lamb chops
  Cherry-Smoked Lamb Chops,
    318
  Lamb Chops in Orange, Garlic
    & Brown Sugar Brine, 319
lamb ribs
  Asian-Style Lamb Ribs, 315
  Honey Mustard Lamb Ribs, 316
  Raspberry Zinfandel Lamb Ribs,
    317
Lamb Meatballs in Marinara Sauce,
  Smoky, 328
lamb sausage
  Lamb Sausage with Apricot
    Maple Glaze, 329
  Perfect Score Lamb Sausage, 330
lemon
  Butter-Basted Whole Trout, 167
  Chicken Breasts, 79
  Herb Garden Leg of Lamb with
    Red Currant Sauce, 322
  Hoisin Pork Skewers, 264
  Lemon-Herb Scallops, 178
  Lobster in Savory Sauce, 173
  Sea Bass Skewers Lemonada, 162
  Smoky Lamb Meatballs in
    Marinara Sauce, 328
  Three P's Shark Skewers, 166
  Whole Trout, 93
lime
  Alder-Smoked Halibut Steaks in
    Orange, Soy & Lime
    Marinade, 151

Buttery Brown Sugar & Lime
  Basting Sauce, 48
Cherry-Smoked Beef
  Tenderloin, 276
Citrus Demi-glace, 68
Coffee Lime Marinade, 41
Garden Catfish, 148
Lime & Ginger Prawns, 179
Lime & Lager Marinade, 38
Lime Cola Marinade, 37
Oak-Smoked Brussels Sprouts
  with Lime & Brown Sugar,
  113
Red Onion & Tomato Salsa, 102
Whitefish in Cumin-Cilantro
  Marinade, 171
Lobster in Savory Sauce, 173
Lobster Tail Kabobs in White
  Balsamic Vinaigrette, 174
Low- and Slow-Smoked Baby Back
  Ribs with Apricot Glaze, 253

M

mango
  Brandied Pineapple & Mango
    Pork Chops, 249
  Caribbean-Style Barbecued
    Meatloaf with Papaya Relish,
    308
  Mango & Chipotle Turkey
    Breasts, 212
Maple & Oak–Smoked Whole
  Hog, 348
Maple-Smoked Pork Loin Roast
  with Cranberry Glaze, 237
Maple-Smoked Whitefish, 172
maple syrup
  Ancho-Herb Pork Shoulder
    Blade, 226
  Apple & Hickory–Smoked Ribs
    in Red Wine Marinade, 258
  Apple-Cranberry Pork Loin
    Chops, 247
  Apple-Smoked Apples, 135
  Apple-Smoked Salmon with
    Green Grape Sauce, 156
  Apricot Chicken Quarters, 199
  Apricot Maple Glaze, 66
  Brown Sugar & Maple Cabbage,
    114
  Cold-Smoked Ostrich with
    Garlic, Honey & Maple, 337
  Corn in the Husk, 115
  Easy Apricot Barbecue Glaze, 66
  French Canadian Barbecued
    Beans, 127
  Maple Honey Marinade, 42
  Maple Mustard Brine, 21
  Margarita-Style Sea Bass, 160

maple syrup *(continued)*
Oak-Smoked Brussels Sprouts with Lime & Brown Sugar, 113
Orange & Maple–Glazed Pork Shoulder Blade, 232
Pork Loin Roast with Raspberry-Mustard Glaze, 236
Salmon "Candy," 158
Salmon in Maple Brine, 185
Sweet & Smoky Turkey Breasts, 211
Margarita-Style Sea Bass, 160
marinades, 18, 36–43
for beef, 36–37, 282, 285, 294, 297
for fish, 36–37, 39–40, 43, 149–51, 160–62, 170–71
for game, 41–42, 344, 353, 354
for game birds, 38, 218
for lamb, 42, 315, 317, 320
for pork, 36–37, 39–40, 42, 230, 234–35, 252, 258, 262, 265
for poultry, 36–39, 41, 43, 197, 201, 203, 206–7, 212, 214–15, 217
for seafood, 36, 38, 39, 178–79, 182
Marinated Tofu, 140
Meatballs in Marinara Sauce, Smoky Lamb, 328
meatloaf, 304–9, 345
Mediterranean Lamb Appetizer Skewers, 324
Mediterranean Marinade, 42
Mediterranean-Style Tilapia, 159
Memphis Barbecue Association, 72
Memphis-Style Barbecue Sauce, 58
Mesquite & Apple–Smoked Deviled Beef Ribs, 293
molasses
Beef Ribs in Pale Ale Marinade, 294
Flower of the Flames Raspberry Barbecue Sauce, 50
French Canadian Barbecued Beans, 127
Kansas City–Style Barbecue Sauce, 55
mops, 18, 44–46
mushrooms
Antipasto Burgers, 302
Brisket-Stuffed Artichoke Bottoms (variation), 292
Buffalo Kabobs with Sesame Marinade, 343
Cold-Smoked Vegetables, 98
Hot-Smoked Vegetables, 112
Mushroom, Garlic & Thyme Meatloaf, 306
Pecan-Smoked Vegetable Skewers, 130

Portobello Mushrooms with Brandied Cream, 122
Sausage-Stuffed Mushrooms, 120
Stuffed Eggplant with Bacon, Garlic & Cream, 117
Stuffed Mushrooms, 76
Stuffed Portobello Mushrooms, 121
Stuffed Tomatoes, 124
Mussels in Apple-Garlic Marinade, 188
Mussels in Passionberry Wine, Hickory-Smoked, 189
mustard
Grand Champion Rack of Lamb, 314
Honey Mustard Barbecue Sauce, 61
Honey Mustard Lamb Ribs, 316
Honey Mustard Pig Roast, 347
Memphis-Style Barbecue Sauce, 58
Mushroom, Garlic & Thyme Meatloaf, 306
Mustard & Marmalade Barbecue Sauce, 60
Pork Chops, 85
Sweet & Spicy Rib Baste, 47
Tangy Mustard Barbecue Sauce, 59

N

New Mexico–Style Ribs, 256
New Mexico–Style Rub, 27
North Carolina–Style Barbecue Sauce, 57
nuts
Brie with Brown Sugar & Pecans, 111
Pecan-Glazed Chicken Thighs, 204
Rosemary Almonds, 144
Smokehouse Almonds, 145
Spicy Nuts, 143

O

Oak-Smoked Brussels Sprouts with Lime & Brown Sugar, 113
olives
Onion & Charred Pepper Salsa, 119
Wheat Berry & Olive Tapenade, 118
onion. *See also* onion, green
Artichoke & Red Onion Relish, 99
Beer & Onion Cabrito Ribs, 351
Buffalo Kabobs with Sesame Marinade, 343

Cold-Smoked Vegetables, 98
French Canadian Barbecued Beans, 127
Gouda with Onion, Jalapeño Pepper & Artichoke Relish, 110
Hot-Smoked Vegetables, 112
Onion & Charred Pepper Salsa, 119
Onion & Garlic Dry Rub, 34
Onion Soy Marinade, 40
Red Onion & Tomato Salsa, 102
Sesame Marinade, 43
Sweet & Spicy Rib Baste, 47
Texas Spit, 54
onion, green
Asian-Style Beef Short Ribs, 297
Asian-Style Lamb Ribs, 315
Blackberry Merlot Marinade, 41
Fiesta Pepper Salsa, 103
Lime Cola Marinade, 37
Rum & Cola Ribs, 262
Smoky, Spicy Turkey Wings, 217
Soy & Green Onion Catfish Fillets, 149
Trout in Lavender Butter, 170
orange
Alder-Smoked Halibut Steaks in Orange, Soy & Lime Marinade, 151
Alder-Smoked Red Snapper with Citrus Spray, 152
Cold-Smoked Fruit, 106
Fresh Fruit Salsa, 107
Fresh Orange & White Balsamic Marinade, 39
Hot-Smoked Fruit, 134
Lamb Skewers with Red Currant–Chili Sauce, 326
Maple-Smoked Pork Loin Roast with Cranberry Glaze, 237
Mustard & Marmalade Barbecue Sauce, 60
Orange, Garlic & Brown Sugar Brine, 22
Orange & Maple–Glazed Pork Shoulder Blade, 232
Orange & Raspberry Country-Style Ribs, 263
Orange & Soy Flank Steak, 281
Orange & Soy Marinade, 39
Pork Loin Roast with Cranberry Glaze, 238
Sweet & Spicy Rib Baste, 47
Sweet Orange Baste, 46
Whole Chicken with Orange & Tarragon, 196
ostrich
Cold-Smoked Ostrich with Garlic, Honey & Maple, 337

Hot-Smoked Ostrich in Bay
Leaf Marinade, 338
oysters
Barbecued Oysters, 176
Flower of the Flames Oysters,
175

P

Pacific Northwest BBQ
Association, 72
Pale Ale Marinade, 294
Papaya Relish, 308
pastes, 18, 26, 35, 196, 314, 322
peach
Orange & Raspberry Country-
Style Ribs, 263
Peachy Barbecue Sauce, 64
Southwestern-Style Turkey
Thighs, 215
Peach-Smoked Apricot Pork Loin
Roast, 241
Peanuts, Smoked, 142
pear
Cold-Smoked Fruit, 106
Fresh Fruit Salsa, 107
Honey Mustard Pig Roast, 347
Lamb Skewers with Red
Currant–Chili Sauce, 326
Orange & Maple–Glazed Pork
Shoulder Blade, 232
Smoky, Spicy Turkey Wings, 217
Three P's Shark Skewers, 166
Pecan Honey, 204
Pecan-Smoked Buffalo Tenderloin,
342
Pecan-Smoked Chicken Wings, 209
Pecan-Smoked Pork Tenderloin
with Fresh Garlic & Herb
Paste, 233
Pecan-Smoked Vegetable Skewers,
130
peppers, bell
Apricot Chicken Skewers, 203
Buffalo Kabobs with Sesame
Marinade, 343
Caribbean-Style Barbecued
Meatloaf with Papaya Relish,
308
Cheese, Vegetable & Pepperoni
Skewers, 109
Cherry-Smoked Beef
Tenderloin, 276
Cold-Smoked Vegetables, 98
Fiesta Pepper Salsa, 103
Hot-Smoked Vegetables, 112
Lamb Skewers with Red
Currant–Chili Sauce, 326
Lobster Tail Kabobs in White
Balsamic Vinaigrette, 174
Mediterranean-Style Tilapia, 159

Onion & Charred Pepper Salsa,
119
Pecan-Smoked Vegetable
Skewers, 130
Sea Bass Skewers Lemonada, 162
Three P's Shark Skewers, 166
Vegetable Chowder, 133
peppers, chili (green)
Lime & Ginger Prawns, 179
Three-Bean Barbecue Casserole,
126
peppers, chipotle
Chipotle Marinade, 36
Goat Cheese & Chipotle Dip, 139
Lime & Lager Marinade, 38
Mango & Chipotle Turkey
Breasts, 212
peppers, jalapeño
Artichoke & Red Onion Relish,
99
Cold-Smoked Vegetables, 98
Corn Relish, 116
Gouda with Onion, Jalapeño
Pepper & Artichoke Relish,
110
Hot-Smoked Vegetables, 112
Red Onion & Tomato Salsa, 102
Vegetable Chowder, 133
peppers, serrano
Beef Short Ribs in Serrano-
Szechuan Marinade, 298
Beefy Barbecue Mop, 46
Cilantro Coconut Pork Loin
Roast, 240
Fresh Fruit Salsa, 107
Hickory-Smoked Mussels in
Passionberry Wine, 189
Italian Antipasto Skewers, 265
Lime Cola Marinade, 37
Margarita-Style Sea Bass, 160
Onion & Charred Pepper Salsa,
119
Spicy Pork Tenderloin, 234
Perfect Score Lamb Sausage, 330
Pesto Salmon Salad, 153 (tip)
Pheasant Breast, Apple-Smoked,
334
pig, whole
Feast of Fancy Suckling Pig, 346
Honey Mustard Pig Roast, 347
Maple & Oak–Smoked Whole
Hog, 348
pineapple
Buffalo Kabobs with Sesame
Marinade, 343
Caribbean-Style Barbecued
Meatloaf with Papaya Relish,
308
Cold-Smoked Fruit, 106
Fresh Fruit Salsa, 107

Hot-Smoked Fruit, 134
Lamb Skewers with Red
Currant–Chili Sauce, 326
Pineapple-Glazed Hot Italian
Sausage, 268
Three P's Shark Skewers, 166
pineapple juice
Ancho-Herb Pork Shoulder
Blade, 226
Brandied Pineapple & Mango
Pork Chops, 249
Coleslaw in Pineapple Soy
Dressing, 101
Feast of Fancy Suckling Pig, 346
Maple & Oak–Smoked Whole
Hog, 348
Pineapple-Soy Turkey
Tenderloins, 214
Pork Shoulder Blade in
Pineapple-Soy Marinade, 230
Pork Shoulder Blade with Peach
Barbecue Sauce, 228
Sugar-Free Barbecue Sauce, 56
Plum Good Ribs, 252
pork. See also specific cuts (below);
bacon; ham and prosciutto;
pig, whole; ribs, pork; sausage
bastes for, 46–47, 227, 263, 348
glazes for, 66, 232, 236–38, 253
marinades for, 36–37, 39–40, 42,
230, 234–35, 252, 258, 262,
265
rubs and pastes for, 28, 30–35,
228
sauces for, 51–52, 57–60, 62–65,
67, 68, 241, 254, 261
pulled, 51, 63, 86, 226–32
pork, ground
Barbecued Meatloaf, 304
Cherry-Smoked Fresh Pork
Sausage, 266
Cold-Smoked Venison Sausage,
340
Perfect Score Lamb Sausage, 330
Smoky Lamb Meatballs in
Marinara Sauce, 328
The Ultimate Slow-Smoked
Burger, 300
pork chops
Apple-Cranberry Pork Loin
Chops, 247
Brandied Pineapple & Mango
Pork Chops, 249
Pork Chops, 85
Tennessee Bourbon–Brined Pork
Chops, 248
pork loin
Apple & Hickory–Smoked Pork
Loin Roast with Ancho-Herb
Dry Rub, 243

pork loin *(continued)*
Cilantro Coconut Pork Loin
Roast, 240
Hoisin Pork Skewers, 264
Maple-Smoked Pork Loin Roast
with Cranberry Glaze, 237
Peach-Smoked Apricot Pork
Loin Roast, 241
Pork Loin Roast in Maple
Mustard Brine, 244
Pork Loin Roast with Hot
Pepper Jelly Glaze, 245
Pork Loin Roast with
Raspberry-Mustard Glaze, 236
Sugar Maple–Smoked Pork Loin
Roast in Lime Cola Marinade,
242
pork shoulder blade
Ancho-Herb Pork Shoulder
Blade, 226
Orange & Maple–Glazed Pork
Shoulder Blade, 232
Pork Shoulder Blade, 86
Pork Shoulder Blade in
Pineapple-Soy Marinade, 230
Pork Shoulder Blade with Peach
Barbecue Sauce, 228
Pork Shoulder Blade with Sassy
Raspberry Vinegar Baste, 227
Pork Steak, Creole-Style, 246
pork tenderloin
Pecan-Smoked Pork Tenderloin
with Fresh Garlic & Herb
Paste, 233
Pork Tenderloin, 84
Pork Tenderloin in White Wine
Marinade, 235
Spicy Pork Tenderloin, 234
Portobello Mushrooms with
Brandied Cream, 122
potatoes. *See also* sweet potatoes
Horseradish Potatoes, 128
Hot-Smoked Vegetables, 112
Potato Casserole, 129
Potato Salad, 104
Potato Salad with Celery &
Pickles, 105
Potatoes, 77
Vegetable Chowder, 133
poultry. *See also* chicken; game
birds; turkey
bastes for, 46, 216
brines for, 22–23
glazes for, 66
marinades for, 36–39, 41, 43,
197, 201, 203, 206–7, 212,
214–15, 217
rubs and pastes for, 29–31, 34,
35, 196, 198
sauces for, 52, 62–65, 67, 209, 220

Q
quail
Bacon-Wrapped Quail, 335
Quail in Blackberry Merlot
Marinade, 336

R
rabbit
Garlic & Spice Rabbit, 354
Rabbit with Apricot Maple
Glaze, 353
raspberry
Chili-Raspberry Beef Short Ribs
(tip), 296
Flower of the Flames Raspberry
Barbecue Sauce, 50
Pork Loin Roast with
Raspberry-Mustard Glaze, 236
Pork Tenderloin, 84
Raspberry Chicken Breasts, 201
Raspberry Molasses Sauce, 294
Raspberry Zinfandel Lamb Ribs
(tip), 317
Ratatouille, 131
red currant jelly
Butterflied Leg of Lamb in Red
Currant Marinade, 320
Lamb Skewers with Red
Currant–Chili Sauce, 326
Red Currant Sauce, 67
Red Onion & Tomato Salsa, 102
red snapper
Alder-Smoked Red Snapper
with Citrus Spray, 152
Red Snapper & Vegetables, 183
Red Wine Marinade, 258
relishes, 99, 110, 276, 300, 308. *See
also* salsa
Rib Roast, 272
ribs. *See also specific types of meat
(below)*
bastes for, 47
rubs for, 32–33
sauces for, 55, 58
ribs, beef
Asian-Style Beef Short Ribs,
297
Beef Ribs in Pale Ale Marinade,
294
Beef Short Ribs in Serrano-
Szechuan Marinade, 298
Chili-Raspberry Beef Short
Ribs, 296
Mesquite & Apple–Smoked
Deviled Beef Ribs, 293
ribs, goat
Beer & Onion Cabrito Ribs, 351
Honey Mustard Cabrito Ribs,
352

ribs, lamb
Asian-Style Lamb Ribs, 315
Honey Mustard Lamb Ribs, 316
Raspberry Zinfandel Lamb Ribs,
317
ribs, pork
Adam & Eve Ribs, 260
Apple & Cherry–Smoked Baby
Back Ribs, 250
Apple & Hickory–Smoked Ribs
in Red Wine Marinade, 258
Baby Back Ribs, 82
Brown Sugar–Rubbed Ribs, 257
Country-Style Ribs with Asian
Plum Sauce, 261
Low- and Slow-Smoked Baby
Back Ribs with Apricot Glaze,
253
New Mexico–Style Ribs, 256
Orange & Raspberry Country-
Style Ribs, 263
Plum Good Ribs, 252
Rum & Cola Ribs, 262
Spicy Cola Baby Back Ribs,
254
World Championship Ribs, 251
Rich & Delicious Brisket Mop, 45
Rich Beefy Brisket, 284
Roasted Red Pepper & Avocado
Relish, 276
Rosemary Almonds, 144
rubs, 18, 26–34, 198, 228
for beef, 34, 280, 287–88, 290
Rum & Cola Ribs, 262

S
Salad Caprese with Mozzarella,
Basil & Tomatoes, 137
salmon
Apple-Smoked Salmon with
Green Grape Sauce, 156
Herb-Brined Salmon, 186
Hickory-Smoked Salmon with
Buttery Brown Sugar & Lime
Baste, 155
Salmon "Candy," 158
Salmon Fillet, 91
Salmon in Bay Brine, 184
Salmon in Maple Brine, 185
Salmon with Sweet Orange
Baste, 154
Salmon with White Wine &
Pesto, 153
Shark Steaks in Orange & Soy
Marinade (tip), 164
Three P's Shark Skewers
(variation), 166
Tuna in Fresh Orange & White
Balsamic Marinade (variation),
187

Whitefish in Cumin-Cilantro
  Marinade (variation), 171
salsa, 102–3, 107, 119, 160
Santa Fe Chicken Breasts in Coffee
  Lime Marinade, 202
Sassy, Spicy Chicken Wings, 205
Sassy, Spicy Pork Rub, 34
Sassy Raspberry Vinegar Baste, 227
sauces, 18
  barbecue, 49–65, 209, 241, 254,
    261, 294, 296, 326
  for beef, 54–55, 68, 70, 294, 296,
    302
  finishing, 49, 54, 66–71, 156, 220
  for fish, 60, 71, 92, 156
  for game, 64–65, 68
  for game birds, 52, 65, 68, 69
  for lamb, 64, 67, 70, 326
  for pork, 51–52, 57–60, 62–65,
    67, 68, 241, 254, 261
  for poultry, 52, 62–65, 67, 209,
    220
  for vegetables, 51, 62
sausage
  Barbecued Beans, 75
  Cheese, Vegetable & Pepperoni
    Skewers, 109
  French Canadian Barbecued
    Beans, 127
  Italian Antipasto Skewers, 265
  Italian Sausage, 81
  Italian Sausage & Artichoke
    Soup, 269
  Lamb Sausage with Apricot
    Maple Glaze, 329
  Pineapple-Glazed Hot Italian
    Sausage, 268
  Sausage-Stuffed Mushrooms, 120
Savory Brown Sugar Rub, 28
scallops
  Lemon-Herb Scallops, 178
  Scallop Martinis, 191
  Scallops, 94, 190
  Scallops in Sesame Marinade,
    177
sea bass
  Margarita-Style Sea Bass, 160
  Sea Bass Skewers Lemonada, 162
seafood. See also specific types of
    seafood; fish
  bastes for, 182
  marinades for, 36, 38, 39,
    178–79, 182
  sauces for, 71
Sesame Marinade, 43
Sesame Turkey, 210
sesame seeds
  Asian-Style Beef Short Ribs,
    297
  Asian-Style Lamb Ribs, 315

Beef Short Ribs in Serrano-
  Szechuan Marinade, 298
shark
  Alder-Smoked Shark Steaks,
    165
  Shark Steaks in Orange & Soy
    Marinade, 164
  Three P's Shark Skewers, 166
sherry
  Creole-Style Pork Steak, 246
  Maple-Smoked Pork Loin Roast
    with Cranberry Glaze, 237
  Peachy Barbecue Sauce, 64
  Pork Loin Roast with Cranberry
    Glaze, 238
  Soy-Sherry Marinade, 37
shrimp
  Alder-Smoked Shrimp, 180
  Honey-Basted Shrimp, 182
  Lime & Ginger Prawns, 179
  Shrimp, 95
  Shrimp in Lime & Lager
    Marinade, 181
slather, mustard, 26, 85
Smoked Peanuts, 142
Smokehouse Almonds, 145
smokers. See also grills
  bullet, 9–10, 13, 15
  ceramic, 9, 15
  charcoal, 9–10, 13, 15
  choosing, 7–8, 17
  electric, 10
  gas, 10, 13–14, 15
  professional-style, 11, 14, 15
  wood pellet, 10, 14, 15
smoking. See cold-smoking;
  hot-smoking
Smoky, Spicy Turkey Wings, 217
Smoky Deviled Eggs, 141
Smoky Lamb Meatballs in
  Marinara Sauce, 328
Smoky Mesquite Brisket, 290
Soft Cheese, 74
Southwestern-Style Turkey Thighs,
  215
soy sauce
  Alder-Smoked Halibut Steaks in
    Orange, Soy & Lime Marinade,
    151
  Asian-Style Beef Short Ribs, 297
  Asian-Style Lamb Ribs, 315
  Beef Short Ribs in Serrano-
    Szechuan Marinade, 298
  Coleslaw in Pineapple Soy
    Dressing, 101
  Easy Asian Marinade, 40
  Herb-Brined Salmon, 186
  Onion Soy Marinade, 40
  Orange & Soy Flank Steak, 281
  Orange & Soy Marinade, 39

Pineapple-Soy Turkey
  Tenderloins, 214
Pork Shoulder Blade in
  Pineapple-Soy Marinade, 230
Salmon in Bay Brine, 184
Sesame Marinade, 43
Soy & Garlic Duck Breast, 218
Soy & Green Onion Catfish
  Fillets, 149
Soy-Sherry Marinade, 37
Spicy Acorn Squash, 123
Spicy Cola Baby Back Ribs, 254
Spicy Nuts, 143
Spicy Pork Tenderloin, 234
spinach
  Flower of the Flames Oysters,
    175
  Sausage-Stuffed Mushrooms, 120
  The Ultimate Slow-Smoked
    Burger, 300
squash. See also zucchini
  Barbecued Buffalo Meatloaf, 345
  Barbecued Meatloaf, 304
  Cold-Smoked Vegetables, 98
  Hot-Smoked Vegetables, 112
  Pecan-Smoked Vegetable
    Skewers, 130
  Spicy Acorn Squash, 123
  Stuffed Portobello Mushrooms,
    121
Standing Rib Roast, 89
Stuffed Cornish Game Hens with
  Apricot Mustard Sauce, 220
Stuffed Eggplant with Bacon,
  Garlic & Cream, 117
Stuffed Mushrooms, 76
Stuffed Portobello Mushrooms, 121
Stuffed Tomatoes, 124
Sugar-Free Barbecue Sauce, 56
Sugar Maple–Smoked Pork Loin
  Roast in Lime Cola Marinade,
  242
Sweet & Smoky Turkey Breasts, 211
Sweet & Spicy Rib Baste, 47
Sweet Orange Baste, 46
sweet potatoes
  Brandied Pineapple & Mango
    Pork Chops (tip), 249
  Hot-Smoked Vegetables, 112
  Potatoes, 77
  Sweet Potatoes, 128
Sweet Wings, 206

T

Tangy Mustard Barbecue Sauce, 59
Tapenade, Wheat Berry & Olive,
  118
Tennessee Bourbon Brine, 23
Tennessee Bourbon–Brined Pork
  Chops, 248

Texas Spit, 54
Texas-Style Barbecue Sauce, 53
Texas-Style Cabrito, 350
Three-Bean Barbecue Casserole, 126
Three P's Shark Skewers, 166
Tilapia, Mediterranean-Style, 159
Tofu, Marinated, 140
tomato sauces and purées. *See also* ketchup
  Apricot, Apricot, Apricot Barbecue Sauce, 65
  Bourbon Barbecue Sauce, 52
  Caribbean-Style Barbecued Meatloaf with Papaya Relish, 308
  Flower of the Flames Raspberry Barbecue Sauce, 50
  Orange & Raspberry Country-Style Ribs, 263
  Sugar-Free Barbecue Sauce, 56
tomatoes
  Cold-Smoked Vegetables, 98
  Fettuccine with Garlic, Tomato & Basil, 132
  Fiesta Pepper Salsa, 103
  Goat Cheese–Stuffed Tomatoes, 138
  Gouda with Onion, Jalapeño Pepper & Artichoke Relish, 110
  Hot-Smoked Vegetables, 112
  Italian Sausage & Artichoke Soup, 269
  Margarita-Style Sea Bass, 160
  Mediterranean-Style Tilapia, 159
  Onion & Charred Pepper Salsa, 119
  Ratatouille, 131
  Red Onion & Tomato Salsa, 102
  Red Snapper & Vegetables, 183
  Salad Caprese with Mozzarella, Basil & Tomatoes, 137
  Stuffed Portobello Mushrooms, 121
  Stuffed Tomatoes, 124
  Tomato Guacamole, 125
  Tomatoes, 78
trout
  Butter-Basted Whole Trout, 167
  Crab-Stuffed Whole Trout, 168
  Maple-Smoked Whitefish (variation), 172
  Trout in Lavender Butter, 170
  Whitefish in Cumin-Cilantro Marinade (variation), 171
  Whole Trout, 93
tuna
  Shark Steaks in Orange & Soy Marinade (tip), 164

Tuna in Fresh Orange & White Balsamic Marinade, 187
Tuna Steak, 92
turkey
  Honey-Chipotle Turkey Drumsticks, 216
  Mango & Chipotle Turkey Breasts, 212
  Pineapple-Soy Turkey Tenderloins, 214
  Sesame Turkey, 210
  Smoky, Spicy Turkey Wings, 217
  Southwestern-Style Turkey Thighs, 215
  Sweet & Smoky Turkey Breasts, 211

U

The Ultimate Slow-Smoked Burger, 300

V

vegetables. *See also specific vegetables*
  Caribbean-Style Barbecued Meatloaf with Papaya Relish, 308
  Cold-Smoked Vegetables, 98
  Vegetable Chowder, 133
venison
  Cold-Smoked Venison Sausage, 340
  Venison Chops in Blackberry Merlot Marinade, 339
Vinegar-Style Barbecue Sauce, 51

W

Wheat Berry & Olive Tapenade, 118
White Wine Marinade, 235
whitefish
  Maple-Smoked Whitefish, 172
  Whitefish in Cumin-Cilantro Marinade, 171
Whole Chicken in Orange, Garlic & Brown Sugar Brine, 195
Whole Chicken with Orange & Tarragon, 196
Whole Trout, 93
wine, fruit
  Blackberry Merlot Marinade, 41
  Blackberry Merlot Sauce, 68
  Hickory-Smoked Mussels in Passionberry Wine, 189
  Maple & Oak–Smoked Whole Hog, 348
  Mussels in Apple-Garlic Marinade, 188
wine, red
  Antipasto Burgers, 302

Apple & Hickory–Smoked Ribs in Red Wine Marinade, 258
Apple-Smoked Salmon with Green Grape Sauce, 156
Flank Steak Skewers in Lime Cola Marinade, 283
Pecan-Smoked Buffalo Tenderloin, 342
Ratatouille, 131
Soy & Garlic Duck Breast, 218
wine, white
  Buttery Brown Sugar & Lime Basting Sauce, 48
  Haddock Fillets in White Wine, Ginger & Horseradish, 150
  Herb-Brined Salmon, 186
  Mussels in Apple-Garlic Marinade (tip), 188
  Pork Tenderloin in White Wine Marinade, 235
  Raspberry Zinfandel Lamb Ribs, 317
  Red Snapper & Vegetables, 183
  Salmon in Bay Brine, 184
  Salmon with White Wine & Pesto, 153
  The Ultimate Slow-Smoked Burger, 300
  Whole Trout, 93
wood
  adding, 12–14, 15–16
  for cold-smoking, 17
  flavors of, 13
  forms of, 12–13
Worcestershire sauce
  All-Purpose Mop, 44
  Easy Asian Marinade, 40
  Honey-Basted Shrimp, 182
  Lobster in Savory Sauce, 173
  Pork Shoulder Blade in Pineapple-Soy Marinade, 230
  Sweet Wings, 206
  Texas Spit, 54
World Championship Ribs, 251

Z

Zinfandel Sandwich Sauce, 302
zucchini. *See also* squash
  Barbecued Meatloaf, 304
  Cheese, Vegetable & Pepperoni Skewers, 109
  Cold-Smoked Vegetables, 98
  Hot-Smoked Vegetables, 112
  Pecan-Smoked Vegetable Skewers, 130
  Ratatouille, 131
  Stuffed Portobello Mushrooms, 121